RONAN McGREEVY

WHEREVER THE FIRING LINE EXTENDS

IRELAND AND THE WESTERN FRONT

The History Press Ireland

For my wife Rebecca and our two children, Rosamund and Leo, with all my love.

This book is dedicated to the memory of Private Michael Ryan (1st Royal Munster Fusiliers) from Knocklong, County Limerick, who was killed during the Battle of Passchendaele on 12 August 1917. Ryan is Rebecca's great-grandfather.

First published 2016, this edition 2017

The History Press Ireland
50 City Quay
Dublin 2
Ireland
www.thehistorypress.ie

The History Press Ireland is a member of Publishing Ireland,
the Irish book publishers' association.

© Ronan McGreevy, 2016, 2017
Map illustrations by Thomas Bohm, User Design, Illustration and
Typesetting

The right of Ronan McGreevy to be identified as the Author
of this work has been asserted in accordance with the
Copyright, Designs and Patents Act 1988.

British Library Cataloguing in Publication Data.
A catalogue record for this book is available from the British Library.

ISBN 978 0 7509 8358 7

Typesetting and origination by The History Press

CONTENTS

FOREWORD

I was inaugurated President of Ireland on 11 November 1997 which is, of course, Armistice Day. Two days earlier I had attended the Armistice Day commemoration service at Dublin's Anglican St Patrick's Cathedral. The congregation was in the main elderly and sparse and it struck me forcefully that day, that since the theme of my Presidency was building bridges, part of the shared future we hoped to build on this island had to involve a retelling of the divided and skewed story of Ireland and the Great War.

We may never know the true figure of how many men from the island of Ireland died in that dreadful war of the vanities of Empires. It is probably somewhere in the region of 35,000 men. Ireland was still then undivided but part of the British Empire. Ours was a small population of some 4 million. Every street, almost every clan, had a returning soldier or a shoebox of medals and memories to mark a tragic death. If they managed to return home alive they certainly did not return unscathed. The Ireland they left in 1914 was not the same Ireland they returned to in 1918.

It was an Ireland radically altered by the Easter Rising, and a Free State with its own fresh narrative of heroic Irish sacrifice for the freedom of its own small nation from the yoke of the British Empire.

Over time, especially with the partitioning of Ireland along sectarian lines, commemoration of the Great War became a divisive issue. Conveniently the story north of the border augmented the role played by Ulster Protestants and the story south of the border diminished the role played by Southern Catholics. It was no way to respect the dead or injured, to play politics with their memory.

Thankfully one of the more benign legacies of Northern Ireland's recent history has been a revisiting of history in order to set the record straight. It is true that we cannot change the past but we can change how we tell the past. In the last few decades, a number of individuals and organisations set about restoring to respected memory those of our people who fought in the First World War.

When the dusty shoeboxes emerged from the attics, it was to give renewed meaning and lustre to those forgotten lives. Ironically they have become part of a divided island's sincere attempt at putting the past behind us and forging a peaceful, collaborative, good neighbourly future. The simple realisation that all religions and shades of politics fought side by side, suffered and died side, brought home to the present generation the common humanity, the common sorrow that the politics of meanness and division had tried to extinguish. Ireland's contribution to the Great War has become a bridge, a safe conduit to those estranged from one another. Its resilient capacity to hold men and women of all politics, faiths and perspectives on this island, was showcased memorably at Messines on the 11 November 1998 when, with King Albert of Belgium and our good neighbour Queen Elizabeth II, I was privileged to open the island of Ireland Peace Park.

The impact was cathartic. A once bitterly contested zone has become a sacred space of shared memory and shared commemoration. The persistence of Paddy Harte and Glen Barr who brought the Island of Ireland Peace Park into existence has been well vindicated. In the two decades since it opened many thousands have taken the journey to Messines, among them Sinn Féin leader Martin McGuinness in the year before his death. Many more have gone the journey in their hearts, taking the path to a new understanding of the past and new hope for the future.

Though a century has passed since the First World War, many in Ireland are discovering its remarkable and continuing legacy for the first time. They are learning that for many on this island it was our war and is our story. Ronan McGreevy's book helps the ongoing unpacking of that complex story. It is a very opportune and important addition to the growing body of scholarly literature on the Irish in the Great War.

Ronan focuses on the monuments the war left behind, providing a useful guide for the growing numbers of visitors to those foreign fields where so many young Irish and many other lives were lost and from where home-coming survivors, for the rest of their lives carried grim memories often too raw to share.

Ronan reminds us that memorials provoke us to ask what story they want us to know. The Flanders memorial to the poet Francis Ledwidge, which I visited in 2004, signals his complex identity as an Irish nationalist and British soldier, and it invokes the complex identities of those of us who share the island of Ireland. In his poem 'In Memoriam Francis Ledwidge', Seamus Heaney says:

I think of you in your Tommy's uniform,
A haunted Catholic face, pallid and brave,
Ghosting the trenches with a bloom of hawthorn
Or silence cored from a Boyne passage-grave.

In the concluding words of the poem Heaney brilliantly observes that too many soldiers, whether British or Irish, all 'consort now underground'.

The cross at Guillemont in the Somme and the Ulster Tower nearby are two monuments which so simply demonstrate the underlying divisions which came to dominate the post-war narrative, the former the repository of the disenfranchised grief of nationalist Ireland when it was unveiled in College Green in 1924, the latter the repository of Ulster Protestant pride in the 36th Ulster Division. The Thiepval Memorial holds the name of 73,000 men missing in action, among them the distinguished intellectual Tom Kettle whose wife's attempts to find his body disclose the agony left to burn unabated for decades in broken hearts of those left with no grave to bring their grief to. Even Rudyard Kipling, the most famous writer of his age, was not spared this trauma.

Ronan's book shows how remembering is never static, but ever changing. The First World War was so colossal in scale, so destructive in its outcome that remembering was always fraught with difficulty. The passage of time has given us the gift of a different kind of remembering.

When I opened the Island of Ireland Peace Park in 1998, we noted how the Irish divisions, the 16th (Irish) Division, Catholic and nationalist, fought side by side with the 36th (Ulster) Division on the same site at the Battle of Messines Ridge. That was remembered as a victory, but their subsequent slaughter at Langemarck during the terrible battle of Passchendaele was virtually forgotten about until now. It is good to see that a new memorial is being erected in Flanders to remember that single day in August 1917 in which 1,200 men from both divisions lost their lives.

It has moved me to tears to walk through each manicured and tranquil grave-yard with row upon row of little white crosses bearing the names and ages of legions of young men whose deaths drained the life out of homes, parishes, counties, communities and our country. You could walk among those graves for ages before finding anyone over the age of thirty. I thought of all the mothers, fathers, wives, children, sweethearts, family, friends and neighbours whose lives crashed sickeningly around them with news of those far-off deaths. It was too great a sacrifice, too great a waste. They were indeed great men, great in courage, great in decency and great in fidelity. Everything about them was great except the war which rewarded them with death. They are entitled to great respect and the memorial of a great peace built between their reconciling successors who have the gift of life, which they would surely have loved and cherished.

Mary McAleese

Mary McAleese
President of Ireland from 1997 to 2011.

INTRODUCTION

In every generation the Irish people have asserted their right
to national freedom and sovereignty; six times during the
past three hundred years they have asserted it in arms.

The Proclamation of the Irish Republic, 1916

In addition to being Irish Catholics,
we have the honour to be British soldiers.

Irish officers at Limburg, 1914

You could not call it war. It is murder and nothing
like the game as it is played in Africa and the
Chitral Expeditions, through both of which I went.

Colour Sergeant John Cooper, 2nd Royal Irish Regiment,
killed at Ypres 1915

If we are going to have a shared history and share
our traditions and share our peace, we have to
share the whole history of the war dead.

Bertie Ahern, former Taoiseach

The heroic dead of Ireland have every right to the homage of
the living: for they proved, in some of the heaviest fighting of the
World War, that the unconquerable spirit of the Irish race – the
spirit, that has placed them among the world's greatest soldiers – still
lives. France will never forget her debt to the heroic Irish dead.

Marshall Ferdinand Foch, 1928

It is perhaps the great paradox of Irish history that more Irishmen died fighting for the Crown than ever died fighting against it.

Irishmen in every generation were willing participants in an army which was regarded by many of their compatriots as an instrument of oppression. The historical reality confounds the modern Irish mind, conditioned as it was until recently, to see the relationship between Britain and Ireland only in adversarial terms. The willing participation of so many Irishmen in the British armed forces was nationalist Ireland's secret and one that it sought to either explain away or conveniently forget after independence in 1922.

More Irishmen fought in British uniforms during the First World War than in any other single conflict, foreign or domestic, before or since. The Irish who joined up between 1914 and 1918 were following a long tradition. Numerous antecedents had been enthusiastic contributors to the great colonial adventure of the nineteenth century which made Britain a superpower. Indeed, they were proportionately over-represented in the armed forces for the whole of that century when British supremacy reached its zenith and the sun never set on Queen Victoria's Empire. The Irish represented 28 per cent of Admiral Nelson's crew at the Battle of Trafalgar in 1805[1] and 30 per cent of the Duke of Wellington's troops at the Battle of Waterloo in 1815.[2]

Catholic soldiers had been banned from joining the British army until 1799. A year later the Act of Union abolished the Irish parliament altogether and brought the country under the direct governance of Westminster. Irish Catholics were not allowed to sit in parliament until Catholic Emancipation in 1829. Yet none of these pernicious circumstances seemed to deter Irishmen from joining the Crown forces in great numbers. Some 159,000 had been integrated into the British army by the eve of the Battle of Waterloo.[3] And they continued their disproportionate prominence in the British army after that date. In 1830, Ireland constituted a third of the population of the United Kingdom, yet 42.2 per cent of all non-commissioned officers and other ranks were Irish.[4] There were more Irishmen than Englishmen in the British army during that decade.[5] Irish numbers in the British army subsequently declined as the century progressed. This was not a measure of waning interest but of catastrophic demographic trends which saw the population of Ireland plummet while that of the rest of the United Kingdom increased rapidly. The Great Famine of the 1840s was the major factor in this devastating diminution of the native population. By 1861, Ireland's share of the UK population had fallen to 22 per cent – but it still made up 30 per cent of the army.[6]

Parallel with the phenomenon of mass Irish participation in the British armed forces was the process whereby nationalist Ireland sought greater freedom from the British Empire. The majority used constitutional means through the Repeal Movement and later the Irish Parliamentary Party and its decades-long campaign for home rule and a peaceful resolution of the differences between Ireland and Britain. A smaller cohort resorted to military action. Of the six rebellions mentioned in the Proclamation of the Irish Republic (1641, 1798, 1803, 1848, 1867 and 1916), those staged in the nineteenth century were poorly organised affairs, lasting only a single day. These rebellions were often quashed in part by fellow countrymen who had become professional soldiers in the British army.

The Irishman in the British army was typically from a rural area. In other parts of the United Kingdom they more often came from urban slums. The Irish recruit was regarded as healthier, better nourished and sturdier than his city-based English, Scots or Welsh equivalent. He was less likely to be turned down for military service. He could bear more hardship.[7]

The Irish also came with a martial reputation, burnished in the armies of the continent, most notably in France during the eighteenth century. The same reputation was also gilded across the Atlantic by their actions in various American wars. The 'fighting Irish' became a cliché but it was one many Irishmen were keen to embrace, most notably the Irish Parliamentary Party leader John Redmond, who could, at the outbreak of war in 1914, summon up 'that gallantry and courage which has distinguished our race all through its history'.

By 1829, the Duke of Wellington had become Prime Minister of the United Kingdom of Britain and Ireland. In the same year, after a long, formidable campaign led by Daniel O'Connell, Catholic Emancipation for Ireland was passed by the houses of parliament in London. In a telling contribution to a sceptical House of Lords, Wellington imagined an exchange he might have had with his Irish Catholic soldiers:

> You well know that your country either so suspects your loyalty, or so dislikes your religion, that she has not yet thought it proper to admit you amongst the ranks of her free citizens; if, on that account, you deem it an act of injustice on her part to require you to shed your blood in her defence, you are at liberty to withdraw. I am, quite sure, my lords, that, however bitter the recollections which it awakened, they would have spurned the alternative with indignation; for the hour of danger and of glory, is the hour in which the gallant, the generous-hearted Irishman, best knows his duty, and is most determined to perform it.[8]

It was, he acknowledged, 'to the Irish Catholic that we all owe our proud pre-eminence in our military careers'.[9]

Wellington was Irish by birth and represented another strand of identity: the Anglo-Irish Protestant ascendancy. The Anglo-Irish were also disproportionately represented in the British armed forces, though they were mainly in the officer class. This would still be the case 100 years after Waterloo.

Why did so many Irishmen join? In 1878, Lady Butler, the well-known artist who specialised in military scenes, painted *Listed for the Connaught Rangers* after honeymooning in Kerry. Two recruits are on the way to join the British army. They are dressed in dun-coloured rags. One has a stooped gait; the other insolently dangles a cigarette from his mouth. The upright recruiting sergeant beside them is dressed in his redcoat and gloves. He is a symbol of organisation and strength of purpose. He represents civilisation. Following him are three drummer boys, suggesting continuity of service from one generation to the next.

The setting is unmistakably the west of Ireland. There are mountains in the background and an austere beauty to the scenery – but you cannot eat scenery. One of the new recruits casts a forlorn look at an abandoned and ruined cottage. The only alternative to emigration for many of these men was a career as a soldier. The inference was clear: the British army was a route out of poverty and a path to the civilising influences of the Empire. But for all the appeal of regular pay and at least one square meal a day, the army was a harsh sanctuary for its lowliest recruits – Irishmen included, as the nineteenth-century ballad 'The Glen of Aherlow' acknowledges:

> Bereft of home and kith and kin, with plenty all around,
> I starved within my cabin, and slept upon the ground;
> But cruel as my lot was, I never did hardship know,
> Till I joined the English army, far away from Aherlow.
> 'Rouse up there,' cried the corporal, 'Ya lazy Irish hound!
> Why don't you hear the bugle, its call to arms to sound?'

But it was a way out, too, for the hordes of landless Catholic boys scattered throughout the country in penury and in rags. If they could withstand the rigours of the regime, the Army represented opportunities not available in civilian life. In 1881, an Irishman could earn £25 a year agricultural labourer, but £40 a year as a private in the British army.[10] The army guaranteed lodgings, a full belly, clothing, steady employment, an outside chance of promotion, a modest pension and foreign adventure. It was not a political act for those who signed up, despite the protestations of some advanced nationalists who considered it tantamount to treason. Neither was it taboo.

The average Irish recruit to the British army was a 'Catholic, poor, sometimes of an adventurous bellicose sort, apolitical and he saw himself as a soldier by occupation', history professor Peter Karsten surmised in his 1983 paper 'Irish Soldiers in the British Army 1792–1922'.

Most Irishmen were neither enamoured by nor hostile to the British Empire. They were professional soldiers. It was as good a living as any other. Karsten points out that Irishmen in the nineteenth century did not join the British army; it was simply 'the army'. It was as much their army as anyone else's. 'Seven centuries of British rule, of one sort or another, had led most Irish people to accept the fact that, like it or not, they were part of the United Kingdom.'

The British army was so integrated into Irish life that even those who sought a violent separation from Britain were mixed up in it. Of the seven signatories of the 1916 Proclamation of the Irish Republic, James Connolly had been in the British army. Tom Clarke was born into it as his father was a sergeant based on the Isle of Wight. Éamonn Ceannt's brother William Kent was a British army regular who was killed during the First World War;[11] their father had served in the Royal Irish Constabulary, the police force which maintained civilian rule in Ireland. Joseph Mary Plunkett, the chief military planner for the Rising, attended Stonyhurst College in Cheshire which had an Officers' Training Corps for the British army. Joseph Mary was too delicate, but his brother George, who participated in the Rising, had been in the OTC. Stonyhurst would produce the first Victoria Cross winner of the First World War, an Irishman named Maurice Dease (the subject of chapter 2). Michael Mallin, one of sixteen men executed after the Easter Rising, had joined the British army as a drummer boy and served for 14 years.[12] Many of those nationalists who had been in the British army protested, by way of explanation, that they had known nothing of their own history when they joined.

The writer Seán Ó Faoláin, who was born in Cork in 1900, grew up during the twilight of British rule in Ireland as the son of an Royal Irish Constabulary constable. But it was not apparent at the time that British rule would soon come to an end. Ireland, he remembered, was then only a geographical entity. It did not exist politically, culturally or psychologically. Ó Faoláin, who would later go on to fight against the British in the War of Independence, was not perturbed by this. Sixty years after the Rising, he remembered:

> I was tremendously proud of belonging to the Empire, as were at that time most Irishmen. I gloried in all its trappings, Kings, Queens, dukes, duchesses, generals, admirals, soldiers, colonists and conquerors, the lot. My childhood had been filled with the colonial glories of Gordon of Khartoum, the Relief of Lucknow, the Charge of the Light Brigade, Irish-born Wellington, the Munster Fusiliers, the glory of the flag, the belly stirring rumble of the preliminary roll of God Save the King, Lord Kitchener, the Angel at Mons, but above all the dream of every well-bred imperial boy of one day becoming a Gentleman.[13]

For Ó Faoláin, the Easter Rising came as such a profound shock that he felt he was living in a different country. His fellow Corkman Tom Barry, who went on to become one of the most feared IRA commanders of the War of Independence, had joined the British army when he was 17. He served in the Royal Field Artillery during the First World War and was present at the siege of Kut, one of the great British military defeats of the war. The Easter Rising changed everything for him too, as he recalled in his well-known memoir *Guerilla Days in Ireland*:

> I went [to join the British army] because I knew no Irish history and had no national consciousness. I had never been told of Wolfe Tone or Robert Emmet, though I did know all about the kings of England and when they had come to the British throne. I had never heard of the victory over the Sassenach at Benburb, but I could tell the dates of Waterloo and Trafalgar.[14]

For the Anglo-Irish class, the army offered greater possibilities. Many, like Wellington, were not particularly wealthy by the standards of their peers in England. Military service was their means of achieving status and income. The British army was often the only route to a successful career for a middle or younger son of the gentry and became increasingly so as the fortunes of the Anglo-Irish waned over the course of the century.

The percentage of Irishmen in the British army continued to decline as the century progressed and Irish depopulation continued. In 1890, the Irish represented just over 15 per cent of the British army, but Catholics constituted 18.7 per cent of the same army, many of them Irish emigrants or their descendents, James Connolly being one of them.[15]

The outbreak of the Second Boer War in 1899 roused a lot of pro-Boer and anti-British feeling in Ireland. Nationalist Ireland saw in Boer resistance to British rule a template for Ireland too. Nationalist sentiment had been running high in 1898, the centenary year of the 1798 Rebellion. Maud Gonne, the wife of Major John MacBride and muse of the poet W.B. Yeats, went on an anti-recruitment drive and reminded the Irish public that it had been the same British army which had put down the 1798 Rebellion. She pleaded with those going off to fight the Boer War to 'even at the eleventh hour remember that they were Irishmen, and cast off the hideous English uniform'.[16] Major MacBride would go on to command an Irish Brigade in South Africa that would fight alongside the Boers. He would later be executed for his part in the Easter Rising.

The battle for hearts and minds in Ireland intensified as the nineteenth century gave way to the twentieth. Nationalists sought to turn back the tide of the Anglicisation of Irish society, which Séan Ó Faoláin alluded to in his memoirs.

The turn of the century brought a revival in Irish nationalist sentiment. The Irish Literary Renaissance, the Gaelic League, the GAA and a united Irish Parliamentary Party all questioned what it meant to be Irish and, just as keenly, what it meant not to be British.

The activists who saw it as the British army, and not just 'the army', were growing in number and getting louder. An apolitical, ordinary Irishman was no longer enlisting in an apathetic vacuum. Nationalist critics were liable to cast aspersions on his decision. The slurs hurled at him if he served in British uniform during the

Boer War were particularly vicious. He was one of the 'meanest curs in creation' and a 'traitor to his country and an enemy of his people'.[17]

Yet popular sentiment was still very much on the side of the Irishman in British uniform. In 1907, the Fusiliers' Arch was erected in St Stephen's Green to remember the Royal Dublin Fusiliers killed in the Second Boer War. A large, enthusiastic crowd turned out for the event, though the Irish Parliamentary Party had called on Irish people to 'inculcate an attitude of aloofness from the Army because it was the Army which held Ireland by force'.[18] It became known to nationalists as 'traitors' gate'. This bitter hostility between those pro and anti the British army would be heightened by the time of the First World War.

—

In 1914 Ireland had eight recruiting districts for the British army:

Royal Irish Rifles: Antrim, Down
Royal Irish Fusiliers: Armagh, Cavan, Monaghan, Louth
Royal Inniskilling Fusiliers: Donegal, Derry, Fermanagh, Tyrone
Connaught Rangers: Galway, Mayo, Roscommon, Sligo, Leitrim
Leinster Regiment: Meath, (King's County) Offaly, (Queen's County) Laois, Westmeath, Longford
Royal Dublin Fusiliers: Dublin, Kildare, Wicklow, Carlow
Royal Munster Fusiliers: Cork, Kerry, Limerick, Clare
Royal Irish Regiment: Waterford, Kilkenny, Tipperary, Wexford.

The home barracks of these regiments were the dominant employers in their towns. Tralee (Royal Munster Fusiliers), Birr (Leinster Regiment), Renmore (Connaught Rangers), Enniskillen (Inniskilling Fusiliers) and so many other rural towns were known first and foremost as 'garrison towns'. Dozens of other towns throughout Ireland had smaller barracks.

In 1888, twenty-one of the fifty-one towns in Munster with a population of more than 2,000 had a military barracks. The pattern was similar in the rest of the country. By comparison, as historian Dr Aoife Bhreatnach has observed, the present Irish defence forces have just sixteen military stations for the whole State. The British army was much more ubiquitous. 'Anyone living in a country with a small standing army will struggle to imagine how pervasive was the military presence,' she states on her blog *Garrison Towns*.[19]

By 1914, just under 10 per cent of the British army, including reservists, were Irish – again proportional to the Irish share of the UK population.[20] This comprised 28,000 Irish-born soldiers and 30,000 reservists. Nearly one in five reservists in the British army was Irish. Within two months, all of them were fighting in France or Flanders.

In 1914, Ireland was in an extreme state of agitation. Two opposing armed militias were smuggling guns with the intention of starting a military conflict if necessary. The Ulster Volunteer Force, founded in January 1913, was the better armed force. It was determined to oppose the introduction of home rule in that part of the province of Ulster which had a Protestant majority. In response, the Irish Volunteers was set up in November 1913, determined to ensure that the British government would not backslide on its commitment to home rule.

In the middle was the British army in all its garrisons. Assumed and obligated to be scrupulously neutral in the political arena, the Curragh crisis of March 1914 came as a shock to the self-same political establishment. Faced with the prospect of moving north to quell unionist unrest, dozens of officers, most of them English or Anglo-Irish and in cavalry regiments, offered to resign their commissions rather than obey government orders. The looming collision between unionist and nationalist forces on the island had now embroiled different factions of the army. This was an extraordinary act of defiance against the will of the sovereign government. It convinced many Irish nationalists that the British army could not be relied upon to enforce the law of the land.

The future British Prime Minister David Lloyd George understood what this nascent mutiny really meant:

> We are confronted with the greatest issue raised in this country since the days of the Stuarts. Representative government in this land is at stake. In those days our forefathers had to face a claim of the Divine Right of Kings to do what they pleased. Today it is the Divine Right of the aristocracy to do what its pleases. We are not fighting about Ulster. We are not fighting about Home Rule. We are fighting for all that is essential to civil liberty in this land.[21]

The Third Home Rule Bill had been introduced into the House of Commons in April 1912. It granted a very limited form of autonomy to a devolved Irish parliament, with Westminster still retaining control over foreign policy, military affairs and taxation. The Parliament Act of 1911 had removed the most significant obstacle to home rule by ending the unelected House of Lords' power of veto over legislation passed in the Commons. Nevertheless, the House of Lords could still delay a bill for two years and did so before the Third Home Rule Bill finally passed all stages.

This two-year delay proved fatal to the prospects of home rule ever being implemented. It was finally put on the statute book in May 1914. It still needed the king's assent to make it the law of the land, but the Ulster question remained intractable. The principle of Ulster's exclusion from any prospective home rule parliament had been conceded by the British Prime Minister Herbert Asquith. But would that exclusion be permanent or temporary? And how many counties would be involved?

Would it be just the four where there was a solid Protestant majority, or six, or all nine counties of Ulster? Irish Parliamentary Party leader John Redmond reluctantly conceded a six-year opt-out for Ulster, but Sir Edward Carson, the uncompromising unionist leader, dismissed this as a mere stay of execution.

Talks convened by King George V at Buckingham Palace in late July ended in stalemate. The respective leaders, Redmond and his deputy John Dillon, Carson and Captain James Craig, departed without agreement. The only semblance of any personal rapport was contained in an offering from Craig to his fellow second in command. 'Mr Dillon, will you shake my hand?' Craig, a Boer War veteran, asked his opponent. 'I should be glad to think that I have been able to give as many years' service to Ulster as you have to the service of Ireland.' Asquith, witnessing this temporary outbreak of bonhomie, observed, 'Aren't they a remarkable people? And the folly of thinking we can ever understand, let alone govern them.'[22]

While all this was going on, the crisis precipitated by the assassination of the Archduke Franz Ferdinand and his wife Sophia had escalated from a regional quarrel into a situation which was rapidly becoming the most serious threat to peace that Europe had ever faced. On 23 July 1914, Austria-Hungary's ultimatum to Serbia, which the country couldn't possibly accept, jolted the British Cabinet into recognising the true gravity of the situation.

The ultimatum was read aloud by Foreign Secretary Sir Edward Gray as other Cabinet members were poring over a large-scale map of Ulster counties. The British Cabinet 'toiled around the muddy byways' of Tyrone and Fermanagh, as Winston Churchill described them, to try to ascertain the religious composition of individual parishes.[23] Tyrone, which had a Catholic majority, proved to be a particularly exasperating county. 'We sat again this morning for an hour & a half, discussing maps & figures, and always getting back to that most damnable creation of the perverted ingenuity of man – the County of Tyrone,' Asquith lamented in a letter to his mistress Venetia Stanley.[24] Churchill, the First Lord of the Admiralty, understood immediately that this regional quarrel was a mere irritant in comparison with the cataclysm that was to come. 'The parishes of Fermanagh and Tyrone faded back into the mists and squalls of Ireland,' he would later recall, 'and a strange light began immediately, but by perceptible gradations, to fall and grow upon the map of Europe.'[25]

The failure of the Buckingham Palace talks had convinced many unionists that the time had come to stage a *coup d'état*. If they couldn't remain within the United Kingdom, then an independent Ulster would be a bearable alternative. Secession and independence were still preferable to home rule. It was time to declare the Ulster Provisional Government. On 29 July, Craig wrote to Carson, 'You may take it that immediately you signify by the pre-arranged code that we are to go ahead, everything prepared will be carried out to the letter unless in the meantime you suggest any modification. All difficulties have been overcome and we are in a very strong position.[26] Food was stockpiled, work on a new currency had begun and plans were afoot to evacuate women and children to Scotland.

In the final days before war was declared, the British army was in bad standing with much of nationalist Ireland. Disquiet about the Curragh crisis turned to outrage when the security forces attempted to stop the importation of arms by the Irish Volunteers at Howth on 26 July. During protests that evening, three unarmed civilians were shot dead by the King's Own Scottish Borderers at Bachelors Walk in the centre of Dublin. The killings maddened nationalist Ireland and generated bitter comparisons with how the authorities had failed to stop gunrunning by the Ulster Volunteer Force that April in Larne. A mass rally was held on 28 July in Dublin city centre. The killings had mobilised all shades of Irish nationalist opinion.

Events elsewhere intervened. From Russia's partial mobilisation on 29 July to 4 August when the United Kingdom declared war – just a week – the major powers embarked upon the bloodiest war in history to that date.

The unionists and nationalists put aside their differences to face a common foe, much to the relief of the British government. 'The one bright spot in the whole of this terrible situation is Ireland,' the British foreign secretary Edward Gray told the House of Commons in a speech on 3 August, the eve of war.[27] Gray's speech, one of the most significant in the history of the British parliament, managed to convince a majority of British MPs that Britain had no choice but to fight and would face dire consequences even if she didn't.

John Redmond responded with equal forcefulness. His voice trembling with emotion, he offered the Irish Volunteers and the Ulster Volunteer Force to the government to defend the shores of Ireland and so release the garrisons based in the country for foreign service. He was satisfied he had secured the measure of control of Irish affairs, albeit within the British Empire, for which he and his predecessors had striven. The shared history of Ireland and Britain was troubled, he acknowledged, but those enmities would not be continued, not in this hour of supreme trial for the British Empire. Redmond became an impassioned advocate for the British war effort. The Empire's war would be Ireland's war. Home rule was given royal assent on 18 September but its implementation was suspended by agreement for the duration of the war. Two days later, Redmond came upon a group of East Wicklow Irish Volunteers who were drilling in the beautiful surroundings of Woodenbridge near his home. Remarking that the wider world beyond this idyllic setting had turned ugly, he told the assembled volunteers that it was time for Irishmen to prove their ancient valour. Their duty was not only to defend the shores of Ireland at all costs from an 'unlikely' foreign invasion, but to venture further afield as 'the interests of Ireland, of the whole of Ireland, are at stake in this war'.[28] There in the beautiful surroundings of the Vale of Avoca, he told Irish nationalists to go 'wherever the firing line extends in defence of right, of freedom and religion in this war'.

For the first time, an Irish nationalist leader had openly encouraged Irishmen to join the British army. Redmond accepted the established wisdom that the war would be short. Prior to the outbreak of the war, his party had gained control of the Irish Volunteers from more strident elements who wanted to foment armed rebellion. But his call for Irishmen to serve in France lost him a wedge of the organisation. Of the roughly 170,000 Irish Volunteers, 158,300 (93 per cent) stayed with Redmond and became the National Volunteers; the remaining 12,300 broke away from Redmond, but retained the title Irish Volunteers. Some 22,000 of those who stayed loyal to Redmond would go on to serve in the British army during the war.[29]

The response to Redmond's early call was a reflection of Irish nationalist support for the British war effort. The war effort had the support of the Irish political establishment, the major Christian denominations and the mainstream press. Most of them sincerely believed Germany was a threat to civilisation. The invasion of Belgium, a small, predominantly Catholic country, was another galvanising factor. Reports of German atrocities there, some of them accurate, some of them exaggerated, had a particular resonance in Ireland.

Redmond had ostensibly triumphed. He was dismissive of the Irish Volunteers who had scorned his cry for unity. They were gadflies and cranks, he believed, who did not represent the bulk of Irish public opinion.

His eventual nemesis Pádraig Pearse, the man who would go on to become the first president of the Provisional Government, was not dismayed by the small numbers who had defied Redmond's call. Better, he maintained, to have a covert, determined cadre of true believers than a leaderless and divided National Volunteers. Within days of the declaration of war, the reservists attached to the National Volunteers were all called up, depriving the organisation of those with valuable military training.

What the remaining Irish Volunteers lacked in numbers, they made up for in a fervent sense of opportunism. They would use the war to fight against British rule in Ireland. England's difficulty would once again be Ireland's opportunity.

It was in this volatile climate that tens of thousands of Irishmen set sail for England and France, while hundreds remained at home to prepare for the forthcoming insurrection.

When the war ended in November 1918, the melancholy audit could begin: those who lived, those who died; the numbers injured; the numbers imprisoned; the numbers lost; the numbers who served. It is estimated that at least 210,000 Irishmen served in British uniform during the First World War. This comprises 58,000 of those already serving at outbreak of hostilities – the 'Old Contemptibles', as they were known – and 140,460 who volunteered later.[30] Conscription was imposed in Britain in January 1916. It did not apply to Ireland, but 95,000 Irishmen had already signed up by then and became part of 'Kitchener's Army'. The remaining 45,460 signed up in the following months and years. Some 10,000 joined up in the last three and a half months before the Armistice of 1918. All of this was achieved without conscription in Ireland.[31]

Historian Keith Jeffery estimates that between a quarter to a third of all Irishmen of military age (15 to 35) signed up to fight in the war.[32] This is a base figure. The naval historian Karen O'Rawe counts more than 10,000 Irishmen who served in the Royal Navy during the war, of whom at least 1,657 died, 350 alone at the Battle of Jutland. In his book *Irish Aces of the RFC and RAF*, Joe Gleeson states that 6,000 Irishmen were in the flying corps during the war.

A total of 19,327 Irish-born men served in the Canadian Expeditionary Force,[33] another 5,774 with the Australian Imperial Force[34] and 1,300 with the New Zealand forces. The number who served in the American Expeditionary Force remains uncertain. The Americans never listed their recruits by country and the records were destroyed by fire in 1973.[35] However, diligent detective work by the historian Megan Smolenyak, based on the New York and New Jersey war dead, concluded that 975 Irish-born men died in American uniform and approximately 16,500 served overseas with the 'Doughboys' during the First World War.[36] In any event, the combined total dwarfs the number of Irish who fought in the Easter Rising and the War of Independence.

The number of Irish dead from the First World War is also disputed. In 1922, a project entitled the Irish National War Memorial Records sought to record all those Irishmen who died to find a definitive figure. By then, however, the Irish Free State was beginning to construct an alternative narrative of recent Irish history. The Irish National War Memorial Records was established by Lord Ypres (Sir John French), the former commander-in-chief of the British army and Lord Lieutenant of Ireland, and compiled by a committee led by Eva Bernard, from a well-known unionist family. The eight volumes, published in 1923, were beautifully illustrated by Harry Clarke, one of the era's most distinguished Irish artists. It was put together at a time when record keepers were still grappling with the scale of the tragedy. As a visual tribute, it is unsurpassed; as a historical record, it is a flawed endeavour with many elementary errors. Recent research proves that more than 10,000 of the men listed within the records to have died in France actually fell in Belgium.[37]

The memorial records name 49,647 Irishmen who died in the war, but these were not all Irishmen.[38] The records include men such as John Kipling (see Chapter 11) and George Edwin Ellison, the last British soldier to die in the war. Both were English, but served in Irish regiments. Service in an Irish regiment or Irish birth was the criterion for inclusion in the memorial records. Many Irishmen who served in regiments based in Britain or who had emigrated to Britain were not listed in the memorial records.

One set of the records was presented to the city of Ypres – or the ruin of Ypres, as it could be more accurately described in the aftermath of the First World War.

The In Flanders Fields Museum is a First World War museum at Ypres Cloth Hall. It is now engaged in updating and correcting the records.[39]

The memorial records list 30,986 men born in Ireland who died in the war and an additional 7,405 with no place of birth. The rest came from elsewhere, most notably England. Of those born in Ireland, 18,946 (61 per cent) came from what is now the Republic of Ireland and 11,299 (39 per cent) from Northern Ireland.[40]

Modern research suggests that this figure for the Irish war dead may be a considerable underestimation. The military historian Tom Burnell has spent seven years attempting to accurately collate the number of Irish dead from the twenty-six counties of the Republic. He has trawled through local newspapers, digitised books, the database of the Soldiers Who Died in the Great War and officers' records, and then checked them against the Irish National War Memorial Records, the records of the Commonwealth War Graves Commission and the two censuses of 1901 and 1911.

Burnell has found confirmation that 23,858 were born in what is now the Republic of Ireland, a 26 per cent increase on the 18,946 listed in the memorial records. However, when the number of servicemen who give their address, their next of kin or are buried in the 26 counties is included, the figure rises to 29,354, a 54 per cent increase.

If extrapolated out to the whole island using the initial 30,986 (born in Ireland) as a baseline figure, it would indicate that the true number of Irish war dead is between 39,042 (a 26 per cent increase) and 47,718 (a 54 per cent increase), more than the 35,000 figure conventionally given as the best rough estimate.

Separate research carried out in Sligo by local historian Brian Scanlon would also indicate the memorial records have underestimated the number of Irish who died. His research has found at least 546 Sligo men who died in the war; the memorial records figure is 395.[41] Some 720 men from Mayo are listed as having died in the war in the memorial records, but the Mayo Peace Park in Castlebar includes 1,100 men on its memorial wall.[42] A similar exercise in Fermanagh found nearly 300 men who were not originally recorded in the records.[43]

The research points to one unmistakable trend – many more Irishmen died than we assumed therefore. Whatever the final figure, and it may never be determined definitively, the First World War was the biggest and bloodiest military engagement ever entered into by the people of Ireland.

—

This book arose from a trip to the Belgian border town of Mons in February 2014. Mons was the place where British involvement in the First World War began and ended. There are four monuments with an Irish theme there.

This prompted me to look for the other memorials on the Western Front. It has taken me on a physical and historical journey across northern France, southern

Belgium and central Germany. From the Ulster Tower, opened in 1921, to the incomparable Island of Ireland Peace Park, built as late as 1998, the Irish have left a remarkable legacy on the Western Front. That legacy is remembered in the many monuments and cemeteries scattered across the region.

Most of the monuments were built in the 1920s, when memories of the war were still vivid and many survivors were able to tell their stories. At the unveiling of the Guillemont Cross in College Green, Dublin, on Armistice Day 1924, a crowd estimated at 50,000 turned up.[44] It was a day of the rawest of emotion. After 1916 and the War of Independence of 1919-21, Ireland was a cold country for those who had served in British khaki, but there was a strong, lingering seam of empathy too. The deaths of tens of thousands of Irishmen and the maiming and traumatising of countless more could not be ignored in an island with a population of just 4.4 million. The British Legion estimated that 164,000 Irish children had lost a parent during the war – mostly a father. Everybody knew somebody who had served or been injured. Even successive Irish Free State governments proved to be surprisingly generous in providing funds for a national war memorial.

Yet the story of the Irish who fought in the First World War faded away as the men themselves faded away. As the decades passed, the Irish State adopted only one national narrative. The opposite happened in the North, where the dead were venerated as proof of Ulster's unswerving loyalty to the Union. The fact that the majority of Irishmen who fought in the war were from a nationalist Irish Catholic background was conveniently forgotten here too. The Ulster and Free State establishments had this much in common. It did not suit the self-images of the two political entities that emerged after the partition of Ireland.

In 1967, a year after the fiftieth anniversary of the Easter Rising, the historian F.X. Martin famously deployed the term 'national amnesia' in his essay 'Myth, Fact and Mystery'. Those who had served in British uniform in the First World War, or those who had been involved in the Irish Parliamentary Party's long campaign for greater autonomy for Ireland, had been subjected to a 'great oblivion'.[45] Martin offered a telling statistic: for every Easter Rising rebel, there were sixteen Irishmen fighting on the Western Front. Furthermore, he suggested four out of five Irish people had been in favour of the British war effort in the beginning.[46]

Despite Martin's intervention, national amnesia remained the prevalent condition well into the 1980s. The decrepit state of the Irish National War Memorial Gardens, on the banks of the River Liffey in Islandbridge, was representative of Irish attitudes at the time. Ireland's national memorial, with its beautiful, sunken rose garden and sturdy pergolas, was only completed in 1939, twenty-one years after the war had ended. It was not officially opened until 2006, for the ninetieth anniversary of the Battle of the Somme, when both President Mary McAleese and the Taoiseach Bertie Ahern were in attendance.[47] This tranquil place of memory, created by Edwin Lutyens, the architect who designed the Cenotaph in London and the Thiepval Memorial in the Somme, had become a graffiti-strewn, rubbish tip. And its location was peripheral, on the edge of the city, out of sight and out of mind.

In the memorable words of the journalist and historian Kevin Myers, who had been one of the few voices to challenge the national amnesia, Irish people had not merely 'forgotten, but they'd forgotten they had forgotten'.[48] In an interview with Myers, Sebastian Barry, whose novel *A Long, Long Way* told the story of one Irishman caught up in the maelstrom of the war and the Easter Rising, also expressed his remorse at official attitudes. 'These men deserved a most wondering thanks for their ordinary divine courage. That they were not thanked when they came home was a profound indictment of a state that could not find it in its narrowing heart – though its own way a brave narrowing heart – to include them.'[49]

—

The monuments erected on the Western Front were built to endure. They were built with a sense of finality, a profound conviction that the human race could not possibly sink to such horrors again. The First World War therefore became the Great War, because those who lived through it could conceive of no greater war. It would be the last catastrophic rupture in the soul of human civilisation. It would be 'the war to end all wars'. Within twenty years, the continent would again be in flames, the machinery of war ever more violent. The trenches of one war led to the gas chambers of the next.

The Irish monuments and gravestones of the First World War have stood the test of time and the vicissitudes of Irish memory. They will remain there in their stoic dignity, open to anyone who stops to visit and contemplate and maybe offer a prayer. In these centenary years, they may be discovered by a few more people who wish to pay tribute to these men of 'ordinary divine courage'.

In the last two decades, a new awareness of those men and their times has seeped into the Irish consciousness. This renaissance of memory has coincided with the Northern Ireland peace process. The two developments are not unconnected. Better relations between Britain and Ireland, and nationalists and unionists have opened up a space for both communities to commemorate their war dead with more open hearts.

In the Republic, the old monocultural history for a monocultural state has been replaced by a deeper understanding of the complexity of the story, with all its competing loyalties and narratives.

It was in this more generous spirit that the Island of Ireland Peace Park was opened in 1998, the year the Good Friday Agreement was signed. The presence at its opening of Queen Elizabeth II and President of Ireland Mary McAleese was probably the most significant act of remembrance for the Irish war dead since the war ended eighty years previously. In 2011, Queen Elizabeth II, during her first visit to the Republic of Ireland, visited the Irish National War Memorial Gardens in Islandbridge and the Garden of Remembrance in Parnell Square, built for those who had died fighting against British rule in Ireland. In 2013, the Taoiseach Enda Kenny and the British Prime Minister David Cameron visited the grave of Major Willie Redmond in Flanders. It was also an acknowledgement of shared history, not only of Irish involvement in the British armed forces, but also the Irish contribution to British parliamentary life. As an MP who fought and died in the First World War, Willie Redmond embraced both traditions.

The last two decades have seen new memorials on the Western Front. In 1998, the Francis Ledwidge Memorial dedicated to the Irish poet and soldier killed at the Battle of Passchendaele was completed. In 2011, the monument to the Iron 12 provided a permanent memorial to the extraordinary execution of twelve men, six of them Irish, a dark chapter of the war which had been almost completely forgotten. In 2015, after many years of negotiation, a sign commemorating the site of the *Last General Absolution of the Munsters*, the most famous Irish painting of the war, was finally erected on the Rue du Bois in Richebourg. In November 2015, the London Irish Rifles Association unveiled a plaque in Loos town centre.

In 2016, the pivotal year in the Irish Decade of Centenaries which remembers events from 1912 to 1922, other permanent reminders were put in place. The gas attack on the 16th (Irish) Division at Hulluch while the Easter Rising was going on in Ireland is remembered in a permanent message board in France. On Remembrance Sunday the French Government unveiled a new memorial in Glasnevin Cemetery to the Irish who died in the service of France. It is modelled on the Ginchy Cross. In 2017 the battles in Flanders will be remembered with a new memorial to Willie Redmond and John Meeke the man who attended to him on the battlefield, while a memorial stone will recall the forgotten Battle of Langemarck.

When the Irish politician Paddy Harte proposed a round tower, a symbol of permanence, for the Island of Ireland Peace Park, he envisaged a memorial that would 'last for centuries and be as meaningful in 500 years time as when it was built'.[50] The round tower is now there. The graves, the cemeteries and the monuments were there long before it. As long as they silently stand sentry, they will tell of the men who left Ireland's shores never to return.

These monuments are a reminder to never forget. These monuments are forever Ireland.

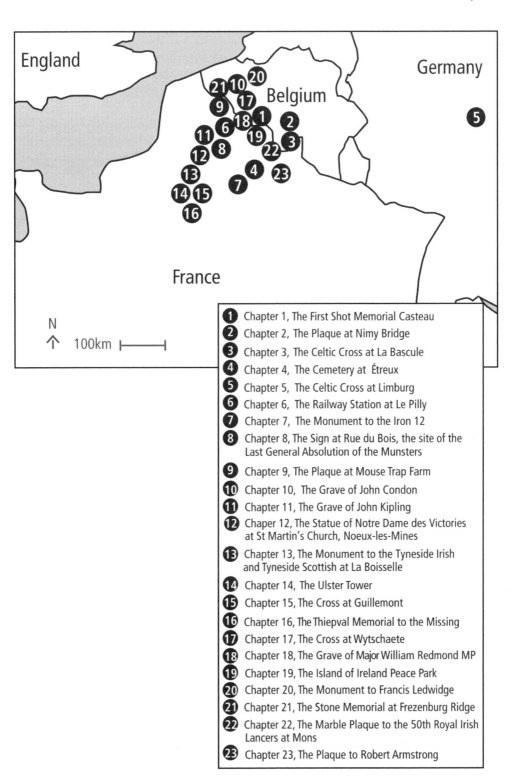

England

Germany

Belgium

France

N

↑   100km |——————|

1 Chapter 1, The First Shot Memorial Casteau
2 Chapter 2, The Plaque at Nimy Bridge
3 Chapter 3, The Celtic Cross at La Bascule
4 Chapter 4, The Cemetery at Étreux
5 Chapter 5, The Celtic Cross at Limburg
6 Chapter 6, The Railway Station at Le Pilly
7 Chapter 7, The Monument to the Iron 12
8 Chapter 8, The Sign at Rue du Bois, the site of the Last General Absolution of the Munsters
9 Chapter 9, The Plaque at Mouse Trap Farm
10 Chapter 10, The Grave of John Condon
11 Chapter 11, The Grave of John Kipling
12 Chaper 12, The Statue of Notre Dame des Victories at St Martin's Church, Noeux-les-Mines
13 Chapter 13, The Monument to the Tyneside Irish and Tyneside Scottish at La Boisselle
14 Chapter 14, The Ulster Tower
15 Chapter 15, The Cross at Guillemont
16 Chapter 16, The Thiepval Memorial to the Missing
17 Chapter 17, The Cross at Wytschaete
18 Chapter 18, The Grave of Major William Redmond MP
19 Chapter 19, The Island of Ireland Peace Park
20 Chapter 20, The Monument to Francis Ledwidge
21 Chapter 21, The Stone Memorial at Frezenburg Ridge
22 Chapter 22, The Marble Plaque to the 50th Royal Irish Lancers at Mons
23 Chapter 23, The Plaque to Robert Armstrong

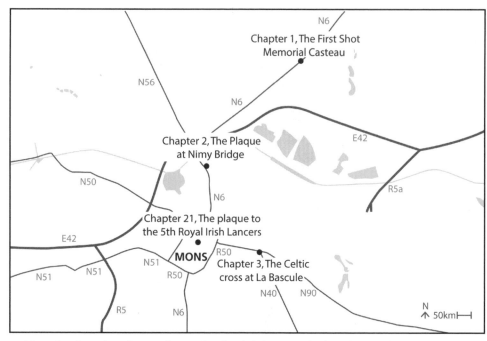

Mons, the place where the British started and ended the war and where there are four Irish monuments.

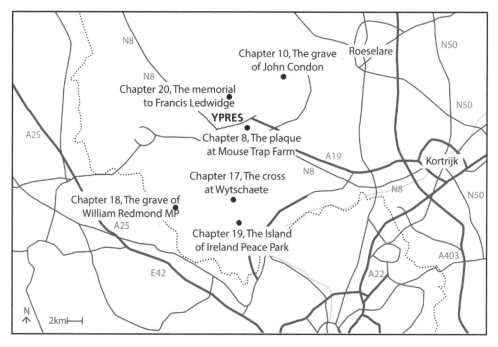

An estimated 12,500 Irishmen died in Belgium during the First World War, most in Flanders fields around the town of Ypres where the Irish have left a tangible presence.

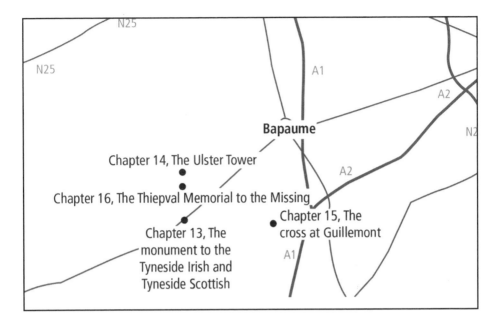

The Battle of the Somme was the biggest of the First World War and the tens of thousands of Irish who fought and died there have left their mark.

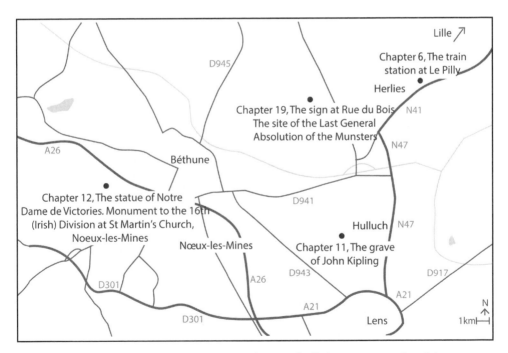

Sometimes called 'forgotten front', the area to the west of Lille has many reminders of the horror of the First World War and the Irish who fought there.

ICI FUT ETABLI, LE 22 AOÛT 1914, À 7 HEURES DU MATIN
LE PREMIER CONTACT ENTRE LE CORPS EXPEDITIONNAIRE
BRITANNIQUE ET LA PREMIERE ARMEE ALLEMANDE. LE
CAPORAL E. THOMAS DE L'ESCADRON C DU 4e ROYAL IRISH
DRAGOON GUARDS TIRA LE PREMIER COUP DE FEU ET LE
CAPITAINE C.B.HORNBY COMMANDA LA PREMIERE CHARGE
QUI REFOULA LES ECLAIREURS ENNEMIS JUSQU'A LA
LISIERE NORD DU VILLAGE DE CASTEAU.

THIS TABLET IS ERECTED TO COMMEMORATE THE ACTION OF
'C' SQUADRON 4TH ROYAL IRISH DRAGOON GUARDS ON
22ND AUGUST 1914
WHEN CORPORAL E. THOMAS FIRED THE FIRST SHOT FOR THE
BRITISH EXPEDITIONARY FORCE AND CAPTAIN C.B.HORNBY
LED THE FIRST MOUNTED ATTACK AGAINST THE GERMANS.

1

THE FIRST SHOT MEMORIAL AT CASTEAU

There are events so cataclysmic in history that it impossible to conceive of the world without them. The First World War was such an event. Had it not happened, Europe might have continued, as it had done in the first decade of the twentieth century, on the path of incremental social and economic progress. Inevitably, there would be regional conflicts and occasional flashpoints between the great powers, but these would have been defused by pragmatic politicians reluctant to commit a generation to the slaughterhouse of total war.

Before the First World War, Germany was a progressive society. The country had only been unified in 1871. Its first chancellor, Otto von Bismarck, sensed the great issues of the day would be decided by 'blood and iron', but it was more iron than blood after their victory in the Franco-Prussian war, which ended in 1871.

Under Prussian leadership, the patchwork of thirty-nine smaller kingdoms and principalities were united into one nation. Germany had an abundance of natural resources, but its greatest resource was the ingenuity and industry of its people. In the three decades before the First World War, Germany's population grew from 41 million to 68 million.[1] Steel production rose twelvefold, coal production by five. Its world-class chemical and machinery industries trebled in size. The Germans grasped how the nexus between research and innovation could generate continuous economic prosperity.[2]

Firms such as Krupps, Siemens, Bayer and Mercedes Benz were already world leaders in their fields. After the United States, Germany was the biggest industrial power in the world.[3] As a potential military power, it was both envied and feared, especially by the British, who resented its desire to challenge the Royal Navy, the guarantor of the British Empire.

The largest party in the Reichstag was the Social Democrats, but Germany was not a truly representative democracy. Ultimate power lay with the unstable Kaiser Wilhelm II, who was given to injudicious sabre-rattling, and behind him a Prussian military elite who saw only threats from Russia in the east and France in the west. They would lead their country to disaster.

Russia, too, was a country making rapid economic progress. It remained an autocracy, but it was catching up with the rest of Europe. Before 1914 it had been Europe's fastest-growing economy.[4] Its vast natural resources were attracting foreign investment, particularly from France, but it laboured under an unaccountable Czar Nicholas II, who promised democratic reforms but never delivered them.

The antebellum Europe of early 1914 was an imperfect place. There were vast inequalities between rich and poor. Poverty, disease and illiteracy were widespread and democracy was limited, but human progress was undoubtedly on an upward trajectory.

Harold MacMillan, the future British prime minister who served in the Grenadier Guards and was wounded three times in the First World War, remembered the summer term at Oxford in 1914 as an idyllic dream:

The term was thus 'devoted' almost wholly to enjoyment. All the summer we punted on the river, bathed, sat in the quad, dined and argued with our friends, debated in the Union, dancing at Commemoration balls. Everything would get better and better. This was the world I was born in … Suddenly, unexpectedly, one morning in 1914 the whole thing came to an end.[5]

In June 1914, Lord Dunsany wrote a preface to Francis Ledwidge's first collection of poems *Songs of the Fields*. (Chapter 20 of this book is devoted to Ledwidge.) The publication was delayed by the start of the war in August 1914. In June 1915, Dunsany and Ledwidge were both in the 5th Royal Inniskilling Fusiliers. Ledwidge was on his way to Gallipoli. Everything had changed and none of it was for the better, Dunsany recalled. 'I wrote this preface in such a different June, that if I sent it out with no addition it would make this book appear to have dropped a long while since out of another world, a world that none of us remembers now, in which there used to be leisure.'[6]

Whatever alternative path Europe would have taken had the First World War not happened, it could hardly have taken a worse turn than it did. The continent produced two global wars in the first half of the century. Humanity inflicted upon itself apocalyptic convulsions of violence, suffering and degradation. From the first great war sprang a second, some twenty-one years later.

Being both German and Jewish, the historian Fritz Stern understood the consequences better than most. He called the First World War as 'the first calamity of the 20th Century, the calamity from which all other calamities sprang.'[7] Without it, Adolf Hitler would have lived out his life in richly deserved obscurity. Without Hitler, the Communists would have struggled to spread their ideology to the whole of Eastern Europe, which in turn led to the founding of the North Atlantic Treaty Organisation (NATO) in 1949.

After these two global cataclysms, even the bitterest of foes realised they would have to become allies. West Germany, therefore, came together with France and the UK under the umbrella of the United States, a country which emerged from its international isolation during one world war and ended the second as the world's dominant power.

The hulking edifice of NATO's SHAPE (Supreme Headquarters Allied Powers Europe) and the memorial to the first shot fired by a British soldier on the Western Front in 1914 are less than a mile apart. They are linked, however, not just by the same road, but by the same avenue of history.

SHAPE moved across the border from France to Belgium in 1967 when Charles de Gaulle took his country out of NATO.[8] The Belgian government finally settled on a disused 200-acre army complex just north of Mons in the village of Casteau. Travelling out of Mons, past SHAPE, the road narrows and leads uphill. Opposite a restaurant, there is a stone monument on the side of the road.

'This tablet is erected,' it says, 'to commemorate the action of C Squadron 4th Royal Irish Dragoon Guards ... when Corporal E. Thomas fired the first shot for the British Expeditionary Force and Captain C.B. Hornby led the first mounted attack against the Germans.'

The memorial was unveiled to mark the twenty-fifth anniversary of the action on 20 August 1939, just two weeks before Britain found itself at war with Germany again. It was neglected for years, rendered smutty by the fumes of countless passing cars. Mons was never part of the lattice of trenches which stretched from the Swiss border to the North Sea. Yet it has both symbolic and military significance as it was the place where the British army began and ended the First World War.

The occasional British visitor, straying off the well-worn commemoration path further south, remarked on how unkempt it looked, but otherwise it remained neglected until the looming centenary of the First World War finally prompted the local authority to clean it up and enhance with a surrounding border of pink stones.

Near this spot, the British army ended a century-long disengagement from Western Europe stretching back to the Battle of Waterloo in 1815. The re-engagement would cost the British Empire 1.1 million dead. [9]

Britain had spent the nineteenth century accumulating a huge empire at relatively little cost in blood or treasure. 'Since the Crimean War, the principal task of the British army has consisted of suppressing relatively ill-equipped native insurrections in the colonies,' observed the military analyst Nikolas Gardner. [10]

The army had engaged Pasthuns, Dervishes, Zulus and Boers. Now they were facing an enemy that was supported by the most industrialised and sophisticated economy in Europe and that outnumbered them two to one.

First Lord of the Admiralty Winston Churchill candidly acknowledged Britain's previous good fortune in a secret memo which was sent to the Cabinet in January 1914. 'We have engrossed to ourselves, in a time when other powerful nations were paralysed by barbarians or internal war, an altogether disproportionate share of the wealth and traffic of the world. We have got all we want in territory, and our claim to be left in the unmolested enjoyment of vast and splendid possessions, mainly acquired by violence, largely maintained by force, often seems less reasonable to others than to us.' [11]

The regiment involved in this first action of 1914 was raised by the Earl of Arran as cuirassiers (heavy cavalry with an armoured breastplate) in 1685 to fight for the Catholic King James II. In 1698, it moved to Ireland and spent almost all of the eighteenth century in the country. It became the 1st Irish Horse and in 1788 the 4th Royal Irish Dragoon Guards, by which time the regiment had become known as 'The Mounted Micks'.

The late eighteenth century was a time of increasing restiveness in Ireland. The regiment was readied to intercept the French fleet due to arrive in Bantry Bay on Christmas Eve 1796, but the landing was aborted. The Dragoon Guards was part of the vanguard in the effort to repulse the 1798 Rebellion, at considerable cost to itself, but at a much greater cost to the rebels, who, inspired by the French revolutionary ideals and by the French themselves, rose up against British rule in Ireland.[12]

The regiment still recruited in Ireland and it was still two-thirds Irish by the time of the Great Famine. It spent most of the late nineteenth century and early twentieth century in India. Corporal Ernest Edward Thomas, who fired the first shot of the British Expeditionary Force, signed up to the British army as a boy soldier at the age of 14 in Kirkee, south of present-day Mumbai in India, and joined the regiment when he was 16. 'When the Great War broke out, I was already an old soldier,' he recalled years afterwards. He was just 29, but had spent more than half his life in the army.[13]

In August 1914, the Mounted Micks were based at Tidworth barracks in Wiltshire. They left England for France on 15 August 1914 and were billeted at Camp Haupont to the south of Mons. On 20 August, the German First Army marched into Brussels and was bearing down on the British Expeditionary Force assembling near the town of Mons in southern Belgium to guard the left flank of the French Fifth Army, itself under severe stress from the German Second Army.

The British knew the Germans were coming but were ignorant of the size of the force they were facing. On 21 August, the 177 men of C Squadron deposited all extraneous clothes in limbered wagons to lighten the load in case they needed to charge or, which was more likely, retreat. That evening and early the following morning were times of near unbearable tension for the cavalry on both sides, who ventured tentatively forward, seeking out the enemy. Benjamin Clouting, a 16-year-old cavalryman and the last survivor of the first shot incident, recalled the men tying handkerchiefs around the horse's necks to stop the reins jangling in the still summer night.[14]

The squadron commander Major Tom Bridges heard reports from fleeing refugees of a massed phalanx of grey-clad Germans travelling south, including one from a general who reported columns amounting to 400,000 troops bearing down on the assembling British.[15] C Squadron retired to a wood for the night. Fires were quenched and absolute silence was observed. At first light the squadron moved to another wood near the village of Casteau. The horses were just being watered when news came through of a German patrol. Observers had spotted a group of four to six German Uhlans (German calvary) coming towards them.

While the British knew the Germans were coming, though they did not know how many, the Germans had no idea the British lay straight in their path and believed they were still near the Pas-de-Calais. Their cavalry patrols even gave off an air of insouciance. Bridges reported his opposite number smoking a cigar as the patrol cantered unwittingly towards the enemy. Then they stopped 'as if they smelt a rat' and turned tail.

The 1st Troop with Captain Charles Hornby gave chase. They caught up with the German patrol in Casteau, then a village with pretty cobbled streets near the River Obrecheuil. The first encounter between Germans and British was a chaotic affair. The Germans with unwieldy lances and the British with swords fought a seventeenth-century engagement during the first encounter of a twentieth-century war. Horses slipped and careered on cobblestones rendered treacherous by a recent shower of rain. 'The men cheered and drove right in amongst them, sabering several and dismounting many, who were taken prisoner,' was how the official history of the regiment put it.[16]

Outnumbered, the Uhlans fled north in the direction of the German lines, pursued by the troop. Edwards was part of the support 4th Troop giving chase. Hornby ordered them to dismount and take cover behind a tree. Further down the road, the Germans were doing likewise. Thomas recalled:

> Possibly because I was rather noted for my quick movements and athletic ability in those days, I was first into action. I could see a German cavalry officer some four hundred yards away standing mounted in full view of me, gesticulating to the left and to the right as he disposed of his dismounted men and ordered them to take up their firing positions to engage us. Immediately I saw him I took aim, pulled the trigger and automatically, almost as if it seemed instantaneously, he fell to the ground, obviously wounded but whether he was killed or not is a matter that I do not think was ever cleared up or ever capable of proof.[17]

Thomas did not know the significance of his actions until after the war. He recalled an air of complete unreality about this first fateful encounter between the British and the Germans, which occurred on the same day that the French suffered their worst one-day losses of the whole war: 27,000 men dead in the Ardennes Forest. Firing the first shot was no different, he remembered, from 'rifle practice on the plains of Salisbury'.[18] Having joined the army as a drummer, he took pride in his accuracy:

> I find lots of people think that bandsmen are not soldiers in the ordinary sense, but they are quite wrong, for every bandsman has got to do his duties. The strange thing about the episode was as far as I can remember, and it seems as clear to me as if it took place last week, that I had not the slightest feeling of being in a battle, not the remotest idea I was taking a very active part in what was to be the greatest war of all time.

One hundred years on from the initial incident, his great-grandson Ben Thomas represented the family at the centenary commemorations on 22 August 2014, which took place at the Casteau Memorial:

I first found out about my great-grandfather's involvement in the first shot when I was 7 and by complete coincidence was living with my godparents in Jurbise, just a few miles down the road, and my godfather was chief engineer at SHAPE. My grandparents had just dropped me off and had mentioned the family connection to my godparents and a few days later we went to see the memorial and had my picture taken. The next time I went there was forty-five years later with the BBC for Fergal Keane's report on the outbreak of war and then the hundredth-anniversary commemorative activities. Being there at the exact spot, 100 years to the day, was very strange and I felt very 'connected' at that minute in time.[19]

For a long time, it was assumed that Ernest Edward Thomas was from Nenagh, Co Tipperary. After learning about the alleged connection, Tipperary-based radio producer Tom Hurley set about making a radio documentary *In Search of E.E. Thomas*, which was broadcast on Tipp FM in October 2014.[20]

Hurley had previously made a documentary about Private Daniel Hough, who was the first casualty of the American Civil War and came from the Nenagh/Borrisokane area of the county. It would be an intriguing coincidence if the first soldier to die in the American Civil War and the first British soldier to fire a shot on the Western Front were from the same area.

According to his own attestation records, Thomas was born in Colchester, Essex, in December 1884, into an army family. His Welsh father Henry was a private in the Essex Regiment stationed at Warley Barracks, Brentwood in Essex.

The Thomas family lived a peripatetic existence, as army families tend to do, and Ernest Edward Thomas joined the 4th Royal Irish Dragoon Guards while his father was stationed in India.[21]

Where did the belief arise that Thomas was from Nenagh? The original source may have been the Tipperary-born Victoria Cross-winner John 'Jack' Moyney, who was interviewed at length in the 1970s by Kevin Myers. Moyney won his Victoria Cross for an incredible act of endurance during the Battle of Passchendaele in September 1917.[22] Moyney led a group of fifteen men who were stranded in no man's land for four days without support, food or water. On the fifth day, they successfully fended off a German assault and Moyney led his men to safety.

Thomas married a woman called Ellen Pont in 1909. She lived until 1964. By 1912, they had two children, Ernest Henry (known as son) and Violet. Ernest Henry would later win an MBE for services to aviation. Violet died in 1946.

After being discharged from the army in 1923, Thomas worked as a commissionaire at the Duke of York cinema in Brighton, a cinema with a beautiful Edwardian exterior, now Britain's oldest working cinema.

Commissionaires performed a dual role. They were front of house and the public face of the cinema and they also acted as bouncers who kept order when things got busy or rowdy. Thomas made for a particularly striking commissionaire. Occasionally, he would wear his medals to work, especially the Military Medal for bravery, which he won at Messines in 1915. It allowed him to carry the letters 'MM' after his name.

Ben Thomas recalls:

> It seems he was very happy after the war, especially in his role as commissionaire at the Duke of York's Cinema. He wore his medals and was regularly feted in the pub across the road. Mrs Thomas, it seems, was a formidable lady and whilst he was clearly an imposing character, I think there is no doubt about who wore the trousers in that family.[23]

Hurley found nothing that linked Ernest Edward Thomas to Nenagh, but he found two siblings of his that had been born in Ireland, Elliott George, born in 1880 in Athlone, who died at the age of 6, and Florence Martha, born two years later. Both were baptised in Curragh Camp. Their father's regiment was stationed in Ireland at the time.[24]

One of the few people left alive who remembered Thomas was Winnie Pentecost, now 97, who was bridesmaid at his daughter's wedding. Pentecost remembered that her mother lent Thomas's wife Ellen money to go to Ireland, but could not recall the reasons why she wanted to go. She did recall, however, that the money was never paid back.

The centenary of the first shot and the Tipp FM documentary also prompted Ben Thomas to re-examine the family history which would appear to corroborate Winnie Pentecost's memories:

> We obtained additional research from one of the Brighton museums who had done some digging. It seems that Ellen Pont was always borrowing money to go to Ireland, for reasons unknown as she was not actually Irish herself. Ernest Edward Thomas's father Henry Thomas (from Pembrokeshire) however, was married to Elizabeth Wright, who had six children born in Ireland, so presumably she was Irish. There does seem to be a strong Irish connection, but the details are vague at this time.

Thomas had a 'good war', so far as any man could, and the worst he suffered was a bad fever/PUO (pyrexia of unknown origin). He died in February 1939 at the age of 54, having caught pneumonia while standing out on in the rain on duty. He never did get to see the monument, which was erected six months after his death. The monument is not quite accurately positioned. The first shot was fired about half a mile further north of where the memorial stands, near the gatehouse of an old chateau.

Ben Thomas says he was informed that the commune of Mons placed it where it did because it was a site where it could be easily maintained. There may be another compelling reason why it is sited there. Directly across the road is a plaque to the 116th Canadian Infantry Battalion, which marks the furthest advance of the Allies on Armistice Day. Here, therefore on the same road, was the place where the British Empire started and finished the First World War.

Five days after the first shot incident, the 4th Royal Irish Dragoon Guards was involved in an incident which led to the most famous British court-martialling of the war. This incident involved another Irish regiment.

The commanding officers of the 1st Royal Warwickshires and the 2nd Royal Dublin Fusiliers surrendered on 27 August 1914. Both regiments were part of 10th Brigade, 4th Division, and endured four days of hell from their arrival in France on 23 August. On the morning of 27 August, men from both battalions arrived in the railway town of St Quentin, the biggest in the Aisne region. Lieutenant-Colonel Arthur Mainwaring, the commanding officer of the Royal Dublin Fusiliers, already suffered from bad health. He was 50. He had not slept for four nights. He and the Warwickshire's commanding officer Lieutenant-Colonel John Elkington tried to get their men to continue their march southwards but none was able to move.

They sought the aid of the newly installed mayor, the previous one having fled the town, in getting their men food, water and a train away from the action, but the train station was abandoned. The mayor informed the two men that the Germans were to the north of St Quentin and approaching rapidly. Resistance was futile. If the regiments sought to fight, the Germans would shell the town, killing civilians. The two men pondered their options and decided to surrender. They signed a surrender document in the presence of the mayor, who intended to dispatch it to the advancing Germans.

But the mayor's information was wrong. The town was surrounded, not by the enemy, but by two Irish cavalry regiments. The 4th Royal Irish Dragoon Guards and the 5th Royal Irish Lancers were providing a cavalry screen for retreating British troops. The Germans were still too far north. Bridges rode into St Quentin and urged the weary men to leave but none was capable of marching.

Finally, he threatened to have them all shot and they reluctantly compiled. What followed was a celebrated incident which showed, even in extremis, that there was room for humour in wartime. Bridges spotted a toy shop in the town centre. He walked into it and got himself a tin whistle and drum. He and his trumpeter proceeded to march in circles around the city square, playing 'Tipperary' and 'The British Grenadiers'. The weary men appreciated the gesture.

In his memoirs, Bridges recalled, 'They sat up and began to laugh and even to cheer. I stopped playing and made them a short exhortation and told them I was going to take them back to their regiments. They began to stand up and fall in.'[25]

The episode gave rise to a famous music-hall song of the time:

> Dreary lay the long road, dreary lay the town
> Light out and never a glint o' moon:
> Weary lay the stragglers, half a thousand down,
> Stand sighed the weary big Dragoon.
> 'Oh! If I'd a drum here to make them take the road again.
> Oh! If I'd a fife to wheedle, Come, boys, come!
> You that mean to fight it out, wake and take your load again,
> Fall in! Fall in! Follow the fife and drum!'

Bridges also retrieved the surrender document from the mayor. It would prove critical in the forthcoming trial. Elkington and Mainwaring were court-martialled the following week. They faced a charge of cowardice in the face of the enemy and a lesser charge of dishonourable conduct, 'having behaved in a scandalous manner unbecoming the character of an officer and a gentleman'.[26]

A party of the 4th Irish Dragoon Guards was readied as a firing squad. Fortunately for both men, they were not needed. They were both cashiered (dismissed dishonourably) from the British army and sent home in public disgrace.

Elkington was to revive his career in the most dramatic fashion. He joined the French Legion as a private, unheard of for a senior British officer, and was wounded at Verdun in 1916.[27] He was reinstated by the king as a lieutenant-colonel, though his war was over because of incapacity. There was no story of redemption for Mainwaring though. He protested his innocence until the end. He disappeared from public life completely and died in 1930 at the age of 64.

TO THE GLORIOUS MEMORY OF
THE OFFICERS, N.C.O.s AND MEN OF
THE 4TH BN. ROYAL FUSILIERS
WHO HELD THIS SECTOR OF THE
BRITISH FRONT IN THE DEFENCE
OF THE TOWN OF MONS
AUGUST 23RD 1914.

THIS MEMORIAL
MARKS THE M.G. POSITION WHERE
THE FIRST V.C.s AWARDED DURING
THE WAR 1914-18, WERE GAINED BY
LT M.J. DEASE.V.C.
AND
PTE S.F. GODLEY. V.C.

2

THE PLAQUE AT NIMY BRIDGE

The morning of Sunday, 23 August 1914, dawned wet and misty in Mons. The British troops strung out along a 15-mile section of the Mons–Condé Canal north of the town had endured a restless night.

The men who lay prone in shallow trenches all night were prey to constant and unnerving rumours. They heard that vast columns of German infantry were bearing down on them. Coming in the opposite direction, British infantry marched wearily up to Mons, a distance of some 20 miles, from their assembly point across the French border in the riverbank town of Maubeuge. When they passed through the Belgian town of Frameries, they were cheered in the streets.

Soldiers rested in the Grand Place in Mons. They were grateful for the respite and appreciative of the warm welcome they received from locals who proffered coffee, pastries and hard liquor.[1]

The British Expeditionary Force was a mixture of hardened, career soldiers, many of whom had seen action in various colonial campaigns, and reservists who had left the British army, but were now recalled to the colours from civilian life. In addition, there were territorials, part-timers were known as 'Saturday night soldiers'. Saturday night was reserved for drilling and firearms training. They were also obliged to attend two weeks of summer camp. For many of them, this was the only holiday they knew. There was also a modest payment for being available for the day – and that day would probably never come – when their services would be required for king and country.[2]

When hostilities began in 1914, the War Office estimated it would take six months for these men to be ready to fight. But here they were, a few weeks later, trudging along the treeless lanes of northern France and southern Belgium, alternately soaked and scorched by the capricious weather. Marching in sultry, late summer heat was hard for everyone, but agony for them. They had been issued with new boots that pinched toes and cramped insteps. The men had been inoculated and many were feeling the effects. They marched with rivulets of sweat trickling down their faces and moist shirts clinging to their backs. Compounding their discomfort was the realisation that they were simply not fit enough for the epic of endurance which was only beginning.

The British Expeditionary Force deployed on the extreme left of the French line, where the French Fifth Army was desperately trying to hold off the German Second Army. These were the most critical days of the early stages of the war. Of the five French armies in the field, two were retreating, the Third and Fourth had been beaten back with catastrophic losses and the Fifth was holding a right-angled salient centred around the town of Namur, due east of Mons.

In this central sector of the huge battlefield, the Germans had numerical superiority of approximately 100 battalions (100,000 men) over the combined French and British forces. The British Expeditionary Force arrived in the nick of time. Fortunately, the French and British had combined to brilliant effect to keep its embarkation a secret.

The soldiers moved north of Mons to spread out along the Mons-Condé Canal, which was a natural defensive barrier. The canal had been developed in the middle of the nineteenth century when the Borinage, Belgium's equivalent of the English Black Country, was the largest coal-producing area in Western Europe.[3] It brought coal to France and Flanders. The region was a bleak vista of pitheads, tightly-packed miners' cottages and slagheaps as far as the eye could see. Soldiers clamoured up on top of the enormous spoils to get a better view of their surroundings only to find their view obscured by even bigger slagheaps.

It was, according to the *British Official History of the Great War*, 'practically one huge unsightly village … a close and blind country, such as no army has been called upon to fight in against a civilised enemy in a great campaign'.[4]

Sergeant John F. Lucy from Cork, one of the 'old sweats' who survived the war, recalled his first sight of Mons in his brilliant post-war memoir *There's a Devil in the Drum*. He viewed it 'through the slag heaps of many mines, on the right front of the marching regiment. This dirty-looking factory town had no particular interest just then for us'.[5]

As the dawn mists cleared to a fine Sunday morning, the British soldiers, now in position in hastily dug trenches along the canal, noticed a scene familiar to the thousands of Irishmen within their ranks. Belgium, like Ireland, was one of the most Catholic countries in Europe. Church bells rang and villagers emerged in their Sunday finery to attend Mass. Soldiers noticed they seemed to be unperturbed by the mighty clash of arms which was building on both sides of the canal. 'It was as if war was utterly distant to them,' the official history records.

Lucy, who would have understood this communal ritual well, wrote, 'The devout inhabitants of our hamlet come out at various hours during the morning to attend Mass in the church at the opposite side of the square, and they presented to our front for several hours. We lay on our stomachs watching them, and from time to time I had to warn them not to group in front of us, and not to converse with the men.'[6] Lucy said some hurried prayers in lieu of Mass for his own safekeeping.

Lieutenant Kinglake Tower of the 4th Royal Fusiliers was on sentry duty 1,000 yards in advance of his regiment manning the canal. One of his reservists spotted a German cavalryman in the distance and shot him dead. His men also captured a German aristocrat who was limping and 'shivering with fright'.[7]

The early morning damp and mist was burning off as Tower returned to his lines. Two armies were about to collide, but the locals remained oblivious. Tower remarked, 'The church bells were ringing and the Belgian peasants could be seen walking quietly to church. What a contrast!'[8]

This Sunday morning there would be no time for Mass for 24-year-old Lieutenant Maurice Dease of the 4th Royal Fusiliers, a regiment raised at the Tower of London. He was the officer commanding a machine gun section at

Nimy Bridge, one of two bridges across the canal where it bends around in a half-moon formation.

This would turn out to be the Mons salient. Salients are to be avoided in warfare as they give the enemy the opportunity to attack on three sides, but there was no avoiding the salient in Mons, which was dictated by the topography of the canal.

Dease had a fairly typical Anglo-Irish upbringing. His family seat was at Turbotston House in Coole, County Westmeath, a Georgian mansion built around 1810 and designed by the architect Francis Johnston.[9] The Deases were in *Burke's Landed Gentry of Ireland*. His father Edmund had written a history of the Westmeath Hunt.[10] Maurice Dease had received an expensive English public school education at Stonyhurst, the Jesuit college in Cheshire.

In one critical respect though, the Deases confound the Anglo-Irish conventions. They were resolutely Catholic from the time they arrived in Ireland in the early 1200s, following the Norman invasions.

The family held on to their faith. The original Turbotston was confiscated in 1601 but a pardon was issued in 1602. The house was confiscated again in 1650 but bought back from the Packenham family soon after. The Deases, as Catholics, held on to their lands despite the Penal Laws because they secretly transferred them to the Protestant Nugent family in County Cavan. Major General Oliver Nugent would be the man who commanded the 36th (Ulster) Division during the First World War.[11]

Another Dease descendant, Thomas Dease, was a founding member of the Irish College in Paris and later became Catholic Bishop of Meath from 1621 to 1652.[12] At a time when fidelity to the Crown and Catholicism were seen as mutually antagonistic positions, Thomas Dease cleaved to both.

In 1642 the Catholic nobility and hierarchy in Ireland sought to exploit the turmoil surrounding the English Civil War by establishing the Catholic Confederacy to rule the two-thirds of Ireland where Catholics, rather than Protestant settlers, still dominated. Until the Cromwellian conquests at the end of the decade, this was an effective parliament for Ireland, independent of King Charles I, with whom the confederacy was nominally aligned.

Despite multiple entreaties from his co-religionists, Thomas Dease refused to join the confederacy. He preached fidelity to the powers that be, however straitened the situation might become, and had a horror of disorder. He did not believe the confederacy had the wherewithal to endure if the Protestant English and Scottish could raise an army to defeat it. (He was prescient in that regard as Oliver Cromwell was to ruthlessly prove in 1649.)

He took to quoting the Gospel of St Luke and Jesus's warning to those whose ambitions were not matched by their means. 'For which of you, intending to build a tower, sitteth not down first, and counteth the cost, whether he have sufficient to finish it?'

Dease's obdurate stand brought him into conflict with the Papal Nuncio Archbishop Giovanni Rinuccini, who regarded him and others like him as nothing more than self-serving cowards. 'Timid, satisfied with mere toleration … and keeping themselves clear of all risk'.[13]

In 1648, Rinuccini heard of Dease's death at the age of 80 with undisguised glee. Dease was a man of 'almost heretical sentiments' and his death was to the 'great gain of the kingdom'.[14] Unfortunately for Rinuccini, reports of Dease's death were untrue. In despair, he wrote to Rome saying Dease still lived 'to try the patience of the good'.[15] Thomas Dease lived for another three years, long enough to see the calamity of the Cromwellian invasion of Ireland, the defeat of the confederacy and the violent suppression of Catholic Ireland.

The Deases were temporarily banished from their lands in Cavan and Westmeath by the Cromwellian soldiers.

James Arthur Dease, Maurice Dease's grandfather, had twelve children. Maurice Dease's father Edmund was the youngest. He was born in 1856. He had ten older sisters and an older brother Major Gerald Dease, the heir to Turbotston.[16] Four of his sisters became nuns. More than race or nationality, religion was what defined the family.

Major Dease spent twenty years with the Royal Fusiliers, based in the Tower of London, leaving just before the turn of the century. His nephew Maurice would join the same regiment.

After retiring from the British army, Major Dease became a committed Irish nationalist and agreed to drill and train the Irish Volunteers in County Westmeath. He was unimpressed with those who had enlisted as he outlined a month before the war broke out:

> The two virtues it will be most necessary for our local corps to practice for some months to come will be patience and self-control (sobriety, of course, I take for granted, as a drunken Volunteer is inconceivable). It will be a time of drudgery for any man worth his salt, for squad and company drill must be thoroughly mastered and we shall have to confine ourselves very much to them while the foundations of the national system are being laid.[17]

His nephew took a different path. Maurice Dease was born in 1889. He grew up in Gaulstown, Coole, County Westmeath. He was sent away to Stonyhurst at 13. He was a popular boy, 'good-natured and amiable' yet full of determination. He looked after the birds at the school, duties he discharged with 'characteristic thoroughness'.

There is a vignette in the *Stonyhurst Magazine* that further illuminates his character. 'To see old Father Myers, then a man of no small weight, limping slowly along to say Mass, leaning on the arm of his favourite server, Maurice Dease, was an object lesson in the respectful and thoughtful sympathy of the right-minded boy for venerable old age.'[18]

After Stonyhurst, Dease attended Wimbledon College, a precursor to entering the army, and then the Royal Military College at Sandhurst, where he was commissioned as an officer.[19] In 1910, he joined the 4th Royal Fusiliers, becoming a lieutenant in April 1912, which would put him in command of a section of eight men. He was trained by an officer of the Indian army in mountain warfare. The prevailing wisdom was that the British army's next major engagement would come on the northern fringes of the Indian sub-continent and not in Europe.

Instead, he found himself in barracks when war came. His letters home to his parents after war was declared were matter-of-fact. He marched his men around the barracks at Cowes on the Isle of Wight before they embarked from Southampton on 12 August for France. Within a fortnight, Dease and his battalion were quickly marched to plug a gap in the French line.

Dease commanded a machine gun section which consisted of an officer, a sergeant, corporal, twelve men and a wagon pulled by two horses with a driver.[20] Each battalion had just two Maxim heavy machine guns; most of the German battalions had eight. The Maxim gun was noted for its reliability, but nobody had tested it in battlefield conditions like this.

Now, on the banks of the Mons-Condé Canal at Nimy Bridge, Dease, his men and their machinery were about to be tested beyond their limits. He ordered his troops to make improvised defences. When no sand was available, he told them to fill sandbags with rocks. One machine gun was positioned on the bridge, the other was sited to the left of the bridge, with a flat trajectory across the canal to the woods on the far side. The rest of the company presented a formidable concentration of rifle firepower to the approaching Germans.

Each rifleman was issued with a .303 Lee-Enfield bolt-action rifle, the best infantry weapon in the world. With a roll of his thumb, a well-trained British infantryman could fire a front-loaded 10-round magazine with barely a pause. The ability to fire fifteen well-aimed rounds a minute, known as the 'mad minute', brought down such a blizzard of fire on the Germans that they believed they were facing many more machine guns than was the case at Mons. The British infantryman shot for his pay. The British army prized it more than any other military skill.

The Battle of Mons began at around 6 a.m. as German cavalry patrols appeared in front of the British lines. Two officers of the 3rd Hussars reconnoitring the woods in front of the 4th Fusiliers were taken prisoner. They imparted the information that the British were about to face overwhelming force. German artillery formations came within 1,500 yards of the British positions, but were forced back by machine gun fire.[21]

It was then the turn of the German infantry from IX Corps of the German First Army. They presented an extraordinary sight to the British troops. Lucy, who was

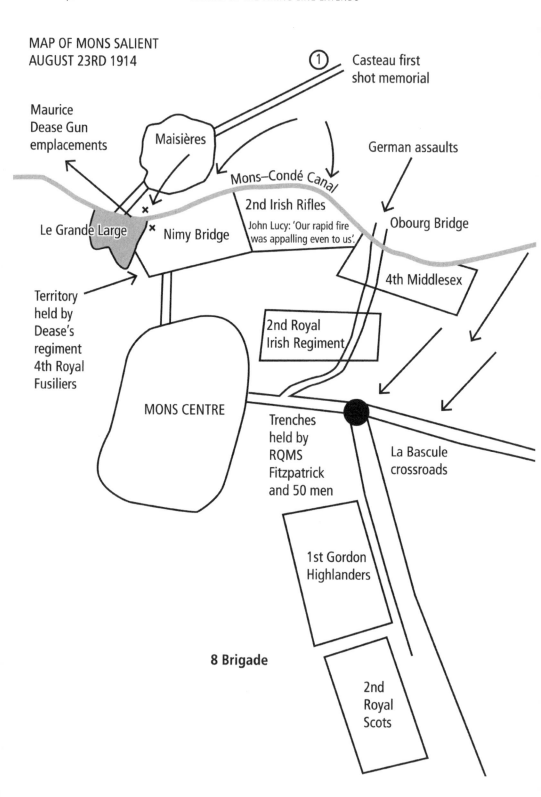

MAP OF MONS SALIENT
AUGUST 23RD 1914

① Casteau first shot memorial

Maurice Dease Gun emplacements

Maisières

German assaults

Mons–Condé Canal

2nd Irish Rifles

John Lucy: 'Our rapid fire was appalling even to us'.

Obourg Bridge

Le Grande Large

Nimy Bridge

4th Middlesex

Territory held by Dease's regiment 4th Royal Fusiliers

2nd Royal Irish Regiment

MONS CENTRE

Trenches held by RQMS Fitzpatrick and 50 men

La Bascule crossroads

1st Gordon Highlanders

8 Brigade

2nd Royal Scots

with the 2nd Royal Irish Rifles, wrote a memorable account of the naive Germans approaching the British lines as if on a parade ground:

> Our rapid fire was appalling, even to us, and the worst marksman could not miss, as he had only to fire into the masses of the unfortunate enemy who on the fronts of our two companies were continually and uselessly reinforced at the short range of 300 yards. Such tactics amazed us, and after the first shock of seeing men slowly and helplessly falling down as they were hit, gave us a great sense of power and pleasure. It was all so easy.[22]

Some accounts suggest the Germans lost 500 men, killed or injured, in the first ten minutes of battle. The British shot them at will. Tower believes it was even bloodier than that and that Dease was responsible for many of the deaths. 'Shortly after this the enemy started to advance in mass down the railway cuttings about 800 yards off and Maurice Dease fired his two machine guns into them and absolutely mowed them down. I should just judge without exaggeration that he killed at least 500 in those two minutes.'[23]

At Nimy Bridge, the 4th Royal Fusiliers was under severe pressure from 8 a.m. onwards, yet it held on against determined artillery and rifle fire. Conditions for the machine gun section were desperate. When a man was hit he had to be removed immediately and another put in his place. The machine-gunners inflicted many more casualties than they took, but they took enough to make their position perilous.

Dease's command post, from which he directed fire, was overlooking the canal, but then the machine-gunner at the bridge was killed and there was nobody left to man the gun. Dease clamoured from his command post and ran to the bridge. He was hit first in the neck and calf, yet managed to muster the strength to continue firing the machine gun. In this pitiless engagement, he would kill many Germans, despite the fact that he was bleeding profusely.

When the gun in the command trench jammed, he climbed back down the embankment and was hit in the arm and chest, this time fatally. The commissioned officer was part of a privileged caste in peacetime, but not in this war where the average life expectancy was six weeks.[24]

There was nobody left in the machine gun section to operate the gun. Company commander Lieutenant Fred Steele, an Australian who joined the British army to see action, asked for a volunteer to man the machine gun while the battalion retired. Private Sidney Godley, from East Grinstead in Sussex, stepped forward. He dragged three dead bodies out of the way and began to fire. Behind him, his company started to retreat. He risked certain death or capture. The same stubbornness and fondness for a barrack room quarrel that made him a querulous individual in peacetime now made him a hero in war.[25]

A shell burst behind him, embedding shrapnel in his back. He held on until felled by a bullet which grazed his head. Seriously injured and faint from loss of blood, he still managed to summon up the strength and presence of mind to dismantle the machine gun and throw it into the canal. He staggered off, looking for medical aid, but was overtaken by the Germans. He spent the rest of the war in a prisoner-of-war camp in Germany. Dease and Godley won the first Victoria Crosses of the war. The citation for Dease's reads, 'Though two or three times badly wounded he continued to control the fire of his machine guns at Mons on 23rd August until all his men were shot. He died of his wounds.'[26]

This was another notable Irish first. The first Victoria Cross ever won was won by an Irishman, Charles Lucas, a navy midshipman from County Armagh who threw a bomb that had landed on the deck of his ship overboard during the Crimean War in 1854.[27] The first soldier to win the Victoria Cross was Sergeant Luke O'Connor from Elphin, County Roscommon in the same year and same war.[28] Now, Maurice Dease would become the first winner of the Victoria Cross in the First World War and one of thirty-seven Irishmen to win Britain's highest award for gallantry in the conflict.[29]

Godley was informed of his award while he was a prisoner of war. He did not receive his medal until 1919. 'If I'd thought about it, I wouldn't have done it!' was the succinct explanation he proffered for the actions that won him the Victoria Cross. [30]

On 22 September, almost a month after the Battle of Mons, the Dease family in County Westmeath, having heard nothing from their usually communicative son, received a telegram from the War Office saying he had been 'dangerously wounded'. How dangerously wounded? Was this a euphemism for being near death or crippled? The lack of information was agony for the Dease family. Dease's sister and only sibling, Maud, wrote to her brother's acquaintances in the army. Their answers offered little hope. They thought her brother was dead, but nobody was absolutely sure. The War Office sent another telegram on 26 September, this time stating that he had been mortally wounded. The family had already suspected as much. At least now there was certainty. But then another telegram came. He was 'wounded and missing'. The agony visited on his parents and sister by this maladroit bureaucracy was unbearable. Confirmation came a month later from another officer, Major T.R. Mallock, the second in command in the battalion, who had witnessed his death. The tribute was stirring in its sentiments; terrifying in its finality:

> You will, I expect, have heard by now of your son Maurice having been killed at the Battle of Mons. He died as a gallant soldier should, defending the passage of a bridge with his machine gun most heroically – nearly all the machine gun detachment were killed – and the guns continuing firing until they were put out of action by the enemy's rifle fire and shells. Maurice set the men a most

splendid example: although wounded quite early in the arm, he refused to leave the guns. It is with the deepest regret and sorrow of all ranks that I acquaint you of his death. We all loved him – one of the best officers we had in the regiment.

Dease's good friend Kinglake Tower was equally effusive. He sought to give Maud Dease some consolation. 'Everyone mourns the loss of one of the most popular and best officers of the regiment.'[31]

Though it was not immediately apparent, Maurice Dease's death would prove to be the end of his family's 700 years of continuous living in Ireland. He was the heir presumptive to Major Gerald Dease's Turbotston House and estate. Major Dease had been childless.[32] Neither Dease's sister nor aunt could inherit the estate.

Major Dease sold Turbotston to the most senior representative of the Dease family, a cousin, Major Edmund James Dease of Rath, County Laois. However, he became confined to a wheelchair after a stroke and the house passed to his son Richard, who had served in the South Irish Horse during the war. He came back from the war with the intention of joining the Royal Irish Constabulary as a police officer.[33] According to his relative Peter Bland, Richard Dease was told he would be killed by the IRA and his parents' house burned out so he left Ireland. He was killed in action in 1940 while serving as a pilot officer in the Royal Air Force Volunteer Reserve. In 1934, the Dease lands were divided into holdings by the Land Commission. Turbotston was used to winter sheep.

Dease's parents left Ireland in 1926 for a new life in Britain. They never returned.

In 2004, Peter Bland, a senior counsel in Dublin, bought Turbotston and restored it to its former glory. He is a great-nephew of Richard Dease. 'I bought it because I was seduced by the romance of retrieving it for the family yet again,' he said. 'As a bachelor at the time, I had little use for nineteen bedrooms!'[34]

———

In April 1939, the plaque at Nimy Bridge was erected. Some fifty veterans of the Royal Fusiliers, including Godley, attended. It was becoming evident by then that the First World War was not the 'war to end all wars'.

The plaque was taken down from Nimy Bridge for safekeeping after the German invasion in 1940. The wooden bridge was replaced by the current structure in 1961.[35] Ten years later, the plaque was restored to the bridge and remained there until it was stolen in January 2011 and had to be replaced.[36]

Maurice Dease and Sid Godley are among the best remembered Victoria Cross winners of the First World War. Dease's portrait is in the hallway of the Fusilier Museum at the Tower of London. The painting was commissioned by the Dease family from a photograph. It was painted in 1915. It depicts a proud and serious young man with a bearskin, sword and gloves. The Fusilier Museum purchased the painting in 2012.[37]

Dease's body was recovered from the canal bank and buried locally. In the 1920s, it was moved to St Symphorien Cemetery, one of the most beautiful and best-known cemeteries on the Western Front.

This is one of the few cemeteries on the Western Front where German, British and Commonwealth soldiers are buried side by side. A Belgian farmer gave the land to the Germans on condition that they bury both German and British soldiers together.

There are just 327 bodies buried in the cemetery, but its smallness makes it possible to comprehend the sadness of each individual death. The obelisk, the German symbol of remembrance, is accompanied by the British Cross of Sacrifice.

The first British soldier killed in the war, Private John Parr, is also buried in the cemetery. So too are the last British soldier to die, Private George Ellison, who was with the 5th Royal Irish Lancers, and the last Commonwealth soldier to die, Private George Price. Price, a Canadian, died two minutes before the Armistice came into force at 11 a.m. on 11 November 1918.

The German dead include Oskar Nemeyer, who won the first Iron Cross of the war. He displayed suicidal bravery when he jumped into the Mons-Condé Canal. Under fire, he loosened the swing bridge from its moorings and swung it across. His comrades rushed across while he lay dying from his wounds. The war destroyed a generation of young German men; Germany suffered 2 million military dead in the war, proportionally more, even given its bigger population, than Britain.[38]

Maurice Dease's sister Maud later married Bertram Leo French, a member of the extended Anglo-Irish French family that gave the Roscommon village of Frenchpark its name and included among its number Field Marshal Sir John French, the original commander of the British Expeditionary Force.[39]

Maud and Leo had three children, Lavinia, Maurice and Arthur French. Maurice carried on the family tradition in the Royal Fusiliers and saw active service during the Korean War.[40] He was present in St Symphorien Cemetery for the centenary commemorations on 4 August 2014, marking 100 years to the day since war broke out on the Western Front. The British chose St Symphorien as the site to commemorate the outbreak of war. There, Prince Harry implicitly acknowledged the Irish contribution to the British war effort by reading from a letter sent by Private Michael Lennon of the 1st Battalion of the Royal Dublin Fusiliers to his brother Frank in May 1915. 'Well Frank, I suppose we are for it tomorrow, if we don't get shelled on the way. I can only hope that we have all the luck to come through the night and if I should get bowled out – well it can't be helped.' Lennon was killed a month later in Gallipoli.

The action at Nimy Bridge was the subject of an hour-long docudrama on the BBC *Our World War* series, in which Dease was played by Dominic Thorburn and Sidney Godley by Theo Barklem-Biggs. This thoroughly modern take on an old story involved headcams and a contemporary soundtrack. It was the war as told for the video-game generation. In 2012, the British government announced that it was going to erect a paving stone for each of the 627 recipients of the Victoria Cross during the First World War, but the gesture would only apply to those who were born in the present-day United Kingdom. This excluded Dease and twenty-six other men from the Republic of Ireland. This was rectified following representations from Stonyhurst College among others.[41] On 23 August 2014, 100 years to the day after the Battle of Mons, a paving stone with Dease's name on it was presented to Glasnevin Cemetery in Dublin by UK communities minister Lord Ahmad, who was leading Britain's commemorations programme.

Paying tribute, Glasnevin Trust chairman John Green described the Dease family as a 'microcosm of Ireland for a long time'. Their story demanded greater scrutiny. 'We're trying to get people to look at this period of history and understand it themselves. We're not in the business of what is right and wrong. The more we look at it, the more complicated it looks. These were extraordinary men of extraordinary bravery. They deserve to be commemorated.'[42]

On 23 August 2016, the 102nd anniversary of his death, Maurice Dease was remembered with the unveiling of a memorial cross and plaque in his home village of Coole. The monuments were placed in the grounds of the Church of the Immaculate Conception near a headstone marking his ancestors who had been in the area since the thirteenth century.

The plaque was unveiled by two people separated by almost 90 years – second World War veteran Ivor Fogg, who lived locally, and three-year-old Lodhi Bland. Lodhi is the daughter of Peter Bland and the 28th generation of Deases from the area.

A Mass was said for Dease and for thirty-three other men from the Castlepollard parish who died in the first World War.

The midlands branch of the Royal British Legion organised the unveiling ceremony. Co-ordinator Michael Duffy said the day was not just about Dease, but the 800 men from Westmeath killed in the First World War. The ones who returned alive received a 'cold and critical acceptance and a lifetime of discrimination' in post-independence Ireland.

'Perhaps this ceremony will provide an impetus in healing wounds, and the sacrifices of so many men 100 years ago will be understood.'

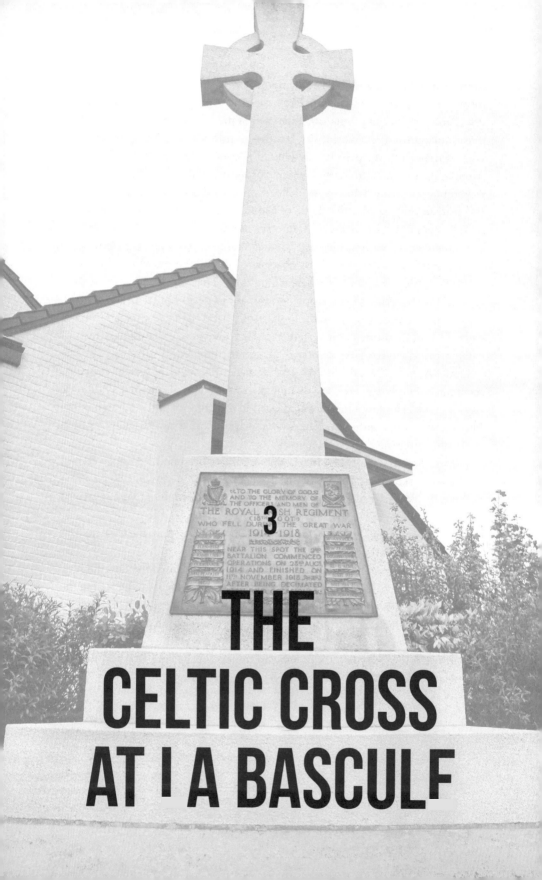

3

THE CELTIC CROSS AT I A BASCULE

Legends endure because they are more potent than the truth. The politician who made a career out of being 'The Man Who Shot Liberty Valance' turned out not to be the man who shot Liberty Valance, but the newspaper men did not want to know. 'This is the West, sir', declared the newspaper editor in the film. 'When the legend becomes fact, print the legend.'[1]

John Ford, the Irish-American director who made the classic western film, understood the power of myth. He would have understood the story of the Angels of Mons.

On 29 September 1914, one month after the Battle of Mons, the writer Arthur Machen published a short story in London's largest-circulation newspaper, the *Evening News*.[2] 'The Bowmen' was a tale of supernatural intervention grafted on to a lurid account of the battle and told in a baroque prose style.

At the moment of greatest peril for the British Expeditionary Force, when it faced an enemy twice its number, St George intervened and sent bowmen from the Battle of Agincourt (1415) to thwart the German forces.

Machen's story begins with the British Expeditionary Force in mortal danger on that 'dreadful day when three hundred thousand men in arms with all their artillery swelled like a flood against the little English company'.[3] This was hyperbole. Large as the German army was at the Battle of Mons, it numbered, in fact, around 160,000 versus the 80,000-strong British Expeditionary Force.

Machen never intended to allow the facts get in the way of his story. He continued:

> There was one point above all other points in our battle line that was for a time in awful danger, not merely of defeat, but of utter annihilation. With the permission of the censor and of the military expert, this corner may, perhaps, be described as a salient, and if this angle were crushed and broken, then the English force as a whole would be shattered, the Allied left would be turned, and Sedan would inevitably follow.[4]

Sedan referred to the cataclysmic French defeat during the Franco-Prussian war in 1871, which sealed the fate of Napoleon III and created the German Empire with whom Britain was now at war.

The 'good Englishmen' – though a sizable contingent were either Irish or Scottish – were assailed by cannon fire so terrifying that it could get no worse, until it did. This 'seven-times-heated hell of the German cannonade' threatened to tear all of them limb from limb. But just as annihilation seemed certain, came divine intervention.

> And as the soldier heard these voices he saw before him, beyond the trench, a long line of shapes, with a shining about them. They were like men who drew the bow, and with another shout, their cloud of arrows flew singing and tingling through the air towards the German hosts.

The arrows came so thick that they darkened the sky above. Within minutes, 10,000 German soldiers lay dead in a thick carpet of field-grey uniform in front of the British lines. According to the story, the Germans suspected the British had used poison gas as their dead bore no sign of injury. Machen was prescient in that detail. Gas was an unsporting outrage at the start of the war and banned by international law, but the Germans were using it within eight months. Initially appalled, the British ended up using gas too.

'The Bowmen' was fiction of course, but it was published as fact on page three of the newspaper, a page reserved for news. To compound matters, Machen was also a respected reporter; he was trusted by readers of the *Evening News* for his weighty deliberations on many contemporary matters.

So the story of the Angels of Mons was widely embraced. In a more credulous age, the British public, in extremis, believed what they wanted to believe. God was always on the side of the British. Did he not give the British an empire on which the sun never sets? And the devil was with the Germans. Reports were widespread in the British press of the Germans burning down the world-renowned library at Louvain and shooting innocent civilians. 'The Hun is at the gate', the poet of the Empire Rudyard Kipling wrote with something approaching religious fervour.[5]

Machen protested that his 'unremarkable' tale had been misinterpreted. The word 'angel' (or 'angels') appears nowhere in his story. He assumed readers would see it as fiction. Instead it became a form of collective wishful thinking.

The 'angel' strand of the myth originated with *The Hereford Times*, which contained an account of two officers from the British Expeditionary Force, 'both of whom had seen angels which had saved their left wing from the Germans when they came right upon them during our retreat from Mons'.[6]

The story was reproduced in the All Saints' church *Parish Magazine* in Bristol to sensational effect. Its editor, Revd Gilson recalled, 'To find that our modest little parish magazine has suddenly sprung into almost world-wide notoriety; every post … has brought letters from all over the country, not asking merely for single copies, but for dozens of copies, enclosing quite embarrassing numbers of stamps and postal orders, the more so since there were no more magazines to be had.'[7]

Machen's continuing protestations were in vain as soldiers themselves began to bring back reports of heavenly interventions. 'This snowball of rumour that was then set rolling has been rolling, growing and getting bigger ever since,' he lamented.[8] The legend of the Angels of Mons had taken wings. The British War Office saw no harm in this flight of patriotic fancy. It too was keen to promulgate the story of the 'miracle of Mons', so called because of the manner in which the British had managed to escape from the Germans.

Machen based his account on what he had read in newspapers. The early exchanges in the war were a profound shock to the British public. In comparison to the unspeakable carnage that was to characterise the war, the British losses at Mons were trifling – some 1,600 dead or injured. But the papers were full of accounts of heavy fighting, fields filled with the dead and dying, and the small British army in full-scale retreat.

Machen was seized with a sense of 'deep despair' by the reports of the gallant British army 'broken to fragments scattered abroad in confusion'. He wrote the story to cheer himself up and, by extension, the British public.[9]

Visitors to Mons in search of the fable's origins are directed to the La Bascule crossroads outside the town. Here, the main road from Mons to Charleroi is bisected by another road from Nimy Bridge to the town of Frameries, which provided the axis of retreat for the British Expeditionary Force. There, they will find a white limestone Celtic cross erected in 1923 to the men of the 2nd Battalion of the Royal Irish Regiment. Founded in 1684, it was the oldest of the Irish regiments in the British army.[10]

The cross is located at exactly the point where a motley outfit of cooks, store-men, drivers and delivery men, about fifty from the regiment in all, held up the German advance for eleven hours. The Angels of Mons story is associated with 8th Brigade of the 3rd Division of the British army. The brigade consisted of four infantry battalions, about 4,000 men in total. These were the 2nd Royal Scots, the 2nd Royal Irish Regiment, the 4th Middlesex Regiment and the 1st Gordon Highlanders. They were the regiments defending the Mons salient where Machen sets his short story.

Few Irish regiments had a more eventful war than the 2nd Royal Irish Regiment. Within a day of the declaration of war, the regiment was seen off from Clonmel by cheering crowds. Significantly, a party of Irish Volunteers, led by Frank Drohan, escorted the drafts from the barracks in the town to the local railway station.[11]

The soldier who inspired the story of the Angels of Mons more than any other was Quartermaster Sergeant Thomas Fitzpatrick from Enniscorthy, County Wexford. The son of a Royal Irish Constabulary policeman, Fitzpatrick joined the Royal Irish Regiment straight from St Aidan's Academy in Enniscorthy when he was 18. The regiment recruited from the counties of Wexford, Waterford, Tipperary and Kilkenny. Its barracks was in Clonmel.

Within a year of joining, Fitzpatrick was posted to the North East Frontier in India, the start of a fifty-two-year career in the British army, during which he rose to the rank of major general. He also received fourteen foreign decorations.[12] Nothing, though, in his long career, would ever achieve the renown of his actions during the Battle of Mons, which happened a week shy of his thirty-fifth birthday.

As a quartermaster, Fitzpatrick was not a frontline soldier. His role was to ensure his regiment was suited, booted, fed and watered. The demands of this particular day, however, thrust him squarely into the frontline. The Royal Irish Regiment was at the base of the salient created where the Mons-Condé canal bends in a semi-circle. The A Company of the 2nd Royal Irish had been overwhelmed.

Captain Walton Mellor had been killed and the company commander Fergus Forbes was badly injured. A member of the family which gave its name to the village of Newtownforbes in County Longford, he would die later that day.[13]

By midday, the situation was already critical. The Germans had breached the salient over the canal. It had been heavily defended at a terrible cost in lives and now the Germans were threatening the flanks of the British Expeditionary Force. There was a real danger that I Corps, half its entire force on the continent of Europe, would be surrounded and find its war at an end before it had barely begun. Sensing the danger, Fitzpatrick gathered up fifty men from his regiment who were not then in the frontline and they took over the hastily dug trench at La Bascule crossroads.

From there, he and his men had a clear line of sight of the German advance in front and at the side where the German 17th Division was pressing hard on the flanks of the two Scottish regiments, the Gordons and the Scots.

Many accounts of the rearguard stand at La Bascule have been written, but the best is probably the one that came from the horse's mouth. Fitzpatrick published his in *The Old Contemptible*, a magazine for ex-servicemen in March 1955.[14]

Fitzpatrick watched the progress of the battle through his field glasses. He saw with alarm that the Germans were starting to surround his battalion.

Shortly after occupying the trench, Fitzpatrick and two others scrambled, under fire, to recover a British machine gun lying on the road in front of them. The gun was jammed and the machine-gunner was dead, but Fitzpatrick recalled being 'delighted' with their 'trophy'. Each regiment had only two machine guns. Without both, they stood little chance of thwarting the Germans.

Fitzpatrick ordered his men to lie still and not to shoot until the enemy was within 200 yards. The tension was unbearable as the enemy drew nearer. Then the men of the Royal Irish Regiment opened up a murderous spray of fire with machine gun and rifle.

Again and again the grey-clad German forms approached; again and again they were repulsed. 'Everyone was now in good form and in good spirits,' remembered Fitzpatrick in the tone of a man recalling a particularly good grouse hunt. 'We felt we were on top of the world and had repulsed the whole German army.'

At one end of the trench, a soldier played Irish airs on his tin whistle and at the other, a soldier asked for permission to go down the local brewery for some beer. Fitzpatrick told him to wait until after dark.

But the cost to his little Irish band of brothers was considerable. Of the fifty or so men in the trench with him that day, only seventeen would end the day unscathed. No medical aid was forthcoming for the wounded and dying.[15] Fitzpatrick was matter-of-fact about it:

> I had no drugs or first-aid appliances and our first-aid station, at nearby Chateau, was in flames. I hoped they would die quickly. My great anxiety all day was to conserve our strength. I lashed out unmercifully at men who were careless and

showed themselves unnecessarily. All the men were useful technicians of a sort and all rather old, but very well trained soldiers so that I took every opportunity of counting our dead and seriously wounded, not from a statistical point of view, but anxious to ascertain if we had sufficient strength to carry on in our highly tactical but vulnerable and forward position, otherwise I would consider moving back as not to be overwhelmed or fall into enemy hands.

The surviving men were hungry and thirsty. Mostly they craved tobacco. Fitzpatrick and two others went looking for food. They saw two German soldiers looting a shop for sweets and shot them both. There were no angels in Mons that day. They then went to look for Captain Forbes and stumbled across the bodies of about fifty German soldiers. Fitzpatrick felt no pity. 'How elated we were to see the result of our afternoon's work.'

It was now night-time. The Germans had been severely mauled. They had closed down the operation to tend to their dead and injured. As they pondered their next move, Fitzpatrick and his men encountered a group of German medical officers in a large Mercedes who approached their trench and demanded access to the German injured.

Bayonets fixed, a stand-off ensued. The senior German officer told them they would be in Paris in five days. 'I hope it keeps fine for you,' an Irish voice piped up. Another German officer observed the Royal Irish badges. 'I presume you must all be Ulstermen,' he asked.[16]

Fitzpatrick was amused. 'This remark was received by my men with hoots of derision. Lydon said he was from Wexford, others shouted their various counties, Waterford, Cork, Tipperary, Kerry etc and I said jokingly, "don't give information to the enemy".'

His men presented a bedraggled sight to the enemy, as Fitzpatrick remembers. 'We looked a motley looking crowd. Some had lost their caps and had tied handkerchiefs over their heads. Others were wearing balaclavas or mufflers instead. Coats were open and packs hanging at all angles, many besmeared with blood after tending the wounded.'

The stand-off melted into something approaching civility when the Germans agreed to tend to the wounded Irishmen. The German senior medical officer offered the men cigars. They were then sent on their way. At 11 p.m., the men decided to move back towards the British lines. They took their dead and buried them in the trench where they had held out for most of the day. A Belgian civilian led them to safety. On the way, they encountered a young Irish officer, Second Lieutenant John Denys Shine from Waterford, who had been taken in by a Belgian woman and was dying from his wounds in an upstairs room. He had been shot through the groin. He would be the first of three Shine brothers to die in the war. His brother Hugh died at the Second Battle of Ypres in May 1915 and a second brother James died during the awful Battle of Passchendaele in August 1917.[17]

Their father Colonel James Shine was a doctor attached to the Royal Medical Corps who also served in the war. He was a veteran of the Boer War and colonial campaigns in Burma and the North-West Frontier of India.

Despite the grievous agony of losing his three sons, Colonel Shine continued his duties to the bitter end of the war. He was mentioned three times in dispatches and rose to the level of deputy director of medical services. The British made him a Commander of the Order of the Bath (CB), but nothing could ameliorate the grief of losing his three sons. His wife Kathleen, who lost all her sons in the war, died in 1924 leaving him a widow. He died seven years later, in 1931, at the age of 70.

Seeing 19-year-old John Shine's life ebb away, Fitzpatrick's earlier feelings of euphoria gave way to depression. 'Was war worth the glory and its adventures, why should men kill one another?' There was no time to ponder the answer.

Eventually Fitzpatrick's seventeen survivors found their way back to their battalion at 2 a.m. as the whole of the British Expeditionary Force began the retreat from Mons, a 200-mile footslog in hot summer weather with the German army in pursuit. At 4 a.m., with just two hours' sleep, they joined the long haul south.

Fitzpatrick was injured twice during the war. In 1915, he was gassed and left for dead. A terse telegram from the British War Office told his mother to come at once to the French hospital in Boulogne. He had not been expected to live. He survived and went on to become a high-ranking functionary in various parts of the British Empire. He was at one time chief of police in Cairo. He retired in 1949.

Reflecting on that fateful day in Mons more than forty years later, Fitzpatrick recalled seeing no 'Mons angels. I honestly think that not one of my men had the faintest idea what they were fighting for. In fact, I was not sure myself – which illustrates the unconquerable spirit of the British soldier of that day – the Irish soldier in our case. They were there to fight without thought of clan or creed but how well they responded to the call of duty and the traditions of their gallant regiment.'

His men, despite their appalling losses, felt 'elation in the same manner as we had won the final in an important football tournament, not because we managed to withstand the German attacks and to cause them many casualties. We were better men and better trained than the Germans who seemed to me a kind of machine levered by their officers, and without initiative.' His abiding emotion, though, was the 'humiliation of being compelled to retire before the Germans. How little did I know what we were up against that day.'

For his actions, Fitzpatrick received the Distinguished Conduct Medal (DCM) from the British government, the French *Médaille militaire*, their equivalent of the Victoria Cross, and the Russian Order of St George.

The efforts of the 2nd Royal Irish Regiment allowed the 8th Brigade to make good its retirement.

Sadly, the 2nd Royal Irish Regiment was nearly completely destroyed two months later when it attempted to take the village of Le Pilly on Aubers Ridge in northern France. This will be the subject of another chapter. The regiment was again decimated at Mouse Trap Farm in Ypres on 24 May 1915, losing nearly 400 men in a single day to a German gas attack.[18]

During the Battle of the Somme, the Royal Irish Regiment was involved in the attempt to take Mametz Wood, which was full of German machine-gunners and snipers. The Royal Irish almost succeeded but were held up by thickets of barbed wire. In October 1916, the regiment became part of the 16th (Irish) Division. It was decimated again in 1918 on the first day of the German Spring Offensive, when the regiment found itself at the forefront of the assault which began on 21 March. The Royal Irish lost 499 killed, wounded or missing.

On the evening of 10 November 1918, the Royal Irish reached a line near the railway in Nouvelles, just south of Mons. It took them four hours, under heavy machine gun and rifle fire, to take the railway crossing. At 10 p.m. they reached the village of St Symphorien, the place where so many of their comrades from four years previous were buried.

On Armistice Day they entered Spiennes, an old tin-mining town south-east of Mons. In the final day of battle, the regiment lost four men killed, fifty-three wounded and six missing. Four days later, all that was left for the victory parade in Mons were six officers and 200 men.[19]

The Celtic cross to the 2nd Royal Irish Regiment was unveiled on Armistice Day 1923, one year after the regiment was disbanded along with the four others which had been recruited in what became the Irish Free State.

Contemporary photographs show huge crowds at the unveiling, including local children who were given the day off. They lined the paths to the cross and laid flowers at its base. The inscription on the memorial alluded to the battalion's presence at the Battle of Mons and at the town's liberation and all its travails in between:

> To the glory of God and to the memory of the men and officers of the Royal Irish Regiment (18th Foot) who fell during the Great War 1914-1918. Near this spot the 2nd Battalion commenced operations on 23rd August 1914 and finished on 11th November 1918 after being decimated on four occasions.

The train from Brussels to Paris made an unscheduled stop in Mons to let the regimental party disembark. Field Marshal Sir John French, now Lord Ypres, gave the address in French. He began, 'No more appropriate spot than this ancient city of Mons could have been found to perpetuate the memory of the glorious heroes of the Royal Irish Regiment who fell on the field of battle.'[20]

French had all the ambivalence of the Anglo-Irish caste. He regarded himself as Irish though he was born and brought up in England. His family owned substantial estates in County Roscommon.

French was a supporter of home rule and passionately believed that Ireland's future was within the British Empire. After the disastrous Battle of Loos in 1915, he was removed as Commander-in-Chief and put in charge of home defence, out of harm's way, or so the British government hoped. As Commander-in-Chief, Home Forces, he was the man in charge when General John Maxwell was dispatched to Dublin to suppress the Easter Rising in 1916. Infamously, it was Maxwell who ordered the execution of the leaders of the Rising.

That deed alone earned French the undying enmity of Irish Republicans. He misjudged the change in mood in Ireland. He thought Sinn Féin was a passing phase. The Irish would grumble but eventually accept conscription. Once they saw the Republicans for what they were, they would 'cast them out like the swine that they are'.[21]

The 1918 general election, which saw the abstentionist Sinn Féin win 73 of the 105 Irish seats, did not change his view. When the War of Independence began in 1919, French, who was now Lord Lieutenant, tried to crush it but complained bitterly that the British government, which had no heart for any more conflict anywhere, was leaving him short of the resources to deal with the rebellion.

In December 1919, a party of eleven IRA volunteers tried to assassinate him as he returned by train to the vice-regal lodge in Phoenix Park. He was hit on the head by a hand grenade and knocked unconscious. Fortunately for him, the grenade did not explode. French remained in his post until April 1921, three months before the truce which ended the War of Independence.

He was hopelessly torn about Ireland. He bought a house in Roscommon and seemed genuinely drawn to living out his days in comparative tranquillity, but he could never retire in Ireland given the deadly animosity between himself and the IRA. Field Marshal Sir Henry Wilson, a southern Irish unionist, who was possessed of no such ambivalence and believed the Irish needed a firm hand, wrote of French, 'Poor little man he is so weak and pliable and then has such inconsequential gusts of illogical passion. He is an Imperialist, a Democrat, a home ruler all at the same time.'[22]

Whatever feelings French had towards the rebellious Irish at home, he had nothing but admiration for the Irishmen in the pay of the British army and made only one oblique reference in his speech at Mons in 1923 to the changed political situation:

Years may pass before the true history of the Great War can be known and understood, but when this moment comes the attitude of the soldiers of Ireland will stand out nobly. They were always where the fighting was hottest and the Irish regiments held their ground with a tenacity which has never been surpassed. Alas the inexorable decree of destiny has caused them to disappear from the ranks of the Army, but the memory of their actions will survive I am convinced for all time.

Fitzpatrick survived the war and the next one. During the Second World War he was chief of police in the Suez Canal area. Latter-day pictures show an old man laughing and joking with the nurses who were looking after him in a Putney nursing home. He died in 1965, aged 84. According to his grandson Tom Fitzpatrick, his memoirs were appropriated by the Ministry of Defence (MOD) because they contained sensitive information about British activities in the post-war Middle East. What stories they would have told. We will hardly see his likes again.[23]

4

THE CEMETERY AT ÉTREUX

There are few military manoeuvres more perilous than a rearguard action. The defenders are separated from the bulk of their comrades; usually they are facing an enemy many times their number. It is a measure which calls for precise military organisation and stout hearts. A general who trusts a rearguard action to a battalion or a brigade does so in the hope that they will stand their ground long enough for the bulk of the retreating army to escape.

At Étreux in northern France on 27 August 1914, the 2nd Royal Munster Fusiliers performed a rearguard action which is regarded as one of the finest of the First World War.

In the preface of his book *The 2nd Munsters in France*, published four years after the war, Lieutenant-Colonel H.S. Jervis, who was taken prisoner at Étreux, wrote the following:

> It is occasionally given to a brigade to hold up a whole division. A division may occasionally stop the advance of an army corps, but for one battalion of infantry – or to be more exact, three companies with the aid of a couple of field guns to stem the advance of an entire army corps is probably an incident without parallel in modern warfare. Yet this was done on August 27th, 1914, by the 2nd Royal Munsters Fusiliers.[1]

The Munsters had departed for France on 13 August 1914 with 1,009 personnel. They were attached to the 1st Division of I Corps of the British army, commanded by Lieutenant-General Douglas Haig, later to be Field Marshal Haig.[2] The Munsters were led by Major Paul Charrier, who had taken over command from Lieutenant-Colonel J.K. O'Meagher. The son of a British army officer and a French mother, Charrier was born into the army in India in 1868.

A child of the British Empire, Charrier spent his formative years as a soldier defending that empire. In 1900, he was mentioned in dispatches after being wounded in the splendidly named War of the Golden Stool, in which British colonists sought to subdue the West African Ashanti Empire in what is present-day Ghana. He also fought in the Boer War. Unusually for the monoglot British army, he was fluent in French and felt the occupation of his mother's country keenly. 'It was claimed that he was the best company commander at Aldershot,' wrote Jervis.[3]

Charrier was distinguished not only by his organisational ability, but by his great height at a time when the average man was several inches shorter than he would be today. At 6ft 7in, he was the tallest officer in the British army. Charrier compounded his striking appearance by wearing a green-and-white hackle in his colonial cap.

The 2nd Royal Munster Fusiliers was to be the rearguard of I Corps, which consisted of the 1st and 2nd Divisions of the British Expeditionary Force. On the morning of 27 August 1914, Charrier wrote tersely in his diary, 'Morning of 27th August 1914 – mission, rear guard'.

The British army's field service regulations instructs that a rearguard:

> carries out its mission best by compelling the enemy's troops to halt and deploy
> for attack as frequently and at as great a distance as possible. It can usually affect
> this by taking up a succession of defensive positions which the enemy must
> attack or turn. When the enemy's dispositions are nearly complete – the rear
> guard move off by successive retirements, each party as it falls back covering the
> retirement of the next by its fire. The action is repeated on the next favourable
> ground. All this takes time, and time is what is needed by a retreating force.[4]

Two days after the Battle of Mons, the British Expeditionary Force found itself at
a fork in the road in the Forest of Mormal. This forest at the foot of the Ardennes
Mountains is one of the biggest in northern France. It was heavily fought over in
both world wars. Today, it is populated with frogs, newts and toads that have made
comfortable homes out of the old shell holes. In August 1914, it was a natural
barrier which threatened ruin on the British army. The forest could only be
traversed on two narrow roads. The retreating British Expeditionary Force had no
choice but to split its bedraggled army in two: II Corps, under General Sir Horace
Smith-Dorrien, headed south-west in the direction of St Quentin and I Corps,
under Haig, headed south-east in the direction of the town of Guise.[5]

I Corps reached the town of Landrecies south of the Forest of Mormal on
25 August. The Allies were to continue their withdrawal in lockstep. I Corps was
to follow a route through the town of Étreux, turning south to Guise, which they
had to clear before going into billets for the night.[6] The narrow streets of Guise
were a potential death trap for the corps. The British 1st Division was to pass
through it after the 2nd Division had gone first. The retreat was already impeded
by fleeing civilians clogging up the roads. Progress was being made at a pace of
just two miles per hour and even this was too much for the stragglers.

The plan was for the 1st Division to provide rearguard cover for the 2nd. Then
the 1st Division would move off, its brigades providing rearguard for each other:
3rd Brigade, followed by 2nd and then 1st Brigade. That brigade would move off
in sequence with each of its four battalions retreating in turn. The final battalion
to depart the battlefield would be the 2nd Royal Munster Fusiliers. The Munsters
would act as the rearguard for the rearguard. In other words, they would be the last
men to retreat.[7] The 2nd Division began the 7-mile march from Étreux to Guise
at 4 a.m. The retreat was carried off with the utmost haste as rumours abounded
that the Germans were already south of the retreating British. It was nonetheless
late afternoon before the 1st Division could follow suit.

The countryside defended by 1st Brigade was and still is one of large, sugar
beet fields, high hedges and dense copses obscuring the field of view in many
directions. Overlooking Étreux, there is high ground which is bisected by the

Sambre-Oise Canal. The road into Étreux is a shallow valley. Whoever controlled the slopes controlled the battle. This terrain would allow the Germans, if they gained it, to observe and then shell the retreating British. It had to be held at costs.

Scouting the landscape, Charrier deduced that the Germans would attack, not across fields, but straight down the roads. They could not do otherwise. The terrain was too difficult.

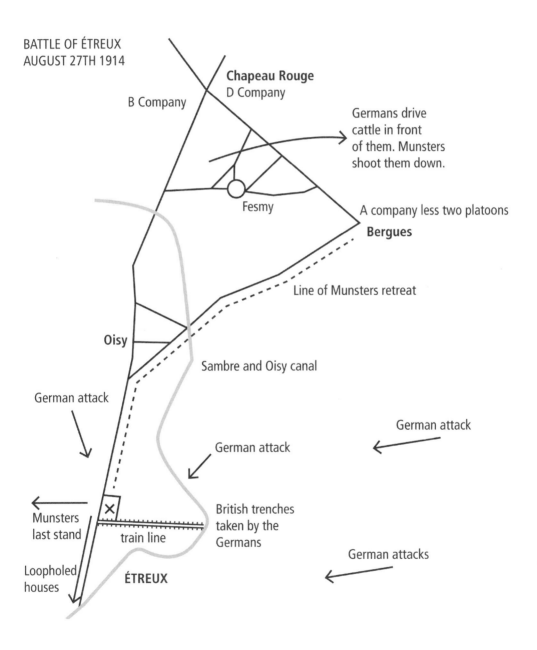

BATTLE OF ÉTREUX
AUGUST 27TH 1914

B Company

Chapeau Rouge
D Company

Germans drive
cattle in front
of them. Munsters
shoot them down.

Fesmy

A company less two platoons

Bergues

Line of Munsters retreat

Oisy

Sambre and Oisy canal

German attack

German attack

German attack

Munsters
last stand

British trenches
taken by the
Germans

train line

German attacks

Loopholed
houses

ÉTREUX

In total, the Munsters held a front of approximately 2 miles, with Fesmy as its centre point. Two companies were dispatched to the north. B and D held the crossroads at Chapeau Rouge. Half of A Company held the line at Bergues to the south. The rest of A and all of C Company were deployed in between. It was a lot of ground to hold with approximately 900 men. As support, the battalion had two 18-pounder guns from the 118th Battery, Royal Horse Artillery (RHA) and two troops of the 15th Hussars, a cavalry regiment, comprising seventy men in total.

This made for a diagonal formation which the Germans would have to breach if they were to access the road to Oisy, which bestrides the canal. From Oisy was the road to Étreux, a town of about 2,000 people, and from there was the road to Guise. This was the only feasible route for I Corps to take, given their numbers.

At 9 a.m., the first German cavalry appeared on the horizon. These were the 17th Brunswick Hussars, a fabled regiment which had fought at the Battle of Waterloo as allies of the British. Known as the Black Brunswickers, their black uniforms and death-head motif made them one of the most distinctive cavalry regiments in Europe. Their role in Étreux was to reconnoitre the enemy rather than attack. They came within 500 yards of the Munsters' line and then disappeared back to their lines.

For an hour or so, an uneasy calm descended on the battlefield. Private Patrick O'Donnell took advantage of the hiatus to climb some apple trees. He recalled being given no indication that they were about to face a much more numerous enemy. 'I was put about for a moment, but soon came to my senses, and looking around me, I could see nobody. I fell off the apple tree. It was the quickest way to get down. I was no sooner down when two shots came ringing over my head.'[8]

The Germans advanced within yards of the Munsters at Bergues and then the heavens opened. It felt like divine intervention, as O'Donnell recalled:

They were all around us. While we were there the rain fell in torrents. Thank God for the rain – that is what saved us from being killed. There we were and our teeth crackling from the cold and hunger at the same time. Our officer was brave and so were our men. We all gave up to be killed and sure to die. We had only one chance to take a certain road, and there were Germans left and right of us. I led my comrades as best I could. We all ran. I was first, but the fire was too heavy and I turned myself under a hedge until all the fire ceased. All my comrades had gone away, and I was alone. I fell nine times under heavy fire, but God must be with me, to say that I could escape. I was lying on the road for ten minutes before I could get up and being then alone, I was in great danger. Our brave officer was wounded and two of my comrades, leaving only three out of five hundred. It was God that saved me.[9]

The 1st Brigade expected to be heavily outnumbered, but they did not know they would be facing an entire corps of between 30,000 and 40,000 men of the German Army.

The X Reserve Corps comprised two divisions from the Westphalia and Hanover areas. They were reservists, not the highest calibre of German soldier, but what they lacked in experience, they made up for in numbers.

Between six and nine battalions assailed the single battalion of the Munsters. These were overwhelming odds. In their favour, the Munsters' actions were essentially defensive. The old regulars of the British army were professional soldiers and were exceptionally good infantrymen. Musketry was paramount. During the South African War of 1899–1902, the Boers had taught the British army a salutary lesson about the necessity for entrenching before facing an advancing enemy. Though small in number, the Munsters could bring impressive firepower down on an advancing enemy. The intensity of the fire from the men of the Munsters, with their Mark III Short Magazine Lee-Enfield rifles, led the Germans to believe that they were facing an unusual concentration of machine guns. The first to be attacked was B Company. The men waited until the Germans revealed their positions. The sultry weather of the preceding days finally broke and the rain came down in torrents. When the thunderstorm cleared, the fighting resumed. The German attack on Chapeau Rouge began at 10.30 a.m. The attack was repulsed at little cost. The Munsters had dug in well and their firepower kept the Germans from advancing.

The men had been in the trenches since first light and by now were ravenous. D Company's cooker came out and the men were served at around midday. The company was split in two by a road down which the Germans directed fire.

The cooks scrambled as they delivered dinners with bullets flying around them. Even in such an extreme situation, there was time for some country Irish humour. 'Don't be emptying all the tae down your trowsies,' exclaimed one wag as the cooks struggled with the large Dixie pots.[10]

Another deluge of rain came. This allowed the men at Chapeau Rouge to evacuate their positions and head in the direction of Fesmy. They did so, according to the regimental history, by 'shooting down the Germans as they showed themselves at the gaps in the hedges'.[11]

At Fesmy, the battalion's two machine guns were placed in the centre of the road, banked on both sides by high hedges. This made the position relatively easy to defend as it could only be attacked at a high cost. The Germans grew desperate and at one stage marched a herd of cattle in front of them to mask their attack. The Munsters shot the cattle down, which exposed the enemy behind, who were then shot in turn. At 2.30 p.m., Charrier sent a message to headquarters. 'The Germans are driving cattle in front of them up to us for cover. We are killing plenty of them.'[12] At the south end of the Munster line, A Company holding

Bergues was forced to withdraw under intense pressure from the German 13th Division. The 2nd Welsh Guards had also withdrawn. The road to Étreux was now open.

The rest of 1st (Guards) Brigade managed to pass unhindered through Étreux and on to Guise. The Munsters' transport, mostly horse-drawn, also managed to get away. Had the rest of the Munsters got the message in time, they too could have made their escape. The message to withdraw was sent by two dispatch riders. Tragically, one was shot and the other was held up for two hours by German fire. By the time he got to the Coldstream Guards at Oisy, which now had a small detachment of Munsters from Bergues with them, it was 3 p.m. The three other battalions of the 1st Brigade reached Guise with 'trifling loss'. The rest of the Munsters were on their own. Charrier's men made slow progress from Fesmy to Oisy, a distance of about half a mile. High hedgerows on both sides of the road created a sniper's alley. The Munsters had to give covering fire for every step they took to ensure that the Germans did not have a free hand to fire at will into the retreating soldiers.

The withdrawal of the Munsters was delayed by the slow movement of B Company, which held the right-hand position. This delay, lasting almost an hour, was fatal. Two platoons of the rearguard stopped the Germans from entering Oisy and just before 6 p.m., the rest of the Munsters crossed the bridge at Oisy and turned south in the direction of Étreux.

They had emerged relatively unscathed from a day of fierce fighting. Their action had been a success and the Germans were nursing heavy casualties. The Munsters had made better use of the difficult terrain. The experience they had gained through hard training and colonial campaigns had trumped overwhelming numbers. The official history of the German 15th Reserve Regiment recalled 'receiving fire at every turn of the road. Whilst marching off it was impossible owing to the 6ft high hedges, threaded with wire and almost impenetrable … everywhere thick hedges. We are always getting fired on, we can't tell from where.'[13]

As they approached the outskirts of Étreux, the Munsters found to their consternation that their way to safety was blocked. The Germans had taken advantage of the Munsters' evacuation of Bergues and the Welsh Guard's evacuation to approach Étreux from the south. The Munsters had been outflanked and the trenches, which had been dug so expertly by the 1st Black Watch parallel to the railway crossing outside Étreux, were now occupied by troops from the 15th Reserve Infantry Division.

The Germans duly showered withering fire upon the Munsters from a couple of houses on the outskirts of the village that they had fortified with machine guns. The Munsters had inflicted many more casualties than they suffered in the first part of the battle. Now it was their turn.

From the east, they were shelled. Their ability to return shellfire was firstly thwarted when a shell killed one battery team and the other began to run out of ammunition. Charrier ordered the destruction of the German-held house with what ammunition the battery had left, but the artillery team was shot down in the attempt. The Munsters were cut off. The German 10th Reserve Division was approaching from the north and the way forward was blocked to the south. The Germans now directed fire from the south, east and west.

Charrier led the Munsters as they attempted to force the passage through Étreux. They charged the fortified house and the railway crossing. They were shot down. One by one their officers were killed or wounded; a wounded Charrier continued to lead his men until he was killed. Jervis and the men from D Company left the death trap that was the road and crossed fields in an attempt to get round the flank of the entrenched Germans. When they were just 70 yards away, they charged the Germans, but were also shot. Jervis, who was one of the few to survive the charge, reached a hedge and shot six of the enemy with his revolver.[14]

The battle continued all evening as the death toll mounted and the Munsters' predicament became ever more desperate. A bayonet charge on the fortified house failed with huge casualties. An officer got as far as one hole in the wall and fired into it, but he was knocked out by falling masonry.

The Germans, too, were suffering grievously. The countryside for miles around was strewn with the bodies of young reservists who just a month previously had been civilians in one of Europe's most prosperous societies.

A thunderous cacophony of shot and shell, accompanied by the groans of dead and dying men and horses, assailed these Aisne villages which had never seen war before. A house that had been a civilian dwelling that morning was hit directly by a German shell and burst into flames. Eventually the remnants of the Munsters gradually fell back on the apple orchard alongside the main road on the outskirts of the town. Here, command devolved to the unwounded officer Lieutenant E.W. Gower. They positioned themselves around the perimeter of the orchard, where they continued to fight until their ammunition was expended. At 9.15 p.m., the officers and men laid down their arms and surrendered.

In an epic twelve-hour action, the Munsters, with support, had held off no less than nine battalions of the German army before succumbing. According to Jervis, the Germans recognised the bravery of the Munsters. But when they realised they had suffered 1,500 casualties at the hands of a relatively paltry number of men, they were furious. And to make matters worse, at least 12 miles now separated the Germans from that of the retreating British.

The day after the action, the Germans allowed the prisoners to bury their dead comrades, which included Hussars and Artillery men. The nine officers who were killed, including Charrier, were buried separately from their men, who numbered ninety, in the orchard. Realising that the Munsters had no chaplain with them, the Germans provided one of their own to officiate over the burials. As a mark of respect to the men who were buried, the Germans had a sign erected over the two mass graves, which read 'Freund und Feind im Tod vereint' (Friend and Foe United in Death).[15]

Of the 800 or so men who had started out that morning with firm instructions to hold the line, just 240 men and four unwounded officers from the battalion who managed to escape or had been held in reserve were available the following day at stand to. The British official history recorded that 'beyond question, they had arrested the enemy's pursuit so that their sacrifice was not in vain'.[16]

Among the dead were eighteen soldiers from Cork, thirteen from Limerick, twelve from Kerry and four from Clare. Shortly after the war ended, a proposal was put forward to erect a Regimental Memorial at Étreux and the following citation was received from the secretary of the Battle Exploits Memorial Committee:

> The action is likely to become the classical example of the performance of its functions by a rearguard. The Battalion not only held up the attack of a strong hostile force in its original position, thereby securing the unmolested withdrawal of its Division, but in retiring drew on itself the attacks of very superior numbers of the enemy. It was finally cut off at Étreux by five or six times its numbers, but held out for several hours, the remnant only surrendering when their ammunition was practically exhausted and only a small number of men remained unhurt. The survivors were warmly congratulated by the Germans on the fine fight they had made. No other claim to a memorial near Étreux is likely to be advanced – certainly nothing which would not take second place to the Munsters.
> (Signed) C. T. Atkinson,
> Historical Section, C.I.D.
> June 7th, 1919.

—

The orchard was purchased in early 1921 by Captain Walter Styles MP, a brother of Lieutenant Frederick Ernest (F.E.) Styles, one of the officers killed and buried there. It would be preserved as a memorial to the men of the Royal Munster Fusiliers who died during the war.[17] A wall was built round it, with iron gates leading to the Étreux–Landrecies road. The cemetery was consecrated by the Revd Archdeacon Lefevre, Dean of Wassigny on 5 October 1921 and a prayer was recited by the Revd Vere Awdry, whose son, Second Lieutenant Carol Edward Vere Awdry, is buried there. Carol Edward's half-brother Revd Wilbert Awdry achieved international fame by writing the Thomas the Tank Engine series of children's books.

With the consecration ceremony over, the regimental buglers sounded the 'Last Post'. It was followed by an interval of silence, after which 'Reveille' was sounded. A very fine Celtic cross was erected in the cemetery with funds collected mainly by the 2nd Battalion and Captain Styles. Standing 22ft tall, it is modelled on a similar cross in Killarney, County Kerry.

The unveiling of the cross on 4 June 1922 was undertaken by Lieutenant-General Sir George Macdonogh, Adjutant-General of the Forces and the highest-ranking Catholic of Irish extraction in the British army.

The dedication ceremony was carried out by Revd Fr Francis Gleeson, who had been chaplain to the battalion for three years. Lieutenant-Colonel Arthur Bent was the last commanding officer of the battalion before the regiment was disbanded. He told the assembled crowd that the cross 'remains a perpetual testimony of the dedication of these brave Irishman who, at the beginning of the war, made the supreme sacrifice in France and for France and may she always remind these two great nations who fought side by side for years that they will always represent liberty, peace and justice'.

Later, the Commonwealth War Graves Commission took possession of the cemetery and placed headstones with the names of the men along the walls of the cemetery in alphabetical order. The Commission continues to maintain this cemetery to the highest standard.

The cemetery is in the same spot where the men surrendered on the Étreux-Landrecies road, past which thousands of British soldiers marched in August 1914. It is slightly out of the way of the remembrance trail and is seldom visited in comparison with many other cemeteries, but its isolation only heightens its attractiveness.

On 27 August 2014, 100 years after the battle, centenary commemorations took place in the cemetery, hosted by the Royal Munster Fusiliers Association. Many of those who attended were descendants of the men who fought at Étreux. Among them was Mike Donoghue from Canada, whose novel *My Kingdom* is based on the story of his grandfather Private Daniel Donoghue, who was taken prisoner at Étreux.

The Irish ambassador to France Rory Montgomery laid a wreath on behalf of the Irish people. The Mayor of Étreux Joël Noisette did so on behalf of the town. Montgomery spoke of his pride representing the Irish State at the commemoration and how there had been a 'real maturing' in attitudes to those Irishmen who had died in British uniforms. 'The time had passed for arguing the rights and wrongs of the conflict or for questioning the motives of those involved. All those on both sides had paid an appallingly high price for the errors of their political leaders and the societies in which they lived.'[18]

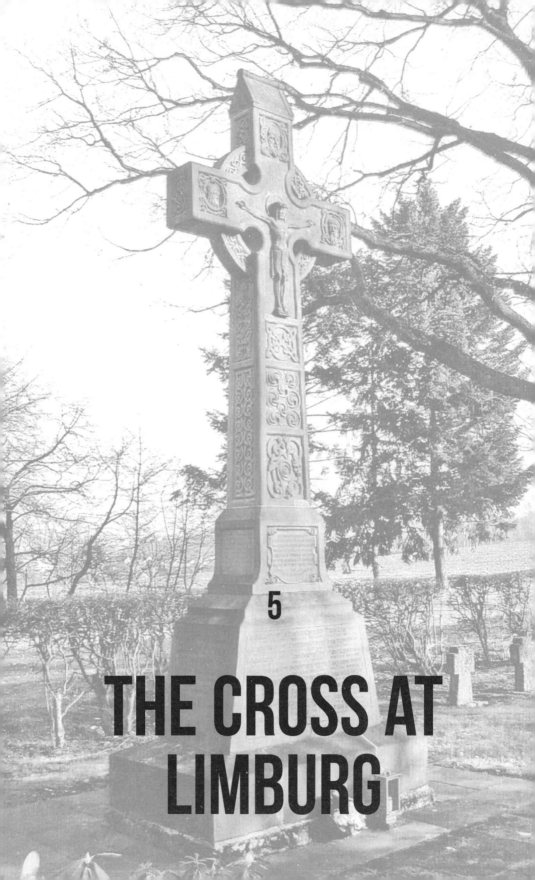

5

THE CROSS AT LIMBURG

Whatever admiration the Germans had for their vanquished Irish foes after the rearguard action at Étreux, it did not last. While the Munsters officers were given preferential treatment and sent straight to prison camps in Germany, the ranks were left for sixteen days in an old mill, subsisting on cabbage water drunk from broken bottles and whatever else their captors deigned to feed them. This meagre diet worsened the condition of many wounded men who needed proper nourishment to aid their recovery.[1]

On the seventeenth day of their capture, the Irish prisoners of war were taken to camps in Germany. These names would resonate for the next four years in homes throughout Ireland – Dulmen, Friedrichsfeld, Giessen, Hamlin, Sennelager and Limburg.

Prisoners of war committees were set up across Ireland to supply food, clothing and small comforts from home for the men. As the Allied blockade of Germany continued and hunger stalked the civilian population, the German authorities did not prioritise feeding the hundreds of thousands of prisoners of war in their care.[2] 'Were it not for the timely aid of our good friends at home we would be sleeping the long sleep under German soil today,' recalled Private William O'Connell of the 2nd Royal Munster Fusiliers, who was captured at Étreux.[3]

The journey from Étreux in northern France to camps in central Germany was a trial for the Munsters. The men expected the relative comforts of being a prisoner of war: namely, a bed, shelter and sufficient food and drink. The treatment of prisoners of war was covered under the terms of the Geneva Convention, but these men were treated abominably.

O'Connell told the *Limerick Chronicle* after the war:

> We were compelled to exist on a drop of black coffee made from burnt horse beans and a small ration of bread for the whole day and had often to work very hard. Many a time, I have seen unfortunate Irish lads driven at the point of the bayonet to walk 2 or 2½ miles to carry heavy railway sleepers and owing to their weak conditions they fainted under the heavy burden. The sanitary arrangements here were very simply abominable. Starvation, misery, and cruel treatment constituted our lot during our time in Sennelager.[4]

On 22 December 1914, the Irish prisoners scattered around the central German state of Hesse were transferred temporarily to Limburg camp, about 22 miles outside Frankfurt. The Germans were prepared to make them an offer and the man responsible for that offer was an extraordinary figure in Irish history – Roger Casement.

Every detail of Roger Casement's upbringing would lead one to assume that his instincts would be unionist rather than nationalist. He was brought up in the Protestant faith of his father, a former British officer, though his mother had him secretly baptised as a Catholic when he was four. Casement's mother died when he was 9; his father when he was 13. Casement's mother had died when he was 9. The orphaned Casement was sent to live with his father's relatives in unionist Ballymena.

Casement left school at the age of 16 to make his way in the world. He joined the British consular service and gained an international reputation for his work in exposing abuses in the rubber industry in the Congo Free State, a kleptocracy set up by King Leopold II of Belgium. His devastating report in 1904 into the abuses of the rubber trade in what is the modern-day Democratic Republic of Congo had a huge effect on public opinion. He chronicled incidences of 'enslavement, mutilation and torture of natives on the rubber plantation'.[5]

His reputation could have rested on that report alone, but he followed it up with another into the exploitation of the Putumayo Indians by the Peruvian Amazon Company (PAC), which was published in 1910. Here, too, 1,900 miles from the source of the Amazon, he found ruthless exploitation of native peoples by colonial invaders.

Casement was knighted for his services in 1911. His friend William Cadbury, of the famous chocolate family, remarked, 'He gave the best 20 years of his life and his magnificent physical frame and constitution ungrudgingly to the service of the British government in the interests of the weaker and downtrodden races of the earth.'[6] Although he accepted this bauble of the British Empire, Casement had already begun the process of becoming an Irish nationalist, seeing in British rule of Ireland echoes of the colonial exploitation he had encountered in other parts of the world. In Casement's worldview, the Irish, too, were one of the 'weaker and downtrodden races' referred to by Cadbury.

Once convinced of the cause of Irish nationalism, Casement threw himself into it with the same sense of single-minded devotion and self-abandon he exercised in the service of the British Empire. Casement was involved in the setting-up of the Irish Volunteers in November 1913 and was one of the organisers of the shipment of arms to them at Howth in July 1914.

He was in the United States raising funds for the Irish Volunteers when war broke out in August 1914.[7] There, he met veteran exiled Republicans John Devoy, a link to the previous Fenian uprising of 1867, and Joseph McGarrity, a member of Clan na Gael, an organisation dedicated to overthrowing British rule in Ireland by force if necessary. Together they contacted the German ambassador to the United States Count Johann Heinrich von Bernstorff.

Devoy made a proposal. If the Germans supplied guns, the Irish would supply the rebellion which would tie up thousands of British troops destined to fight Germany on the Western Front. Later, at Casement's behest, Devoy and a group of other Irish Republicans penned an unctuous letter of support to Kaiser Wilhelm II written by Casement and signed by all the members of the executive of Clan na Gael:

Sire,

The undersigned, representing many millions of the people of this country, either of Irish birth or Irish descent, desire very respectfully to place before Your Majesty what we believe to be the view of the vast majority of Irishmen not only in the United States but throughout the world.

In the first place, we seek to give voice to the feeling of Irishmen in America. That feeling is chiefly one of sympathy and admiration for the heroic people of Germany ... We feel that the German people are in truth fighting for European civilisation at its best. We recognise that Germany did not seek this war, but that it was forced upon her. We wholeheartedly hope for the success of the German people in this unequal struggle forced upon them ... It is by sole possession of Ireland that Great Britain has been able for two centuries to maintain an unchallengeable mastery of the seas and by this agency to convert a small trading community into the wholly arbitrary judges of war and peace for all mankind.[8]

In October 1914, the Germans arranged for Casement to sail under an assumed name from the United States to Norway and from there to Germany. Before he left, Casement penned a letter to the *Irish Independent* setting out his opposition to Irishmen fighting in the war:

Ireland has suffered at the hands of British administrators a more prolonged series of evils, deliberately inflicted, than any other community of civilised men. The cause of Ireland is greater than the cause of any party; higher than the worth of any man; richer in its poverty than all the riches of Empire no Irishman fit to bear arms in the cause of his country's freedom can join the allied millions now attacking Germany, in a war that at best concerns Ireland not at all.[9]

While in Germany, Casement spent many weeks trying to persuade them to take his offer of Irish support seriously. In November 1914, he finally succeeded in securing a declaration from the German government 'that under no circumstances would Germany invade Ireland with a view to its conquest or the overthrow of native institutions. Should the fortune of this great war bring German troops to Ireland, they would land there, not to pillage or destroy, but as forces of a govern-ment inspired only by goodwill.'[10]

In early December 1914, the Germans concentrated some 2,300 Irish-born prisoners together in the Limburg camp. The men were drawn mostly from the ranks of the Royal Munster Fusiliers, the Royal Dublin Fusiliers, the Royal Irish Regiment, the Connaught Rangers and the Leinster Regiment, all of which had lost hundreds of prisoners to the Germans in the early stages of the war.

Casement and the Germans had a plan. He would enter the camp as a potential liberator and offer the men a deal: turn and fight against the British and they would be in the vanguard of a joint German-Irish force which would liberate Ireland from British rule.

Fanciful as it might seem in retrospect, the Germans were confident that the men could be persuaded to switch sides. Their military attaché in Washington, Franz von Papen, a man who would go on to be German chancellor before Adolf Hitler, reported back to Berlin, 'Success and cooperation of all Irishmen in British army then beyond doubt. In northern France strong discord between Irish and English, therefore use of volunteer Irish prisoners against British again suggested.'[11]

Casement visited the beaten, half-starved men who had been brought from the various camps and addressed them. He promised them liberation, good treatment, better food and better conditions. He appealed to them as an Irishman to Irishmen. Did they not want to fight for their own country? Why were they fighting for Ireland's 'hereditary enemy'? Why were they fighting on behalf of Belgium, a country that meant no more to them than Fiji? He reminded them of the three civilians shot dead by British troops at Bachelors Walk in Dublin just a week before the war broke out. John Redmond was a traitor for suggesting Irishmen should go and fight for the British. Home rule was a 'pretence' because the British could never be trusted.

King George III had paid money to foreign mercenaries to slaughter Irish rebels during the 1798 Rebellion. Queen Victoria only regretted that the Irish had not rebelled during the famine so they could be put down. There was an oath of allegiance to serve only one country, but what was that country if it was not Ireland?[12]

Casement then dealt with the practicalities of his offer. Men should not need money to fight for their country, but he understood these men were poor. He would endeavour to pay them at least £10 for joining the Irish Brigade from his own resources as they should not, as a matter of principle, be paid by Germany.

Casement is now regarded as a great Irishman, especially after his execution for treason in August 1916, but in late 1914 and early 1915, the Irish prisoners assembled at Limburg regarded him as a charlatan and a nuisance. They listened with mounting incredulity and no little irritation.[13]

Casement and his fellow Irishmen would seem to have been united by nothing other than a common loathing. In his diary Casement described the men he saw in Limburg as 'the scum of Ireland – literally ... the more I see of these alleged Irishmen – the less I think of them as being Irish. They are a black blot on our claim to nationality – these so-called soldiers in the English army'. They were not imbued with any sense of patriotism, he believed, but many were 'more English than the English themselves' and spoke of going 'home to England'.

Many of the prisoners were the same men who were captured by the Germans at Étreux. One of the Munsters was Private John Cronin from County Cork, who was part of a prisoner swap later in the war. He was a witness for the prosecution at Casement's trial for treason in London after the Easter Rising of April 1916.

According to Cronin, Casement had promised the men they would no longer have to live in hunger or misery. Should they join the Irish Brigade, they would be treated as guests of the German nation.

In the event of the Germans winning a sea battle with the British (a big if, given the disparity in naval resources between Britain and Germany), the Irish Brigade would land in Ireland as a friendly invasion force. Cronin was unimpressed. 'When I knew what he was about, I avoided him.'

Casement was also physically attacked. 'As soon as the men realised who he was and what was his aim, they set upon him, and he was only saved by the German sentries from serious injury,' Cronin recalled.[14] Corporal John Robinson of the Royal Army Medical Corps recalled that when the men assaulted Casement, he fended them off with his umbrella. Rations were stopped for the Irish prisoners of war for three days.

The Germans increased the pressure by allowing those few who signed up to his Irish Brigade to appear in front of cold and hungry prisoners wearing smart, German-made uniforms. 'They [the Germans] had them sitting there smoking cigars, and with wine, in good German uniforms, with food before them and enjoying themselves properly,' recalled one sergeant.[15]

Despite all the pressure that was put on the men, Casement's attempt to raise an Irish Brigade was an extraordinary failure. All his entreaties were in vain. In May 1915, he made a last-ditch attempt to get the men to enlist. Addressing their concerns that he was a German agent, he responded:

> You may believe me, or disbelieve me (and nothing I could say would convince you as to my own motives), but I can convince you, and I owe it to yourself as well as to myself to convince you, that the effort to form an Irish Brigade is based on Irish interests only, and is a sincere and earnest one, so far as my actions with the German government are concerned.[16]

Out of some 2,300 Irishmen in Limburg, he managed to recruit a paltry contingent of fifty-six. Even in extremis, the men were not inclined to break their oath of allegiance to the king. A British report into the Irish Brigade concluded those who joined were mostly motivated by hunger, others had questionable records and 'only a dozen or less could be classed as political malcontents'.[17] The senior Irish non-commissioned officers (NCOs) sent a blunt message to the camp commandant that no attempt to bully them into joining an Irish Brigade would succeed. 'In addition to being Irish Catholics, we have the honour to be British soldiers.'[18]

This led Casement to conclude with great sorrow, 'How could anybody truly Irish really survive the free entry into the British army? No. These are not Irishmen but English soldiers – that is all.'[19]

Even if the captured men had no great love for the British Empire, they detested the Germans. They had seen their comrades killed by the enemy. They witnessed how badly the Germans treated them as prisoners of war. To have switched sides would have been tantamount to an admission that their sacrifices and the sacrifices of their comrades were in vain. This was too much to bear. The men chose captivity over the relative freedom offered to them.

'Irishmen despise the Germans and would cut their throats if they had the chance,' Private James Wilson from Dublin told Casement. 'If you are waiting for any of us to join and you are going to shoot us or ill treat us if we don't, you'd better start now', to which others replied 'hear! hear!'[20]

Casement was shocked by his reception. Even the presence of two Catholic priests as interlocutors had little effect on his efforts to raise an Irish Brigade.

Casement was also joined by Joseph Mary Plunkett, who was sent by the Irish Volunteers. Plunkett arrived in Berlin via a circuitous route through Britain, France, Spain, Italy and Switzerland. In Berlin, he met with German government officials, Casement and a few of the Irish Brigade who had joined up. One, Private Timothy Quinlisk from Wexford, was unimpressed with this future signatory of the 1916 Proclamation. 'One would never associate the soldier and burning patriot with the rather sickly looking young man, who looked more like a dreamer and a poet than anything else.'[21]

Plunkett had no more luck than Casement in persuading the men to join the Irish Brigade. Casement too became increasingly disillusioned. In the spring of 1915, he wrote to McGarrity, 'I could be far more useful now in the USA than here. I have done my work here. It is impossible to do more or go further.'[22]

He grew to despise the Germans, who he now understood had no interest in the liberation of Ireland and were only interested in creating mischief for the British. Casement wrote in his diary, 'Oh, Ireland – why did I ever trust in such a Govt. as this – or think that such men would help thee! They have no sense of honour, chivalry, generosity. They are cads. That is why they are hated by the world and why England will surely beat them.'[23]

Despite the bitter sense of betrayal Casement felt, the Germans did provide weapons for the Irish rebellion, albeit a token amount given that the Irish Republican Brotherhood requested 200,000 guns. Some 20,000 confiscated Russian rifles, ten machine guns and a million rounds of ammunition were loaded on to the SS *Libau*, disguised for the purposes of the long voyage to Ireland as the Norwegian vessel, the *Aud*.

Casement travelled in a U-19 submarine behind the ship. He had now made up his mind that the Rising was doomed as the Germans had offered insufficient support and he wanted to do what he could to stop it. Muddle and mess followed. The *Aud* arrived in Tralee Bay off the coast of County Kerry on Thursday, 20 April 1914, but without a radio. There was no one there to meet it. Tragically, three Irish Volunteers who were to signal the *Aud* ashore and disable the wireless station at Caherciveen were drowned when their car went off the edge of Ballykissane pier.

The *Aud* was trapped by a British navy squadron outside Queenstown (now Cobh), whereupon the crew changed into their German naval uniforms, ran up the ensign of the German Empire, scuttled the ship and then surrendered. The *Aud* is one of the 'what ifs' of Irish history. Had it landed its cargo, the British would have had much greater difficulty putting down the Easter Rising.

Casement meanwhile arrived off the coast of Kerry on Good Friday, 1916. He was sick after a difficult journey and was suffering from the effects of malaria, which he had contracted on colonial duties. He was accompanied by two other men: Robert Monteith, sent by the Irish Volunteers, and Robert Bailey of the 2nd Royal Irish Rifles, who was one of the few prisoners to join the Irish Brigade.

The three rowed ashore. Monteith and Bailey went looking for the Irish Volunteers who were supposed to meet them while Casement took refuge in McKenna's Fort in Ardfert as he was too weak to move. He was exhausted, soaked to the skin and had a sickening sense that the forthcoming rebellion would fail. Yet, with that came a sense of serenity because he was at home again. He wrote to his sister Nina from prison:

> I was happy for the first time for over a year. Although I knew that this fate waited on me, I was for one brief spell happy and smiling once more. I cannot tell you what I felt. The sandhills were full of skylarks, rising in the dawn, the first I had heard for years – the first sound I heard through the surf was their song as I waded in through the breakers, and they kept rising all the time up to the old rath at Currahane … and all round were primroses and wild violets and the singing of the skylarks in the air, and I was back in Ireland again.[24]

Four months later, Casement was tried and convicted of treason. He appealed unsuccessfully and was hanged in Pentonville Prison on 3 August 1916, the last of those involved in the Easter Rising to be executed.

His fellow countrymen remained in Limburg for four years. In 1917, at the request of their 'beloved sagartaroon' Fr Thomas Crotty, the men raised the money for a Celtic cross to remember the Irish prisoners who had died in Limburg.

The cross cost 7,000 German marks (£350) and was financed by the men through the paltry sums of money they were paid for work around the camp.

Crotty, a Dominican father from County Kilkenny, was sent by the Vatican to minister to the men in Limburg. More than anyone else, his intervention ensured that Casement's bag of Irish prisoners would be a small one. At Mass one morning, he told them:

Men of Galway, Clare and Connaught, the German Emperor wants you to go
and fight on his side, and some people have been telling you that it is a proper
thing for you to do. And I have been asked to tell you the same. But I have been
sent to you by his Holiness the Pope, not to talk politics to you or to mislead
you or to be the procurer of any King or Kaiser on earth, but to tell you in the
name of God and of the Holy Church what is good and right for men to do.
As the priest of God I tell you it is your duty as good Catholics to keep the oath
you have taken to be loyal to your King. And that's all I have to say to you this
day. May the Grace of God rest upon you and help you.[25]

The German captors were dismayed by this address. *The Times* reported,
'The German officer had to look on helpless and see his prey slipping from his
fingers. But he dared not interrupt his priest in his holy office.'

It was planned that the Limburg cross would be made in Ireland and shipped to
Germany, but wartime conditions made that impossible. Though it was designed by
Messrs Harrison and Sons in Dublin, it was constructed in Germany. It was made
of sandstone, measured just over 10ft in height and weighed 10 tons.[26]

The engravings at its head are the patron saint of Ireland, St Patrick, the patron-
ess St Bridget and, significantly given its location in Germany, St Kilian. Kilian was
an Irish missionary who brought Christianity to modern-day southern Germany.
The cross was erected with the permission of the camp commandant. It was the
only one permitted in any prisoner-of-war camp run by the Germans during
the war. It was consecrated on Trinity Sunday, 3 June 1917, and some 200 Irish
prisoners of war from the surrounding districts were allowed to attend.

The cross lists the names of forty-five Irishmen who died in either Limburg or
surrounding camps during the war. Permission was also given to build a garden
around the memorial. The cross at Limburg has survived both world wars and
remains peaceful place known locally as the Russian cemetery because of the
number of Russian prisoners of war who were buried there in the First and
Second World Wars. No other trace of the prisoner-of-war camp that once accom-
modated 12,000 prisoners remains. The cross is in a peaceful place, popular with
local walkers and joggers. There is an entrance with four small palm trees and
a gravel path around the cross. The outside boundary of the walk is trimmed
with evergreens and there is a large palm tree in each corner. The village of
Dietkirchen has named a nearby street *Fredrick-Reilly-Straße* after Frederick Reilly
of the Cheshire Regiment, the first man to die in Limburg.

The cross would forever be the memento of the suffering and death of so many
men who endured horrible conditions in Limburg, according to those who spent
the war there. O'Connell concluded his letter to the *Limerick Chronicle*:

We have today erected a cross to their memory which cries out to the Almighty God for vengeance for the excruciating torture they were subjected to. It was very often the case to find many of our brave Irish lads hunting around the cook houses for scrapings of potatoes and carrots, and many more discovered in iron dustbins, in order to secure some sort of staples.[27]

Over the years, the cross at Limburg had fallen into a state of neglect and disrepair. The names of the forty-five men were faded away from the base.

The initiative to restore the cross came from members of the local community of Dietkirchen, where Limburg is located, and in particular Franz Prox, an ex-soldier of the German army. A series of fundraising events were organised. Two Irish folk festivals were held and the military band of Koblenz staged a beneficiary concert. In Ireland, the 'Friends of the Limburg Celtic Cross' was established by Anthony O'Brien and Dr Tadhg Moloney, both members of the Royal Munster Fusiliers Association. Anthony O'Brien's father, T.P. O'Brien, had been a Royal Munster Fusilier and prisoner of war. Moloney's grandfather, Lance Corporal John Joseph Cleary, was captured at Étreux. He was taken to Limburg to be addressed by Casement. Moloney says his grandfather, like most of the other Irishmen at Limburg, took their oath to their king seriously.

'Standing with other comrades, he observed the older veterans and what they were going to do to be guided by their actions,' Moloney says. 'They, having decided not to move, he also did not move. There was also the fact that he had taken an oath of allegiance and was not going to break it.'[28]

The two men contacted various historical and regimental associations for dona-tions. The Royal Munster Fusiliers Association, the Irish Guards, the Scots Guards, the Royal Inniskilling Fusiliers Regimental Association (Ballymena & Limavady Branches), the Bandon War Memorial Committee and the Irish Seamen's Relatives Association also contributed, as did a number of private individuals. The Irish government made a significant contribution, with an overall total of €25,000 between Ireland and Germany collected to restore the cross. Restoration was undertaken during the months of spring and summer of 2007.

The monument was cleaned and cracks in the stone were filled with fibreglass. Holes were drilled into the sandstone to stabilise the structure and make it water-tight. A new bronze plaque was fixed to the cross with the names of all the Irish prisoners of war who died there.

The restored Celtic cross was reconsecrated on 18 November 2007. A large delegation from Ireland was present. During his speech, Mr Bernhard Eufinger, head of the community of Dietkirchen, referred to the cross as 'a sign of concili-ation, but at the same time reminding us of the immeasurable pain of two world wars of the last century. In preserving the cross, we keep the memory alive of those who died.'[29]

6

THE RAILWAY STATION AT LE PILLY

Somewhere in the soggy terrain of French Flanders lie the bodies of 164 Irishmen who died in a battle hardly anybody remembers. Millions of men died in the First World War and have no known grave, but it is rare, despite all the carnage, that the dead of a whole regiment would disappear without a trace.

The 2nd Royal Irish Regiment was part of 8th Brigade, 3rd Division and II Corps of the British army. As mentioned in a previous chapter, it had performed a redoubtable rearguard action at Mons on 23 August 1914, which inspired the legend of the Angels of Mons. Eight weeks later it suffered a catastrophe in the French hamlet of Le Pilly.

The Battle of Le Pilly was part of the 'Race to the Sea', one of the First World War's great misnomers. There was no race to the sea, just the Allies and the Germans who sought to avoid full-frontal attacks by attacking each other's flanks. Slowly but inexorably the war turned north-westward across innocent French and Belgium territory. The tide of battle turned into a stagnant pool where place names of the Somme, Vimy, Arras, Aubers Ridge, Ypres, Verdun and so many other places were sullied forever. Battle once engaged in would never be broken off in these places until the Germans were pushed back across the Belgian border in the autumn of 1918.

The Royal Irish had followed the great retreat south from Mons. It fought at both the Battle of the Marne and the Battle of the Aisne in September 1914 and suffered relatively light casualties.

The Royal Irish was put in charge of guarding 540 German prisoners after the battle. In Jean Renoir's cinematic masterpiece *La Grande Illusion*, class trumped nationality so that the French and German officers dined convivially together. Similarly, the German and Irish officers dined together. The men, as ever, were an afterthought.[1]

The Germans had dug in on the north bank of the River Aisne. The French and British made an attempt to dislodge them, which failed. They dug in opposite the Germans. On 14 September, the British dug their first trenches on the south bank of the River Aisne. In early October, the French commander General Joseph Joffre requested the British army move to the left of the French and take up positions from the Somme River to Ypres. This was a logical step that brought the British closer to the channel ports and home. It would also find them closer to an evacuation route if things got too hot, as was the case in 1940.

The Royal Irish Regiment force marched for three days and then travelled 36 miles in motor cars, a novelty for some of the men, to Béthune in the Pas-de-Calais.[2] The 3rd Division was sent to reinforce an area of front around La Bassée, a strategically important town which sits astride the canal of the same name, and the road from Lille to La Bassée.

The unseasonably chilly days of mid-October 1914 were the last during which opposing forces faced each other in the open before trench warfare became the

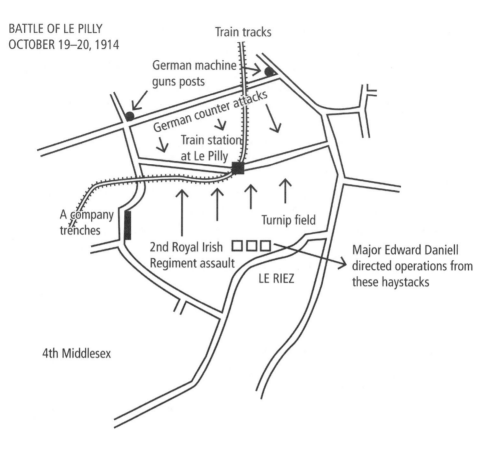

BATTLE OF LE PILLY
OCTOBER 19–20, 1914

Train tracks

German machine
guns posts

German counter attacks

Train station
at Le Pilly

A company
trenches

2nd Royal Irish
Regiment assault

Turnip field

LE RIEZ

Major Edward Daniell
directed operations from
these haystacks

4th Middlesex

norm. The Battle of La Bassée lasted just over three weeks from 10 October to 2 November. From the Belgian coast to La Bassée, the Germans sought a breakthrough to the Channel coast. The combined Allied force of Belgian, British and French troops sought to stop them and to retake Lille.

II Corps wanted to drive the Germans off Aubers Ridge, the higher ground in the area. The term is relative as Aubers Ridge would, by most definitions of typography, be classified as scarcely a perturbation on the landscape. It is no more than 65ft in height, but this is some of the flattest land in Europe. Any elevation was an advantage.

The British and French attempted to retake territory occupied by the Germans in October 1914. On 12 October, the German army walked into Lille, finding the city undefended save for a force of 4,500 French territorials.[3] The defenders of the city were surprised by the German Sixth Army, which marched nearly 150 miles in seven days and took Lille without a struggle.

This was a momentous loss for the Allies. Lille was north-west France's administrative and industrial capital. With a population of some 227,000, it was the biggest

French city to fall to the Germans. The French wanted it back, but, in the event, it would not be liberated for four years.

The Royal Irish Regiment was attached to 8th Brigade, which was based at Aubers, a village which gave its name to the ridge and to the disastrous battle of 1915, one of many in that most dismal and fruitless of years for the Allies.

On 14 October, the 3rd Division suffered the loss of its general, Hubert Hamilton, who was killed by a shrapnel shell. Nevertheless, it was decided five days later that a concerted push would be made to drive the Germans out of Le Pilly and open the way to take the ridge.

Intelligence gathered in advance of battle ought to have given the British commanders pause for thought. Company Sergeant Major John Cooper from Clonmel went out to reconnoitre and found the Germans entrenched in Le Pilly village. He estimated they outnumbered the Royal Irish ten to one.[4]

The battalion was to give support to the French who were attempting to liberate the neighbouring and larger village of Fournes. The Irish were ordered to attack at 2.30 p.m. on the afternoon of 19 October, supported by a section of Royal Field Artillery which shelled the German lines from 2 p.m. Most of the shells fell short.

At 3 p.m., a half an hour later than planned, the men crossed a turnip field and attacked the German line with the commanding officer Major Edward Daniell directing operations from behind a haystack. Half of A and B Companies were in the vanguard, C was in support and D was in reserve.[5] The Irish successfully drove the Germans out of Le Pilly on 19 October under heavy shelling. They fixed bayonets and charged the enemy up the street which runs through the village. Cooper recalled, 'When the Germans see our bayonets fixed they run like a pack of sheep. They commenced squealing like pigs when they saw them [the bayonets], and are running yet.'

A Company reached a farmhouse which stands there to this day, but had to retreat because of friendly fire from shells which fell short. The whole of the regiment was now engaged in holding Le Pilly, but the attack had caused 165 casualties (the number of dead was not calculated).

Even those who were evacuated were not spared. 'I often heard of the brutality of the Germans and never believed it, but from personal experience I now know it is an absolute fact,' recounted Cooper. The Germans opened up with their Maxim machine guns on the dead and wounded. They also shelled a temporary field hospital. Cooper was appalled. 'You could not call it war. It is murder and nothing like the game as it is played in Africa and the Chitral Expeditions, through both of which I went.'[6]

During the night of 19 October, Daniell asked for reinforcements to protect the flanks of his men who had dug in and made shallow trenches. The 4th Middlesex, now occupying the trenches at Le Riez previously dug by the Royal

Irish, promised to assist at first light, but were prevented from doing so by fierce German shelling. The Irish were now on their own.[7]

The exposed men faced fire not only from the front but also from the village of Fournes, which the French were supposed to have secured.

The German Sixth Army sensed vulnerability. As soon as first light came, the Germans opened ferocious artillery fire on the Middlesex regiment. It was forced to retire a further 400 yards back, far enough away not to be in a position to come to the rescue of the Royal Irish. The Germans attacked from left and right. They were repulsed by accurate machine gun fire, but these were soon silenced by German artillery. At 3 p.m. Daniell met his death trying to warn A Company to turn and face the enemy attacking from in front and behind.

The last hour was an agonising death throe for the regiment. The Germans put machine guns and snipers into surrounding houses. Between 3.30 p.m. and 4 p.m. on the afternoon of 20 October, three companies of German infantry closed in on the beleaguered Irish regiment from front and rear under the cover of machine gun and artillery fire. The devastation was almost total; only four men escaped the carnage. One who made it back to British lines recounted that many of the Irishmen had been shot in the back of the head.

When the end came, 177 men of the regiment were dead. Just thirteen have known graves. Some 303 were injured. Of those, approximately 100 were able to stand.

On 19 October 1914, the strength of the battalion had been twenty officers and 881 men. Two days later, it was one surviving officer, a transport officer and 135 men. The regimental diary is chilling in its succinctness. 'Unfortunately little evidence is obtainable of what occurred on this day.'[8]

The Royal Irish Regiment had endured almost twelve hours of torment against overwhelming odds with no gain. It was a hopeless struggle, which achieved nothing other than the destruction of a fine regiment of regular soldiers. Should Daniell have withdrawn when he had the chance or surrendered earlier, long before his losses became overwhelming? The only German account of the battle is instructive. It came from a Lieutenant Martens, who was taken prisoner by a reconstituted version of the Royal Irish Regiment after the battle.

Martens commanded the 6th Company of the 56th Active Infantry Battalion. His interrogators were anxious to get a German account of a battle about which they had scant information. Martens was brutally frank about his vanquished enemies:

> The Irish regiment was in a hopeless predicament. There seemed no escape except they surrendered, and it was exceedingly foolish that they did not. Our artillery continued to fire on your men and enfiladed their main trench throughout the day until we had you all surrounded. And then we opened a heavy fire on your rear and flanks. The British regiment was in a bad way, indeed, as you had no protection whatsoever against our rifle fire.[9]

One of the youngest to die was Private Stephen Collins from Philip Street in Waterford city. He was just 16, three years under the minimum for serving abroad. All of Thomas and Agnes Collins's six sons served in the war. Four of them died.[10] Private Michael Collins died in the same area and with the same regiment at the disastrous Battle of Aubers Ridge in May 1915. He was 24. A year later, Private John Collins (22) died at Ginchy during the Battle of the Somme. His body was never found and he is remembered on the Thiepval Memorial to the Missing. The last to die was the eldest son Patrick, aged 30, a second corporal in the 173rd Tunnelling Company of the Royal Engineers. He was killed on 29 March 1918 during the German Spring Offensive. A fifth brother, Joseph, was repatriated from Salonika with bad shrapnel wounds.

After Patrick's death, William, the one son who had survived the carnage unscathed, was repatriated back home. Saving Private Collins became a moral imperative. His surviving grandchildren and great-grandchildren have worked to keep his memory alive, as well as that of his unfortunate brothers who died.

Rachel Collins, William Collins' great-granddaughter, wrote of the comparison between her family and the film *Saving Private Ryan*, which was based on the true story of an Irish-American family, the Niland brothers:

> I've never watched *Saving Private Ryan*. An aversion to violence, bloodshed and the sad inevitability of war films means I haven't seen the epic 27-minute opening scene, where Tom Hanks and his comrades face the carnage of the Normandy landings. Besides, the plot has always seemed a bit far-fetched. A family of boys wiped out by war; an army that was only too happy to send its sons to slaughter suddenly pulling out all the stops to save the last remaining brother. Then earlier this year while talking to my father, I learned that not only was such a story entirely plausible, it had played out in our family.[11]

Among those who died at Le Pilly was Lance Corporal John Brien from John Street, Wexford, had cherubic features which belied his 35 years. He was a Boer War veteran and had come through that conflict 'without a scratch', according to an obituary published in the *Wexford People*. He also served several tours of India. Like so many of the 'old sweats' who had done their soldiering in colonial campaigns, he found to his ultimate cost that the Germans were a more terrifying, efficient and ruthless enemy and the First World War a war of slaughter beyond the imagination.

Brien was in the special reserve at the outbreak of war and was called up immediately. His wife Nellie endured months of uncertainty after the battle. He was first reported missing, though his own brother, who also fought at Le Pilly, believed he was dead. Confirmation finally came in June, eight months after his disappearance, that he was indeed dead. At the time, his three brothers and four nephews were still in the firing line.

A new recruit to die was Second Lieutenant Alan Anderson from Dublin, described by his father Robert as someone who 'had just come down from Oxford, a boy of fine promise, full of love of his country'.[12] Alan Anderson was just 21 when war broke out. He was a champion boxer at school and university. His father Robert was involved in the Irish co-operative movement, as was Alan Anderson, who was already on the committee of the Irish Agricultural Organisation Society, despite his young age.

Robert Anderson recalled decades later, 'He had won the heart and the confidence of Horace Plunkett [founder of the Irish co-operative movement] in a way which I had utterly failed to do. Time and again our leader used to appeal to him: "What do you say, Alan?" I felt no sort of envy but rather pride.'

At the outbreak of war, Alan Anderson joined Oxford's Officers' Training Corps and was commissioned in the Royal Irish Regiment immediately. His death at Le Pilly came in only his second day of action.[13]

The most high-profile Irishman to die as a result of the battle was Captain James Arnold (J.A.) Smithwick, the son of Parnellite MP John Francis Smithwick and a scion of the famous Kilkenny brewing family. Smithwick was 34 years old when he died. A Boer War veteran, he appears to have been a popular member of the community in Kilkenny. He was wounded at Le Pilly, rescued by the Germans and brought to Crefeld prisoner-of-war camp. His wounds were so serious that the Germans agreed to exchange him after ten months, concluding that he would be of no further use to the British.

He survived and wrote a letter to his brother Richard from Crefeld, which was subsequently published in *The Irish Times*:

I am here, wounded and a prisoner, and am being well treated. As you have seen by the casualty list, the regiment suffered very heavily. It is bad luck being here, but I'm lucky to be above ground. I escaped until half an hour before the end without a scratch, then while trying to retire with some of my men to deal with a machine gun which was enfilading us from our left rear and was grazed twice on the shoulder and on the hand. They next got me plumb on my right breast. It hit my compass, then on to a rib and through the muscles on top of my stomach and out at my left side. Narrow squeak! It knocked me clean out at the time and I'm a bit stiff and sore, but it is going on well and there is no danger.[14]

His optimism was sadly premature. Three months after being repatriated Smithwick succumbed to tuberculosis, 'directly traceable to his injuries'.[15] He had been visited by King George V at Wandworth Military Hospital and then removed to a sanatorium. He died in London in November 1915 and is buried in Kilkenny. His gallantry, according to local magistrates, was 'worthy of his regiment and his race. Physically, he was a splendid type of a gallant Irish officer and in Kilkenny, where his family were so respected, he was extremely popular among all classes'.[16]

The missing from the 2nd Royal Irish Regiment are commemorated on two panels at the Le Touret memorial on the Rue du Bois overlooking Aubers Ridge.[17]

The loss of so many young men must have cut a swathe of grief and uncertainty through the counties of Waterford, Wexford, Tipperary and Kilkenny, from where the regiment drew its soldiers. Yet, the battle left no folk memory in the south-east. It also disappeared from the consciousness of local people in Le Pilly and Herlies, the village into which Le Pilly is now incorporated.

The Battle of Le Pilly was a significant engagement by most standards. Some 177 Irishmen and probably around the same amount of Germans were killed. A battalion was reduced to the size of a company, but 'most standards' do not include the First World War.

This section of French Flanders from Armentières to La Bassée saw cataclysmic fighting after it became part of the Western Front in October 1914 for the next four years. This was British-held territory for most of the war. Neuve Chapelle, Loos, Aubers Ridge, Festubert and Fromelles were all bloody encounters which costs the lives of tens of thousands of combatants yet never achieved the notoriety of the Somme or Passchendaele. On the well-trodden remembrance trail bookended by Ypres and Somme, this is often called the 'forgotten front'. In such circumstances, the loss of hundreds of men could be forgotten about, wiped from memory or supplanted by a myriad of even bloodier encounters.

The house where the long-time Mayor of Herlies Marie-Françoise Auger was reared features in a 1916 photograph taken of Le Pilly. It is still there today, but it took almost 100 years before she knew a battle had taken place in her home village. On 7 October 1914, her grandparents were forced to flee the village when it fell to the Germans. They did not return until the end of the war. For generations afterwards, the people of Herlies and Le Pilly believed the war had somehow passed them by.[18]

Surrounding them was a necklace of villages devastated by the war – Neuve Chapelle, Aubers and Fromelles – yet somehow Le Pilly escaped. The village was damaged but not extensively. Locals thought a stray shell might have hit some of the homes. The 'iron harvest', where farmers turn up tons of rusted munitions, never turned up anything significant in Le Pilly.

Yet there was one tantalising clue that hung in Herlies town hall for generations but attracted hardly any attention. It is an oil painting that depicts purposeful German troops, bayonets fixed, advancing across a battlefield. There is a burning building and the distant sight of a church spire peering through the smoke. It looks very like the spire of Fournes church. Nobody paid much attention to the caption in German, which stated, '*Sturm auf das dorf Herlies bei La Bassée. Nach einem olgemalde des kriegsmalers Hans Weinberg*' [Combat in the village of Herlies near La Bassée. An oil painting by the war correspondent Hans Weinberg].

As the centenary of the battle approached, locals in Herlies decided to host a 'bistro' – an evening out to discuss how to commemorate the First World War locally. They studied maps, particularly the British offensives in the area. They realised there was a gap in the lines where the modern village of Herlies is now situated. Internet research uncovered another painting by Hans Weinberg on the same theme and revealed details of a talk given in Waterford city by the Tipperary-based historian Michael Desmond in 2013 about the Battle of Le Pilly.

Herlies' locals were astounded to find that not only had a battle taken place in Le Pilly but it had been well chronicled. A detailed account of the battle was given in the *Campaigns and History of the Royal Irish Regiment 1900-1922* by Brigadier General Stannus Geoghegan, which was published in 1927, complete with maps of Le Pilly. It is also mentioned in the British official history of the war.

Much of the battleground from Le Riez to Le Pilly is the same as it was in 1914. There is a wide expanse of open field broken by the odd wind-bent tree. It is the same open field the Royal Irish Regiment crossed to take the village on 19 October. The terrain slopes slightly upwards towards Le Pilly. Steep-gabled, red-roofed houses of a type common in northern France mark where the German frontline used to be in 1914. The battlefield is framed in the distance by the spire of Fournes church. The same farmhouse captured by the Royal Irish Regiment is still there, as is the railway station where the wounded were treated after the battle. The road from Lille to La Bassée is now a wide stretch of two-lane highway which carries commuters to and from the city.

From behind Le Riez, you can see where the Middlesex Regiment was based within sight of its fellow battalion and yet so far away. The realisation that a battle had taken place locally now made sense to Franck Gil, a French army veteran of the First Gulf War. He bought the old railway station at Le Pilly on Rue du Pilly in the early 2000s and converted it into a home for himself and his wife Dorothée in 2005. The garden around it had grown wild with plans, some of which were 6ft high. The station had been abandoned for twenty-five years.

The station was built as part of a private railway line in 1904 to transport sugar beet to local processing plants. It was used by travellers at weekends. After the Second World War, the French government nationalised all the railways and closed those that were superfluous to requirements, including this line. A woman lived in the converted railway station until her death.

When Franck and Dorothée Gil bought the house, they noticed marks consistent with bullet holes in the façade. It was as if somebody had taken a chisel and hammer and randomly chipped off pebble-sized chunks.

'It is at this point that I have noticed the impact around the station. It was gunfire,' Franck Gil says. 'What surprised us is that all the walls are affected, especially the door frames and windows. Something violent had happened, but the mystery remained. I inquired with neighbours, but nobody had any precise information. Everyone knows that our area has been a battleground for centuries.'[19] The Gils made inquiries from neighbours but none seemed to know what had happened. Charles De Gaulle called it the fatal avenue, the sweep of northern France from the Pas-de-Calais to the German border, which is flat and difficult to defend.

Inside, in one of the beams of the open-plan interior, there is a bullet hole. How did it get there? It must have come through the upstairs window of the old railway station, which was fired upon during the battle.

From the angle of entry, it can be deduced that German bullets riddled the back of the house, where they commenced their attack, and the bullet marks at the front came from the Irish firing back. Different calibre weapons were used. It is clear the railway station was at the apex of the battle.

By the time Michael Desmond arrived in Herlies to mark the centenary of the battle, the locals were more than intrigued. Desmond knew more about this forgotten battle than anyone else. The town hall was full to its 160 capacity and others were left outside. They wanted to be told about the battle which had taken place in their locality but about which they knew nothing.

Desmond remains convinced that the tragedy of Le Pilly should never have happened. When confronted with the same numerically superior enemy, the French had made a decision to carry out a strategic retreat. He believes the death of Hubert Hamilton and his replacement by General Colin McKenzie, only in the job a week, and Daniell's premature promotion to temporary battalion commander had left a dearth of experience in the top ranks.

When II Corps commander General Horace Smith-Dorrien realised the Irish predicament, he ordered a retreat, but it was too late. McKenzie was sacked after just two weeks in the job. He would reappear as one of the generals involved in the nearby Battle of Fromelles in July 1916.

Among the prisoners taken by the Germans at Le Pilly was one Maurice Meade, one of the few who joined Roger Casement's Irish Brigade and fought with the Germans in Egypt. He returned to Ireland after the war, joined the IRA and then the pro-Treaty forces.

Meade lived a remarkable life. He was born into a poor family in County Limerick. When he was a teenager he worked for a local farmer, but all his wages were taken by his father.[20] In 1911, at the age of 17, he did what many frustrated Irish teenagers did at the time – he joined the British army.

'I thought I saw some prospect for gaining my personal independence,' he told the Irish Bureau of Military History. He was approached by a smartly-dressed sergeant. 'I say, young man, why don't you join the British army'?' the sergeant asked. 'Begorah, sir,' Meade replied, 'I was just thinking of doing that.' Meade's memory of the Battle of Le Pilly, which he recounted to the bureau in 1953, is succinct and vivid. After his commanding officer died (whom he mistakenly called Cox, not Daniell), the men surrendered. They were cut off for days without rations or ammunition.

'We were in such a bad way at the time and surrounded by dead bodies that, in fact, we used the dead bodies as barricades, heaping them up to give us cover from the German fire.'

Meade became a prisoner of war. He, too, recounted how they were badly treated, half starved and left to sleep out in the open in all weathers. The men were so hungry that they licked spilt soup off stone floors and scavenged potato peelings from the bins. It did not, however, stop him from joining his erstwhile tormentors when he became one of only fifty-six Irishmen to sign up to Casement's Irish Brigade. The few who did join were given smart uniforms and were introduced to Kaiser Wilhem II.

Meade claimed to have been one of the few of them to have actually seen service in a German uniform. He fought in Egypt. After the war, he returned to Germany and was arrested in Gdansk by the British, who heard his Irish-accented English.

Meade was returned to Britain in a Royal Navy warship. In 1919, he was tried and convicted of high treason and sentenced to death. He languished in the Tower of London for a fortnight before being informed he had received the king's pardon. British control of Ireland was slipping away. King George V was anxious not to create any more martyrs to the Irish cause.[21]

Meade returned to Ireland and was rearrested for high treason, but escaped the Royal Irish Constabulary. He joined the IRA's East Limerick Flying Column, which was one of the most active columns during the War of Independence, targeting Royal Irish Constabulary officers and Black and Tans during the War of Independence.

In February 1921, Meade was involved in the attack at Dromkeen, where eleven policemen and eight Black and Tans were killed in an IRA ambush. Two uninjured Black and Tans were also captured. Meade executed both of them after a summary trial, claiming that it was an order from GHQ in Dublin that all captured British auxillaries and Royal Irish Constabulary men were to be shot on sight in retaliation for a similar order from the British. He gave a chilling account of his actions to the Bureau of Military History:

O'Hannigan called me and said, 'Hey Maurice will you shoot one of them?' I agreed to do so. He gave Stapleton the job of executing the other. I took my man down the road and shot him. Then I went down to see how Stapleton was getting on and found that he disliked the job and did not want to do it, so I took the fellow over and executed him.

After the War of Independence, he joined the Free State Army, served until 1924 and then was invalided out.[22]

His old comrades-in-arms lie beneath French soil undiscovered and, for the most part, unremembered. The Le Pilly battlefield is not extensive. It is probably not much bigger than half a mile square. Usually Germans buried the dead near where they fought. Where did they bury the dead of Le Pilly?

Some locals speculate that they might be buried in the Chateau de L'Eau in Illies, but this is a distance of 3 miles away. How would the bodies have been brought there? Maybe the Germans used the captured rail lines to transport the men's bodies to a location away from Le Pilly.

Just 3 miles north of Le Pilly, the Australians have been involved in an ongoing process to find the bodies of their men who were slaughtered at the Battle of Fromelles on 20 July 1916. This was meant to be a diversionary attack from the Battle of the Somme raging to the south. Yet, in magnitude and bloodiness, it ended up being every bit as ghastly. By the time the battle ended, some 1,300 Australians were reported missing in action. Many had died and their bodies could have been left in the French earth forgotten and forlorn, but the Australians resolved to find and identify the bodies of all of their 61,270 soldiers who died in the war, however long it takes.

The Fromelles project began with the efforts of a Melbourne schoolteacher, Lambis Englezos. He calculated there were 163 Australian casualties from the battles whose bodies were not accounted for. He set about accumulating the evidence. Critically, he found an account in a German archive from Generalmajor Julius Ritter von Braun, the commander of the German 21st Bavarian Reserve Infantry Regiment, who had ordered the digging of a mass grave behind Pheasant Wood.

The British and Australian governments agreed to look for the graves and identify bodies using DNA techniques. The bodies were found in 2009 and the process of identification began. It was necessary to match the DNA from these men with that of living relatives. A public call for relatives to come forward attracted an astonishing pool of potential relatives – 60,000 in all. DNA testing kits were sent out and 1,800 individual profiles were accumulated. Skull fragments were checked against head and shoulders photographs of the men. Nothing was left undone.

To date, the Australians have positively identified the remains of 150 men of the 251 found in a mass pit.

But what of the Irish dead at Le Pilly? Their bodies have disappeared as resolutely as memories of them and the terrible battle they fought in have disappeared from the public conscience.

The six Collins brothers who fought in the First World War, of whom four were killed, are now remembered with a blue plaque at the site where their home once stood. The plaque, a joint endeavour between Waterford Civic Trust and the Royal British Legion, is located on the site where the family home once stood at Philip Street in Waterford city. Eighty members of the Collins family gathered for the ceremony which took place on Remembrance Sunday 2016.

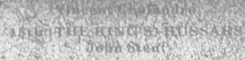

THE MONUMENT
TO THE IRON 12

On the evening of 22 February 1915, an armed convoy of two cars and a lorry set off from the German-occupied chateau at Guise in the Aisne department of northern France. A short time later it arrived in Iron, a hamlet on the River Iron nestled in a hollow surrounded by high-banked roads.[1]

The German party was led by Lieutenant-Colonel Richard Waechter, the military governor based at Guise. Four times in as many months he had issued ultimatums to Allied soldiers hiding behind enemy lines: surrender and be a prisoner of war or be captured and shot as a spy.

Upstairs in the spacious attic of a retired local silk weaver named Vincent Chalandre, eleven fugitive British soldiers were preparing for supper. Some were performing their ablutions, others were repairing their threadbare clothes. This attic space had been their home for more than two months. They lived in constant fear. Normally they would stay in the attic, though sometimes one or two of them would venture out.

The previous December, German troops arrived in the village looking for escaped soldiers. An alert young woman in the village warned the men that 'les Boches' were coming. The men escaped and hid for the day, knee-deep and shivering in a nearby stream.

The soldiers had been on the run for four months. Nine were discovered by Chalandre hiding in nearby woods on 15 October 1914. They were scavenging for raw carrots and the rutabagas (a swede-like vegetable) that were commonly grown in northern France at the time.[2]

Chalandre was doing casual labour for the Logez family, who owned a mill in the village. M. Logez had suffered a stroke and the onset of senile dementia on 4 August 1914, the day war was declared and France's nightmare began.

His wife Mme Leónie Logez was a determined, compassionate woman, a 'good patriot', according to local accounts.[3] She pitied these soldiers, who had been reduced to the status of mendicants. To her they were '*pauvre enfants*'; the youngest was just 19.[4] There was no equivocation about her decision, despite the fearsome risks involved. It was her 'simple duty'.[5]

Mme Logez kept cows, which allowed her to move around with a degree of impunity. She carried food and drink to the men in milking pails. They initially slept in a hut. Its walls were heaped with manure to make it look like a dung heap. But as winter arrived and the weather deteriorated, she and Chalandre agreed to take the men inside. Five went to her mill and four to Chalandre's house, but dividing the group doubled the risk. After some weeks, it was agreed they would all sleep in Chalandre's attic. In December, two more British soldiers were found hiding in the woods. Mme Logez was unfazed. 'If I can keep nine, I can keep 11.'[6]

Between the Logez and Chalandre families, these men were fed, clothed and sheltered despite the constant presence of German forces, who were under pressure to deal with the hundreds of Allied soldiers trapped behind enemy lines once and for all. Across Belgium and northern France, the occupiers repeated the same message: surrender and survive as a prisoner of war or be caught and shot.

The Germans meant it. At Le Nouvion, north of Iron, in October 1914, north of Iron, they kidnapped the mayor and threatened to shoot him if the British soldiers hiding in the woods did not give themselves up.[7] In early 1915, in St Quentin, the largest town in Aisne, they ordered the mayor to find three coffins for French soldiers caught sheltering in the town. They, too, were shot. The Germans believed that those caught behind enemy lines were fugitives and spies and therefore not subject to the protections of the Hague Convention of 1907 which governed the treatment of prisoners of war.[8]

By late October 1914, the Western Front consolidated into an unbroken series of trenches from the North Sea to the Swiss border. The Germans dug in on the north bank of the Aisne River. The frontline was just 20 miles from Iron.

The eleven men became known locally as '*les onze Anglais d'Iron*', the eleven English of Iron. It had an alliterative and therefore memorable quality in both English and French, but six of the men were Irish. The nuances of national identity in the British army, the subtleties of accent, outlook and religion which made a soldier English, Irish, Scottish or Welsh, were lost on both the Germans and the French. They were all '*les Anglais*'.

Of the eleven men, ten were from Irish regiments: five each from the Connaught Rangers and Royal Munster Fusiliers. The eleventh was a private in the 15th (The King's) Hussars, the cavalry regiment which provided support to the Munsters at Étreux. They were all either privates or lance corporals. They had the presence of mind to retain their rifles and some 1,000 rounds of ammunition.

The five Munster Fusiliers had become detached from their battalion during the Battle of Étreux in August 1914. They were Private Denis Buckley (34) and Private Daniel Horgan (19), both from Cork; Private Fred Innocent (26) from Bradford, Private John Nash (21) from Sneem, County Kerry; and Lance Corporal James Moffatt (30) from Birkenhead near Liverpool. Not much is known about these men. John Nash was one of nine children. He had three older sisters, three younger brothers and two younger sisters.

The five Connaught Rangers were Private George Howard (28) and William Thompson (24), both from Sheffield; Private Terence Murphy (29) from Ballisodare, County Sligo; Private John Walsh (33) from Tullamore, County Offaly; and Private Matthew Wilson (31) from Ahascragh, County Galway. Kent native Lance Corporal John William Stent (24) completed the eleven.

Buckley (34) was the oldest of the eleven soldiers and had seen service in the Boer War and along the North-West Frontier in India. Horgan grew up in a one-room tenement with his parents and two siblings in Cork. Innocent was another Englishman in an Irish regiment. He was a reservist who worked in a wine merchants before mobilisation. Moffatt was a second-generation Irishman from Liverpool who joined the Munsters in 1903. His brother Tom also fought at Étreux and was captured by the Germans.

Howard from Sheffield had no known Irish connections. He worked in his father's cutler business. Thompson also worked in Sheffield's steel industry. Both men may have joined up when the Connaught Rangers recruited in the city in 2008. Wilson from Ahascragh, County Galway was a reservist who had seen service in the regular army in India. His military records indicate a fondness for drinking and sex, he was treated for gonorrhoea, but also for self-improvement. He was working as a coalminer in England when the war broke out. Lance Corporal John Stent, the sole cavalryman to be executed, had a sister Edith who did much to keep the story of the Iron 12 alive.

Terence Murphy had married nine days before embarkation. He already had a son. Back in Ireland, John Walsh's mother Mary Anne was in such straitened circumstances that she made an application for relief from the Tullamore Union – the local poorhouse. She told the Union that she had three sons away at the front, fighting for the Empire. 'I am compelled to seek some relief as I am destitute. I have no one to earn anything for me, and I cannot get anything to earn myself at the present time. I hope you will consider my case.'[9]

When the Germans arrived on the evening of 22 February 1915, the eleven men knew they had been betrayed. 'We realised when we saw the road suddenly covered with Boches that the crisis had come,' Mme Logez told *Worldwide Magazine* many years later. 'I tried as I had done on the occasion of the first perquistion [search] to warn the soldiers who were again in the granary. But it was impossible to do anything, for the Germans had been told that they would be likely to find the men in that very place.'

The eleven men could have fought it out and might even have escaped, but they chose neither course. They surrendered without a fight. To do otherwise would have led to savage reprisals against the locals who had risked their lives to shelter them. The men had made it easy for the Germans, who reciprocated by binding them together two by two. They then kicked, beat and humiliated them in the street while villagers were forced to watch. One of the men was slashed across the thigh with an officer's sword.

The Germans were determined to make an example of the men and the community that had defied them. They also arrested Chalandre, his wife Olympe, their son Clovis and daughter Germaine. The Chalandre home was torched in front of the locals.

The soldiers and the Chalandres were all taken to the chateau in Guise. The men were held in a building that is now the town hall, which is opposite the steep-banked ramparts of the Chateau de Guise. That night they were tortured. Locals could hear the screams coming from the prison.[10]

The only local account of the incident was published in France in 1920 in a pamphlet entitled *Les Onze Anglais d'Iron*. The author is unknown. It is worth quoting in full:

On the morning of 25 February the English and (Vincent) Chalandre were woken up and subjected to terrible beating with punches, whips, cudgels; blunt instruments and rubber hammers were used in an orgy of joyous and strictly administered callous cruelty. Half conscious, the twelve victims were put in a cart and led into the fort at Guise by the night-gate. A ditch had been dug. Everyone understood its significance. The soldiers were stood along the edge of the ditch in two batches of six.

One of the soldiers spoke briefly. 'Let's pray, chins up. Remember – Englishmen were never slaves. No-one can say that.' Then the English saluted.

The order to fire was given twice; gunfire rang out and the Englishmen were mown down and fell into their communal grave. A German soldier gave them the coup de grâce. Then their bodies were covered with soil.

The veracity of this account cannot be confirmed. It is hightly unlikely locals witnessed the execution, so how can the author know what happened? A degree of poetic licence is understandable given the legacy of bitterness left in its wake. When the men's bodies were exhumed after the war, they were found with their hands tied behind their back. There could have been no pre-death salute. Chalandre had a bullet in the back of his head.

The first locals heard about the mass executions was on Sunday, 28 February 1915, in the propaganda sheet disseminated by the occupying forces, *Le Moniteur de la Ville de Guise*. Published in German and French, the account of the arrest and execution was signed by Waechter, who evidently believed he had acted with restraint:

In spite of my repeated warnings, Chalandre, a weaver from Iron, had been hiding and feeding eleven Englishmen from the end of December. I took them all prisoner, as well as Chalandre's family and I had their house burned. The English were in possession of loaded guns. I had them all shot along with Chalandre. Madame Chalandre, her son and her daughter have been tried by a military tribunal. Madame Chalandre has been sentenced to four years in prison; her daughter Germaine to two-and-one-half years' imprisonment; and her son Clovis to three years' imprisonment. The wife of the mentally-incompetent miller at Iron [Logez] kept and fed seven of the soldiers on her property from the end of November to the end of December, bringing them food until the end. She too deserves death, but I do not want to shoot women unless it is absolutely necessary. She has been tried by a military tribunal along with her son and daughter and I had her buildings burned.[11]

The tribunal has sentenced Madame Logez to five years' imprisonment and her daughter Jeanne to one year's imprisonment. I repeat my warning to those wanting to help enemy soldiers: you will be sentenced to death. I request all mayors to publicise this order in their communes. I want order, peace and security in the countryside. All those who oppose me will suffer the consequences.

This would be the largest single execution of its kind on the Western Front.

Reports appeared in many British and Irish newspapers. The execution of the English nurse Edith Cavell later that year caused worldwide outrage, yet the execution of these men merited only a footnote.

Executions were more common within armies than between armies. The French executed more than 600 men and could have executed thousands more after the Nivelle revolt of 1917, when thousands of Frenchmen refused to obey orders to go over the top.[12] The British shot 306, including 28 Irishmen. All of these men were pardoned posthumously in 2006.[13] At the Tower of London, the British executed eleven Germans suspected of spying between 1914 and 1916.[14] The execution of the leaders of the Easter Rising in 1916 has also to be seen in the context of the First World War.

Governments everywhere used the ultimate sanction with a degree of enthusiasm which would never be countenanced in western society today. Indeed, the Irish Free State government executed seventy-seven anti-Treaty rebels in 1922 and 1923 during the Civil War.

Executions have a special resonance in Irish history. Robert Emmet, the Manchester Martyrs, the leaders of the 1916 Rising, Roger Casement, Kevin Barry and so many others are better known for the manner of their deaths than anything else. Yet, hardly anybody in Ireland knows about the Irishmen executed by the Germans behind enemy lines, of whom there are at least nine.

—

The story of the Iron 12 begins in the chaos of the massed retreat of the British army following the Battle of Mons. The retreat was an unbearable trial for the ordinary Tommy. The alternative to death or capture by the Germans was to continue marching southward, despite a lack of sleep, food or direction, all the time being harassed by German cavalry or outposts of infantry. Nobody knew when or where this march would end.

Men stumbled along, lost in a delirium of sleep-deprived exhaustion. The imperative to keep ahead of the Germans made sleep a dangerous luxury. Many nodded off while standing or slumped by the side of the road. Their comrades were too lost in their own exhaustion to notice. When these men woke up, their battalions were long gone. Between them and their units lay mile after mile of the human detritus of war.

Soldiers fleeing the advancing Germans shared the roads with civilians carrying their worldly belongings. They could move no quicker than the slowest among them. This might be a child who had just learned to walk or an elderly person shuffling towards a grim fate. One French civil servant, Michel Corday, witnessed Belgian civilians 'weeping with weariness'.[15] It was a 'dreadful cavalcade of old men and little children'. Belgium and occupied northern France were some of the most prosperous places in Europe, with an industrial heartland producing iron and coal augmented by abundant harvests from fertile farmland. In just a month, the lives of some 8.5 million civilians were irrevocably changed by occupation. This was the end of everything they knew. An atmosphere of fear and panic permeated these early weeks of the war.

The 2nd Connaught Rangers had arrived in France just ten days after the declaration of war. Before they saw any action they were already making their mark. They had adopted a recently composed music hall ditty as their marching song. 'It's a Long Way to Tipperary' would become the most famous marching song in the British army. The Connaught men had heard the tune being played by an itinerant musician in Galway city.

Their barracks was in Renmore, County Galway, and most of them had been recruited from the counties of Connacht. The Connaught's regimental nickname was 'The Devil's Own' and, as the name suggests, they had a reputation for bravado and fearless determination in battle. They attracted many non-Irish soldiers to their ranks because of this reputation. As they disembarked at Boulagne in high spirits, they were seen by a *Daily Mail* reporter who heard them singing this rousing tune about Tipperary. He sent back a stirring report with lyrics attached.

The Rangers were spectators at the Battle of Mons on 23 August, much to their own frustration. They watched the action from a trench 2 miles south of Mons. 'Everyone was very keen at the idea of meeting the enemy and we were all in the best of spirits,' wrote Captain Ernest Hamilton in a letter home. 'We had a splendid view of the battle from where we were entrenched. The time before was a perfect summer evening and it was a wonderful sight to see the shells bursting.'[16]

This characteristic enthusiasm, so prevalent at the start of the military engagements, quickly gave way to the grim realities of war. The Rangers were commanded by Lieutenant-Colonel Alexander Abercrombie, the son of a British civil servant based in Bengal. He had seen nearly thirty years of service in the British army, but had never risen above the rank of battalion commander.

With the vast movement of British forces from Mons underway, the Rangers, like their colleagues in the Munster Fusiliers, were ordered to perform a rearguard action. Haig, I Corps commander, had moved his headquarters to Le Grand Fayt, a small village some 6 miles south-east of the town of Landrecies. At 2 a.m. on the morning of 26 August, the Connaughts set off in the direction of Le Grand Fayt. Having got a fitful and troubled few hours' sleep, the battalion took eleven hours to reach a crossroads outside the town, a distance of no more than 3 miles. At every step, they were thwarted by French troops retreating across their line from west to east. The French 5th Division was falling back and French reservists had also been mobilised to meet the danger. Everybody was on the move in these chaotic days.

It was now late morning. As they waited, Abercrombie and some of his men went to investigate firing coming from the east, leaving two companies of the 2nd

Connaughts at a crossroads without orders. When German shells began to land on their positions, Hamilton, who had been waiting at the crossroads, took his A Company southwards into Le Grand Fayt.[17]

It was a beautiful late summer's day. When they reached Le Grand Fayt, it was peaceful. Then all hell broke loose. 'At 3.30pm another officer and myself were sitting on the bridge over the stream which runs through the village, when, without the slightest warning a shell burst within 50 yards of us. In five minutes what had appeared to be a peaceful hamlet became a positive inferno.'[18]

Hamilton took the sensible course and marched his men southwards out of the village to join up with the rest of the retreating I Corps. Three hours later, Abercrombie with C Company and a platoon of D Company, some 280 men in all, marched in the direction of Le Grand Fayt. A French civilian told them the village was empty. The civilian was either misinformed or deliberately misled the men.

The Germans were waiting for the Rangers and opened fire from every direction. The Rangers spread quickly into nearby fields and returned fire as best they could. They escaped in the direction of Maroilles, a town best known today for its rather pungent cheese. Bizarrely, it is back towards the German lines instead of south. The reasons why they went in this direction remain a mystery. On arriving in Maroilles, the remaining men met a Colonel Thompson from the Royal Army Medical Corps, who was evacuating the village. He recommended the men spend the night in a couple of abandoned houses that were being used as hospitals.

The weary men lay down to sleep. When they woke, they were surrounded by German troops. For almost 280 men and their hapless commander, the war was over. Fatalities in the engagement at Le Grand Fayt were low, but only in relative terms as some seventeen Rangers had been killed. Most are buried in Le Grand Fayt communal cemetery. There is one plot in the cemetery where German and British soldiers are buried together, a rarity on the Western Front. A grey slab commemorates nine unidentified British soldiers from the Connaught Rangers and seven German soldiers. The named Rangers are Captain William Leader from Coachford, County Cork; Lance Corporal J.J. Wiley, born in Bandon, County Cork; and Lance Corporal Edward McCann from Dundee, Scotland.

The rest of the regiment got away and marched southwards. They were in a state of delirious exhaustion compounded by extreme hunger. Hamilton was too tired even to sit on his horse. His men were equally fatigued as they trudged onwards. 'Some of them fell out and lay down in the road – it exhausted all one's vocabulary of entreaty and abuse, and even called for a liberal use of the boot to get them going again. Even, so in spite of our efforts, I'm afraid some half dozen were left behind.'[19]

The tide of battle swept southwards towards the most important battle of the war on the Western Front: the Battle of the Marne, where the German advance was stopped and the war of movement degenerated into a war of deadly stagnation in the trenches. The soldiers and civilians trapped behind enemy lines were reduced to simply surviving. The British soldiers hoped against hope that the war would end before they were discovered or that their units would turn the tide of battle northwards and roll back the German advance.

Alternatively, they would try to make their way back to their own lines or the English Channel to be picked up or to neutral Holland. It was not an unrealistic hope. Nurse Edith Cavell helped hundreds of soldiers, including many Royal Munster Fusiliers and Connaught Rangers, to escape to Holland and from there to England.[20]

The eleven British Soldiers were among that lost and frightened tribe of wandering fugitives. They hid in the dense woods and copses in the area. German army maps from the time show two large forests either side of Étreux, big enough for a large body of men to hide in without being detected.

There was safety in numbers. The same woods were full of Belgian and French refugees. The Germans had turned villagers out of their homes in reprisal for perceived civilian collaboration with the Allies. Atrocities were committed by the Germans on the pretext that occupied France and German was full of *francs-tireurs* (free shooters), irregulars disguised as civilians, a legacy of the Franco-Prussian war. These civilians had either fled the Germans in fear or had had their properties confiscated.

The French Resistance of the Second World War is firmly lodged in the public imagination. Less well known is the German occupation of Belgium and northern France in the First World War, which was no less traumatic for the civilian population.

The Germans occupied a crescent-shaped portion of France from the Pas-de-Calais to the Swiss border. The shooting of innocent civilians by the Germans during the early stages of the war had hardened civilian attitudes. Mostly this took the form of passive resistance, active subversion being severely punished.

The Germans cited military law to justify appropriating the resources of the areas they had occupied. Industry was destroyed or shipped to Germany. Five-sixths of the 1914 harvest in occupied France was seized by the Germans. The movement and sale of livestock needed the permission of the local commandant.[21]

Able-bodied men who had not yet signed up to the French war effort had to report twice a week to the occupiers to ensure they were still present and not fomenting rebellion. Many French and Belgian men were deported to labour camps in Germany. By 1918, the population of Aisne, 500,000 before the war, was reduced to a third of that figure.[22]

It took bravery and ingenuity to hide out from the Germans. The Iron 12 might just have survived the war were it not for an embittered, old Franco-Prussian war veteran called Louis Bachelet. Aged 66, he was sharing the affections of a married woman in the village named Blanche Griselin. And those affections were also being shared with none other than Vincent and Olympe Chalandre's 16-year-old son Clovis. The 1920 pamphlet, which recounted their story, refers to Mme Griselin as the 'local married slut'. The Germans too 'wallowed in this filth', according to the same account.[23]

When Clovis Chalandre found out about his rival, he went to Bachelet's lodging and threw stones at his window. In a rage, Bachelet shouted back that he would inform on the Chalandre family. He was as bad as his word. On 22 February, Bachelet went to the military headquarters in Guise and told Waechter about the men hiding in Chalandre's attic.

While he was there, Madame Logez arrived to renew her weekly permit. She suspected nothing. Waechter acted swiftly on the information given to him by Bachelet.[24] Three days later, the eleven British soldiers and Vincent Chalandre were executed. The ordeal for the Logez and Chalandre families did not end there. Leonie Logez was arrested and taken to Guise Chateau. She was left out in the rain in the courtyard of the chateau for two nights. Her senile husband was turned out of their home. Their mill was burned to the ground and all their livestock was shot.

Both families were taken to a prison in eastern Germany where common criminals were housed. 'We suffered greatly from cold and damp,' Leonie Logez told the journalist Herbert Walton in 1928, 'and it sends a shiver through me even to this day to think of the food we were forced to eat'.[25]

Olympe Chalandre died prematurely in 1919. Tragically, her three youngest children, Leon, Marthe and Marcel, all died in the 1920s. Olympe had come home from the prisoner-of-war camp with what was believed to have been tuberculous meningitis, with which she infected her children, who were in a weakened state as a result of years of neglect.[26] Mme Logez's husband also died before the war was over. They too can be regarded as fatalities of this appalling episode.

The Iron 12 executions were followed in May 1916 by a similar incident. This war crime was carried out in the village of Villeret, just north of St Quentin. Four more British soldiers were executed here. Two of the men were Irish: Private David Martin from Newry, County Down, and Private Thomas Donohoe from Belturbet, County Cavan. Both men were with the 1st Royal Irish Fusiliers.[27] The story of the Villeret Four bears many similarities to that of the Iron 12. There are resolute soldiers who refuse to surrender, brave locals who shelter them, a poignant love affair and a callous betrayal.

The ringleader of the Villeret Four was Private Robert Digby from Hampshire. He fell in love with the teenage daughter of the family who sheltered him. Their child, Hélène Cornaille-Digby, was born in 1915 and died in 2005, at the age of 90.

Somebody betrayed the four men. They were arrested by the Germans. The two Irishmen and Private Willie Thorpe from Liverpool were shot the next day. Digby fled into a nearby wood. He was found by the acting mayor Emile Marié, who told him that he if he did not give himself up, all the villagers would be shot.

Faced with either losing his own life or being responsible for the deaths of dozens of innocent people, Digby gave himself up and was executed three days later. Villeret was burnt to the ground by the Germans in 1917. The story of the Villeret Four was the subject of a BBC radio documentary *An Act of Remembrance* and *A Foreign Field*, a bestseller by the former *Times* Paris correspondent Ben MacIntyre.

Though the Iron 12 affair was the biggest incident of its kind in the war, it remains hardly known. Herbert Walton published the first English-language account of what really happened.

The relatives of the eleven British soldiers had assumed that their men were missing, presumed dead, on the field of battle, like millions of others in this ghastly war.

News of their execution came after the war but even then the details were blurred. The locals in Iron only knew who these men were from a pathetic scrap of paper found years after, under a stone near the burnt-out mill. The men had scribbled the details of their own names and regiments on the piece of paper.[28]

The story was almost entirely forgotten until it came to the attention of an English academic, Hedley Malloch. Malloch's grandfather was from Mitchelstown, County Cork, and had been in the Royal Munster Fusiliers. Malloch joined the Royal Munster Fusiliers Association (RMFA) to find out more about his grandfather. In 1994, he first came across the story in the association's magazine.

Malloch's move to France to work at the Catholic University in Lille allowed him to spend more time researching the story of the Iron 12. His research brought him to Iron. The first person he met was the Mayor of Iron André Gruselle, who happened to be the great-grandson of Léonie Logez. The story had lodged itself in the folk memory of the villages of Iron.

It was, and remains, for Malloch, 'one of the great untold stories of the first World War. It works as story. It has everything: courage, endurance, duty, suffering, patriotism, jealousy, betrayal. If the story was scripted and cast in Hollywood, nobody would believe it. Yet it all happened.'[29]

It was discovered that Chalandre had been reburied in St Médard Cemetery in an unmarked grave close to where the eleven British soldiers shot with him were buried. The neglect of his grave reflected the devastating impact that his execution had on his family. In 2006, the grave received a new marker and memorial plaque.

Malloch, in his capacity as chair of the Iron Memorial Fund, set about raising the money for a memorial to the Iron 12. The three regimental associations involved and the people of the village of Iron all gave generously. Several years later, on 17 September 2011, the stone memorial was unveiled in Iron with full military honours.

The memorial is made from Wicklow granite, with a bronze plaque by Clare artist Seamus Connolly. It was created by Feely Stone from Boyle, County Roscommon, a town closely associated with the Connaught Rangers. The memorial to the Iron 12 is located next to the village's own war memorial, on which the name of Vincent Chalandre is written.

The bronze plaque on the new monument tells the story of the Iron 12 incident. The names of the twelve executed men are on the front of the monument. The right-hand panel gives the names and dates of the battles at Le Grand Fayt and Étreux. The back panel depicts the regimental insignias and the left-hand panel shows a mill, representing the village of Iron.

A simple plaque was also erected in the grounds of the chateau at Guise. It reads, 'On this spot, on February 25 1915, eleven British soldiers and one French civilian were executed by the Germans. Their names are commemorated on the Guise War Memorial.'

On 25 February 2015, memorial services were held in Iron and Guise to remember the Iron 12. Both places have seen better days. Iron is a rather forlorn place, its population now no more than 250. At the outbreak of the war, the population was 900 because of its thriving silk industry. Guise too is struggling and its population is in terminal decline a century later. This part of the upper Aisne has never really recovered from the First World War. The disruption was so profound as to render it impossible to return to the status quo.

Bachelet died after the war while awaiting trial for his treachery. He appears to have died of natural causes, a better death than he deserved, according to *Les Onze Anglais d'Iron*. Waechter's reward for his brutality was the role of military governor of Belgrade. Alexander Abercrombie died in a German prisoner-of-war camp in 1916 at the age of 50. His son, also called Alexander, also died because of the war. Tragically, he succumbed to wounds three months after the Armistice.[30]

Mrs Mary Anne Walsh lived in hope that her son John had somehow survived the conflagration, despite being officially listed among the missing, presumed dead. A year after he was executed, her desperate hopes were raised by news from Germany, only then to be cruelly dashed. A neighbour had come across a report in a Dublin newspaper which appeared to suggest that John Walsh was still alive in a German prisoner-of-war camp. Her local newspaper, the *King's County Chronicle*, took up the story:

The long pent-up feelings of the mother found vent in tears of joy, as hope returned that she would yet welcome again her favourite son; and with her own hand she wrote him a true mother's letter, saying, 'Oh, John, John, I am still your mother, as I ever will be even unto death!', and asking him to write and she would send him anything he asked for. But it was not to be. That reply was anxiously awaited from day to day and, at length, a post-card was delivered, bearing the mark of the German Eagle. It was from Sergt. Hogan, detained at the prison camp to which she had written – a kind-hearted Irish soldier, who expressed his regret to have to inform her that the only soldier in camp of the name of Walsh was a native of Listowel, Co. Kerry. Tears well up in her eyes, and blot out from her the vision of the resolute yet kindly face of a brave man which smiles from the photo in the poor woman's hand, as a mother's heart is moved with its strongest emotion.

Mrs Walsh's impoverished circumstances were never alleviated either. The *King's County Chronicle* added that 'she never got a half-penny from either the Government or anyone else. All she gets is two shillings worth of provisions from some ladies in the town and she has nothing to pay rent.'[31]

Many of John Nash's large, extended family emigrated to the United States. His niece Bridget Nash married a Kerryman, Jeremiah Riordan. Their son is Michigan appeal courts judge Michael Riordan. 'My mother used to talk about the execution of her uncle John Nash,' Michael recalled in an email exchange with the author. 'She did not know the details, but she knew he was executed by the Germans in World War I. She knew there was a woman involved and she thought her uncle and the others were executed in a cave. My mother said there was a big medal in their home and that she and her siblings would play with it when they were children.'

This would have been the bronze medal known as the 'death penny'; it was British policy to issue the medal to every family that lost a loved one serving in the armed forces during the war.

Michael Riordan recalled:

> Private Nash was, and still is, held in high regard by his family. My grandfather named his second son after him and the name John Nash lives on in my family through many others. Private Nash was a teen when he joined the army. Whatever the army paid him was far more than he could have earned at home as his family struggled with the few fields they had hewn out of the rocks to sustain the many mouths that had to be fed. While Rossmore Island is a beautiful place, unfortunately, back in those days one could not eat or carve out a living from the beauty alone.
>
> It is now a hundred years since the Germans killed the Iron 12. The valiant local French families, the Logez's and the Chalandre's, along with many of the villagers in Iron, did all they could to help the young, many Irish, enlisted men who had no officer to lead them. Each of the men fulfilled the duty to which they had obligated themselves. While I am not an expert in military law, the brutality of their treatment and murder shocks the conscience, even a hundred years later. I have often wondered about the last thoughts that may have gone through Private Nash's mind as he awaited, in pain, his execution. Did he think of his family that he would never see again? Did he think of Ireland or wonder about the aspirations he would never achieve? Did he wonder if his family would ever know what became of him? Did he look forward to meeting his late-mother in the next life? Did he think of the beautiful plot of land on which he was raised? Or, did he say a prayer for himself and the others? None of us will ever know. But, I do know that the German commander, Lieutenant-Colonel Waechter, wanted the deaths of these men, and the punishment of those who bravely aided them, to be an example. An example of what, I am not sure. But, in the end, as history has shown us, his actions were a foreshadowing of the brutality that would grip the European continent for decades to come. A brutality that, before it was finished, extracted a toll on humanity that before then may have been unbeknownst to mankind.[32]

Dans la soirée du samedi 8 mai 1915, le 2ème Bataillon du Royal Munster Fusiliers, fort de 800 hommes, commandé par le lieutenant-colonel Victor Rickard, s'est arrêté sur ce site, face à la chapelle Notre Dame de Seez, sur la route avant de prendre place pour l'attaque de la crête d'Aubers, prévue pour le lendemain matin.

Le Sergent-major John Ring appela ses hommes qui formèrent un carré devant la chapelle. A cheval face à eux, le Lieutenant-Colonel Rickard, le Père Francis Gleeson, aumônier du bataillon et le Capitaine Thomas Filgate, le Sergent-Major Ring s'est placé à l'arrière.

En face de chaque compagnie, un drapeau vert avec la harpe irlandaise et le nom "Munster" brodé. Les drapeaux sont un cadeau de Lady Gordon, épouse d'un Lord Lieutenant Irlandais.

Les armes brillent à la semi-lumière d'un soir de printemps; des tirs et des bruits d'explosions rappellent à tous l'épreuve à venir. Le Père Gleeson a déplacé son cheval pour être plus près des hommes et mis son étole pourpre de confession autour de son cou. Tous, têtes nues, les cheveux ébouriffés par une brise légère et les drapeaux flottant dans ce merveilleux crépuscule. Le Père Gleeson débuta la célébration de l'absolution en entonnant des chants et des hymnes, y compris le "Hail Glorious St. Patrick."

Après le service, le Père Gleeson est passé le long des rangs en encourageant et en demandant aux hommes de soutenir l'honneur du régiment.

Puis, en réponse au commandement du sergent-major Ring, le Bataillon s'est reformé en colonne et a repris sa marche vers la ligne de front.

Le lendemain matin après la bataille, le nombre de tués s'élève à 19 officiers, dont le commandant du bataillon, 270 sous-officiers et soldats.

On the evening of Satur...
the men of 2nd Battalio...
siliers, some 800 strong...
Lieutenant-Colonel Victo...
this site, by a way-side s...
to take their place for th...
Ridge, ordered for the fo...
Sergeant Major John Rin...
order and formed them...
in front of the shrine. Fac...
back, were Lieutenant-C...
Father Francis Gleeson,...
and Captain Thomas Filg...
tant. Sergeant-Major Rin...
In front of each company...
with the Irish harp and th...
embroidered on it, a gift...
wife of the Lord Lieutena...
Gun flashes added to the...
spring evening; gunfire a...
reminded all of the ordea...
Gleeson moved his horse...
and put the purple stole o...
around his neck. All bareo...
the light breeze ruffled ha...
flutter the green company...
that wonderful twilight, Fa...
toned a general absolutio...
the singing of hymns, inclu...
ous St. Patrick."

Following the service, Fath...
along the ranks, encouragi...
well and telling the men to...
honour of the Regiment.
Then, responding to the co...
Sergeant-Major Ring, the B...
in column and the march co...
the front line.

Casualties in the battle on t...
morning amounted to 19 off...
the Battalion commander, a...
commissioned officers and r...

8

The painting of the "Last Absolution of the Munsters" was commissioned by Jessica Rickard, wife of Lieutenant-Colonel Rickard, from the famous war artist, Fortunino Matania, and first appeared in 1916.
It is based on a sketch by a sergeant who was present at the event and on information given by Mrs. Rickard who had received it from some of those in attendance.
The sketch and the various accounts of the "Last Absolution" confirm that there were three men on horseback: Lieutenant-Colonel Rickard, Father Gleeson, Chaplain, and Captain Filgate.
However, for the purpose of the painting, the artist has depicted only two men on horseback, Lieutenant-Colonel Rickard and Father Gleeson, Captain Filgate is shown standing in the foreground with Sergeant-Major Ring to his left near the shrine.

* A copy of the painting can be seen in the town hall of Richebourg.

La peinture de la "Dernière Absolution des Munsters" a été commandée par Jessica Rickard, épouse du Lieutenant-Colonel Rickard, célèbre artiste de guerre, à Fortunino Matania et est vue pour la première fois en 1916.
Il s'est basé sur un croquis réalisé par un sergent présent lors de l'événement et sur des informations données par Mme Rickard qui avaient reçu certains militaires présents ce jour-là.
Le croquis et les différents récits confirment que lors de la "Dernière Absolu-tion" qu'il y avait trois hommes à cheval: le Lieutenant-Colonel Rickard, l'aumônier, le Père Gleeson et le Capitaine Filgate.
Cependant, sur la peinture, l'artiste n'a représenté que deux hommes à cheval, le Lieutenant-Colonel Rickard et Père Gleeson. Le Capitaine Filgate est représenté debout au premier plan avec le Sergent-Major Ring gauc...
Une copie du ... visit... mairie de Ri...

Plaque commémorative du centenaire l'Absolution des Munsters posée le 8 mai 2015 en leur souvenir par la commune de Richebourg

THE SIGN AT RUE DU BOIS:

THE LAST GENERAL ABSOLUTION OF THE MUNSTERS

The Rue du Bois is a long road running through the heart of French Flanders. This is prosperous agricultural country, semi-rural for the most part. Behind the neat red-brick farmhouses which line the road are fields of wheat, potatoes, onions, sugar beet and green beans. Here is some of the flattest terrain in Europe, disturbed only by the whitewashed monuments to the terrible events of the First World War. At one end of the Rue du Bois are memorials to the soldiers of two countries that were sucked into a global conflict to no obvious end.

The Indian Memorial remembers nearly 5,000 soldiers from Britain's largest colony. They signed up to the British war effort believing they would be fighting in the Middle East and ended up filling gaps in the British lines on the Western Front instead. Behind the Indian Memorial is the monument to the Portuguese soldiers who died in the war. Portugal was a late entrant and joined the Allied side because of tensions with Germany over its colonies and the targeting of its merchant shipping. At the other end of Rue du Bois is the Le Touret Memorial to 13,404 British soldiers who were killed in the first year of the war and have no known grave.

With so many imposing reminders of the war, the unsuspecting traveller was unlikely to grasp the significance of a lay-by and council depot where mounds of sand and gravel were kept behind a dull, dun-coloured wall and a green gate. Yet this most prosaic of locations is the site of one of the most famous paintings of the First World War and one of the most culturally significant Irish paintings of the twentieth century.

Fortunino Matania was not even there when he painted *The Last General Absolution of the Munsters at Rue du Bois*. Neither was the novelist Jessie Louisa Rickard, the wife of one of the officers destined to die a short time after the general absolution took place. Yet these two artists conjured up something that has more than verisimilitude; they managed to create works with an enduring emotional resonance strong enough to lodge in our collective imagination. The ominous sky in the painting with its evening tints of red and yellow gives the viewer a sense of foreboding, which would be more than justified by what happened subsequent to the scene depicted.

The war was just nine months old when the 2nd Royal Munster Fusiliers marched out to battle on the evening of 8 May 1915. The battalion had already been decimated twice, once at Étreux on 27 August and then at Festubert, near the Rue du Bois, before Christmas 1914.

The 2nd Munsters had barely recovered from losing three quarters of its strength at Étreux when it was pitched into a dreadful quagmire before the first Christmas of the war. The men had been looking forward to a quiet festive season behind the lines, but, four days prior to Christmas Day, the battalion was pressed into action to defend trenches seized by the Germans from Indian troops who had been subject to a merciless bombardment.

The Munsters achieved their goal in an epic of endurance that lasted sixty hours. 'We lay in the ditch all day, thirsty, hungry, cold, longing for darkness to fall and give us an opportunity to stretch our legs, hoping that food and supports would be brought up to us,' one of them wrote afterwards.

On Christmas Day, Mass was offered for the seven officers and 200 men killed at Festubert on that 'dreadful night of carnage', according to the battalion's chaplain Fr Francis Anthony Gleeson, a 31-year-old diocesan priest from Templemore, County Tipperary.[1]

Gleeson was an Irish speaker and a nationalist. Yet when war broke out he did not hesitate to accept a commission with the rank of captain as a chaplain in the British army. Catholic chaplains were known for their bravery and selflessness. They frequently found themselves in the firing line delivering the last rites to dying soldiers. Gleeson had already seen enough:

> Such desolation. Such suffering! If all militarists had hearts at all they should bleed, if they saw the scene of frozen men I saw today – this Christmas day of 1914 AD. How I felt on that death region today! Good Saviour of the world – will you deem to bring peace and abolish all war forever![2]

The war was not over by Christmas. Euphoria had dissipated. Enthusiasm foundered as summer gave way to autumn and then to a bitter and fruitless winter. By the turning of the year, friend and foe alike had come to the grim realisation that this conflict would be protracted and bloody beyond what anyone had imagined.

The German gamble on a quick war had failed. In late 1914, they decided to switch their attentions from the Western Front to the Eastern Front. This strategy was the reverse of the Schlieffen Plan, which had envisaged a swift defeat of France, thereby freeing Germany to concentrate its whole strength on Russia.

France would not be defeated in the short term. It was a much tougher and more determined foe than the nation defeated in the Franco-Prussian War of 1871. Now France had the British on its side, a small but growing presence.

The Germans believed that the Russians, despite their vast reserves of manpower, were critically weak when it came to equipment and leadership. This was not an inaccurate calculation on the part of the Germans. Russia would eventually be defeated, but not for another two years and by then it was too late.

In early 1915, the Germans moved 100,000 men from west to east and resolved to stay on the defensive in France until the Russian threat could be dealt with. In May, the Central Powers opened up the Gorlice-Tarnów offensive in modern-day Poland.[3] The Germans remained confident they could switch troops from one front to another without affecting their war effort as they were unimpressed by French efforts to dislodge them from conquered soil. They were also contemptuous of the British Expeditionary Force, judging it, not inaccurately, to still be of insufficient size to pose a serious threat. Nothing they had encountered to date from the British had worried the Chief of the Imperial German General Staff Erich von Falkenhayn, who observed that '[t]he English troops, in spite of undeniable bravery and endurance on the part of the men, have proved so clumsy in action that they offer no prospect of accomplishing anything decisive against the German Army in the immediate future.'[4]

In May 1915, the French and British planned a joint offensive either side of the La Bassée Canal in the Pas-de-Calais, which marked the demarcation line between both armies. Undeterred by scarcely believable losses of 750,000 dead soldiers and twice that number injured, the French commander-in-chief, the endlessly optimistic Joseph Joffre, believed the Allies could make a telling breakthrough as the winter gave way to spring. His British counterpart Field Marshal Sir John French remembered that 'Joffre was very hopeful … said he was bringing up even more troops and really thought he would break the line past mending, and that it might be, and ought to be, the beginning of the end. He talked of getting to Namur and the war being over in three months.'[5]

South of the canal, the French were to attack Vimy Ridge and Arras, drive the Germans off the high ground in the area and on to the Douoi plain in the direction of Noyon. This town on the Oise River was the apex of the 'Noyon elbow', the right-angled salient which marked the furthest point of the German advance into France. It was just 60 miles from Paris.

The British objective was to take Aubers Ridge from the Germans. As encountered in the previous chapter on Le Pilly, the ridge – to call it a hill would be to exaggerate – gave the Germans an elevated position overlooking the dead-flat land around it.

The British First Army, which was leading the assault, had purloined every gun it could find. It had 276 18-pounder field guns, 84 quick-firing guns and 181 howitzers. Sir John French believed this was inadequate for the assault, but he could get no more from the War Office as the Second Army was involved in a desperate struggle at Ypres.[6] The plan was to use the field guns to break up the German barbed wire with shrapnel shells. The heavy-calibre howitzers would then pound the German breastworks and raze their parapets to the ground.

The guns were lined up on the Rue des Berceaux, a parallel road behind Rue du Bois, some 1,600 to 2,000 yards from the targets. The attack on Aubers Ridge was designed as a pincer movement. IV Corps was in the north, I Corps in the centre with the 1st Division (including the Munsters) and the Indian Corps, comprised of two divisions, south of that. I Corps and the Indians occupied a front of about 2,500 yards parallel to Rue du Bois.

Aubers Ridge was a mile and a half beyond the British jumping-off positions. A secondary target was a redoubt called La Clicqueterie Farm, another mile and a half distant from that.[7]

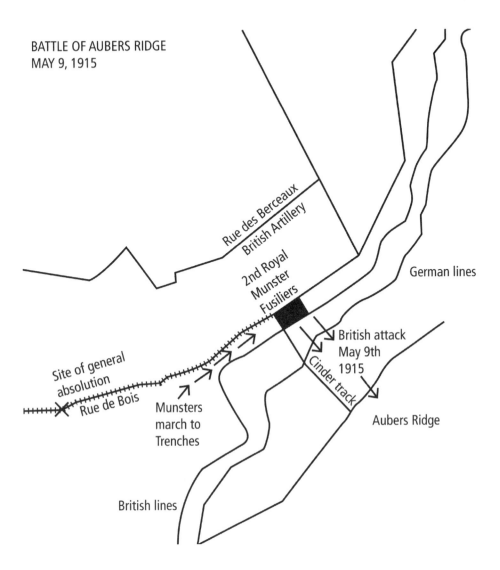

BATTLE OF AUBERS RIDGE
MAY 9, 1915

The Munsters knew for several weeks that they were to be involved in a spring offensive. Many of the men were already battle-hardened but, like so many of the other old regiments of the British army, the Munsters had made up for horrendous losses with drafts of men drawn from the reserves at home. For many of these rookies, the forthcoming battle would be their first, and in some cases last, experience of combat.

The men were billeted in a farmhouse at Locon, about 6 miles north of Rue du Bois. The joint French–British attack was postponed twice because of bad weather. On the evening of 7 May, Gleeson watched the rain sheeting down and was pleased the men would not be leaving their comfortable billets. Things would be hard enough without going into battle wet and chilled to the bone.

The following evening was clear. This time the attack was going ahead. Despite the horrors they had already seen, the men were in good spirits. 'The scenes of enthusiasm are outstanding,' Gleeson wrote in his diary. These men were resolute Catholics and the constant presence of death made them an 'army of prayers', according to Company Sergeant Major James Leahy.[8]

'I have seen sights, but the faith, piety, and sincerity of that congregation, each man knowing that death was staring him in the face, would make anyone in this world proud to be a Catholic.' In his diaries, Gleeson kept an extensive list of his men and when they had last received the sacraments. His sorrowful letters back home to grieving relatives offered one consolation – the men had died in a state of grace.

As they marched down the Rue du Bois towards the British trenches, Gleeson spotted an exposed altar at a lay-by near a bend in the road. This was the shattered remains of a roadside family chapel, the Chapel of Notre Dame de Seez, which had been hit by a shell in the early part of the war. The men halted. Gleeson walked up and down the ranks giving what comfort he could to the 900 men of the battalion, reminding them of the honour of their regiment. At this moment of solemnity, they sat on the grass, read their Bibles or fingered their rosary beads 'silent, absorbed, reverential to a degree'.[9] Leahy also remembered the occasion being tinged by solemnity:

> There were no ribald jest, or courage buoyed up with alcohol, none of the fanciful pictures which imagination conjures up of soldiers going to a desperate charge; no, there were brave hearts without fear, only hope that God would bring them through … Every man had his Rosary out reciting the prayers in response to Fr. Gleeson, just as if at the Confraternity at home, instead of having to face death in a thousand hideous forms the following morning.[10]

Confession, one of the seven sacraments of the Catholic Church, was usually administered in the privacy of the confession box. Canon law sets out two conditions under which general absolution can be administered. Firstly, there must be a shortage of priests available to hear confession. Secondly there must be no alternative. The battalion was overwhelmingly Catholic and, with the men about to go into battle, Gleeson was satisfied that the circumstances were appropriate for such an extreme measure. Sitting on his horse, Gleeson raised his hand in a prayerful gesture and spoke out loud the words of the Catholic rite of absolution for sinners.

During this moment, each man was left with his own thoughts, each beseeching the Queen of Heaven before entering the mouth of hell. The silence was broken by the men singing 'Hail Glorious St Patrick'. The ritual over, they dispersed to march a mile to the assembly trenches, which were to the left of the Cinder Track, a laneway which led to the German lines and which is still there today.

Adjutant Captain Thomas William Filgate, who came from a prominent County Louth family, later reported they were able to assemble in the front-line trenches by midnight without any enemy harassment. It was time for whatever fitful sleep the men could get. It would be scarcely another five hours before they would go over the top. One wonders if any of the men slept at all.

The Battle of Aubers Ridge was a diversion to the main attack. The French had allocated a whole army, the 10th, to capturing Vimy Ridge, the steep escarpment which dominated the region north of Arras. The British objective was the same as at Neuve Chapelle in March 1915 – to capture the slight rise of Aubers Ridge and drive the Germans back further.

Neuve Chapelle had almost been a success. An oval-shaped area of ground including the village of Neuve Chapelle was taken but at a cost of more than 11,000 men. The British were unable to exploit their initial success because of a fatal delay in bringing up reserves. Now the British were back, slightly further south, but with the same goal in mind. This time, though, it was the Germans who had learned the lessons of that battle.

They set about strengthening their defences. The land is low-lying and soggy. The Germans built up and out. Their parapets were 7ft high and 7ft wide. The breastworks were so well fortified that only a direct shell hit could shatter them. Each parapet had a wooden structure for a machine-gun team and shelter for men from heavy shelling. Again and again this structure would confound the heaviest shells and the bravest men the British Empire could throw at them.

The British did not know this when they were preparing for the Battle of Aubers Ridge in May 1915. The high command had brought up every available heavy gun to soften the German defences. They believed a hurricane bombardment lasting half an hour would be sufficient to allow the British soldiers time to leave their trenches and creep towards the enemy lines. The Germans would be either dead or sheltering from the barrage.

It had to work. No man's land in this part of the front line was no more than 100 yards in places. In front of the Munsters it varied from 380 yards to 550 yards. If the bombardment did not work, the British infantry would not stand a chance.

At 5 a.m., the British guns opened fire, firing shrapnel shells into the German front line and then switched to high explosives as the bombardment wound down. From the perspective of the British command, the bombardment seemed to be working. The noise was apocalyptic as shells whistled overhead and crashed into the German breastworks. Smoke and flames coming from the German lines obscured the view. But when the smoke cleared, the men assembled at the front to go over the top could see the Germans moving about in front of them, seemingly undaunted by the pounding. Alarmingly, the breastworks were still in place, but no one decided to call a halt to the offensive.

The 2nd Munsters and the 2nd Royal Welsh Fusiliers had crept up to within 80 yards of the German lines under the cover of the bombardment, waiting for it to lift. A and B Companies from the Munsters led the assault, with C and D in support. As soon as the bombardment lifted, A and B rushed forward. Those from A Company were mown down by German machine guns. The machine-gunners trained on B Company hesitated long enough for two platoons of the Munsters to get into the first and second line German trenches.

Some sixty men found themselves alone and isolated in the German trenches. They pressed on as per their orders and found themselves at a stream several hundred yards beyond the enemy front line. They ambushed a party of Germans who were using a communications trench to retreat to the rear.[11]

The rest of B Company and D Company following on in support were racked with machine gun fire. Approximately half an hour after the attack started, Lieutenant-Colonel Victor Rickard rallied his men and went over the top. He had barely stepped off the parapet when he was killed by a bullet to the neck.

At 10.30 a.m., the remaining men from the battalion awaited further instructions to go over the top, but those orders never came. As evening approached, the British started another bombardment to assist the brave men who had got into the German trenches. Unfortunately, they succeeded in killing many of the Munsters who had held out bravely all day. Of the B Company who got into the German trenches, only two of the men made it back to the British lines. One of them, Lance Corporal Meehan, was of the view that 'the situation was hopeless. All our officers were gone and I, alone in the German trenches, found myself in command. I was then a lance corporal. Of the eight men with me, but three returned. I got off the field that night between 8 and 9 O'Clock.'[12]

Meehan, from Limerick city, had been a journalist living in Canada when war broke out. He had left the army in 1911, but rejoined at the outbreak of war. He wrote vivid dispatches for the *Cork Examiner* under the pen name Patsy.

It was a 'splendid failure', according to the author of *The 2nd Munsters in France*, Lieutenant-Colonel H.S. Jervis, who was taken prisoner at Étreux. 'General Sir Charles Munro, commanding the 1st Army Corps, and Major-General Haking, commanding the 1st Division, joined in congratulating the Munsters on being the only unit which reached the enemy's lines.'[13]

The battle in the northern sector began more promisingly. Here the opposing trenches were literally a stone's throw away, between 150 and 200 yards in most cases. Five battalions, including the 1st Royal Irish Rifles, went over the top. Twenty minutes after the first attack, two underground mines were blown and a London battalion rushed forward to occupy the trenches. Some progress was made here, but the men could not hold on. The German defences remained intact and no man's land was strewn with corpses.

Haig ordered a bayonet charge for 8 p.m. All day long the remains of traumatised battalions and fretful reserves waited for the order to go over the top, knowing it would add considerably to the appalling losses. Mercifully, it was called off as not enough fit men could be assembled for it. It was the only wise decision made all day.

Within twenty minutes, the Battle of Aubers Ridge was effectively over. The German machine guns cut through prone men. The casualties were enormous. At 6.15 a.m., the British initiated another artillery barrage, but only succeeded in hitting many of their own men who were lying against the breastworks. Haig ordered another attack in the afternoon. The 1st Division reserves were thrown into the action and suffered the same fate as those they replaced. The 3rd Brigade suffered more than 1,000 casualties within minutes.

In the early hours of 10 May 1915, all the men who managed to get themselves into German trenches were withdrawn because they could not be supported.

The Battle of Aubers Ridge was an absolute catastrophe for the British. Some 11,000 casualties had been suffered without a single yard of ground being gained. The Munsters sustained 398 casualties bad but not as bad as the Royal Irish Rifles with 467 casualties. 'It had been a disastrous fifteen hours of squandered heroism, unredeemed by the faintest glimmer of success,' wrote Alan Clark, whose 1961 book *The Donkeys* did much to reinforce the enduring belief that the ordinary British Tommies were lions led by donkeys.[14]

The British commanders had gambled on a short but furious artillery bombardment softening up the German lines. The gamble was a disaster. When the bombardment ceased, many of the front-line British infantry had already crept into no man's land. They made for a pitiful sight for the incredulous German infantry who had been forewarned of the attack.

'There could never before in war have been a more perfect target. There was only one possible order to give – fire until the barrels burst,' was how the incident was remembered in the German 57th Regiment diary. A sombre commanders' conference was called for 9 a.m. the following morning. There was no way the attack could be rejoined. The British guns were out of ammunition.

The post-mortem was damning. The British artillery barrage had been wholly inadequate. There had not been enough shells and too many of the shells that were fired were duds. Others fell short, mortally wounding their own men. The 4.7-inch guns were so worn out that the copper driving bands which kept the shell on an accurate trajectory unravelled and the shells fell all over the place. Gun barrels were worn out and fatally inaccurate.

The blunders of British generals generated a pitiful aftermath. 'Spent all night trying to comfort, aid and remove the wounded,' Gleeson wrote in his diary on 10 May, the day after the battle. 'It was ghastly to see them lying there in the cold, cheerless outhouses, on bare stretchers with no blankets to cover their freezing limbs.'

It took several days for the magnitude of the disaster to filter back to Britain and Ireland. The public were preoccupied with the sinking of the *Lusitania*, which had occurred two days before Aubers Ridge and the unfolding catastrophe in Gallipoli.

Sir John French was reduced to a sullen rage over this latest debacle and blamed Lord Kitchener, the minister in charge of munitions, for leaving him desperately short of shells and high explosives. Kitchener grasped before many others that this would be a long and attritional war which would require the whole resources of the Empire to prosecute, yet he was strangely reluctant to utilise the whole of British industry for the war effort.

French had a gift for intrigue and briefed his friend, *The Times* war correspondent Count Repington, about the shell shortage. His dispatch in the paper on 12 May was the most significant of the whole war and had long-term political consequences. 'Need for Shells, British Attack checked, Limited supply the cause, A lesson from France.' The unwieldy headline, typical of the period, had, nevertheless, a momentous impact. 'The want of an unlimited supply of high explosives was a total bar to our success,' Repington wrote. 'The brave infantry were confounded by the want of shells which left the German defences intact. The infantry did splendidly, but the conditions were too hard.'[15]

Two days later the First Lord of the Admiralty John Fisher resigned over the Gallipoli debacle. The Liberal government's prosecution of the war was now untenable. British Prime Minister Herbert Acquith was forced into forming a coalition government with the Conservatives and unionists. He offered a seat in Cabinet to John Redmond, but Redmond declined, citing his party's long-time opposition to serving in British governments. Edward Carson had no such compunction and became attorney general. The presence of such an avowedly anti-home ruler at the heart of British government compounded Redmond's political isolation.

Waiting anxiously for news of her husband was Lieutenant-Colonel Victor Rickard's widow. The couple's only child, Justin, had been born two years previously.

Jessie Louisa Rickard was the daughter of Canon Courtney Moore from Cork, a Protestant Irish nationalist. She had divorced her first husband, Robert Dudley Innes Ackland, an army officer who went on to be one of the last British soldiers to die in Gallipoli.[16] Rickard published her first novel, *Young Mr Gibbs*, in 1912. After her husband died, she wrote an account of the Battle of Aubers Ridge which appeared in the *New Ireland* magazine. The article is suffused with a sense of grief and loss. It is told with a novelist's eye:

> It was a clear spring evening, dark under a green sky, the orchards through the country heavy with blossom, their scent recalling manifold recollections. The poplar trees, many of them shell-scarred and broken, were very still in the windless twilight, dark spires against the clear clean sky. At the entrance to the Rue du Bois there stands a broken shrine, and within the shrine is a crucifix.

It was not a broken shrine but the broken remainder of the small road chapel, which was destroyed in the first months of the war.

Rickard imagined the scene. 'Colonel Rickard halted the battalion. The men were ranged in three sides of a square, their green flags, embroidered with the Irish harp and the word "Munster" a gift from Lady Gordon, placed before each company.'

In the middle were Father Gleeson, Colonel Rickard and Captain Filgate, the adjutant, on their chargers and in that 'wonderful twilight Father Gleeson gave a general absolution. To some present, certainly, the '*vitam æternam*' was intensely and beautifully manifest, the dayspring of eternity very near. '*Miseratur vestri Omnipotens Deus, et dimissis peccatis vestris, perducat vos ad vitam æternam.*' The whole regiment, with their heads bared, sang the Te Deum, the great thanksgiving, the Sursum Corda of all the earth:

> There are many journeys and many stopping-places in the strange pilgrimage we call life, but there is no other such journey in the world as the journey up a road on the eve of battle, and no stopping-place more holy than a wayside shrine. The morning of the 8th broke incredibly still and fair, touching the land with the strange suggestion of unreality, which is part of the mystery of early dawn; and the Rue du Bois, for all its desolation, was for a moment beautiful with the spaciousness of peace. Night dews were still in the air, and the first coming of the sun was not far distant when sustained thunder pervaded the whole world.

Rickard's account of the battle is vivid and triumphalist, despite the terrible carnage which ensued. She describes how Captain John Campbell Dick led the men who stormed the German trenches. 'As he reached the second line of the German trenches he stood on the enemy's breast-works, quite indifferent to the danger which lay on every side, and standing as he often stood cheering a winner in the old days in Ireland, he waved his cap and shouted to his men, "come on, the Munsters!"'

Her account of her husband's death is indicative of how she regarded him and the cause for which he gave his life:

> As they crossed the first hundred and fifty yards to the given point Colonel Rickard fell, killed by a bullet that struck the spinal column of the neck … no one who knew him could ever doubt that he would have chosen any other end than to die leading the regiment he so loved all his life. He gained the perfect death that takes no thought of self, and which, in all truth, is swallowed up in victory. In a garden near a place called Windy Corner, Colonel Rickard is buried at the head of a line of graves. As Father Gleeson wrote, 'The Munsters who gave their lives so heroically and cheerfully, have, even in death, at their head, their kindly and loving leader, who so much inspired them and cheered us all'.

Rickard decided to expand the article into a book and to extend her tribute to her late husband's battalion by including chapters on the Munsters at Étreux and at in

1914. The book, *The Story of the Munsters*, published in late 1915, was a bestseller and was later updated.

Her vivid and passionate writings came to the attention of Fortunino Matania, who was born in Naples, Italy, in 1881. He was the son of an illustrator and displayed prodigious talent by the age of 3. He was illustrating commercially at the age of 11 and was a special artist with a daily Italian newspaper by the age of 15.[17] His talent took him to London, where his illustrated news magazines sold hundreds of thousands of copies every week. Matania had many gifts. He had a photographic memory, an ability to work quickly and a desire for verisimilitude. In 1902, he was asked to illustrate the coronation of King Edward VII. He did it from memory as no drawing materials were allowed inside. In 1922, he painted an accurate depiction of Howard Carter's discovery of Tutankhamun's tomb, though he was 1,500 miles away in London, thus displaying his great imaginative powers.[18]

When war broke out, Matania was commissioned by the British government as an official war artist. With characteristic verve, he threw himself into his work. His early work was all based on eyewitness accounts. He would interrogate injured soldiers and those at home on furlough. His illustrations were uncannily accurate and loved by the men who were his subjects.

He could have earned a comfortable living for the rest of the war, but Matania was not satisfied. He used his influence to get sent to the battlefield. While painting the detritus after the Battle of Neuve Chapelle in March 1915, a shell landed within 5 yards of him. When he returned to his billet behind the lines, he burst into tears. Upon his return to Britain, he constructed a reproduction of what he had seen in Neuve Chapelle. His most famous painting was *Goodbye Old Man*, an emotionally dramatic rendition of a British officer saying goodbye to his wounded horse as his comrade beckons him to return to safety.

Matania was commissioned by *The Sphere* to paint a scene to accompany Rickard's description. He read her heartbreaking account of an Irish battalion stopping by a wayside shrine to pray and reflect on the eve of going into battle. He also interviewed Meehan, who had been present at the general absolution. It is clear from Matania's painting that he forensically interrogated Meehan about the positioning of each of the protagonists. Who was standing where? Fr Gleeson and Lieutenant-Colonel Rickard are clearly identifiable, as is Rickard's adjutant, Captain Thomas Filgate. The man standing in front of the massed ranks of infantry and its green Munster flag with the uncrowned harp is Regimental Sergeant Major John Ring.

In Rickard's version, her husband and Filgate are both mounted. In Matania's painting, only Victor Rickard is mounted. The men's heads are all bowed. There are puddles on the track in front of Gleeson's horse, though none of the written accounts mention a recent shower of rain. In the background, the sky is an ominous reddish pallor. Many of these men would never see another sunset.

There is one curiosity, which was either a rare aberration on the part of Matania, a case of mistaken recollection by the subject interviewed or a playful addition by the artist. There is a windmill on the horizon on the right-hand side of the picture, but the windmill had been destroyed by shelling in the early stages of the war.

Gleeson gave many clues about the location of the general absolution site, but for many years it could not be found. A group from the Royal Munster Fusiliers came to the area in 1971 looking for it but could not find it. The issue remained unresolved until the advent of the internet. In August 2005 a contributor to the Great War Forum set up a thread inquiring as to the exact location of the Last General Absolution of the Munsters.[19] The thread caught the attention of Michel Knockaert, from Locon, France, where the Munsters had been billeted before they went into battle at Aubers Ridge.

Some twenty-five years previously, he had found a tag belonging to a British soldier, Second Lieutenant Robert William Stead from Liverpool. Assuming the soldier had died, he searched the records only to find that Stead had survived the war, but died of a cerebral haemorrhage at the age of just 30. Through his search for Stead, he came across the story of the Munsters and a copy of the Matania painting which hangs in Richebourg town hall.

Six months later, Knockaert had a breakthrough. He bought a local history book which recounted the story of the Munsters at Rue du Bois. The book told the story of how the event happened at the Chapel of Notre Dame de Seez in the hamlet of Epinette in Richebourg l'Avoué.

A copy of the painting was given to the rebuilt church by Mrs Rickard in 1935. When Knockaert went looking for the church, he found that it had disappeared. It had been destroyed in 1970 when the local council decided to straighten a sharp bend in the road.[20]

Another book, *Richebourg Mon Village*, yielded more critical details. The roadside chapel was built in 1867 by the Leroy-Pottier family and badly damaged during the First World War. It was reconstructed in 1929. The book contained the telling detail that it was on the site of this destroyed roadside chapel that the men of the Royal Munster Fusiliers gathered for their last general absolution on Saturday night, 8 May 1915. A plaque given to the Leroy-Pottier family read:

À cet endroit le samedi soir 8 mai 1915
Le 2è Royal Munster Fusiliers
Commandé par le Lieutenant-Colonel Victor Rickard
Reçut de son aumonier le Rev Père Gleeson
Une dernière absolution
Avant d'entrer dans la bataille de la côte d'Aubers
Où le Colonel Rickard devait trouver la mort

Avec un grand nombre de ses hommes.
Souvenons nous d'eux dans nos prières!
[At this place on Saturday night, 8th May 1915
The 2nd Royal Munster Fusiliers
Commanded by Lieutenant Colonel Victor Rickard
Received from their chaplain the Rev. Father Gleeson ·
A final absolution
Before entering the battle of Aubers Ridge
where Colonel Rickard found his death with a large number of his men.
Let us remember them in our prayers!]

Michel Knockaert tracked down the descendants of the Leroy-Pottier family and found that they had kept all the artefacts, including a statue of the Virgin Mary, a crucifix and, most importantly of all, the plaque given to the family.

He had now established the whereabouts of the lost chapel. The small, narrow-gabled, brick chapel destroyed when the road was realigned was beside the site of the original chapel.[21] The bend the council had straightened out was now a lay-by. Behind it was a council yard for sand and gravel. Nevertheless, Knockaert's discovery elicited a lot of emotion in people who had been following his quest. 'Living in Australia, so far from the scene of this event, I can still feel the emotion you must have felt,' one wrote on the *Great War Forum* thread. 'It's amazing how we can all feel about a field!! People probably just pass by – not knowing the significance of it!!'[22]

Knockaert had rediscovered the place where the Munsters had reposed before spending a fretful night in the trenches. The original painting of the *Last General Absolution* disappeared during the Second World War. According to the Imperial War Museum, it was destroyed in the London Blitz, along with many other paintings held by the *Illustrated London News* and other publications.

On 8 May 2015, 100 years later to the day, the commune of Richebourg and the Royal Munster Fusiliers Association unveiled a roadside marker marking the exact site. The sign was the result of many years of patient negotiation.

Adrian Foley, a bandsman with the Irish army and a member of the Royal Munster Fusiliers Association, played the 'Last Post'. The Mayor of Richebourg Gérard Delahaye broke into 'La Marseillaise'. The French joined in. The Irish hummed the tune. It brought an end to the years of searching for this moment of spiritual grace in an inhuman war. The Rue du Bois has been a long road for all concerned.

SGT. WILLIAM MALONE

No. 7522 2nd. Bn., Royal Dublin Fusiliers,
One of many who died in the attack here at
Mouse Trap Farm, may 24th 1915.
On behalf of his wife Rose, sons Brian and John.

Willie Malone Kilmainham Art Foundry Dublin 2002

9

BROTHERS IN ARMS:

THE BRONZE PLAQUE AT MOUSE TRAP FARM

In the spring of 1915, Dublin was a city in shock. Black crêpe hung on doors, churches were full of the broken-hearted, the casualty lists published in the newspapers grew ever longer. Everyone knew someone who had lost someone.

'Dublin was full of mourning, and in the faces one met there was a hard brightness of pain as though the people's hearts burnt in the fire,' observed the writer Katharine Tynan of the succession of military disasters which befell the city in 1915.[1] In the space of a single calendar month, between 24 April and 24 May, hundreds of the Royal Dublin Fusiliers were slaughtered. These were the regular soldiers, working-class lads for the most part, for whom soldiering was the best chance of stable employment and adventure.[2]

The deaths hit the poorest parts of the city hardest. The inner-city areas, immediately north and south of the River Liffey, with their densely packed tenements, were hit hardest of all. Dublin had some of the worst slums in Europe. The harshness of army life was a comfort by comparison.

The theatres of war could hardly be more different – the narrow beaches, bluffs, steep cliffs and parched landscape of Gallipoli in Turkey and the soggy flatlands of Flanders – but the outcome was the same. Faraway places delivered death on an unprecedented scale to the streets of Dublin.

When the First World War broke out, the 1st Battalion of the Royal Dublin Fusiliers returned from India. It had been stationed at Fort St George in Madras.

The colonial battalions, which also included the 1st Royal Munster Fusiliers and the 1st Royal Inniskilling Fusiliers, were cobbled together into a 29th Division to be dispatched to the Eastern Front and to Gallipoli, Winston Churchill's folly. The attempt to take the peninsula and force a passage through to Constantinople was one of the greatest military disasters in history.

The Munsters and Dublins were cast adrift figuratively and literally on the southernmost tip of Gallipoli, V Beach, during the landings of 25 April 1915. Three companies of the 1st Dublins, some 750 men in total, were dispatched to the beaches in rowing boats and lighters. The boats drifted broadside into the path of the Turkish defenders, who poured a murderous hail of machine gun fire and artillery down on them. Helpless and prone, many of these men did not reach the shore alive. At the other end of V Beach, a single company of the 1st Dublins found themselves in the SS *River Clyde*, a converted collier turned Trojan horse turned coffin ship. Many of the 2,100 men on board did not reach the shore either. They were shot down as they emerged from the sally ports cut out of the sides of the ship.

In just two days of fighting, the 1st Battalion of the Royal Dublin Fusiliers suffered some 600 casualties, including nearly all its officers. Only eleven men in the battalion that landed in Gallipoli in April 1915 would leave it without having been killed, wounded or captured.[3]

The Royal Munster Fusiliers suffered similar losses in Gallipoli. Such were their collective losses that the two Irish battalions were merged for a short time to form the Dubsters. The losses of the Dublins would be compounded during the assault on Suvla Bay in August 1915, when the 6th and 7th battalions took a pounding. The 7th Royal Dublin Fusiliers included the celebrated D Company, which was drawn from the middle classes of Dublin and would become known as the 'Pals at Gallipoli'. The well-off now felt the same pain as the working classes.

While the 1st Battalion died on the sands of Gallipoli, the 2nd was engaged in its own terrifying struggle a thousand miles away in Flanders. On 22 April 1915, the Germans launched the Second Battle of Ypres in an attempt to take the town and the salient around it from the Allies.

When the Western Front solidified in late 1914, the Ypres salient was an aberration on a 450-mile front that ran for the most part in straight lines from the Belgian coast to the Swiss border.

A small contingent of Germans entered Ypres on 12 October to acquire provisions. They left without taking the town and never returned. Ypres was strategically important. It became symbolically important too, the Verdun of the British army, a symbol of absolute determination to be held at all cost. It was the only significant town in Belgium still in Allied hands. Behind it, just 30 miles to the south-west, were the channel ports of Dunkirk and Calais.

The Germans were blocked from making a coastal advance when the Belgians flooded the polders they had spent centuries reclaiming from the North Sea. The opening of the sluice gates on the River Izer stopped the Germans more assuredly than any army could have.

The British held Ypres, but also the semi-circle of ridges which surrounded it. Of no great significance geographically, militarily Passchendaele, Messines, Frezenberg, Gravenstafel and Bellewaerde ridges would become places of dread.

The Allies concluded that the town of Ypres could not be held without holding all or some of the high ground around it. To do otherwise would leave them open to observation and shelling by the enemy.

There were some who did not agree. General Horace Smith-Dorrien was the hero of Le Cateau in August 1914. His rearguard action then saved the British Expeditionary Force from disaster, but his suggestion that the salient should be abandoned and a more defendable line established on the outskirts of the town was rejected by British commanders and he resigned.[4]

The Germans regarded the salient as an affront to their ambitions and wanted to take Ypres, but at minimum cost to themselves and a maximum cost to the enemy.

German commander Erich von Falkenhayn had just six corps for the job, approximately 200,000 men in total, less than was deemed adequate to take a place that was so heavily defended. The Germans had another compelling reason for launching an assault in April 1915. They had recently moved the 11th Army, compromising of ten divisions, to the Eastern Front to participate in the successful Gorlice-Tarnów offensive against the Russians in modern-day Poland.

They wished to disguise their troop movements by launching an offensive to keep their western foes busy.

The Germans had come close to taking Ypres during the First Battle of Ypres in October and November 1914. This was a particularly brutal encounter characterised by desperate rearguard actions by numerically inferior French and British troops. The British often fought on with no support. The thin line of Tommies held, but at an awful cost. The First Battle of Ypres broke the regular British army. The old sweats who marched off to war in August 1914, veterans of colonial adventures, professional soldiers and reservists, rough diamonds and toffs alike, were broken men from broken battalions by the time the First Battle of Ypres was over.

The battle had been a terrible experience for the German army too. Tens of thousands of raw recruits, eager students plucked from their tranquil lives, were fed into the maelstrom of a vicious battle by callous generals who believed one more great sacrifice would achieve the necessary breakthrough. Frequently they advanced in line with only enthusiasm, patriotism and a little training. Courage was no match for the cold steel of accurate British rifle and machine gun fire.

The Germans called it 'Kindermord' (the murder of the children). That legacy is remembered in Langemark Cemetery outside Ypres. A spectral place, with its dun-coloured wooden panels and skeletal figures, it bears testimony to the terrible losses the Germans suffered in this battle. One of those who fought at Ypres and witnessed the slaughter was an Austrian living in Munich named Private Adolf Hitler. In Mein Kampf, he wrote, 'There in October and November 1914, we had received our baptism of fire. With the love for the Fatherland in our hearts and with songs on our lips, our young regiment had marched into battle as to a dance. For under it there slumbered the best comrades, almost children still, who once with beaming eyes had run into the arms of death for the only and dear Fatherland.'[5]

Germany had no inclination to throw away lives so cheaply again. They had no excess of men this time around, so they turned to another weapon, one so taboo that it was banned under international law – poison gas. The man tasked with developing this weapon for the German army was Fritz Haber, one of the most important German scientists of the twentieth century. He won the Nobel Prize for Chemistry in 1919 for the synthetisation of ammonia, a process which took nitrogen, the most abundant element in the Earth's atmosphere, and turned it into artificial fertilisers and explosives.

Haber believed Germany must do all it could, by fair means or foul, to win the war. He rationalised that poison gas would shorten it and save lives on both sides, however much it would be condemned initially. The same rationale of 'casualties now, peace later' was used to justify the dropping of the atomic bombs at Hiroshima and Nagasaki.

Haber would lose his good reputation as a scientist, despite winning the Nobel Prize, and his wife Clara, also a scientist, who could not bear the shame that her husband had inflicted on his reputation and that of his country by facilitating the use of poison gas. She killed herself just a fortnight after the first gas attack at Ypres. Haber was born Jewish, but converted to Protestantism. Neither his patriotism nor his Protestantism would save him from the Nazis. It was bitterly ironic that this uber-patriot was driven out of Germany when the Nazis took power in 1933.[6]

Haber's invention of synthesised ammonia allowed Germany to stay in the war much longer than it could have expected. It lessened the effects of the Allied blockade, which cut Germany off from its leading fertiliser markets in South America. Additionally, synthesised ammonia allowed the Germans to manufacture as much explosives as it needed. Haber's discovery was one of the scientific finds of the century. A 2008 paper in *Nature Geoscience* estimated that without Haber's discovery, the Earth could only sustain 3.5 billion people.[7]

Taking life, though, rather than sustaining it, was Haber's goal when in April 1915 the Germans moved 5,700 small and large steel cylinders to the Ypres front. The gas would be released from pressurised cylinders and carried by the wind into the opposing trenches.

Unfortunately, for the Germans attacking at Ypres, their front was the wrong way round for the prevailing winds, which are south-westerly in Belgium. The Germans identified the extreme north-east section of the Ypres salient manned by French colonial troops as the weakest link, but they needed a north-easterly wind to carry the gas across. At 5 p.m. on the evening of 22 April, the Germans finally released chlorine gas into the French lines. The impact was felt immediately. The dense, yellowish gas caused panic in the ranks of French and Algerian troops. The gas initially had the desired effect. The Germans didn't have to take the trenches with heavy loss of life; the French simply abandoned them.[8]

They had no protection against this infernal weapon. The faces of the dead men 'turned a sort of saffron-yellow which after a time changed to purplish blue'.[9] Chlorine gas turned to hydrochloric acid in the lungs. It was a terrible, slow death – men effectively suffocated from the effects of gas. The experience has been described as 'drowning on dry land'.

Within an hour of the gas being released, the Germans had penetrated 3,000 yards on an 8,000-yard front. A gap had opened up between the British and the French. The shock of these actions were profound. The use of poison gas was not only forbidden but also regarded by most military commanders as a blunt and counterproductive weapon that was dependent on the capricious nature of whatever breeze was blowing. The gas was only effective at a forward wind speed of between 6-8mph. Any slower and the gas tended to linger; any faster and it tended to break up. If the wind changed direction, it became a menace to the attacker as much as the defender.

Both the French and British were warned that a gas attack was imminent by a German deserter Private August Jager, who told his French interrogators that only unfavourable winds had thwarted previous attacks. The Germans had distributed

20,000 mouth protectors to their own troops and believed they now had the means to make the breakthrough they sought.

Still the French and British commands did not believe him. Jager's testimony was too detailed and therefore too convincing. He must be a decoy sent to spread confusion and fear in the Allied ranks, they reasoned. Though gas is intimately associated with the First World War now, it was then a new weapon. It had been used on the Eastern Front in January 1915, but the gas sublimated in the freezing air and was useless.[10]

Some German generals were queasy about its use. 'The mission of poisoning the enemy as one would rats affected me as it would any straightforward soldier – I was disgusted,' wrote General Bernard von Deimling, the commander of the XV Corps charged with following up the gas attack at Ypres.[11]

The breakthrough would have been complete had the Germans made a more comprehensive attack, but they failed to release gas on the Canadians on one flank and the Belgians, defending the last few square miles of their own territory, on the other. The long delay that meant the gas was not released until the evening was also critical. German infantry might have pushed on for Ypres but the gathering dusk inhibited further attacks.

Nevertheless, the Germans had taken command of seven bridges across the canal and the situation was grave. The next phase was the Battle of Saint Julien, the village north-east of Ypres. Before the battle started, it was comfortably behind Allied lines and occupied by the Canadians in their first major encounter of the war. The Germans drove the Canadians out in heavy fighting, creating a breach in the lines.

The Canadians proved to be magnificent soldiers. On the evening of 22 April, they staged a midnight attack through Kitcheners' Wood near Saint Julien and drove the Germans out with the points of their bayonets. This one near-suicidal operation was described by Ferdinand Foch, Supreme Allied Commander, as the single 'greatest act of the war'.[12]

As its sister battalion, the 1st Battalion of the Royal Dublin Fusiliers, was sailing to the shores of Gallipoli, the 2nd Battalion left its comfortable billets in Bailleul, across the border in France, to march north-east of Ypres to fill the emerging gap in the Allied lines and to aid the Canadians in their struggle. The Royal Dublin Fusiliers was part of 10th Brigade and the 4th Division of the British army.

It took the Dublins twenty-four hours, resting overnight, to reach Ypres on the evening of 24 April. At midnight, they marched again, this time in the direction of St Julien, with orders to take the village back from the Germans. The march was 30 miles in total and the men were carrying heavy packs and rifles. They had barely slept. Now they were expected to charge heavily fortified positions.

'It was a desperately difficult undertaking,' wrote the historian of the Royal Dublin Fusiliers, Colonel H.C. Wylly, in his book *Crown and Company*. 'The night was extremely dark, the ground, which had not been reconnoitred, was honeycombed with trenches and strewn with barbed wire, and, moreover, the artillery had not been able to "register" – that is to say, gets it range of the terrain.'[13]

The 2nd Dublins, along with the 1st Royal Irish Fusiliers, counter-attacked the German positions. The Dublins and the Faughs (as the Fusiliers were known) suffered heavy casualties from German machine-gunners in the village. 'If proof were wanted as regards the direction of the attack, it would be the lines of dead Irish Fusiliers who lay east and west just south of St Julien,' one eyewitness recalled years later.[14] The air was 'thick with bullets' and the German heavy guns in the rear 'spouted a continual torrent of shells over the fields through which the assault was delivered'.[15]

The two Irish regiments were assailed by machine gun fire in front and from an occupied farm behind. Snipers in the fields took their toll too. The British official history departs from its usual measured tone to lament the carnage:

> A few men tried to crawl back into cover, but the majority of those in the lead-ing lines never returned; mown down, like corn, by machine guns in enfilade, they remained lying in rows where they had fallen.[16]

The attempt to take back St Julien effectively lasted twenty minutes. The men of 10th Brigade were brave and resolute but they did not stand a chance. The Germans had chosen their ground well. The losses of 10th Brigade were catastrophic: some 73 officers and 2,346 other ranks in a failed assault. Lieutenant Walter Critchley of the 10th Canadians could see the attack breaking down on his right flank. 'The Huns opened up on them with machine guns. They were just raked down.'[17] Of the 405 Dublins who died during the Second Battle of Ypres, some 137 died during the charge on St Julien.

After the battle, the Dublins took up positions near Van Heule Farm in the vicin-ity of St Julien. Even when withdrawn from the line, they suffered severe shelling. Three times they were deployed in the front line, ready to attack, and three times the attacks were called off because of punishing German machine gun fire.

On 18 May, they moved into trenches in front of Shell Trap Farm, north-east of Ypres, 500 yards from the outskirts of St Julien. The British were queasy about the moniker they put on this exposed farmhouse and changed it to the less sinister-sounding Mouse Trap Farm.

On 22 and 23 May, the Irish noticed reconnaissance aircraft overhead. A lot had changed even in the month since the first gas attack. The men in the front line had been given makeshift respirators with a damp solution to lessen the effects of the gas.

At 2.45 a.m. on the morning of 24 May, four flares were released from the German lines. The flares were accompanied by the hiss of gas from canisters, some of them only 30 yards away. It was the middle of the night, but the men were awake, anxiously awaiting the attack. Hurriedly, they put on their respirators. The gas rolled over their lines, turning everything living in its path – grass, hedges and trees – to withered entrails. The men were prepared for it, but could do little about the German infantry in its wake. Under cover of the deadly fog, German infantry were quickly on top of the Dublins, bayoneting and shooting as they went.

The Germans captured Mouse Trap Farm and the Royal Irish Regiment trenches to the left of the Royal Dublin Fusiliers. The Germans worked their way around to the right. The Dublins fought back and held on until all hope was gone. Commanding officer Lieutenant-Colonel Arthur Loveband from Naas, County Kildare, called on the 9th Argyll and Sutherland Highlanders to the rear to come and reclaim Mouse Trap Farm. The Highlanders went in the wrong direction. Loveband then sent a message back to headquarters which was wondrously restrained in its understatement. 'Reinforcements are required. Situation not satisfactory.' Shortly afterwards, he was struck by a bullet from behind, possibly friendly fire, and died immediately.

Command of the battalion passed to Captain Basil Maclear, the commanding officer of A Company. Maclear was 34 and a Boer War veteran. An Englishman who joined the Royal Dublin Fusiliers after graduating from Sandhurst, he played international rugby eleven times for Ireland while stationed in Cork. He was, according to *The Irish Times*, a man of 'outstanding football genius'.[18]

In 1906, he scored a wonder try against South Africa. 'In all his matches Captain Maclear displayed remarkable dash and his magnificent pace, deadly tackling and promptitude in availing of opportunities always constituted a strong asset to the side,' the paper reported.

Maclear was killed leading a bombing party to thwart the enemy.

At every turn, the Royal Dublin Fusiliers were assailed by impossible odds. The situation became ever more desperate. The German gas attack covered nearly 5 miles of front – the largest attack of the war to date. Each battalion was engaged in its own struggle for survival, making it impossible to reinforce the Dublins. Another officer, Second-Lieutenant Robert James Kempston, sent an urgent message to headquarters. 'For God's sake send us some help, we are nearly done.' He too died that day.[19]

Captain Thomas Leahy, the only officer to survive Mouse Trap Farm unscathed, remembered afterwards, 'When the wounded were sent away after dark there were no Dublins in front of battalion headquarters from about 2.30pm. Everyone held on to them to the last. There was no surrender, no retirement and no quarter was given or accepted. They all died fighting at their posts.'

The battalion strength at the start of the action was 17 officers and 651 other ranks. All that was left that evening was one officer and twenty other ranks. Rarely, in this most terrible of wars, was such a devastating loss visited on a single battalion in a single day.

Four days after the catastrophe, what remained of the battalion was visited by Lieutenant-General Sir William Pulteney, who was commanding III Corps. It was a melancholy sight. He gave them what encouragement he could muster. The men should 'console themselves with the knowledge that those who had gone had done their job'. In the grim, zero-sum game of attrition, he may have had a point. The Germans called off the Second Battle of Ypres the following day. They too were bleeding and exhausted.

Some 143 Dublins died at Mouse Trap Farm. For the most part, they lie buried where they fell in the fields of Flanders. Their bodies were never found. The lamentable roll call of the dead can be found instead on the New Menin Gate in Ypres.

Between 24 April and 24 May, the battalion sustained 1,500 casualties more than its total strength of 1,027. As men fell, others took their place.

Sergeant William Malone from the South Circular Road in Dublin died at Mouse Trap Farm. He was 36, married and had two young children, Brian and John. Malone was born in 1880. He was already in the part-time Dublin City Artillery militia and listed his occupation as labourer when he joined the Royal Dublin Fusiliers at the age of 19 in 1901. He joined at a time of quietude in the fractious relationship between Ireland and Britain. An Irishman then joining the British army was not considered to be engaging in a political act.

Like many men of his time, Malone was short (5ft 6in) and weighed just over 8 stone when he enlisted in the Royal Dublin Fusiliers on 26 July 1901 as Private No. 7522.[20] His early years in the army would appear to have been troubled. In 1903, he spent time in jail for stealing a pair of boots. The incident clearly retarded his career in the army and he had to wait seven years to be appointed to the lowest rank of non-commissioned officer – lance corporal.

He saw service in Malta, Egypt and in Sudan, where he was involved in putting down the short-lived Blue Nile Province Rebellion in May 1908. The rebellion was fomented by a man named Abdul-Kader who thought of himself as Jesus and was involved in the murder of two colonial officials. Abdul-Kader was hanged. While in Sudan, Malone also trained in Camel Corps duties.

In February 1912, he married Rose Cox from County Meath. Their first child, Brian, was born in August 1912 and John came along in April 1914. Neither would remember their father.

William Malone was shipped to France with the rest of his battalion in late August 1914. The trials of war visited the 2nd Royal Dublin Fusiliers as they did all the other battalions of the old British army.

On 27 August, Malone's battalion was involved in the surrender at St Quentin during the retreat from Mons. Things got no easier for the battalion. After the Battles of the Marne and the Aisne, the battalion's last major engagement before the Second Battle of Ypres was during the Battle of Armentières in October and November 1914, in filthy, mud-clogged conditions.

For men like William Malone, there would no respite from the fighting other than death, injury or being taken as a prisoner of war.

A week before the first Christmas of the war, Malone wrote home to his wife. He thanked her for the long letter she had written him and enclosed £2:

I hope you will get it in time for Christmas. I spoke to the adjt [adjutant] about the allotment showing him the answer you got from the pay office and he says he will see about it. Dearest Rosie if anything happens to me, see that you get all the pay I am entitled to. I only got 18 francs since I came to the country and I should be lots in credit. But I hope in God I will have the pleasure of spending some of it with you. I wish the censor was done away with until I wrote a good long letter to you, but I have to pick and choose my words. I was delighted with one part of your letter what you underlined and about Bardie. I am sure he is a great pet. Did he take to your mother and Nell? … Dear Rose you might write a long letter to me like the last one as soon as possible and don't forget the photo. I asked for a new one of yourself and babies. It will be the next best thing to seeing you. Goodbye dear for the present. Wishing yourself, Bardie, Jackie and Dad a very happy Christmas, a bright and prosperous New Year and hoping to be with you soon. Fondest and best wishes, Love from Willie xxxxx[21]

In April 1915, Malone was promoted to the rank of corporal and then on 9 May, 1915, just two weeks before he died, to sergeant. In the terrible aftermath of the incident at Mouse Trap Farm, his terrified widow did not know if he was alive or dead. On hearing that most of the men taken prisoner were sent to Limburg prisoner-of-war camp, she wrote to the most senior Royal Dublin Fusiliers officer there, Sergeant T. (Thomas) W. (Wardrop) Byrne in August 1915 and he wrote back a month later with devastating news:

> I regret very much having to inform you of the very sad news re your husband the late Sergt. Malone. He was killed in the trenches at St Julien, Ypres, on the 24th of May. I obtained the information from the men who were captured on the same day, who were in the same trench and saw him hit by shrapnel. He died immediately. The men were captured in the trench. I am very sorry having to inform you of the same news. You have my deepest sympathy.

Almost a year later, on 6 May 1916, Rose Malone placed a notice in the *Irish Independent*:

> In sad and loving memory of my dear husband Sgt William Malone, 2nd Royal Dublin Fusiliers, who was killed in action at St Julien on May 24th, 1915. Sweet Heart of Jesus have mercy on his soul. Inserted by his loving wife and children.[22]

Just ten days earlier her brother-in-law Michael Malone had died a violent death fighting against the same army in Dublin his brother had died fighting for in Flanders. The Malones would go on to become a well-known nationalist family. Michael

Malone's sisters Áine and Bridget were both members of Cumann na mBan. Michael and William Malone's mother Mary provided safe houses during Easter Week 1916 and the War of Independence. She would eventually get a pension from the State.

In one notorious dispatch from the Office of the Director of Intelligence in 1925, the Minister for Defence was advised that the Malones were a 'whole family tainted by irregularism'.[23]

Michael Malone, who was 28 when the Easter Rising broke out, was a committed nationalist. A carpenter by trade, he joined the Irish Volunteers' Cyclist Corps. He was a member of the St Patrick's Branch of the Gaelic League in Ringsend. He was 'a fine, well built young man with good features, serious minded but with an excellent sense of humour, but when occasion arose could be a very strict disciplinarian', according to his comrade-in-arms Seamus Grace.[24]

On the morning of Easter Monday, Michael Malone and the other members of C Company, 3rd Battalion of the Irish Volunteers assembled at Earlsfort Terrace and at 11 a.m. marched to Upper Mount Street.

With him was Grace, who had joined the Irish Republican Brotherhood in 1912. He had gone to America and then to Canada to get weapons training.

Malone, Grace and two youngsters, Paddy Rowe and Michael Byrne, smashed the lock and occupied 25 Northumberland Road, an imposing three-storey house at the junction of Haddington Road and Northumberland Road. The house was chosen carefully because it was positioned on the road to Mount Street Bridge some 300 yards to the north and to the left of Beggars Bush barracks. The Irish Volunteers, who were under the command of Éamon de Valera at Boland's Mills, set themselves up well. They also occupied Clanwilliam House, which overlooked the bridge and the schoolhouse, which is today a restaurant.

No. 25 Northumberland Road is much as it was in 1916. The family who owned it, the Cussens, had already vacated it when Malone and his small band arrived. On Easter Monday, Grace and Malone opened fire on a party of elderly volunteer soldiers known as 'Georgius Rex', an auxiliary militia and the Irish equivalent of Dad's Army. They were known to the people of Dublin as the 'gorgeous wrecks'. Malone and Grace killed several of them, including Francis Browning, the president of the Irish Rugby Football Union. Browning had recruited hundreds of middle-class Irish rugby players to the British cause, most notably to the 7th Royal Dublin Fusiliers. Many died at the landings in Suvla Bay in August 1915.

On the Tuesday of Easter Week, Seamus Grace had a lucky escape when he poked his head out the window and a sniper took his cap off. The Rising was only thirty-six hours old when Michael Malone concluded they had no hope of winning.[25] The countermanding order signed by Eoin MacNeill, the commander of the Irish Volunteers, had caused confusion in the ranks and severely depleted the numbers participating in the Rising. In addition, the failure of the German arms to reach their destination after Roger Casement's *Aud* was intercepted led him to the logical conclusion that their stand had no chance of military success.

Accordingly, he sent away Paddy Rowe and Michael Byrne, both under 16, who had been barricaded into the house with them. Both left unwillingly.[26]

Having seen the hopelessness of the situation, Michael Malone nevertheless resolved that he and Grace would do their duty. On Wednesday, 26 April, Malone and Grace were told by some women delivering food that 500 British soldiers had arrived in Kingstown. 'This is it,' Grace told Malone. 'Yes,' Malone replied. 'This is it.' Grace recounted to the Bureau of Military History decades afterwards, 'We would have to make our stand where we stood for the khaki clad figures were approaching',

Michael Malone took up position on the third-floor window, Grace on the floor underneath. As the Sherwood Foresters marched from Kingstown into the city centre, the two men ambushed them. Malone used a Mauser C36 pistol, a semi-automatic weapon capable of great accuracy known as 'Peter the Painter'. It was part of the consignment of guns the Irish Volunteers had smuggled into Howth in July 1914. Malone's prowess with a gun had seen him rise rapidly through the ranks of the Irish Volunteers.

Grace had a Lee-Enfield .303, a rifle used to great effect in the First World War by the British and now used against them during the Easter Rising.

One of the first to die was Captain Frederick Dietrichsen, a 33-year-old barrister who had every expectation of a comfortable middle-class existence in Nottingham, where he practised.[27] His wife Beatrice Mitchell was a middle-class Dublin unionist. The couple had two young children. He could have been excused service, but he signed up to the British army. He was commissioned in November 1914 and promoted to temporary captain in October 1915.

He thought his wife and two children were in England with her sister. She thought he was in France. By a remarkable coincidence the couple met each other on the fateful march into Dublin from Kingstown. Dietrichsen, of Danish extraction, abandoned his soldierly bearing and embraced his wife and children, aged 2 and 5, in Kingstown. Hours later he was dead. Those not caught by Grace and Malone were shot by men operating from Clanwilliam House and the schoolhouse.

The Tommies were bewildered, unable to locate the source of the volleys, and their casualties grew. Soon, however, they had possession of almost every house within point-blank range.

In his statement to the Bureau of Military History given thirty-three years after the Rising, Grace could recall vividly the sense of fear he and Malone felt as the British rallied, despite the terrible casualties they had endured:

> Do not believe any person who tells you he does not know what fear is because there were moments from about 5.30 onwards when the fire was so intense that I could not reply, that I trembled from head to foot in a panic of fear and it was only when I was able to reply to the fire that I could overcome the fear.

Grace had taken up position on the hall floor. The crashing of glass signalled that the British had broken through the back door. Grace emptied out his clip into the soldiers as they crossed the threshold.[28]

Malone bravely rushed down the stairs to confront the British as they entered the house. 'There was a crash of a volley from above and afterwards I heard a few shouting, "get him, get him" and it was in that volley that Michael Malone died,' Grace remembered. Malone's body was taken into the grounds of 25 Northumberland Road and Fr Wall from Haddington Road church performed the last rites.

Alone now, Grace retreated to the cellar and fired at an officer at the front door. He continued firing from his automatic pistol, which became so hot that he had to regularly douse it in cold water. He took cover behind a gas stove.

That evening, as the British were assembled for a bayonet charge in the direction of Mount Street Bridge, Grace made an audacious escape out a cellar window. For the next two days, he hid behind enemy lines, hungry and thirsty. He fired on patrols at night.

He took shelter in a shed at the rear of 50 Haddington Road and was discovered by a servant girl. A neighbour five doors down reported his presence. Within minutes, Grace was surrounded by a posse of British soldiers numbering twenty-five in total. They took everything from him, 'even my rosary beads'. He had been four days and four nights without food or drink. Grace was sent to Frongoch prison camp, but was released on Christmas Day 1916, along with hundreds of other Republican prisoners.

Together, the seventeen volunteers engaged in the action at Mount Street Bridge had exacted a toll on their enemy. The volunteers lost four men, including Malone. The British were left with 220 men killed or wounded. It was the worst day of the Rising for the British. The men who died were, for the most part, raw recruits and volunteer soldiers with little training. They expected to fight in France or Belgium against Germany. They had not expected to be engaged in what many British regarded as a civil war.

When Grace returned to Ireland, Michael Malone had still not been buried. Grace was called upon to identify the body. 'I had a last glimpse of my leader and comrade in his blood-stained olive green uniform. Micheál and Sean Cullen of Boland's Garrison and myself fired three volleys over his grave in salute of one of Ireland's most faithful sons – a loyal comrade, a gallant leader, a brave and fearless soldier. *Ar dheis Dé go raibh a anam.*'[29]

A year after the Rising, Éamon de Valera wrote to Michael Malone's mother Mary from Lewes jail, where he was imprisoned after the Rising. She had sent him shamrock for St Patrick's Day:

What gift could be so affecting as that of a box of shamrocks from an Irish mother on behalf of her patriot son, to a comrade whose duty it was to bid him take that post, in the defence of which he so gloriously fell. No wonder that Ireland is still unconquered ... Michael did deeds which will be on record for ever – accomplished in a few hours what other men fail to accomplish in a life full of years. This Easter from his place in paradise he sees us still struggling through this valley of tears. His fate is one for envy not sorrow.

The paradox of Irish history, with families and individuals divided for and against British rule, was manifest in the Malones and in so many other Irish families.

Had fate ordained otherwise, Michael and William Malone might have ended up fighting against each other on the streets of Dublin.

One of the first British officers to die during the Easter Rising was Lieutenant Gerald Neilan from Ballygalda, County Roscommon. He was commanding a platoon of the 10th Royal Dublin Fusiliers on the first day of the Rising when he was shot and killed on Ellis Quay by rebels who had occupied the Mendicity Institute. The soldier and writer Stephen Gwynn recorded in his book *John Redmond's Last Years* that Neilan was 'strongly nationalist in his sympathies'.

His brother Arthur Neilan joined the Irish Volunteers at the age of 18 and took part in the Rising three years later. He was part of the Four Courts garrison under Ned Daly. Arthur Neilan was arrested after the Rising and released under amnesty in 1917.[30] He served with the 4th Battalion of the Dublin Brigade in the War of Independence, but was pro-Treaty during the Irish Civil War and remained with the national army. He died in 1944 and is buried in the same plot as his brother in Glasnevin Cemetery.[31]

Éamonn Ceannt was one of the executed leaders of the 1916 Rising. His brother William Kent rose to be a sergeant-major in the Royal Dublin Fusiliers and was killed at the Battle of Arras in 1917.

Some of the leaders of the Easter Rising had seen service in the British army. Connolly faked his age to join up when he was 14 and served for seven years. Born and brought up in Edinburgh, he was mostly stationed in Ireland, where his social radicalism developed. He was barely a man when he left at the age of 21.

His fellow Citizen Army volunteer Michael Mallin spent fourteen years in the British army. He was 15 when he joined the Royal Scots Fusiliers as a drummer boy. He served in India for six years, where his experiences putting down insurgent tribes on the north-west frontier fomented his anti-colonial views. Prophetically, he wrote home to his parents that he wished 'it was for Erin that I was fighting and not against these poor people'. He left the British army in 1902, shortly after William Malone had joined it.[32]

By the time of the Easter Rising, the Malones were a determinedly nationalist family despite William Malone's sacrifices for king and country.

Other members of the Malone family were also involved in the Rising. Anne Malone, who gaelisised her name to Aine Malone joined Cumann na mBan, the women's equivalent of the IRA. She married Theobold Wolfe Tone Fitzgerald, the man who painted the Irish Republic flag which flew over the GPO. She was injured on the Monday of Easter Week while carrying a dispatch to Jacob's biscuit factory. A bullet lodged in her hip. She claimed years afterwards that the injury prevented her from taking up employment as a seamstress.[33]

Anne, who would later gaelicise her name to Áine, allowed her home to be used as a safe house and a place to store guns.

During the War of Independence, Dan Breen was one of eleven IRA men who attempted to assassinate the British Lord Lieutenant Viscount French in December of that year.

Breen, along with his fellow Tipperary man Seán Treacy, had started the War of Independence in January 1919 when they killed two Royal Irish Constabulary men at Soloheadbeg. This act, at first condemned even in nationalist circles, would prompt two and a half years of guerrilla warfare, which would eventually lead to Irish independence.

French had been commander-in-chief of the British army when William Malone died at Ypres. The assassination attempt failed and Breen was injured in the shoot-out which followed. While recuperating, he stayed with Áine Malone and there he met her sister Bridget Malone. She too was an Irish Republican. The pair fell in love and were married eighteen months later, at a time when Breen was the most wanted man in Ireland. He is pictured in his wedding photo grinning mischievously, with a pistol in his hand.

Breen was strongly against the Anglo-Irish Treaty signed in December 1921, which established the Free State but left Ireland partitioned and with the British monarch as head of state. Breen would come to be regarded in his latter years as a patriot, but the new Free State government regarded him as a menace. When Áine Malone applied for compensation for the injuries she received during Easter Week, she was refused.

Not only was the whole family 'tainted with irregularism', according to their file in the Irish Military Pensions Archives, but they were 'antagonistic to the present Government. The mother [Mary Malone] is an intimate friend of De Valera and one of the daughters is married to Dan Breen.' Another brother, Brian Malone, was a 'sympathiser with the irregulars during the Civil War but was not known to have taken an active part himself'.[34]

Another sister, Marie Malone, received a pension many years afterwards because of her brother Michael's service. In her application she did not even mention her brother William by name, referring to him only as 'another brother – also dead'. Mary Malone successfully claimed a gratuity because of Michael Malone's death. She had been dependent on Michael's income. He earned £3 a week as a carpenter and handed it all over to her. Two grants of £100 each were raised to £150 each on request.

In May 1956, just after the fortieth anniversary of the Rising, President Seán T. O'Kelly unveiled a plaque at 25 Northumberland Road to the memory of Michael Malone. Éamon de Valera, who was there, had been Taoiseach for most of the last twenty-five years.

O'Kelly said Malone had given to Ireland 'devoted service, consummated by the sacrifice of his life' and should be remembered by later generations of Irish people because he fought for the 'priceless value of liberty because they never knew its lack'.

In 2002, William Malone's grandson Willie Malone, was commissioned by the Office of Public Works in Ireland to cast some bronze plaques for the Island of Ireland Peace Park in Messines, near Ypres. The plaques in English, Irish, Flemish and French remember the 'thousands of young men from all parts of Ireland who fought a common enemy, defended democracy and the rights of all nations, whose graves are in shockingly uncountable numbers and those who have no graves'. These were dedicated to men like William Malone who had been forgotten in Ireland except in the hearts of those who mourned them.

While he was in Flanders, Willie Malone realised he was close to where his grandfather had died. He had kept his grandfather's death plaque, which was given to the closest relatives of every British soldier who died in the First World War, and also the 'Mons Star' medal as William Malone had been a regular soldier at the time of the outbreak of war.

Willie Malone believes his grandfather joined the British army at a less radical time and because he was the oldest and needed to make his way in the world.

'I kept all the bits and pieces, but families get on with their lives,' he said. 'We were basically a Republican family as everybody seemed to be in the 20s and 30s. When my grandfather joined the British army in 1901 Britain was doing very well and Ireland was coming along nicely as well.'[35]

Through Tom Burke MBE, the chairman of the Royal Dublin Fusiliers Association, he contacted the family that own Mouse Trap Farm and they agreed to allow him to place a small bronze plaque on the wall.

Willie Malone was told when he was growing up that his grandfather had trained the Irish Volunteers in small-arms fire in the Phoenix Park while on leave from the army. 'I hope that's true. I like to think that it was.'[36]

Mouse Trap Farm was rebuilt after the war. It is now a handsome red-brick Flemish farmhouse with outhouses where pigs are kept and the fertile soil yields up bountiful harvests of wheat, sugar beet, green beans and occasionally, still, the rusted detritus of war. From the farmhouse you can see the twin spires of Ypres Cathedral and the Cloth Hall in the distance. So near and yet so far.

The tiny bronze plaque on the wall of Mouse Trap Farm reads, 'Sgt William Malone: No. 7522. Bn., Royal Dublin Fusiliers. One of many who died in the attack here at Mouse Trap Farm, May 24th 1915. On behalf of his wife Rose, sons Brian and John. Willie Malone, Kilmainham Art Foundry Dublin 2005.'

10

THE GRAVE OF
JOHN CONDON

Among the rows of war dead at Poelcapelle military cemetery in Flanders, there is one grave which is usually a riot of colour set against the surrounding neat white slabs. John Condon's last resting place beside a dahlia tree, next to the far wall of the cemetery, is one of the most visited graves on the Western Front.

So many graves in this cemetery are forlorn reminders of forgotten men who are unnamed and unremembered. Condon's is unmistakable. All year round it is festooned with poppy crosses, flowers, wreaths, the occasional Irish tricolour and small denomination coins which are placed on the top of the headstone.

One holiday company operates five coach tours a week to Poelcapelle Cemetery.[1] His grave is especially popular with schoolchildren from the UK, Belgium and the Netherlands. They are asked to pause and think about a young man, a teenager like themselves, who handled a gun before he handled a razor blade and died when he was just 14.

There is no lowly British soldier better known from the First World War than Private John Condon, No. 6322, of the 2nd Royal Irish Regiment, buried in grave LVI F8.

The Commonwealth War Graves Commission has decreed that of the 888,246 British servicemen and women who died in the First World War, John Condon was the youngest of all.[2]

He has been the subject of a novel (*Age 14 – An Irish Boy Soldier* by the Flemish writer Geert Spillebeen); a play (*Boy Soldier* produced by the Waterford-based Red Kettle Theatre Company); at least one song ('John Condon',[3] recorded many times by folk singers); a documentary (on RTÉ's *Nationwide*); and poems in English and Flemish.

A memorial in his honour was erected in Waterford, his home town, almost 100 years after his death: the memorial is a bronze, tapered cylindrical vessel with a hollowed-out chamber and it is located in Cathedral Square. It is designed to resemble an explosive shell, but the motifs are traditionally Celtic.

Death may be the great leveller, but during the First World War the deaths of officers and men were recorded separately: officers first, then all the 'men' grouped together. The names of officers who died were recorded in local and national newspapers and on the walls of churches and local memorials. Privates, usually uneducated and unconnected, were accorded no such distinction. It makes the attention lavished on John Condon unique and remarkable.

If John Condon was not buried in Poelcapelle Cemetery 6 miles north-east of Ypres, few people would visit. There are 137 British war cemeteries in the area, far more than most visitors could possibly go to.

There are 7,479 British and Commonwealth war dead buried here, but only 1,248 are named soldiers, the best known of which is John Condon.[4]

John Condon is the personification of the 'doomed youth' written about by the war poet Wilfred Owen. In 1919, W.B. Yeats wrote his famous apocalyptic vision 'The Second Coming'. Its first verse contains this couplet, 'The blood-dimmed tide is loosed, and everywhere / The ceremony of innocence is drowned.' The great conflagration was no more than a year past when Yeats dreamt up this magnificent poem of cosmic foreboding. Yeats wouldn't have heard of the boy-soldier by then, but Condon was the very epitome of 'the ceremony of innocence drowned'. If the First World War was a theatre of godless cruelty, then Condon came to symbolise our fallen humanity. And if its vast, bloody canvas could be condensed into the image of a single soldier, that soldier would be a chubby-faced Irish child with a rifle.

Yet, almost inevitably, his story is a mixture of fact and mythology. John Condon may well be an accidental icon. He was probably not 14. He may have been 18 – still young, but not remarkably so in the context of the grim demographics of this war. Doubts have surrounded his status as the youngest soldier for decades. If he was really 14, nobody has proved it. His birth certificate lists a John Condon born in Jenkins Lane, Waterford on 16 October 1896. His parents are listed as John and Catherine Condon.[5] Investigators at the In Flanders Fields Museum in Ypres had puzzled over the contradictions in the John Condon story for years. In the 1901 United Kingdom census, he is recorded as being 4 years old.[6] In the 1911 census, he is recorded as being 15,[7] which would make him at least 18, if not 19, in 1915. The Army Overseas Death Certificate records him as being 20 when he died.[8]

He may not even be buried in Poelcappele. It may be his brother Patrick who was killed in the war. Or was there another John Condon born after the first in the same family who died in the fields of Flanders?

All the documentary evidence suggests that John Condon was 18; all the anecdotal evidence suggests he was 14. The Commonwealth War Graves Commission decreed that he was the youngest when his family sent back the Final Verification (FV) form, stating that he was 14.[9] Why would they lie? His cousin Nicholas was so close to John Condon that they were known as the Condon twins. He was convinced John Condon was 14. Why would he lie?

Doubts have surrounded the story for decades, yet these have not diminished the numbers who come to visit his grave, nor the power of his story to inspire. Much of the mystery surrounding John Condon's grave arises from the manner in which his body was discovered in 1923, eight years after he was killed during the Battle of Mouse Trap Farm on 24 May 1915.

The cemetery where John Condon's grave is located was created after the Armistice. The Belgians granted land to the Imperial War Graves Commission to build cemeteries for bodies recovered from the battlefields around Ypres.

When men died during the First World War they were buried where they fell or as close as possible to that place. Some 3 million soldiers who died on the Western Front have no known grave. It is truly an astonishing number. Most men were killed by shelling, their bodies dismembered and scattered. These are unknown soldiers in every language of the combatants, 'unbekannt', 'inconnu' or 'onbekende'.

Corpses were often buried hurriedly by soldiers who were themselves desperately fighting to stay alive. Battlefields turned to mud and bodies shifted in the sodden earth. Soldiers died in shell holes or in underground tunnels. They fell in no man's land and their bodies were left to putrefy in the mire.

The number of missing soldiers is simply staggering. Some 526,816 British and Commonwealth soldiers who died in the war have no known grave. They are simply missing.[10]

The process of battlefield clearance after the war took the best part of the next decade. It was driven by a desire to help as many relatives as possible find somewhere – anywhere – to grieve a soldier whose status could be changed from missing to found. There was also the need to return the injured countryside to its original state.

Hundreds of millions of bullets and shells, rusting and live ordinances, lay in the earth with the remains of millions of men.

Battlefield clearance was a ghastly business carried out by demobbed men (who were paid 2s 6d above the going rate for a soldier), German prisoners of war or Chinese labour gangs. One man involved in battlefield clearance was Private John McCauley, who opted for the Grave Concentration Units rather than return to the front. Though not as dangerous as front-line duties, battlefield clearance came with its own hazards. The ground was treacherous due to unexploded bombs, poisoned waterholes, yielding shell holes and sinkholes. Bodies were often found where the grass was uncommonly thick – human remains had decomposed and acted as fertiliser.

In the autumn of 1918, as the Allies reclaimed battlefields soaked in blood, McCauley was recovering bodies. He found the job unspeakably awful, but hardened to the task. He never could get the images out of his head:

> Often have I picked up the remains of a fine brave man on a shovel. Just a little heap of bones and maggots to be carried to the common burial place. Numerous bodies were found lying submerged in the water in shell holds and mine craters; bodies that seemed quite whole but which became like huge masses of white, slimy chalk when we handled them. I shuddered as my hands, covered in soft flesh and slime, moved about in search of the disc, and I have had to pull bodies to pieces in order that they should not be buried unknown. It was very painful to have to bury the unknown.[11]

It was during one of these battlefield clearances, in July 1923, that the remains of John Condon were recovered. This was his final resting place, a long way from the port town in the south-east of Ireland where he grew up.

John Condon lived in Jenkin's Lane. He was reared in a two-roomed dwelling with his parents, John and Catherine Condon. They had five children: Kate, Peter, Margaret, John and Patrick. John was the second youngest.[12]

Just a few streets away was Ballybricken Green, where many of 'the quality' lived in handsome, three-storey Victorian homes. The same green would be turned into a cattle mart on designated days. Much of what we know about John Condon comes from an account by his cousin Nicholas Condon in the *Waterford News* from 8 July 1938.

According to a report in the *Waterford News*, the *Sunday Express* had reported the story of Rifleman Joe Strudwick of the Rifle Brigade. Strudwick was from Dorking in Surrey and died in January 1916 at the age of 15 years and 11 months. He is buried in Essex Farm Cemetery in Ypres. The *Sunday Express* believed he was the youngest British soldier to die in the war.

The *Waterford News* responded that he was not the youngest. Instead, that 'sad honour' belonged to one of the town's own. 'It is to Private J Condon falls the sad honour of being the youngest British soldier killed in the war.'[13] But far from adding to our store of knowledge about John Condon, the article only reinforces the confusion which has surrounded him ever since.

Nicholas Condon, a veteran of the war and then working as a boot repairer and a veteran of the war, told a story which has baffled his son William, known as 'Sonny' to this day. 'We were playing together, Patrick and I, near the Waterford quays towards the end of 1914,' recalled Nicholas in the 1938 newspaper report. 'Patrick was thirteen years old. I was a few years older. On a sudden impulse we got on board the small steamer SS Clodagh which plied regularly between Waterford and Liverpool.'[14] (The SS *Clodagh* was subsequently renamed the SS *Coningbeg* and was sunk by a German submarine in 1917 with the loss of 83 lives, the biggest civilian death toll of the war from Waterford.)[15]

Immediately one is confused. How did 'Pte J Condon' – presumably John Condon – morph into his younger brother Patrick? No explanation is forthcoming. Nicholas and John (or was it Patrick?) woke up in Liverpool and made their way to Salford to an uncle. Nicholas told the *Waterford News*, 'We saw so many young men in uniform passing to and fro that we joined the Army. Patrick was a strapping lad for his age and when he said he was 18 they asked no questions. We enlisted with the Lancashire Fusiliers and were transferred later to the East Lancashire's. But my cousin wasn't satisfied. He wanted to join the Royal Irish Regiment.'

Patrick – or was it John? – returned to Ireland and joined the Royal Irish Regiment in Clonmel, County Tipperary. The pair never saw each other again. Nicholas recalled, 'I came through the war all right. But my cousin was killed by a bursting shell. He could have only been a few months fighting.'

Patrick Condon was three years younger than his older brother John. Nicholas Condon did not die until 1974, aged 78.[16] He served in the York and Lancaster Regiment during the war and was invalided out in 1915 after getting hit by a shell. He had a silver plate in his head and was finally discharged from the British army in 1922. Sonny Condon says his father was not in the habit of making things up or embellishing the truth, which makes both the *Waterford News* interview and subsequent controversy over John Condon's age an enduring puzzle.

'If something was unpopular to say, he'd say it,' says Sonny Condon. 'Even before I knew we were related, I knew he [John Condon] was the youngest soldier to die in the First World War. If he wasn't, the people in Waterford, which was a small little city, would have known.'

Sonny Condon regrets never asking his father about his famous relative. 'He never talked about the war. He never spoke about John Condon and that's what's killing me now. All the answers I could get now are all gone because he's dead.' Sonny Condon had an uncle in the First World War, another John (Johnny) Condon, but this one survived the war and would talk about it. He, like his namesake, had been a reservist with the Royal Irish Regiment before the war:

> He [Johnny] was telling me that they went up to Clonmel once a year to train. They did it for a few drinks and a few bob like we did in the FCA [Fórsa Cosanta Áitiúil (the former name of the Irish army reserve]. Then when war broke out he went over to serve. He would talk about it after a few pints at Christmas or at a party I'd get some little thing out of him. He lost a leg over there. One of his friends was wounded so Johnny went out to bring him back and he was hit by a shell burst. He couldn't have a family because he had a wooden leg all his life.

Sonny Condon does not care if John Condon was really 14. He believes the people of Waterford and the people in Belgium share the same sentiment. The inscription on the memorial in Waterford attributes the claim to the Commonwealth War Graves Commission.

Sonny Condon has another theory. The John Condon who died in Flanders may not have been the one born in 1896. Infant mortality was terrible at the end of the nineteenth century in Ireland. It was common for children to be named after one who had died in the family before, but if that is the case, why does the younger John Condon not surface in the two censuses of 1901 and 1911? It is an interesting theory, but one without evidence.

'There's a friend of mine who does family trees for people and he said to me that it was a common thing that if a child died within a year or so and another baby came along they would automatically call him the same name, but we can't find any documentation to that effect,' Sonny says.

Patrick is recorded as being 1 year old in 1901, which could conceivably make him 14 or 15 at the time when his brother died. But how could John have swapped identities with Patrick Condon and kept up the ruse even after the war ended? Wouldn't somebody have noticed in a relatively small place like Waterford? The most plausible explanation is that the anonymous *Waterford News* reporter mixed up Patrick and John.

The confusion over whether it was Patrick or John inspired the Flemish children's author Geert Spillebeen. In his novel *Age 14*, published first in Dutch and then in English, it is Patrick, who pretends he is his older brother John and runs away to war.

The novel opens with John Condon being informed that his remains have been found eight years after he died at Mouse Trap Farm. 'Today was a hard one for John Condon, even after all these years. They had finally found his body.'[17] He sees the letter from the War Office informing his father that a piece of his boot has been found. 'So it's true, I'm now really dead.'[18]

John Condon had survived the war because he never fought in it. 'The real Patrick Condon was dead, he had reported to the front as John. Patrick had given his older brother's name because he himself was too young to be a soldier.'

Patrick Condon is a dreamer who finds his dreams stifled by a lack of opportunity. His father gets him a job on the docks and tells young Patrick to lie about his age. The family needs the money so Patrick complies. While working as a young man on the docks, he resolves to become a soldier. His head is filled with the military triumphs of the British Empire, as was the case for many young Irishmen at the time. Through his father, he gets the idea to fake his age. He walks 30 miles to Clonmel to join the 3rd Battalion of the Royal Irish Regiment. 'If my father lets me lie about my age to get work, I can add a few years to the army too.'

There he meets Thomas Carthy, who is in his mid-40s. Carthy lives with his wife in River Street. They have no children. In *Age 14*, Thomas Carthy is a kind-hearted soul who recognises the youthful Condon's vulnerability. Together the pair go off to war and oblivion.[19]

The real Thomas Carthy is the soldier buried beside John Condon in Poelcapelle Cemetery. He was 47, too old for the front line. In different ways the teenage soldier and the middle-aged man were physically unsuited to the rigours of combat, yet these two graves encapsulated the dilemma faced by a British army, which was desperately short of fighting men in 1915.

The real John Condon was a restless soul, according to his nephew, also called John Condon (Patrick Condon's son). 'He was always running away. From an early age he wandered around the streets of Waterford with a wooden gun and would tell everyone in Jenkins Lane that he was going to join the army. He was never happy at home. He was always wanting to run here and run there and play soldiers. He was never at home. He was always running from one house to another.'

According to his nephew, John Condon, the soldier came back to Ireland after having run away to England and he joined up with the 3rd Royal Irish Regiment. He hid as a stowaway to go to France. 'He wasn't quite 14 when he joined up in Tipperary. When he was killed the War Office sent a letter to my father to say that John was killed. His father and mother didn't know he was in France. They thought he was still in barracks.'

John Condon jnr spent forty-three years working in England and still retains the trace of a north of England accent. He has no time for the conspiracy theories about his father Patrick being the real John Condon.

In 2002, he and Sonny Condon visited the cemetery in Poelcappelle for the first time. No Condon had ever visited the grave before. They were taken aback by how popular his grave was with visitors. 'When I saw all the flowers on the grave I assumed someone had put them there for our visit,' said Sonny Condon, 'but I was told that they had actually taken a lot of flowers off and cleaned up the grave.'[20]

If his military records are to be believed, John Condon was not one of those unfortunate youngsters who signed up in the first flush of patriotic fervour after war was declared. He had actually enlisted in the 3rd Royal Irish Regiment in Waterford on 24 October 1913. Condon gave his date of birth as 24 October 1895, making him 18 years old on attestation, the minimum age for service. This was a lie. He was born on 16 October 1896, according to his birth certificate. He was 17 years and 8 days old. [21]

The 3rd Battalion was a reserve battalion composed of soldiers who served on a part-time basis but were liable to be called up for regular service in the event of mobilisation. This eventuality was considered unlikely. There was no major European war imminent in 1913. Like countless others, he lied when joining the British army. Nobody cared in those prelapsarian days.

He completed his recruit training in February 1914. He was drafted into the diminished 2nd Battalion of the Royal Irish Regiment after the Battle of Le Pilly in October and November 1914. As we have seen in a previous chapter, the regiment was reduced to company size following the disaster at Le Pilly.

In November, it was ordered to reorganise on a two-company basis. In December, commander-in-chief Field Marshal French inspected the battalion and was told only one company was ready and a second was awaiting NCOs. He told their commanding officers that things were so bad he might need both companies, ready or not. In this context, it is not surprising that the British would press every available man into action.[22]

In the space of two months, the battalion was guard of honour for King George V, the French President Raymond Poincaré, the French commander-in-chief General Joseph Joffre and the Russian ambassador.

The Second Battle of Ypres would find the regiment severely depleted for the third time in a war which was not yet a year old. Even on quiet days, casualties were between four and eighteen a day. On 9 May 1915, the battalion was heavily shelled and suffered some 200 casualties.

Worse was to follow during the attack at Mouse Trap Farm on 24 May. The Royal Irish Regiment was to the left of the Royal Dublin Fusiliers. The battalion stood to arms at 2 a.m. and the gas came rolling over at 2.20 a.m. The Germans occupied the Royal Dublin Fusiliers' trenches and began to enfilade the Royal Irish

Regiment trenches. The Royal Irish Regiment casualties were appalling: some 400 in total, including John Condon and Thomas Carthy. The fierce fighting at Mouse Trap Farm saw the bodies of so many men disappear into the gas-blasted, shell-torn Earth.

When Condon's body was found more than eight years later it was at Railway Wood, 2 miles south of Mouse Trap Farm. He was identified by the stamp on a scrap of boot. It was normal practice in the army for clothing to be marked with the service number and regiment of the soldier. The boot bore the stamp '6322 4/RIR'. The Imperial War Graves Commission assumed that the boot must belong to Private John Condon No. 6322 of the Royal Irish Regiment.

Also recovered beside him were the clothing and braces of an unknown British soldier. It was marked with the number '656 4/RIR'. The soldier who most closely matched that description was 6566 Private Thomas Carthy of the 2nd Royal Irish Regiment. Both men were interred beside each other in 1924.

Thomas Carthy's story is interesting in itself. Decades later, *The Irish Times* journalist Kevin Myers made inquires about the identity of this soldier. He wrote to the occupant of 34 River Street, Clonmel, where Carthy is listed as having lived. He received a letter from a woman in Nenagh, who was the great-grand-niece of Thomas Carthy.

'She told me the family history,' recalls Myers. 'The Carthys were poor, small-town Protestants, and her great grandmother had been Carthy's youngest sister. That girl was already married when Carthy died, but with a new name, address and religion, having become a Catholic on marrying and later moving to Nenagh.'[23]

The poignancy of the soldier too young to serve beside the soldier too old to serve adds another dimension to the Condon story.

In later years, Condon's story came to the attention of Belgian schoolteacher Aurel Sercu from Boezinge, a village next to Poelcappele. He started examining the circumstances behind the discovery of the body in John Condon's grave.

Condon's body had been recovered more than 2 miles away from Mouse Trap Farm. On 24 May, the whole of the British line had been under the severest assault from the Germans. It would have been impossible for Condon to end up so far away from the rest of his battalion and it is unlikely that his body would be moved such a distance under heavy fire.

If John Condon is not buried in Poelcappele Cemetery then it stands to reason that Thomas Carthy is not buried there either. 'Let me emphasise, it was not at all my original intention to expose what might be nothing but a myth,' says Sercu. 'I even started with the belief that maybe I could find out that John Condon indeed was only 14, and that there was an explanation for the fact that his remains had been found too far away from the battlefield near Mouse Trap Farm.'[24]

Instead, his research led him to conclude that the body in John Condon's grave was that of another Irishman, Rifleman Patrick Fitzsimmons from Belfast.

The research he had carried out was leaked online in 2003, much to his chagrin as he had no intention of going public with it until he had tracked down members of the Fitzsimmons family. He wrote to every Fitzsimmons in the Belfast phone book, but for eleven years he received no response. 'All in vain. So disappointing and then I gave up, some time towards the end of 2003 or in 2004. I put everything behind lock and key, trying to forget my Condon/Fitzsimmons file. And then, on 16 November 2014, I received an e-mail, the subject line of which, 6322 Rfn. Patrick Fitzsimmons, made my fingers tremble when I opened it.' The email read:

> Good afternoon,
> I have picked up your information on genealogy.com when looking for infor-
> mation about my Great Uncle Patrick. … I would be most pleased to make
> contact to discuss your very significant findings. Rfn Patrick Fitzsimmons was
> my Great Uncle and indeed from Ballymacarrett, Belfast in the province of
> Ulster, Northern Ireland. … I am pleased that correct identification has finally
> been made and intend to visit his final resting place.
> Kind Regards,
> Ken

This 'Ken' turned out to be Kenneth Hanna, a retired British army officer, whose father was from Belfast. Kenneth Hanna's grandmother was Elizabeth Fitzsimmons, a sister of Patrick Fitzsimmons. The Fitzsimmonses were Northern Catholics. After the war, if one was a nationalist in the north of Ireland, it was no more popular to disclose one's links with the British army than it was in the south.

Kenneth Hanna, however, had maintained the family tradition of service in the British army. He served in the Queen's Royal Irish Hussars for 32 years, having joined at the age of 15. His time in the British army included a tour of duty in Northern Ireland during the Troubles, patrolling the same streets where his great-uncle grew up. The British army that recruited from the Catholic community in the First World War was the same one now regarded by some nationalists as the enemy.[25]

Hanna says he is persuaded by Sercu's research that the man buried in John Condon's grave is his relative. 'Clearly from the stamping identified and because of regimental battle histories, it cannot possibly be John Condon. Those remains buried in John Condon's grave, I'm convinced are Patrick Fitzsimmons.'[26]

There is one other critical piece of evidence that would strongly suggest that this is the case. The body was found in Railway Wood. Fitzsimmons was killed during the Battle of Bellewaarde. On the evening of 15 June 1915, the 2nd Royal Irish Rifles assembled between Wittepoort Farm and the railway line to support the 9th Infantry Brigade in an attack on Bellewaerde Spur. Crucially, this is just 200 yards from where the body reputed to be that of John Condon is found. The attack by the 9th Infantry Brigade was preceded by an early morning bombardment lasting some ninety minutes before the men went over the top.[27]

The British advance was met with ferocious German artillery fire. It was during this exchange that Kenneth Hanna believes his great-uncle was killed. 'It is clear that having been posted from the fourth battalion to the second battalion of the Royal Irish Rifles, my uncle had taken part in that engagement,' he says. 'As a result of the early morning barrage, they would have gone from the jumping off point. He would have been taken out by machine gun, rifle or even artillery fire. The rolling bombardment would still have been answered by German fire anyway.'

The only way the matter can be definitively resolved is through an exhumation and a DNA test. This would not be a palatable option for anyone involved. Hanna says he is 99.7 per cent certain about Patrick Fitzsimmons, but concedes that nothing will happen while the 0.3 per cent doubt remains:

> I am very much of the opinion that the IWGC [now Commonwealth War Graves Commission] have misidentified the remains of my great uncle and allocated the wrong identity to him. After much discussion with Aurel and also some of his colleagues; I am quite convinced of the accuracy of their discovery. The sad thing is that when they were missing in action they were engraved on the New Menin Gate for nine decades. To erase it would be wrong. Both soldiers are commemorated albeit incorrectly. To switch that now would create a huge controversy. My honest feeling is that both soldiers gave their lives for the cause of freedom. That they [the Commonwealth War Graves Commission] are in error is a fact of history.

On 16 June 2015, 100 years to the day after Patrick Fitzsimmons died, Kenneth Hanna and his son Adrian visited the grave of John Condon. There, they remembered Patrick Fitzsimmons and John Condon.

That is where the matter rests. The Commonwealth War Graves Commission has invited interested parties to apply to the Joint Casualty and Compassionate Centre, the unit of the British army which investigates First World War burials, if they wish to have the matter investigated further. At the time of writing, nobody has come forward. Would they dare? Who would benefit if the Commonwealth War Graves Commission was to turn around 100 years after both men died and change the headstone?

It would be unfortunate for the Commonwealth War Graves Commission to decide at this remove that it made a mistake, that John Condon was not really 14 and that the wrong man is buried in his grave. The coaches would stop coming, the poets and dreamers would have to find another icon of war, the precedent would open the way for thousands of reinterments. As we will see with John

Kipling in another chapter, John Condon is not the only high-profile disputed burial from the First World War. There are many others.

Those who value historical veracity above all would be satisfied, but would anybody else? The John Condon story has proved to be remarkably resistant to anything as inconvenient as the facts. If the story of John Condon is replete with mistakes, they were innocent mistakes made by overworked clerks processing the detritus of misery in the pre-computer age.

John Condon is the only Irish fatality of the First World War that many Irish people can name. He has become a symbol of all the boy soldiers who fell in the war, those whose enthusiasm and youth were exploited by ruthless recruiting sergeants who were paid 2 shilling 6 pence (half a crown) a man to find the cannon fodder.

The unscrupulous recruitment in the early stages of the war was only ended by the crusading zeal of one man, the wealthy industrialist and Liberal MP Sir Arthur Markham. He led a campaign to end the scandal of boy soldiers. He was overwhelmed by petitioning parents seeking to get their children off the front line. On one day, he received 300 letters.[28] The haphazard, turn-a-blind-eye approach to underage soldiers exhibited by the War Office was replaced by a much tougher, more rigorous regime.

It was too late for John Condon and thousands like him. It is often forgotten in the speculation surrounding his age that if John Condon was born in October 1896, he was still underage when he died in May 1915. The minimum age for serving overseas was 19.

When he joined the British army in 1913, Ireland was still a part of the British Empire. By the time his body was found 10 years later, his part of Ireland had gained its independence. Boys and men like John Condon did not fit the new national narrative, which is why he remains better known outside Ireland than at home.

The evidence that he was not 14 is much more compelling than the evidence that he was 14, but it has not been definitively proved and the Commonwealth War Graves Commission will not yield when it comes to its belief that he was the youngest soldier. Irrespective of the facts, the tourists will keep coming and teenagers will keep reflecting at his grave. John Condon, this accidental icon, has served a greater purpose than what the mere facts might allow.

LIEUTENANT
JOHN KIPLING
IRISH GUARDS
27TH SEPTEMBER 1915 AGE 18

11

THE GRAVE OF
JOHN KIPLING

On 24 June 1992, a Commonwealth War Graves Commission truck entered St Mary's Advanced Dressing Station (ADS) military cemetery carrying a new Portland stone headstone.

This little cemetery, with just 218 marked graves, sits on the road between Vermelles and Hulluch in open country in the Pas-de-Calais. The land around here is dead flat, a 'dull brown low monotonous level', as the novelist and soldier Patrick MacGill described it when he fought there in the autumn of 1915.[1]

The wind blows, unhindered by any shelter, across the plains of French Flanders from the English Channel. The only elevation in the background is a distinctive double crassier, a pair of slag heaps which dominates the old mining town of Loos-en-Gohelle that gave its name to the terrible Battle of Loos. This industrial landscape has been designated as a UNESCO World Heritage site.[2]

In the foreground of St Mary's ADS are two tiny war cemeteries, their Crosses of Sacrifice visible above the surrounding sugar beet fields that are everywhere in this fertile area of northern France.

The Commonwealth War Graves Commission truck stopped opposite a row of graves near the south wall of the cemetery. Workmen carefully removed the existing headstone from its underground concrete I-beam, which had kept it in place for seventy-three years. The inscription on this Headstone 2, Row D, Plot 7 read, 'A lieutenant of the Great War Irish Guards'.

The process of identifying the remains of unknown soldiers has never ended. The discovery which led to the replacing of this headstone was made by a former Canadian metallurgical engineer, Norm Christie, who spent his summer holidays in the early 1980s travelling around war cemeteries.

These cities of the dead haunted his thoughts. His obsession became all-consuming. 'You can't be a little bit interested in the First World War,' he says.[3] At the age of 36, he handed in his notice at the Algoma Steel company in Ontario, Canada. 'I'd become a cemetery expert so the Commonwealth War Graves Commission recruited me in 1990 to go to England,' he recalls. Christie became the chief records officer dealing with the 30,000 inquiries which the commission receives every year.[4]

Many of those who sought his help were looking for details of men who had no known grave. He thought that many of the more than 400,000 soldiers who were only 'known unto God' could become known unto man with a little intuition and research.[5]

Christie found the process easier than he expected. A Canadian cavalry captain who won the Military Cross was easily identified; a brigadier general at Tyne Cot Cemetery, the largest Commonwealth War Graves Cemetery, likewise.

He also found the grave of one of the most famous British casualties of the First World War: Second Lieutenant John Kipling, the son of the poet of Empire, Rudyard Kipling. While looking through some files for St Mary's ADS, he noticed the grave of a single unidentified Irish Guards lieutenant who was killed on 27 September 1915, the third day of the Battle of Loos. Even by the horrific standards of this war, the Battle of Loos had been particularly dreadful.

According to the Commonwealth War Graves Commission, 25 September 1915 was the bloodiest day of the war for the British army, eclipsed only by the first day of the Battle of the Somme on 1 July 1916.[6] Some 10,292 men are recorded as having died on the first day of the Battle of Loos. The 'field of corpses', as the Germans called it, produced 20,000 British deaths in total, mostly in the first three days.

Christie looked through the Irish Guards casualty lists for lieutenants. He assumed a 'tonne of them' had been killed on 27 September, the third day of the battle, but only three had been killed. Immediately, he knew the odds of a positive identification were one in three.[7]

He looked at the grid reference map of where the body was recovered in 1919. He was puzzled. The grid reference map of G25 was at least 3 miles behind where the Irish Guards attacked the German positions.

Christie also found another critical piece of evidence, which came from Rider Haggard, one of Rudyard Kipling's fellow writers and best friends. Haggard did what he could to help a heartbroken father find his son. He had interviewed some of the Irish guardsmen who had fought with John. One, Sergeant Michael Bowe, encountered a badly injured Kipling as he was staggering back towards his own lines to get medical treatment. He was holding field dressings to his mouth, bleeding profusely and crying. 'I shall not send this on,' Haggard wrote in his diary, 'it is too painful.'[8]

Christie knew the potential significance of his discovery. John Kipling was not some unfortunate subaltern forgotten by all except his descendants. Rudyard Kipling had made him famous. His poetic lamentation for his son, 'My Boy Jack', and his high-profile work with the Imperial War Graves Commission were precipitated by the heightened agony of not only losing his son, but having no place to grieve him.

Britain's first Nobel Prize-winning laureate, a man so famous that he stopped writing cheques because they ended up being framed, had to endure a very public agony as he searched in vain for his missing son.

It was Kipling who, upon joining the commission as its literary advisor, came up with the apposite phrase to describe all those nameless dead, 'known unto God'.

In 1919, Rudyard made a very public visit to the area around Loos. He did so again in 1924, when he even visited St Mary's ADS, but at that stage he had no idea his son might be buried there.[9] Christie therefore expected a great deal of documentation relating to the search for John's body, 'but there was just nothing'. He also noted that John Kipling's name was on the Loos Memorial to the Missing at Dud Corner, where some 20,615 British soldiers with no known grave are remembered.

He expected the Spanish Inquisition from the commission, but they were quickly convinced. 'I was very surprised how straightforward it was about Kipling.

I remember going down in the office and I looked on the panels at Duds Corner [Loos Memorial to the Missing] and there was only one [Irish Guards] lieutenant. I was saying that this was just too easy.'

John Kipling was Rudyard Kiping's only son; he also had two daughters. He took an intense interest in his children. He encouraged and cajoled and loved them demonstrably. He was especially devoted to John. Father and son wrote to each other several times a week with a familiarity that was at odds with the formality of the time. They addressed each other with the mutual greeting 'dear old man'. Kipling cherished their mutual bond. 'The relations between a man and his father are the most precious in the world and depend quite as much upon the son as the father,' he once told Oliver Baldwin, the son of his cousin, the future British Prime Minister Stanley Baldwin.

John Kipling was six weeks past his eighteenth birthday when he was killed leading a charge at Chalk Pit Wood near Puits 14 bis, a mineshaft in the Loos sector that the Germans had turned into a machine gun redoubt. He was reported as missing, which was a torment for the Kipling family, who did not know whether he was dead or in a German prisoner of war camp.

In 'My Boy Jack', published a year after his son disappeared, the John becomes Jack and the crater-strewn landscape of Loos becomes the seas around Jutland:

'Have you news of my boy Jack?'
Not this tide.
'When d'you think that he'll come back?'
Not with this wind blowing, and this tide.

'Has any one else had word of him?'
Not this tide.
For what is sunk will hardly swim,
Not with this wind blowing, and this tide.

'Oh, dear, what comfort can I find?'
None this tide,
Nor any tide,
Except he did not shame his kind –
Not even with that wind blowing, and that tide.

Then hold your head up all the more,
This tide,
And every tide;
Because he was the son you bore,
And gave to that wind blowing and that tide!

Two years after John's birth in 1897, his sister Josephine died of pneumonia on an Atlantic crossing. The tragedy bound John and his sister Elsie closer to their parents.[10] John Kipling enjoyed all the privileges of being the only son of a world-famous and wealthy author. He had a private education and experienced foreign travel; he was presented with a motorbike bought for his seventeenth birthday. John was sent to Wellington College in Berkshire. Martial in name, martial in character, Wellington, named after the Irish-born hero of Waterloo, turned out generations of English public schoolboys for the armed forces.

John Kipling wanted to be a naval officer but switched his attentions to the army when he was 16. His father worried about him. John Kipling was neither particularly robust nor particularly accomplished. Unlike his father, described by the author Henry James as a 'complete man of genius', John was no genius. His grades were never great, though he tried hard. Letters between them suggest a conscientious young man who was anxious to please his father.

John Kipling should never have been a soldier. He inherited his father's poor eyesight. John's War Office file reveals that he had 6/36 vision in both eyes without glasses.[11] He was unable to read even the second line on an eye chart. An officer with such poor eyesight was a danger to himself and to the men under his command.

Like his father before him, John was turned down for an army officer's commission. He applied a second time and was rejected again. He considered enlisting as a private, but this would be too ignominious for father and son. He had been a member of the Officers' Training Corps (OTC) in Wellington, an incubator for the officer corps of the British army. His whole orientation, education and background led towards him becoming a commissioned officer.

John Kipling might have had to resign himself to civilian life were it not for the outbreak of the First World War. Though not Irish, he joined the Irish Guards. This was not unusual. The War Office usually included English officers in Irish battalions, all the better to ensure the Irish were kept in line.

John Kipling's father knew many Irishmen in the British army, the best known of whom was Field Marshal Lord (Frederick) Roberts. These sons of Empire, both born in India, had a friendship going back to the time when Kipling was a cub reporter in India and Roberts was commander-in-chief of the Indian army. Bobs, as he was affectionately known, was already Britain's most popular soldier when he was sent to the Boer War. Irish regiments distinguished themselves in that South African adventure, especially the Royal Dublin Fusiliers. So, in 'grateful thanks', Queen Victoria set up a new regiment of guards, the Irish Guards, in 1900. Roberts, the former commander-in-chief in Ireland and scion of a well-regarded Anglo-Irish family, was made honorary colonel.[12]

Roberts and Rudyard Kipling were imperialists who shared a common outlook. Both were united in their belief that Britain needed to introduce compulsory military service, as many other countries in Europe had done. Roberts enlisted Kipling's aid in pressing for conscription. At Roberts' prompting, Kipling wrote a poem on the subject. 'The Islanders' was published in *The Times* in January 1902. He didn't hide his contempt for the perceived complacency of the British establishment. The 'flannelled fools at the wicket or the muddied oafs at the goal,' he wrote, were 'unmade, unhandled, unmeet' for the military and political challenges of the new century.

Roberts was still a serving soldier and could only privately approve. He kept his counsel until he retired shortly afterwards and joined the newly created National Service League in 1902. The league wanted there to be four years of compulsory military training for every male between 18 and 30. Such ideas were embraced by a very fervent section of the British public and ignored by everyone else. There was no political appetite for conscription and no public desire for it either.

Relations between Germany and England deteriorated in the years leading up to the First World War. Germanophobia was by no means as universal as it was to become in Britain after two world wars. The Germans and British had ancestral kinship through the Angles and the Saxons. The British Royal Family were Anglophone Germans by heritage. The German states had been on the British side at Waterloo. Germany was admired for its innovation, industry and its social model, developed by Bismarck, which was the first comprehensive social welfare system in Europe. Many within the British establishment desired an alliance with Germany, not the historical enemy France, but Kipling dissented. As early as 1899, he was describing Germans as the 'shameless Hun'.[13]

Germany's desire to build a navy which could challenge the Royal Navy was an affront to the very notion of British domination of the seas. The erratic Kaiser Wilhelm II, a grandson of Queen Victoria, gave an interview to the *Daily Telegraph* in 1908 in which he appeared to mock the British.

In 1911, Germany and Britain had come close to war over the Agadir incident. This largely forgotten event was an example of how seemingly trivial incidents could escalate to cause a war between the major powers. The status of Morocco had never been properly resolved following an earlier crisis in 1906. France, which asserted its right to control the territory, sent in 20,000 troops to quell an internal rebellion. Germany sent a gunboat to the coast off Agadir, claiming to protect its economic interests in the south of the country. The French took this as an affront and an act of war. The British took the side of the French. The issue was only resolved when stock markets across Europe crashed.

For Roberts, the Agadir incident only reinforced his belief that Britain was utterly unprepared for a continental war. On 22 October 1912, he made a speech in Manchester which showed uncanny prescience:

Germany strikes when Germany's hour has struck. This is the time-honoured policy relentlessly pursued by Bismarck and Moltke in 1866 and 1870. It has been her policy decade by decade since that date. It is her policy at the present hour. It is an excellent policy. It is or should be the policy of every nation prepared to play a great part in history.[14]

Roberts ended with a chilling refrain, 'Arm and prepare to quit yourselves as men, for the time of your ordeal is at hand.'

Kipling was thrilled, writing to Roberts, 'I cannot refrain from offering you my heartiest congratulations on your Manchester speech. If, as I believe, the effect of such pronouncements is to be judged by the amount of abuse elicited, it looks as if the rewards of your long labours were in sight at last.'[15]

Yet few took Kipling seriously. 'Kipling could get an audience for tales and ballads and jungle-books; but the moment he tried to speak nationally, he could not get an audience. Even now, they would rather read H. G. Wells,' the American academic Katharine Fullerton Gerould observed after the war.[16]

Both Roberts and Kipling were vindicated by the outbreak of the First World War in August 1914. Kipling wrote to a friend, 'I told you so.'

Kipling toured Britain, giving speeches to aid recruitment, yet how could he demand that others serve if his own son was not able to serve? John Kipling went to the War Office on 10 August to seek a commission. He was rejected. Rudyard Kipling was dismayed. 'I took John over to Maidstone yesterday [for a commission] and they turned him down for eyes. Passed as physically fit every other way. But surely, in view of our butcher's bills, they are not going to stick to this. They seem to be turning men down here very freely.'[17]

On 17 August, John Kipling tried again and was again rejected. It was at this stage that Kipling approached his old friend Bobs. It would appear from his correspondence that Kipling and Roberts met on 2 September, a day after Kipling's incendiary poem 'For All That We Are' was published in *The Times*. The poem portrayed the war as a battle for national survival:

> For all we have and are,
> For all our children's fate,
> Stand up and take the war.
> The Hun is at the gate!
>
> …
>
> There is but one task for all –
> One life for each to give.
> What stands if Freedom fall?
> Who dies if England live?

On 10 September, John Kipling finally secured his commission with the Irish Guards and went to Warley Barracks in Essex for training.[18]

The Irishmen who signed up to serve in the Irish Guards were the type of Irishman Kipling and Roberts admired. They were loyal to and shared in the glories of the British Empire. Neither man could accept nor understand the Irish desire for home rule.

Though he was born in India and brought up in England from a young age, Frederick Roberts regarded Ireland as his home. The Robertses had settled in County Waterford in the 1700s. His great-grandfather John Roberts was responsible for some of Waterford's finest buildings, including its two cathedrals, both Anglican and Catholic. John Roberts Square in Waterford is named after him. In November 2015, a bust of Lord Roberts was presented to Waterford city by the Irish Guards.

Frederick Roberts hunted with the Waterford Hounds and met his wife, Nora Henrietta Bews, among the family's social circle there. The couple were married in 1859. He subsequently became commander-in-chief of Ireland at a time when there was no indication of the tumult that was to come.[19]

In September 1914, on hearing that a new battalion of the Irish Guards was being raised, Roberts wrote to the commanding officer, Colonel Byrne, 'I am proud of being an Irishman and I appeal to my fellow countrymen to uphold the honour of their land. Every man we raise is needed in this great struggle of giants.'[20, 21]

Though he had tenuous Irish roots himself, Kipling also took an abiding interest in Ireland, though his relationship with the country was profoundly ambivalent. Kipling was not anti-Irish. He had the greatest affection for the cheerful Irish denizens of Empire stationed in India, whom he had known from an early age. Two of his greatest fictional characters were unmistakably Irish: Terence Mulvaney, 'the tallest man in the regiment', is one of three characters in Kipling's *Barracks Room Ballads*; in his novel *Kim*, the central character is Kimball O'Hara, the son of an Irish-born soldier and his Irish wife.

Kipling's political interest in Ireland began in the 1880s when he intervened in the Pigott forgeries scandal. *The Times* sought to link the Irish nationalist leader Charles Stewart Parnell with the 1882 Phoenix Park murders of the Chief Secretary for Ireland Lord Frederick Cavendish and the Permanent Under-Secretary for Ireland Thomas Henry Burke. Nothing could be more injurious to the case for home rule being patiently assembled by Parnell than an association with cold-blooded murders, which had shocked Britain and Ireland.[22]

Parnell condemned the murders outright, but five years later *The Times* published the notorious Pigott forgeries, produced by the vengeful Richard Pigott, an Irish nationalist turned blackmailer. The worst of the letters suggested that Parnell was a hypocrite.

Parnell protested his innocence and was cleared by the Parnell Commission. Kipling was not so convinced and wrote an incendiary poem, 'Cleared', suggesting that Parnell had a more equivocal attitude to violence than he admitted to and was happy to take money from the 'blood-dyed Clanna Gael' when it suited him.[23]

Kipling saw no contradiction between his regard for the Irish and his antipathy to Irish nationalism. The American critic Edmund Wilson put it best in his 1941 essay 'The Kipling That Nobody Reads', which was published in *Atlantic Monthly*:

> So long as the Irish are loyal to England, Kipling shows the liveliest appreciation of Irish recklessness and the Irish sense of mischief: Mulvaney is Irish, McTurk is Irish, Kim is Irish. But the moment they display these same qualities in agitation against the English, they become infamous assassins and traitors.[24]

Kipling's relationship with Ireland reached a nadir in the early years of the 1910s. In 1911, he and the Oxford academic C.R.L. Fletcher published *A School History of England*.[25] This nasty, mean-spirited book, replete with the most vulgar stereotypes even by the standards of the time ('a few bananas will sustain the life of a negro quite sufficiently'), was particularly injurious towards the Irish. Lamenting that the Romans never conquered Ireland, they wrote, 'So Ireland never went to school, and has been a spoilt child ever since; the most charming of children, indeed, full of beautiful laughter and tender tears, full of poetry and valour, but incapable of ruling herself, and impatient of all rule by all others.'

Kipling had written something similar in his short story 'The Mutiny of the Mavericks', in which he described the Irish as this 'quaint, crooked, sweet, profoundly irresponsible and profoundly lovable race'.

The pair also laid bare their opposition to home rule in terms which had everything to do with the welfare of Britain and nothing to do with that of Ireland:

> Most people fear that a separate Irish parliament would be followed by a complete separation between Ireland and Great Britain, by the establishment of an Irish Republic, and by the oppression of the well-to-do and intelligent classes of Irishmen who are certainly loyal to the British Crown. All British politicians, on both sides, have, during the last 70 years, made haste to remove every real, and, indeed, every imaginary grievance of the Irish people though they had earned no gratitude by doing so.[26]

Even by the standards of the base and crude stereotyping of the time, this book had the power to shock and was condemned on the floor of the House of Commons. Kipling found himself rebuked by the British government, with Joseph Pease, the President of the Board of Education, dismissing the offending passages as 'by no means suitable for children in public elementary schools'.

A year later, Kipling's antipathy morphed into a call to outright violence in his incendiary poem 'Ulster', published on 9 April 1912, at the height of the home rule crisis, in the *Morning Post*:

> Rebellion, rapine hate
> Oppression, wrong and greed
> Are loosed to rule our fate,
> By England's act and deed.

The intemperate, violent language was at odds with the reasonableness and non-violent means by which the Irish Parliamentary Party leader John Redmond, and nationalist Ireland in general, pursued the Irish dreams of home rule.

Kipling was not taken seriously by most of those with a liberal opinion in Britain and his intervention went unappreciated by most. In May 1914, home rule passed all stages of parliament and just needed the king's assent. In the same month, Kipling made an appalling speech at Tunbridge Wells in which he accused the British government of treason:

> The Home Rule Bill broke the faith of generations. It officially recognised sedition, privy conspiracy and rebellion. It subsidised the secret forces of boycott, intimidation, outrage and murder. Understand, I do not for an instant blame the nationalists. They are what they are. They are what their particular type of their race has always been since the beginning of recorded history.

Kipling had clearly discarded in his conscience the democratic will of the majority of the Irish people, expressed in every election in which the nationalist majority had the vote.

Feelings were still running high when war broke out in August 1914, yet on 3 August, a day before Britain declared war on Germany, John Redmond, leader of the Irish Parliamentary Party, made an extraordinary statement in the House of Commons, declaring nationalist Ireland's full support for the British war effort. 'I honestly believe that the democracy of Ireland will turn with the utmost anxiety and sympathy to this country in every trial and every danger that may overtake it.' Redmond went further on 20 September in a famous – ultimately infamous – speech at Woodenbridge in Wicklow, where he urged Irish Volunteers to 'go wherever the firing line extends in defence of right, of freedom and religion in this war'.

This was not the treasonable behaviour Kipling continually alluded to when referring to Irish nationalism. Many of the same Irish Volunteers would join his son's battalion of the Irish Guards, seeing no contradiction between their aspirations for home rule within the British Empire and defence of that same empire.

John Kipling was commissioned as a second lieutenant in the Irish Guards, the lowest rank of commissioned officer. The next year was spent in training. In August 1915, the battalion was mobilised for war and landed in France, just as John Kipling was about to turn 18. He needed his parents' permission to go.

John wrote home whenever he could. He bore the privations of the ordinary soldier with stoicism and good humour:

> We work like friends, if we get two hours for meals & stand easies in a day we think ourselves damned lucky, usually getting up at 4am & going to bed about half past nine in the evening. Many is the time I've thought of a hot bath; evening clothes; dinner at the Ritz; going on to the Alhambra [London hotel] afterwards! You people at home don't realize how spoilt you are. You don't realize what excessive luxury surrounds you. Think of a hot water tap alone.[27]

Ominously, his last letter home would ask, matter-of-factly, for an aluminium disc to replace the dog tag he had lost. This would have the most tragic significance later.

Meanwhile, Kipling and his men were preparing for 'the Big Push'. For months, men and materiél were assembled at an area of the British front south of the La Bassée Canal and north of the town of Lens. This is France's Black Country, with slag heaps and pit heads the only elevation in an otherwise dreary industrial landscape. The British did not like the terrain. It was exposed and the advantageous ground was occupied by the Germans. Nor was the timing right: Kitchener's New Army would not be ready until the following year. But the British were not masters of their own fate. The French insisted on a grand gesture from their ally to aid their assault further south.

Thus far, 1915 had been a dismal year of serial military failure for the Allies.

Undeterred, French commander-in-chief Joseph Joffre made plans for an autumn offensive. It had been a year of success for the enemy, with the Germans routing the Russians during the Gorlice-Tarnów Offensive in May and June 1915. The Central Powers now occupied the whole of modern-day Poland while German troops in the west stood on the defensive.

Success had been achieved by stripping the Western Front of divisions. The Allies now had a clear superiority in numerical terms – 132 divisions as opposed to 102 German divisions – but the Germans made up for it by defence in depth. In a war where the machine gun was paramount, defence trumped attack.

Joffre's instructions were clear. The French would strike north across the Artois plain in the direction of the rail junction in the Noyon area. Simultaneous attacks would also occur in the Champagne region and in Verdun.

The British First Army was to 'take a powerful offensive on the north of the French Tenth Army … your attack will find particularly favourable ground between Loos and La Bassée'. The French intended to throw seventeen divisions into the assault, the British six, with an army corps of three divisions and two cavalry corps in reserve.[28]

Though the junior partner, this was the biggest battle the British army had ever fought to that date. It was to be, according to General Richard Haking, the commander of IX Corps, which included Kipling's Guards Division, 'the biggest battle in the history of the world'.

The commander of First Army, General Douglas Haig, did not believe he had sufficient men or artillery to achieve the breakthrough Joffre sought, so he turned to the weapon the British had so resolutely condemned the previous spring – poisonous chlorine gas.

The attack was set for 25 September 1915 and was preceded by four days of bombardment, which served to warn the Germans of the coming attack. Haig consulted his meteorologist and asked him to decide when the gas should be used. The meteorologist demurred and told Haig it was his decision. At 5.50 a.m., the gas was released and 75,000 men went over the top.

The British had early success, taking the village of Loos and Hill 70, a slightly elevated patch of ground on which the Germans had built fortifications known as the Lens Road Redoubt. The 15th (Scottish) Division advanced into Loos village. The Germans were driven back from their front-line positions.

This was the moment of maximum danger for the defenders. A concerted push by the British might have turned victory into a rout, but, for reasons not fully understood to this day, the British commander-in-chief Field Marshal Sir John French refused to release the two divisions under his command until that evening. This fatal decision hastened the end for French as commander-in-chief.

Eventually the attack petered out and the Germans retook Hill 70. The first day of Loos had been a bloody slaughter for the British.

The second day was also a catastrophe. One German regimental diary records, 'Never had machine guns such straightforward work to do with barrels becoming hot and swimming in oil, they traversed to and fro along the enemy's ranks; one machine gun alone fired 12,500 rounds that afternoon.' Alan Clark, in his coruscating account of 1915, *The Donkeys*, wrote that the second day of Loos was comparable 'under conditions of infinite squalor and magnified in scale a hundredfold of the charge at Balaclava'. In three and a half hours of fighting, the British suffered 8,264 casualties, out of 15,000 men who advanced. German losses were trifling by comparison. They dubbed Loos the 'Leichenfeld' – the field of corpses.

While the battle was progressing, Kipling and his men were slowly making their way towards the front. Whatever optimism these men might have had a year earlier surely dissipated as they traipsed past mile after mile of casualty ambulances, wounded soldiers and exhausted pack animals floundering in the other direction.

Kipling wrote home, 'We've been marching for the last two days … The front line trenches are nine miles off from here so it won't be a very long march. We marched 18 miles last night in pouring wet. It came down in sheets steadily.' By the time they reached their front line, Kipling's battalion was in no position to fight. They were exhausted, soaking wet and numbed with fatigue. Nevertheless, they were pressed into action on 27 September. The goal was to capture and this time hold Hill 70, come what may.

The three brigades of the Guards Division were to attack Hill 70 from different directions. The 2nd Battalion was tasked with crossing half a mile of open territory to reach Chalk Pit Wood. Hill 70 was already a heap of corpses when Kipling and his platoon attacked some coalmine outhouses just beyond the wood. The Germans had turned the Puits 14 bis mine works into a fortress, buttressed by the Bois Hugo and Chalet Wood behind. The Irish Guards were met by deadly machine gun fire from the Bois Hugo. The 1st Scots Guards attacked Puits 14 bis, assisted by some of the Irish. It was during this assault that John Kipling was killed.

The family received a telegram after four days stating he was 'missing presumed injured'. This gave them an agonising sense of hope and precipitated a fruitless search which went on for years. The Kiplings clung onto the fact that some men turned up months after going missing, usually in German prisoner-of-war camps. John's mother Carrie wrote to the Swiss Red Cross, the Irish Guards depot and hospitals where casualties were treated. Rudyard wrote to anyone in the regiment he thought might help. 'I should be most grateful if you could tell me anything you may remember about the fight on that day, or if you are able to give me the names of any men who you think may be able to help me with information,' he wrote to a Private W. Fitzpatrick.

Yet he was resigned to the worst, 'The wife is standing it wonderfully tho' she clings to the bare hope of his being a prisoner of war. I've seen what shells can do, and I don't.' But they still campaigned in the hope that he might somehow be still alive. They toured the Western Front and searched hospitals. They dropped fliers over German lines. They beseeched the royal families of neutral Holland and Sweden to intervene with Germany and find out if John was a prisoner of war.

By this stage, Kipling had a partial but telling impression of what had happened. He wrote to his old school friend General Lionel Dunsterville:

> He led the right platoon over a mile of open ground in face of machine gun fire and was dropped at the further limit of the advance after having emptied his pistol into a house full of German machine guns. His CO and his company commander told me how he led them and the wounded have confirmed it. He was a senior ensign tho' only 18 years and six weeks, had worked like a devil for a year at Warley and knew his Irish to the ground. He was reported on as one of the best of the subalterns and was gym instructor and signaller. It was a short life. I'm sorry that all the years of work ended in that one afternoon but lots of people are in our position and it is something to have bred a man.

By December of that year, all hope had gone. Outwardly, Rudyard Kipling kept up appearances, busying himself writing letters while continuing to support the war effort in public. Privately, he was a broken man. Grief and guilt assailed him and he questioned all his old certainties. He told an old friend, Julia Depew, who came to visit, 'Down on your knees Julia, and thank God that you have not a son.'

Kipling sublimated his grief into two great endeavours which would occupy his later years. In 1917, he was approached to write a history of the Irish Guards in the Great War. Kipling confessed himself to be no expert on military matters but his application to the task made up for his lack of knowledge. He wrote assiduously to commanders, read regimental and divisional diaries, soldiers' letters, and a steady stream of Irish Guards came to his Suffolk home at Batesman to offer their reminiscences. He walked the blood-sodden earth of every battlefield from Mons to the Marne. Where was this company deployed? Where did the reserves come in? Who was deployed in which trench? What was the axis of attack?

The result is a two-volume series, one for each of the two Irish Guards battalions, which are among the most comprehensive and best-written regimental histories of the war.

In 1918 Kipling also wrote a poem, 'The Irish Guards' in which he suggested the Irish Guards were the direct descendants of the famous Irish Brigade, which fought with the French against the British at the Battle of Fontenoy in 1745, a battle at which France won a decisive victory:

> For we carried our packs with Marshal Saxe
> When Louis was our King,
> But Douglas Haig's our Marshal now,
> And we're King George's men.
> And after one hundred and seventy years
> We're fighting for France again.

His other great endeavour was to become the literary advisor to the Imperial War Graves Commission. He threw himself into a project he described as the 'biggest single bit of work since the Pharaohs and they only worked in their own country'. Kipling was tasked with encapsulating and articulating the grief, numbness and sense of loss which had settled across the traumatised nations of Europe.

Kipling's undeniable genius for the apt phrase is evident in many inscriptions chosen by him: for example, 'Their names liveth for evermore' or 'Their glory shall not be blotted out', both of which are from Ecclesiastes.

In 1922, King George V toured the battlefields of the Western Front. Kipling composed the poem 'The King's Pilgrimage' and the speech in which the king made a heartfelt plea for peace:

> I have many times asked myself whether there can be a more total advocate of
> peace upon earth through the years to come, than this massed multitude of silent
> witnesses to the desolation of War.

In the same year, Kipling composed 'Common Form', less a poem than an epigram:

> If any questions why we died,
> Tell them, because our fathers lied.

It has become one of Kipling's most famous couplets. But what exactly did he mean by it? Was he referring to the myths and legends the older generations tell in order to legitimise war for the younger generations? Or was he referring to himself and the deceit he practised when using his influence to get his son a commission, after he had been turned down by the medical board?

His grief also surfaced in his poem 'The Children', in which he imagined his son's terrible death:

> To be senselessly tossed and re-tossed in stale mutilation
> From crater to crater. For this we shall take expiation.
> But who shall return us our children?

In 1997, the actor David Haig, who bears more than a passing resemblance to Rudyard Kipling, wrote a play called *My Boy Jack*. He played the part of Rudyard Kipling. It premiered at the Hampstead Theatre. The play was turned into a €15-million film in 2007 and shown on ITV on Remembrance Sunday. It featured Haig as Rudyard Kipling and two of the most prominent actors of the time – Daniel Radcliffe (Harry Potter) as John Kipling and Kim Cattrall (*Sex and the City*) as Carrie Kipling.

The play and film both depict Kipling as a man tormented by the guilt that he had, in effect, killed his own son. 'Do you think a single day passes when I don't consider that possibility? I think about it all the time, all the time … How could I condemn my son to oblivion? How could I do that to Jack?'

The discovery of John Kipling's grave also inspired *My Boy Jack*, a book by the well-known military authors Tonie and Valmai Holt. The book took issue with the findings of the commission. Their research determined that John Kipling could not be buried in the grave ascribed to him in St Mary's Advanced Dressing Station. They based their findings on two critical pieces of evidence: the grave determined to be that of John Kipling belonged to a lieutenant in the Irish Guards, but Kipling was a second lieutenant when he died and was only 'gazetted' (mentioned in the *London Gazette*, the official journal where all officer appointments are announced) after he died.

His last letter home, sent just days before he died, specifically requested an aluminium tag with the inscription '2nd lieutenant', not 'lieutenant'. There was no evidence, they concluded, that he was a lieutenant before he died.

They also took issue with Norm Christie's findings about where the body was found. The grid reference map shows he was found in G25, some 6,000 yards behind where he is reported to have fallen. They reasoned that Christie's explanation for Kipling's body being so far from the front line – that his death should have been recorded in H25, not G25 – was stretching credulity. In addition, the remains of an identified British soldier were found near where Kipling's body was allegedly discovered. The identified soldier, Private P. Blaber of the London Civil Service Rifles, was operating in the G25 area at the time of his death.

The Holts first made their argument in 1998 and in later editions of their book buttressed it with commentary from experts who had reviewed their evidence, including a former circuit judge Anthony Babington QC, the curator of the Guards Museum Captain David Horn and military historian Michael Johnstone.

It took a long time for the Commonwealth War Graves Commission to respond in detail to the Holt claims. In September 2015, just before the centenary of the Battle of Loos, the commission explained its rationale for sticking with its original decision. It had discovered precedents that second lieutenants were promoted to lieutenant before being gazetted and often in the days before battle. Therefore, it was probable that Kipling was wearing the uniform of a full lieutenant when he was killed.

The commission also examined the grid reference maps 18 Labour Company had used when it found the body. Contrary to the presumptions of both Christie and the Holts, it discovered that G25 and H25 are next to each other and not 6,000 yards apart, as had been presumed. The evidence was also accepted by the Ministry of Defence, which reviewed the files in the case.

In correspondence released through the UK government's Freedom of Information Act an unnamed Ministry of Defence (MOD) official (the name is redacted) concluded that Kipling was probably not promoted to a full lieutenant before he died, but the Grave Registrations Unit probably used lieutenant as a generic term. He also concluded from his own research that the 2nd Battalion Irish Guards did fight in the area covered by G25, where Kipling's body was found.

Further corroboration that the Commonwealth War Graves Commission decision was correct came in January 2016 in an article published in *Stand To!*, the Western Front Association journal. The authors, Graham Parker and his daughter, Joanna Legg, concluded that 'on the balance of probabilities' the identification was correct. They did so on the basis that original map referencing was wrong and that documentary evidence had shown that John Kipling was indeed a lieutenant when he died.

A definitive answer could only be obtained by DNA evidence, an unpalatable prospect for all involved.

It has all been a century too late for Rudyard Kipling and his wife Carrie, who ended their lives with that desperate vacuum at the heart of their grief. It was a fate that they shared with the families of 526,816 British soldiers who have no known grave to this day and probably never will.

—

One of the newest memorials on the Western Front is the plaque to the London Irish Rifles in Loos town centre.

It was unveiled on 26 September 2015, 100 years and a day after the start of the Battle of Loos. The London Irish Rifles will be forever associated with that battle because of the story of the 'footballer of Loos'.

Private Frank Edwards cheerily kicked a football across no man's land as the 1st Battalion of the London Irish Rifles went over the top. The football was shot but Edwards survived the war.

The plaque reads, 'Presented to the citizens of Loos-en-Gohelle by the London Irish Rifles Regimental Association on the occasion of the commemoration of the 100th anniversary of the Battle of Loos 26th September 2015.'

The London Irish Rifles had, in their ranks, the novelist Patrick MacGill, whose book *The Great Push* tells the story of the Battle of Loos from the regiment's point of view. MacGill was a stretcher-bearer and was injured on the first day of the battle.

MacGill also wrote memorable poetry about the war. One of his poems, 'In the Morning', was read out at the unveiling ceremony for the plaque in Loos town centre:

> Food of the bomb and the hand-grenade
> Still the slushy pool and mud –
> Ah, the path we came was a path of blood,
> When we went to Loos in the morning.

12

THE STATUE OF NOTRE DAME DES VICTOIRES AT ST MARTIN DE NOEUX-LES-MINES

Easter Week 1916 dawned dry and bright in northern France. It had rained incessantly for the last week and it would rain the following week, but this day – Easter Sunday, 23 April – was beautiful.

In the blue skies above, German aircraft buzzed over the lines held by the 16th (Irish) Division. The men looked up with trepidation. Aircraft meant activity. The Germans were planning something.

The division occupied an area of the front line from north of the large mining town of Lens to south of Hulluch. On a large map, the front line looked straight, but it was full of deadly kinks and salients. From the air, the Irish section resembled a broken nose prodding into the German lines.

The ground was a sodden mass of shell holes, broken drains and blasted earth. The British Tommy hated this section of the frontline. It was always wet and bleak. The monotonous vistas of slag heaps, broken railway tracks and industrial machinery hurt the eyes and offered no visual relief to the men.

It was a 'jagged, scarred and mutilated sweep of mining villages, factories, quarries, slag-dumps, chalk pits and railway embankments,' according to Rudyard Kipling, who tramped these killing grounds looking for traces of his son John.[1]

Water in many of the trenches was never less than ankle deep. The soldiers spent tedious days at the Sisyphean task of bailing water and repairing trenches only to have them trashed by shellfire and flooded by rain all over again.

'The trenches are a sight to see,' the Irish chaplain Fr Willie Doyle wrote to his father, 'it is just a big ditch full of slush and water'. Doyle was a chaplain with 49th Brigade of the 16th Division, though he looked on the whole division as his flock. He likened the men's abodes to St Patrick's Purgatory, the place of penance in Lough Derg, County Donegal. Trench foot, the painful and frequently gangrenous infection from standing for hours in cold water, was common. Rats proliferated among the human debris.

The most important day of the Christian calendar was no different from any of the days preceding it. The devil's work continued, as it must in wartime, on Easter Sunday. The men of the 8th Royal Munster Fusiliers, a service battalion mostly recruited in County Limerick, spent the day doing bombing training, wiring and practising night attacks. There was sporadic shelling and sniper fire from the German lines opposite them, near the red-brick mining village of Hulluch.[2]

The 8th Royal Dublin Fusiliers spent their day practising wire-cutting while dodging shells. Three men were injured from a shell attack. The battalion diary noted that the town of Noeux-les-Mines, where the divisional HQ was based, had been shelled.[3] There was no respite, even away from the front line. 'The period when a battalion was not holding the front trenches was so filled with fatigues, raids and back breaking work parties that many a tired man welcomed the return to the death-dealing lines,' lamented Second Lieutenant J.F.B. O'Sullivan of the 6th Connaught Rangers.[4]

The area had been a place of dread first for the French and then for the British, who took it over from the French in 1915. Parties sent out to repair wire or spy on the enemy often encountered the putrefying remains of bodies from previous battles. The whole place smelt of death. It was, according to Doyle, the essence of the biblical 'abomination of desolation'.[5]

The area occupied by the 16th (Irish) Division was a salient captured by the British during the Battle of Loos. At its southern extremity was the ruined town of Loos. At its northern extremity was the Vermelles-Hulluch Road. The front line meandered around quarries, slag heaps, chalk pits, streams and two woods, the Bois Hugo and Bois Báse. The Tommies called the salient the horseshoe. They could be observed and attacked from three sides. Facing them was the 5th Bavarian Division and its reserve division. The Germans still retained most of the defendable ground but they wanted to recapture Loos.

On this bright Easter Sunday morning, in rear trenches, bombed-out buildings and churches, the men of the 16th took Sunday Mass where they could find it. This was an overwhelmingly Irish Catholic and nationalist division. Some 98 per cent of men in the ranks were Catholic. They had already attained a reputation for piety, which delighted Doyle. He was a Jesuit of a nervous and timid disposition, unsuited, one would imagine, for front-line services in the trenches, yet he conquered his fears through a deep faith that helped him deal with the terrible sights he witnessed.

He was 42 when war broke out. His entire adult life had been lived in the relative comfort and security of the Jesuit order from the time he entered the Jesuit novitiate in Tullabeg, near Tullamore, in County Offaly as an 18-year-old.

He had been a teacher, a preacher and a traveller. His life had been a figurative and literal journey of faith. He travelled widely throughout Catholic Europe and gave some 140 missions and retreats.[6] He was under no obligation to volunteer for chaplaincy service in the First World War, but he did so anyway. He saw the experience as a sacrifice worthy of Christ. He was prepared to lead a life that was 'truly crucified'.[7] If he died he would become a martyr, he reasoned. Therefore, why worry? He cared little for his personal safety.

One Sunday he cycled through a notoriously shell-shattered section of road from one battalion mess to another to say Mass. He ignored warnings and dodged shells, which he likened to being charged at by 'ten mad bulls'. He knew there was a possibility he would be killed, but also a certainty that many of the men moving up to the front would die before receiving the sacraments again. When he reached his destination, the shells exploding nearby rattled the walls of the church, terrifying the men inside. Doyle did not flinch. 'Call it a miracle if you will, but the moment I turned the corner the guns ceased firing, and not a shell till I was safely in the village church. I felt quite happy and quite ready to be blown from the altar.'[8]

He drew comfort from the men who drew comfort from him. This first Easter Sunday Mass in the trenches of Hulluch was an improvised affair. 'My church was a bit of a trench, the altar a pile of sandbags,' he wrote to his father. 'Though we had to stand deep in mud, not knowing the moment a sudden call to arms would come, many a fervent prayer went up to heaven that morning.'[9]

There were 1,200 Catholics in 49th Brigade. The men had a hunger for the sacraments of the Catholic Church which even Doyle, in his boundless enthusiasm, found hard to cope with. 'I have positively a pain in my arm giving Absolution and Communion in the morning.' He noted how the men of the 16th filled the pews of local churches vacated by the more secular-minded French:

> They are really a fine lot of fellows and make a good impression on the people wherever they go, more especially here in the North of France, the mining district, where most of the men are too busy washing the dirt out of themselves on Sunday to bother about much else. Hence it is an object lesson to the parlez-vous to see the crowds who come to Mass and Communion daily and Benediction in the evening. There is nothing like the prospect of a German shell for putting the fear of God into one. Our poor lads are just grand. They curse like troopers all the day, they give the Boches hell, purgatory and heaven all combined at night and next morning come kneeling in the mud for Mass and Holy Communion when they get the chance.[10]

Wherever a shell burst, Doyle was there, often smiling despite the carnage. 'Is it any wonder that … he was worth several officers in any hot spot when endurance was tested,' Lieutenant Frank Laird of the Royal Dublin Fusiliers observed.[11]

Doyle would become, according to Major General William Hickie, the general commanding the 16th (Irish) Division, 'one of the bravest men I know'.[12]

The omnipresence of death made devout men out of those inclined to indifference about their religious observance.

'Your brother used to take every opportunity of going to the sacraments,' a priest wrote to the brother of Lieutenant Louis Quinlan, who was killed during Easter Week 1916 while serving with the Royal Inniskilling Fusiliers on the Western Front. 'He received Holy Communion on the Sunday before his death. You can be perfectly satisfied that his soul is safe. He was always prepared to die.'[13]

Doyle's men, as well as being Catholics, were nationalists. They had put aside their earnest desire for home rule to fight a common enemy. 'Remember Belgium,' the recruiting poster said. The former nationalist MP Tom Kettle certainly did. When war broke out in August 1914, he was buying arms in Belgium for the Irish Volunteers. He was horrified by the atrocities carried out by invading German troops and concluded that the war was one of 'civilisation against barbarians'. He was commissioned into the 9th Royal Dublin Fusiliers.

The 16th (Irish) Division was the closest to John Redmond's dream of an Irish army in all but name. It was one of the volunteer divisions raised by Lord Kitchener. The 36th (Ulster) Division was almost exclusively (in the beginning, at least) Protestant; the 10th (Irish) Division was mixed with a slight preponderance of Protestants over Catholics; the 16th was Catholic. In October 1914, *The Times* announced that Redmond had agreed to regard the 16th as the 'Irish Brigade about which so much has been heard'.

Many of the men who joined it were from the Irish Volunteers, which had been founded in November 1913 as a nationalist counterweight to the Ulster Volunteer Force. The Irish Volunteers was set up to defend the promise of home rule. It was envisaged as a defensive force, though many within the organisation had other ideas.

Home rule was given royal assent in September 1914 but its implementation was suspended for the duration of the war. Redmond envisaged an Irish brigade staffed by Irish officers who understood their men. Recruitment, though, was slow relative to the rest of the United Kingdom. There was a residual antipathy towards service in the British army in some parts of Irish society, but the essentially rural nature of Ireland was another factor. Young farmers opted to stay at home. There was lots of money to be made during the war.

Redmond's generous offer of making the volunteers available for the British war effort was not reciprocated by any imaginative gesture on the part of the War Office or Lord Kitchener, who, despite being Irish-born, had little sympathy for Irish nationalist sensitivities.

Though the 16th (Irish) Division would fulfil Redmond's dream of a Catholic, nationalist division in the ranks, some 85 per cent of the officers were either British or Protestant Anglo-Irish, reflecting the institutional and class bias which existed in the British army at the time.[14] The 16th would eventually have the standard British army formation of three brigades of four battalions each: the 47th, 48th and 49th brigades:

The 47th Brigade

6th Royal Irish Regiment
6th Connaught Rangers
7th Leinster Regiment
8th Royal Munster Fusiliers

The 48th Brigade

7th Royal Irish Rifles
9th Royal Munster Fusiliers
8th Royal Dublin Fusiliers
9th Royal Dublin Fusiliers

The 49th Brigade

7th Royal Inniskilling Fusiliers
8th Royal Inniskilling Fusiliers

7th Royal Irish Fusiliers
8th Royal Irish Fusiliers

The 47th Brigade was billeted in Fermoy, the 48th at Buttevant and the 49th in Tipperary. Their overall commander was Major General William Bernard Hickie, an Irish Catholic. He took over from Lieutenant General Lawrence Parsons, a member of the famous family from Birr, County Offaly, which included William Parsons, the man who in 1845, at the start of the Irish Famine, had built the biggest telescope in the world. Lawrence Parsons had overseen the drilling and training but, aged 66, was deemed too old to take them to France.[15]

After initial training in Ireland, the 16th moved to England in September 1915. A week before Christmas, they left Aldershot by train for Southampton and from there they sailed to Le Havre. They were only a day in France when they heard the distant rumble of guns. Christmas away from home was spent in billets in Béthune. For most of them, it was their first time away from home; many would never return home at all. The horrors of the following year would include the Battle of the Somme.

Their first weeks at the front found them dispersed among other divisions in order to 'blood' fighting units before facing the Germans. The policy of pitching brand new divisions, composed almost entirely of inexperienced volunteers, into the deep end had been discredited by the debacles of Gallipoli and the carnage of Loos. These instructive lessons for the British commanders had been measured by the deaths of thousands of men who had left their civilian lives for what they assumed would be a short stint in the army. The history of the 7th Royal Inniskilling Fusiliers records that experience on the front line could only be gained by 'the analysis of the thousand-and-one things which happen, or don't happen, daily'.[16]

The 16th was then transferred to the Loos sectors. Arriving in Loos, Doyle traversed a battlefield that had not been cleared after eighteen months of fighting. 'Almost the first thing I saw was a human head torn from the trunk, though there was no sign of the body,' he recorded. 'One poor fellow had been buried, surely, before the breath had left his body, for there was every sign of a last struggle and one arm was thrust out from its shroud of clay.'

On 29 February 1916, 47th and 48th brigades moved into the trenches in front of Hulluch. At the same time 49th brigade, newly arrived in France, took over a section of trench vacated by a brigade from the 15th (Scottish) Division. This was where the British had expended an ocean of blood during the Battle of Loos the previous autumn.

The 16th (Irish) Division was attached to I Corps, commanded by General Hubert Gough, one of the army intriguers behind the Curragh crisis of March 1914. His antipathy towards Irish nationalists was softened by regular contact with those with whom he disagreed, particularly the two nationalist MPs within his ranks:

Among many whom I knew there were Captains Willie Redmond and Stephen Gwynn [who were both nationalist MPs]. Brought up, as I have been, in an atmosphere of hostility to home rule and all who supported it, I found in these two, and in many other Irishmen in this division, home rulers though they may have been – a loyalty, a devoted sense of duty, and a gallant spirit which won esteem and affection.[17]

In September 1914, the Irish Republican Brotherhood, a secret revolutionary organisation that had infiltrated the Irish Volunteers, made the fateful decision to plan a Rising while Britain was distracted by the war. It was the same month the 16th (Irish) Division was sanctioned. Eighteen months later, at home and abroad, the aspirations of both sets of armed Irishmen would be put to the proof.

During this Easter Week, these men, who shared the same nationality, religion and political aims and many of whom had been comrades-in-arms in the Irish Volunteers less than two years previously, would face death and injury. Only one group would emerge as heroes, only one would be feted and officially commemorated, their names attached to streets, schools, railway stations, tower blocks, hospitals and GAA grounds, only one would enter the pantheon of Irish national martyrs, only one would be venerated in the official history of the new Irish state.

In Dublin, the Rising began before midday on Easter Monday when volunteers seized weapons from the magazine fort in Dublin's Phoenix Park. At 12.20 p.m., the rebels marched into the General Post Office (GPO), the seat of all communication in Ireland, and seized it. They hoisted the Irish tricolour from the roof.

Then Pádraig Pearse, the president of the 'Provisional Government', emerged onto the steps of the GPO and read the Proclamation of the Irish Republic. The proclamation refers to 'our gallant Allies in Europe' – namely, Germany, which, somewhat reluctantly, had agreed to support the planned Rising. The Germans believed it had little chance of success. Nevertheless, they made a gesture of solidarity by shelling the English ports of Yarmouth and Lowestoft.[18]

The first fatality of the Rising was Dublin Metropolitan Police officer Constable James O'Brien who was guarding the gates of Dublin Castle, the seat of British rule in Ireland. Irishmen in the service of the British security forces would be, from now on, regarded as legitimate targets.

Earlier that same morning, on the Western Front, the 8th Royal Dublin Fusiliers suffered their first fatalities of Easter Week. Private Patrick Rourke from Clane, County Kildare, and Private George Lloyd from Dundalk, County Louth, were both killed by a German bomb.

On Easter Tuesday, a bombing party from the Dublins went to clear a crater in no man's land of Germans. That same evening in Dublin, Irish Volunteers killed or wounded twenty-three soldiers from the 8th's sister battalion, the 10th Royal Dublin Fusiliers, who were caught in an ambush on Parliament Street.[19]

In France, news of the rebellion began to spread. One Jesuit priest reported calling into brigade headquarters on his way to the front 'and heard of the outbreak in Dublin. The news was naturally alarming as it was not easy to find out exactly what had happened.'[20] John 'Max' Staniforth, an English officer in the 7th Battalion of the Leinster Regiment scribbled in his diary, 'Poor old Dublin. Always in the wars.'

In France the Irish regiments holding the front line were engaged in their own life-and-death struggle with 'our gallant Allies in Europe'.

The warning signs had been apparent on 26 April, the day before the Hulluch gas attack. In response to reports of gas canisters being spotted in front of the German lines, the trenches of the 8th Royal Irish Fusiliers were evacuated to bring up 8-inch guns to fire on the enemy. Ominously, the battalion diaries records, 'The shooting was good, but no gas was discovered'.[21] A German deserter also warned of an imminent gas attack and rats were observed fleeing the German lines into no man's land – another telling sign.[22]

The Germans had hidden the canisters well. They had also erected observation balloons over their trenches.

Early the next morning, the German attack began. The weather was 'fine and warm' with a light breeze – perfect conditions for a gas attack. The attack was made by regiments of the 4th Bavarian Division, which held the front line near Loos. Those who bore the brunt of it were 48th Brigade in the south and the 49th Brigade in the north.

In the north, the 8th Royal Irish Fusiliers and the 7th Royal Inniskilling Fusiliers of 49th Brigade faced the German trenches in front of the town of Hulluch.

In the south, the 8th and 9th Royal Munster Fusiliers, with 48th Brigade, were north-east of Loos and opposite Puits 14 bis, a mineshaft which the Germans had turned into a fortress. It was a thin khaki line that the Germans attacked that morning. It was the Thursday of Easter Week. The superior British numbers and equipment was beginning to tell in Dublin, but the Irish on this section of the Western Front had no time to ponder the news from home.

At 4.35 a.m., the Germans opened fire on the Irish lines with machine gun and artillery. They knew the Irish would have no choice but to return fire: they would all approach the fire step to respond in kind, the front-line trenches packed with men. Ten minutes later, and according to their plan, the Germans released chlorine gas from 3,800 cylinders on to the Irish lines.

A 'dense cloud of black gas and smoke between us and the sun' drifted across the Irish lines, according to the RDF's commanding officer, Lieutenant-Colonel Edward Bellingham from County Louth. It was followed by heavy bombardment and more gas, a whitish substance that seemed to drift from the saps (trenches dug into no man's land) and craters occupied by the Germans for the assault.[23]

Under cover of the gas, the German assaulting troops entered the Dublins front-line trenches and the German artillery switched to the communication and rear trenches to prevent reinforcements arriving.

The density of the gas was such that two kittens belonging to the commanding officer of the King's Own Scottish Borderers 3 miles behind the lines started exhibiting signs of gas poisoning. Soldiers on leave behind the lines in Noeux-les-Mines 5 miles behind the front found their tobacco tasted different and the gas could be smelled 15 miles away.[24]

HULLUCH GAS ATTACKS APRIL 27–29, 1916

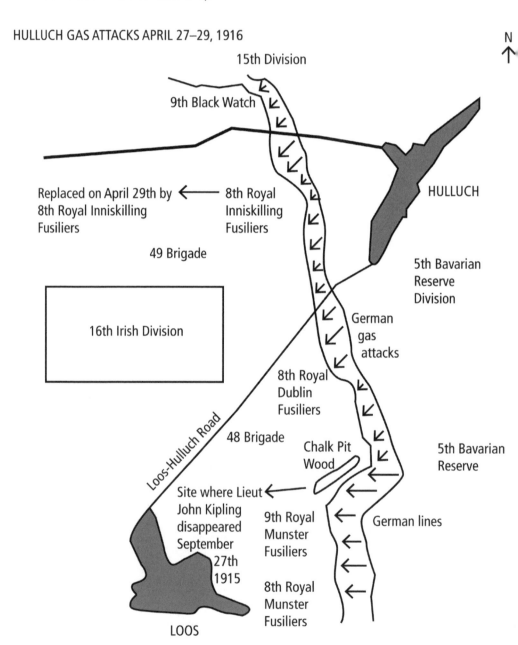

N

15th Division

9th Black Watch

Replaced on April 29th by 8th Royal Inniskilling Fusiliers

8th Royal Inniskilling Fusiliers

HULLUCH

49 Brigade

16th Irish Division

5th Bavarian Reserve Division

German gas attacks

8th Royal Dublin Fusiliers

Loos-Hulluch Road

48 Brigade

Chalk Pit Wood

5th Bavarian Reserve

Site where Lieut John Kipling disappeared September 27th 1915

9th Royal Munster Fusiliers

German lines

8th Royal Munster Fusiliers

LOOS

The soldiers on both sides dreaded hand-to-hand combat most. Shells and machine gun bullets at least had a degree of anonymity about them, but, in the trenches, face-to-face and man-to-man, it was kill or be killed. Rifles or machine guns were useless at close quarters. It was pistols, bayonets and grenades. The dead and wounded lay together in a congealed mass of blood beneath the choking gas, which lent a greenish, deadly pallor to everything it touched.

During this encounter, the Dublins came off worst. 'Nearly all the men were killed or wounded,' Bellingham recorded in the regimental diary. 'They [the Germans] were put out again and the line held for the rest of the day by the remnants of the two companies.' The impact on A and D Companies was devastating. A Company had twenty effective soldiers left; D Company forty-five. The 16th (Irish) Division counted approximately eighty dead German soldiers in front of the Irish lines.

The night of 27 April was spent evacuating the injured and burying the dead, 'identifying where possible'. Some bodies had been so badly pulverised by shelling that they were unidentifiable.[25]

Among the officer casualties were Lieutenant Robert Valentine, the assistant geologist for the Geological Society of Ireland, who used his scientific skills to devise a better way of operating the Lewis machine gun. He was a volunteer who joined the war in September 1914 and was commanding B Company. Bellingham wrote to his parents, 'Your boy was one of the best and most thorough officers I had, and his loss will be deplored by all. He was a favourite with the officers and very popular with the men. I had formed great expectations of him.'[26]

In two days, the 8th Royal Dublin Fusiliers lost 368 men out of a full battalion strength of 946. The list of casualties, which is included in the regimental diary, stretches to ten pages.[27]

Further north, on the front of the 7th Inniskilling Fusiliers, the Germans infiltrated the trenches and separated B and C Companies. Hand-to-hand combat ensued. Men who had escaped the artillery and gas shells found themselves confronting bayonet-wielding German troops with grenades. Several prisoners were taken.

In this intense outburst of savage combat, the 7th Inniskillings suffered 263 casualties, including 137 men gassed. Some 66 men were killed in the initial assault, but the Inniskillings held on and expelled the Germans.

Their brigadier-general Philip Leveson Gower commended their bravery. 'You have proved yourself to be good men of your country. Ireland can be proud of you. In future when asked what battalion did you belong to, you can say with pride you were in the 7th Royal Inniskilling Fusiliers, a fighting battalion, and you will not have to say anything further.'[28]

Though they had the advantage of gas and surprise, the Germans also suffered terribly in the dreadful business of trench raids. As they were driven back, they blew up a mine between two craters named Tralee and Munster and, under the cover of dust and debris, retreated back to their own lines. Their own dead numbered in the hundreds. Enemy dead counted in front of 48th and 49th brigades numbered in hundreds. Many were killed on 29 April when the gas blew back into their faces.

The following day was quiet as the wind was blowing unfavourably from the south-east, but the Germans resumed hostilities on 29 April, the last day of the attack and also the last and bloodiest day of the Easter Rising.

The chlorine gas was carried over to the Irish lines on a light breeze and seemed to linger. It took forty-five minutes for it to drift from the German to the Irish lines, a distance of about 1,000 yards. British air reconnaissance found a trail of dead vegetation across the path of the German gas 'down to the last blade of grass'.[29]

The lingering gas killed many more men. 'Scarcely a man could survive the attack,' Bellingham wrote. 'The casualties from gas poisoning were more severe than on the 27th owing presumably to the gas clouds meeting and remaining stationary and concentrated over the trenches.'[30]

On 29 April, the 8th Royal Inniskilling Fusiliers had replaced the 7th and it was their turn to face the German onslaught. They suffered some 62 fatalities and 214 casualties.

'Warfare of previous generations had given to the British language the word "decimated" as signifying a tragic and hard-to-endure degree of loss,' wrote the regiment's historian Sir Frank Fox. 'But the 7th and 8th Inniskillings had suffered casualties not of one in ten but of more than one in three, but yet had held fast.'[31]

The 8th Battalion of the Royal Munster Fusiliers was pressed into action on 28 April and was confronted with a ghastly sight. 'I saw hundreds dying all round me,' wrote Private Michael Ridge of the Munsters. 'I went from the support to the front line about a quarter of a mile. I was practically walking on dead bodies all the way.'[32] It suffered twenty fatalities on 29 April.

The grim business of burying the dead was left to the men of 47th Brigade, who had been in reserve. 'I thought I was accustomed to war and all its frightfulness, yet this fairly staggers me,' Captain Charles Weld of the 7th Leinster Regiment recorded in its diary.[33] 'It was a ghastly sight. Hundreds of men who were gassed lay three deep on the fire step. They had died in terrible agony with faces like purple from the gas. Many others not yet dead gasped out green foam, and dead rats likewise gassed. This is about the most fearful sight I have ever seen.' The following day he wrote, 'Weather turned very hot and as a result the dead, some of which were not buried, began to stink.'

Fr Doyle was equally confounded by the dreadful spectacle:

Many men died before I could reach them and were gone before I could pass back. There they lay, scores of them (we lost 800, nearly all from gas) in the bottom of the trench, in every conceivable posture of human agony; the cloths torn off their bodies in a vain effort to breathe while from end to end of that valley of death came one long unceasing moan from the lips of brave men fighting and struggling for life. I don't think you will blame me when I tell you that more than once the words of Absolution struck in my throat, and the tears splashed down on the patient suffering faces of my poor boys as I leant down to anoint them. One young soldier seized my two hands and covered them with kisses; another looked up and said, 'Oh! Father I can die happy now; sure I'm not afraid of death or anything else since I've seen you'.[34]

Tragically, there was even a husband and wife killed on the same day during Easter Week. Private John Naylor of the 8th Royal Dublin Fusiliers died on Saturday, 29 April, during the last German gas attack. His wife Margaret was caught in the crossfire during the last day of the Easter Rising and died two days later. The couple's three children, Margaret, Kitty and Tessie, were left as orphans.[35]

The gas attack was over. The 16th (Irish) Division had suffered 2,128 casualties, of which 538 were fatalities, nearly ten times the number of rebels killed during the fighting in Easter Week (58).[36]

While their fellow countrymen lay dead in their hundreds in France, Dublin residents jeered and booed the rebels as they filed, defeated and exhausted, through the streets of Dublin. The rebellion prompted a sense of outrage among soldiers serving at the front, who felt betrayed by men who had sought the support of the enemy in their enterprise.

'Nothing has affected Irishmen out here more than this,' the Jesuit chaplain Fr Henry Gill wrote just three days after the rebellion ended. 'We cannot think of anything else than the terrible things which have been going on in Dublin. We only see accounts in English and French papers.'[37]

Constitutional nationalists felt betrayed, especially John Redmond, who would see his life's work for home rule destroyed in the broken shell of the GPO. He told the Central News of America agency:

Is it not an additional horror that on the very day when we hear that the men of the Dublin Fusiliers have been killed by Irishmen on the streets of Dublin we receive the news of how the men of the 16th Division – our own Irish Brigade, and of the same Dublin Fusiliers – had dashed forward and by their unconquerable bravery retaken the trenches that the Germans had won at Hulluch. This attempted blow at home rule is made the more wicked and the more insolent by the fact that Germany plotted it, Germany organised it, Germany paid for it.

The scale of death shocked the British army commanders. After the Second Battle of Ypres, the British had introduced a new 'box respirator' and had drilled 'gas discipline' into their infantry. They believed sufficient precautions were in place to deal with any gas eventuality.

The British official historian Brigadier General Sir James Edmonds concluded that any attempt to blame the men of the 16th (Irish) Division for lack of gas discipline would be unjust. 'The helmet was obviously insufficient protection against the strong concentration of gas which the enemy was able to produce, the heaviest incidence of casualties and the highest mortality occurring at those parts of the front line nearest to the enemy's trenches.'[38]

The Germans also suffered terrible losses. The 9th Bavarian regiment recorded 163 fatalities from the gas when it blew back across their lines on 29 April.

The British anti-gas committee investigated the attacks at Hulluch. Some of the men were gassed before they could be roused from their dugouts. Many officers succumbed to gas because they were so busy exhorting their men to put on their gas masks that they neglected to do so themselves.

The men were not warned that even with the gas masks on, they would feel a degree of irritation to their throats and lungs that was relatively harmless. Consequently, many thought their gas masks were not working and took them off, exposing themselves fully to the poison fumes.

On one section of the line on 27 April, the Germans had let off smoke bombs first, lulling the Irish into believing the attack had passed. As many of the Irishmen had taken off their masks, they were caught by the second wave of chlorine gas.[39] 'These men had had practically no training for the use of helmets.'

The 16th had been through hell, but had held on to their trenches. It was an achievement. Loos was not retaken.[40]

—

On 1 May, the Germans hung out two placards in front of the trenches occupied by the 8th Battalion of the Royal Munster Fusiliers, each imparting bad news to the British soldiers opposite them. 'Irishmen! Heavy Uproar in Ireland. English guns are firing at your wifes [sic] and children'. For men like Private Martin Ridge, this was the first they heard about the Rising. He wrote home, 'We knew about the trouble in Ireland very soon as the Germans had it up on a board in front of our trenches between Loos and Hulluch.'

The Germans also imparted bad news about one of the great British debacles of the First World War: the siege at Kut and the surrender of 13,000 British troops in modern-day Iraq to the Ottoman Empire, which also occurred on 29 April 1916. The attempt to lift the siege on Kut involved one Tom Barry, then a gunner with the Royal Field Artillery, later to become one of the most feared IRA guerrilla commanders of the War of Independence.

The placard read:

Interesting War News
of April 29th 1916
Kut el Amara has been taken in
by the Turcs and the whole English
army theirin
--- 13000 men ---
maken [*sic*] prisoners.

The roughly improvised signs were made from packing-case timber nailed to a stake made from sapling, with the bark still attached. The placards were shot by the outraged Munsters, who regarded them as taunts. Their ranks were further thinned by the proximity of the German trenches just a few hundred yards away. 'There is enemy activity every day,' the battalion war diary recorded. Trench mortars and snipers were responsible for many deaths.

Observing the taunting placards was Major Laurence Roche from Dromin, County Limerick. Roche was born in the parish of Dromin in west Limerick in 1869. A near neighbour was Éamon de Valera, the most senior rebel leader to survive the Easter Rising, future Taoiseach and Irish president.

Roche was a rate collector for Limerick County Council, a Justice of the Peace and stalwart of the community, but it was his sporting ability that would draw people to him. 'Roche was one of my boyhood heroes, a man of magnificent physique,' the prominent Republican and future Irish government minister Seán Moylan remembered. 'A great all-round athlete, he had been a member of Limerick's victorious All-Ireland football team. He had thus all the qualities that appealed to youth.'[41]

He was 6ft 1in, an extraordinary height at a time when men were much shorter than they are today.[42] He won an all-Ireland senior football medal with Limerick Commercials in 1896 (the final was not played until 1898) and represented Ireland in a match against London exiles at Stamford Bridge in 1896.[43]

He excelled in other sports too. 'I heard a man say recently that Larry Roche had the finest puck of a hurling ball he ever saw,' wrote the popular sports columnist Carbery in May 1916.[44] He won three Irish championships for weight throwing between 1894 and 1897 and 110 first prizes at various sports meetings. He was capable of a long jump of 22ft and was a renowned sprinter.[45]

He went on to become chairman of the Limerick County Board and vice-president of the GAA Central Council. A Catholic nationalist heavily involved in the GAA, Roche was present at the foundation of the Irish Volunteers at the Rotunda Rink in Dublin in November 1913. He remained loyal to John Redmond after the split in the Irish Volunteers at the start of the war.

Roche was 45 when the war began. He was married with four children and had just bought Ballynamuddagh House in Bruree and 70 acres of land for £3,170 in 1913. The sale also included an adjoining farmhouse and 40 acres. Any of these circumstances were compelling reasons in themselves not to go to war, but Roche chose to join up. His decision was a boon to the British recruiters, who resolved to exploit his fame to aid their recruitment campaign. Roche's photograph appeared on recruitment posters across the province:

> The Irish Brigade – come and join us. We must all be Irishmen, officers and men, no others need apply. Any of our splendid manhood, our athletes, national volunteers, members of the Gaelic League and other Irish National Associations willing to join in the defence of Ireland are invited to correspond with Captain 'Larry' Roche (the old athlete), Bruree, Co Limerick.[46]

Roche claimed later to have been responsible for some 1,300 joining at the Strand Barracks in Limerick and 2,000 in total in Limerick, Cork, Kerry and Clare. At one rally in Kerry he appealed to the men in this most storied of GAA counties to yell 'Up Kerry' if they charged the German lines.[47]

Roche was given a commission in the 8th Battalion Royal Munster Fusiliers, a predominantly Limerick battalion. He rose to the rank of major (second in command of a battalion) and it was in that capacity that he ordered the offending placards be removed. An initial attempt to seize them was thwarted. It was simply too dangerous. It demanded near-suicidal courage.

Eventually, Lieutenant Francis Joseph Biggane from Shanakiel, Cork city, and Private Timothy Kemp from Lismore, County Waterford, volunteered their services. Both men were typical Catholic recruits to the British army. Biggane had been a student at University College Cork; Kemp was a part-time actor and a forward with his local GAA club. Both were to die later in the war.

According to S. McCance in his *History of the Royal Munster Fusiliers*, the men carried out a daring raiding party, 'strafed the Huns' and recovered the placards. When they returned to their trenches they sang 'God Save the King'.[48]

This account is probably fanciful. The regimental diary records that at 1 a.m. on the morning of 10 May 1916, the party crawled through no man's land to an unoccupied enemy sap and brought back the two signs.[49] No mention is made of anybody singing 'God Save the King'.

Kemp was promoted to Lance-Corporal for his actions. He wrote to a friend, 'We got the boards all right from dear old cousin Fritz, and we intend getting a lot more off him before we are finished. We are all longing for the day to come when we can get at them with the bayonet, and you may bet that we will make them shout "Merci, comrade".'[50]

Within a month, the signs were touring Limerick city and were 'naturally the object of much interest and curiosity', according to the *Limerick Leader*. The paper noted that the signs were peppered with bullet marks and had been on the end of a 'very warm fusillade' from the Munsters.

Above the report was news that a beautiful banner of the Sacred Heart had been made by the nuns of the Good Shepherd convent in Limerick for the 8th Battalion. This mixture of piety and bare-faced belligerence was typical of many Irish Catholics engaged in the war.[51]

Roche survived the war. In December 1917, he relinquished his commission on account of ill health. His war was over. He had been feted for his recruitment activities in 1914, but returned to a country where he became, by his own admission, a marked man.

In June 1921, during the War of Independence, the IRA seized Ballynamuddagh House. They put cattle and sheep on the land and cut down trees on the estate.

'My wife and I were threatened to be shot for attempting to remove them,' he would recount. Many of those who had been loyal to the Crown during the War of Independence and Civil War were targeted. The IRA burnt down some 275 'big houses', mostly of the Anglo-Irish ascendency, between 1919 and 1923.

In 1922, the British government set up the Irish Distress Committee (later the Irish Grants Committee) to compensate those who had lost their living or their homes during the War of Independence. In 1926, the Irish Grants Committee was extended to include the Civil War. During the civil war, anti-Treaty rebels seized and occupied the homes of many 'loyalists'. Huge damage was done and many of the old ascendancy families were intimidated and had to flee Ireland.

Roche applied to the committee but refused to go to court to testify about the damage done to his home because was he regarded as an 'alien' and 'damaged goods'.[52]

'No witnesses were available as they would not risk their lives by appearing with a British Officer in public courts, who was still an official of the British government,' he told the committee. 'This is my first claim. Being a resident still, I was under the enforced necessity of keeping quiet and not raising an alarm. I never reported the raids to the Crown forces. Reasons obvious.'

This was a reference to his post-war employment as a supervisor in a disability centre for ex-servicemen in Tipperary on a salary of £500 per year.

He was offered £270 for the damage done to his lands and property during the War of Independence, but rejected it on the basis that it would take £600 to repair the house alone.

By the time a second Irish Grants Committee (IGC) was set up in 1926, Roche had left Ireland and moved to Manchester. Once the disability centre closed down, Roche was out of work and had no prospect of getting employment in Ireland. His circumstances were judged to be 'very poor indeed'.

He again applied to the IGC. He pointed out that anti-Treaty forces had occupied the house during their battles with the Free State forces in July and August 1922. This time the house was 'totally wrecked under circumstances which made it impossible for the applicant to produce proofs which would entitle him to compensation'.

Roche was also physically threatened. 'I was a marked man and was several times threatened and revolvers pushed into my ribs,' he said. He was eventually offered and accepted £250 compensation from the British government.

His lands were sold off in 1927 under a Compulsory Purchase Order. 'I haven't a home or land in Ireland now and not a penny of the proceeds of the land sale reached me,' he told the committee.

He died in Manchester in May 1947.

—

The 16th (Irish) Division had its divisional headquarters in Noeux-les-Mines.

In honour of their fallen comrades, General Hickie ordered a subscription to be raised to buy a marble statute which would be located in the nineteenth-century St Martin's church in Noeux-les-Mines. It would be modelled on the one in the basilique of Notre Dame des Victoires (Paris). The statue features the Madonna and child. The infant Jesus has his feet on a globe with stars symbolising his dominion over the universe.[53]

The statue left Paris on Friday, 16 March 1917, with a view to being installed on St Patrick's Day. It finally arrived on site nine days later, just before Passion Sunday Mass was due to start on 25 March 1917. The workmen turned up at the door of the church about fifteen minutes before Mass started. The parish priest sent them away to return later.

The sacristan had left and the altar boys were playing outside, waiting for the priest to finish his office, when a huge German armour-plated shell from a land-based naval gun smashed through the walls of the building and exploded on impact. The church was destroyed in an instant. In May, on leave from Ypres where the 16th (Irish) Division was preparing for the Battle of Messines Ridge, Fr Doyle called into the church. He was incredulous when he saw the 'perfect ruin' where he had so often said Mass.

He wrote to his father:

When I went into the ruin I exclaimed to Mons le Curé 'surely you have had fifty shells in here!' 'No', he answered, 'only one. The havoc you see is the work of a single shot.' Not a trace of the beautiful altar where I so often offered the Holy Sacrifice remains. The carved stalls, the altar rails, benches and chairs are smashed into splinters, the roof and parts of the walls are stripped of plaster. I have never seen such a scene of desolation and destruction, the explanation being that the explosion took place inside the church and the liberated gases rushed round like ten thousand mad animals, rending and tearing all they met, seeking for an exit. Pictures, organ, statues, all are gone, the door of the sacristy blown in and the vestments torn to ribbons, while not a particle of the beautiful stained glass, which filled the twenty large windows, remains now.[54]

There was only one consolation in the desolation. The statue had not been installed and escaped destruction by minutes. Doyle rejoiced. 'Our Blessed Lady is only waiting for the Boche to be driven back to occupy the site prepared for her.'

The statue was stored well behind the lines in the village of Bruay-en-Artois, south of Béthune, for the duration of the war. The church was rebuilt again after the war and the statue was finally installed on 2 October 1921 in a dimly lit section of a side altar, where it remains to this day.

The Irish are long gone. The inscription under the base reads:

Partout et toujours fidèles.
À la mémoire des officiers, sous-officiers et soldats de la 16ème Division Irlandaise tués
au champ de bataille ou morts par suite de blessures ou maladies contractées à la guerre,
en France, en 1916 R.I.P.

[Everywhere and always loyal.
To the memory of the officers, subalterns and soldiers of the 16th (Irish)
Division who died on the field of battle or who died of wounds or diseases
contracted during the war in France in 1916 RIP.]

On the 100th anniversary of the gas attacks, the village of Hulluch unveiled a permanent message board to remember the Irishmen who died there during Easter Week 1916.

The plaque is located in St Mary's Advanced Dressing Station (ADS) Commonwealth War Graves Cemetery between Hulluch and Loos where Lieutenant John Kipling is buried and it overlooks the battlefield where the Irishmen died 100 years earlier. It was designed by the Durand Group who have been involved for years in engineering the system of tunnels from the first World War in the Loos area.

One of the speakers was Bill Byrne from Perth, Australia. His grandfather Billy Byrne was with the 8th Royal Dublin Fusiliers who counted more than 150 dead from the gas attacks.

Billy Byrne survived and died in 1976. His grandson told those assembled for the unveiling: 'He told me the terror felt during the attacks. The pain and burning sensation in the lungs due to gas were so intense that he had not realised his arm was shattered by a bullet.'

The Battle of the Somme – An Introduction

The Somme battlefield, more than any other on the Western Front, is a landscape on which one could imagine titanic battles taking place. This part of northern France is big country. The endless skies and russet-coloured soil, the chalk hills and great meadows, the sweeping panorama that rolls unbroken to a distant horizon – everything contributes to the impression of a vast, bloody canvas upon which the war has done its bloody worst.

The Battle of the Somme made an early claim on the public imagination. It began on 1 July 1916. It lasted until mid-November. But in August of that year a documentary film, *The Battle of the Somme*, shot by two British cinematographers at the front line, was released. It was enormously successful. This was still the early days of motion picture technology. People were captivated by its magic from the start. But this was not the kind of whimsical entertainment that other producers were already churning out for the new picture houses. This was a shocking blast of cinema verité. A silent film, lasting seventy-seven minutes, an estimated 20 million Britons flocked to see *The Battle of the Somme* in its first six weeks of general release.

Circumstances dictated that the cameramen often had to film the battle from a distance. The troops are sometimes barely visible, no bigger than dots. But these images of the soldiers, small as insects and equally anonymous, became a visual metaphor for the wider reality of the war: men in their nameless multitudes being remorselessly fed into this gargantuan killing machine.

'A great noise and a smoke filled the valley in which now and then one saw distant figures moving, aimlessly it seemed, like ants in a disturbed anthill,' was how the author Charles Carrington remembered the first day of the Battle of the Somme.[55]

The heart of the Somme battlefield is the old Roman road between the towns of Albert and Bapaume. Bapaume was then in German hands. Albert was an unremarkable little market town with one standout feature – the Basilica of Notre-Dame de Brebiéres with its prominent statue of the Golden Virgin . The statue was used by the British for artillery spotting and by the Germans for artillery practice. For years it hung at a right angle to the basilica, held up only by bent steel supports. Soldiers on both sides believed that if the Virgin fell from her pedestal, the war would be over. She finally fell in April 1918. The war ended six months later.

The distance between Albert and Bapaume is 10 miles or, as the historian Richard Holmes put it in his television series *War Walks*, the longest 10 miles in British military history.[56] Along the route are villages and signposts with innocent-sounding names that chilled a generation – La Boisselle, Pozières, Contalmaison, Courcelette, Martinpuich. The Somme was to be the big Allied offensive on the Western Front in 1916. It turned out to be the biggest battle of the war, with 1.2 million casualties.

In December 1915, a momentous decision was made at the Chantilly conference outside of Paris: the combined Allied forces of France, Britain, Russia and Italy would launch simultaneous attacks on the Central Powers the following summer. Faced with war on all fronts, Germany, the principal enemy, would not be able to concentrate her forces. On St Valentine's Day 1916, the French and British settled on the area north of the River Somme in Picardy for their joint offensive. France would muster forty-two divisions, Britain twenty-five.

The region itself was of no great tactical significance. It had no industrial base, no railway junction or natural feature which would make the decisive difference. As far as the British were concerned, it was the wrong place and the wrong time. The British commander-in-chief Field Marshal Sir Douglas Haig, promoted in late 1915, believed his million-strong new army would not be ready to fight until August 1916 at the earliest, but the British were still the junior partner.

Haig wished to concentrate his forces further north in Flanders, where there was more strategic infrastructure, most notably the ports of Ostend and Zeebrugge, which were being used by Germany to launch U-boat raids. Haig would get his wish the following year. The result would be the Battle of Passchendaele. The Somme was chosen because it marked the area where the British and French front lines converged.

The best-laid plans, though, were brutally pre-empted by the German attack on the fortress of Verdun in February 1916. The German chief-of-staff Erich von Falkenhayn hoped to effect a telling German breakthrough on the River Meuse. His plan, as outlined in an infamous (and disputed) memo to Kaiser Wilhelm II in December 1915, was to 'bleed France white'.[57]

The year of 1916 would give rise to the dreaded word 'attrition' in military circles. It was used to describe that harrowing state of stalemate in which commanders would hurl their forces at the enemy time and again, to little avail and with enormous loss of life. Those who managed to inflict more casualties than they suffered, or those armies that could bear greater proportional losses, would win a small victory. The hope was that by repeating the process over and over, the enemy would become worn out.

Heavy losses were inevitable. According to Haig, they simply had to be endured. On 1 June 1916, a month before the Somme offensive, he gave a rare briefing to war correspondents which was remarkable in its bluntness:

The nation must be taught to bear losses. No amount of skill on the part of the higher commanders, no training, however good, on the part of the officers and men, no superiority of arms and ammunition, however great, will enable victories to be won without the sacrifice of men's lives. The nation must be prepared to see heavy casualty lists … To sum up: The lessons which the people of England have to learn are patience, self-sacrifice, and confidence in our ability to win in the long run. The aim for which the war is being waged is the destruction of German militarism. Three years of war and the loss of one-tenth of the manhood of the nation is not too great a price to pay in so great a cause.[58]

Seemingly desensitised by nearly two years of catastrophic warfare already, the public back at home received his comments without demur. It seems astonishing to the modern mind that any public figure could justify the death of one man in ten in Britain. Such statements would be denounced as insane, not just unwise, but the public in all the combatant nations had been conditioned to accept extreme sacrifice. The press was full of the valedictory words of 'sacrifice', 'valour', 'heroism', 'gallantry'. The views expressed by James Connolly in December 1915 were minority ones, 'Any person, whether English, German, or Irish, who sings the praises of war is, in our opinion, a blithering idiot.'

When Haig issued his chilling warning, the Battle of Verdun had already raged for a hundred days. Verdun sat astride the River Meuse, surrounded by hills and huge fortresses buttressed by large gun turrets and bomb-proof shelters.

It was here, on 21 February, that the German Fifth Army unleashed the biggest bombardment of the war. In order to do so, it had assembled the greatest concentration of artillery fire in world military history. At dawn that day, they opened fire with 1,400 artillery pieces on a 8½-mile front – one heavy gun for every 10 yards of ground.

'Imagine if you can, a steadily growing storm raining only paving stones, only building blocks,' was how one French officer remembered it. Many of the French who survived the initial bombardment were then confronted by another grotesque weapon: flamethrowers, which incinerated men trapped in their trenches. The Germans had swift success but, despite their enormous firepower, could not follow it up with a decisive breakthrough.

The French transported division after division down the road of resistance, the *Voie Sacrée* (Sacred Way), which was the only open road from Verdun to the rest of France. It was the one artery that prevented France from being bled white. At one point in March, a convoy of lorries was rumbling through every fourteen seconds. Verdun was to become a symbol of French resistance. '*Ils ne passeront pas!*' (They shall not pass!) became the battle cry. They suffered 337,000 casualties at Verdun, of whom 162,308 were killed. The Germans had almost exactly the same number of casualties, but significantly fewer fatalities.

While both armies were in this death grip, the greater responsibility for the Somme offensive fell on the British.

By June, the original large-scale offensive had been narrowed down to twenty-one British and eighteen French infantry divisions, a reduction of 40 per cent from the initial plan. Eventually fourteen British and five French divisions would take part in the first day of battle. Small in number, but with experienced troops and more accurate artillery, the French would achieve significant breakthroughs in the south of the Somme sector on 1 July. But the first day would be about the British.

Two miles north of Albert, outside the village of Ovillers-la-Boisselle, there is a road sign that marks where the British front line was on 1 July. A further 4 miles up the same road there is another sign indicating their position on 1 September. The final sign is 2 miles south of Bapaume. It indicates the furthest advance of the British army during the Battle of the Somme, achieved on 20 November 1916. It took them four months and nineteen days to advance 7 miles. The cost for this paltry amount of ground was over 1 million British, French and German casualties.

The British lost 127,000 men between 1 July and 13 November. Thousands of other men would have succumbed to their wounds in field hospitals elsewhere.[59] British casualties were 416,000 in total; the French 196,000, of whom 37,000 were killed. The best estimate for German casualties is approximately 450,000 casualties, with 160,000 dead or missing.[60]

The final audit for the Allies reads like a military and moral apocalypse: some 78 square miles of ground gained at a cost of forty casualties per square yard.

The Battle of the Somme was the bloodiest battle in British history. The first day was the bloodiest day in the history of the British army. It lost 19,240 dead, among 57,470 casualties. Most of those not killed were injured as very few prisoners were taken.

In a single day, therefore, the British army suffered more battle casualties than in the Battle of Waterloo, the Crimean War and Second Boer War combined.[61] It is much more than what British forces sustained in the entire Battle of Normandy in 1944.[62]

Yet that was only the start of the bloodshed. On all sides, an average of almost 3,000 men a day died during the Battle of the Somme. 'It was the muddy grave of the German Field Army,' Captain Werner Otto von Hentig of the Guards Reserve Division said of the Somme.[63] This has become the conventional wisdom; however, the battle's pre-eminent historian, Martin Middlebrook, believed that the Somme was not a pivotal setback for Germany:

> The German army, 'broken' on the Somme held back the British advance at Arras in early 1917, drove the French army to mutiny at the Chemin des Dames that spring and held the British for months in the third battle of Ypres later that year. That same Germany army, admittedly reinforced after the collapse of Russia on the eastern front, almost broke through and won the war in 1918 before it was finally worn down by the Allied advance that summer. So much for an Allied victory on the Somme.[64]

Bapaume was never reached, despite multiple offensives as summer turned to autumn. Haig remained almost psychotically indifferent to the carnage as he committed tens of thousands of men to the charnel house. On 2 July, he wrote in his diary, 'Casualties are estimated at 40,000 to date. This cannot be considered severe in view of the numbers engaged and the length of front attack.'[65] For this and many other futile offensives, Haig became known by the sobriquet 'the butcher of the Somme'.

The British Prime Minister David Lloyd George, who despised Haig, eventually withheld troops from him in 1918, lest they be used for further futile attacks. Haig came to epitomise the squanderous reputation of Britain's top brass.

The war poet Siegried Sassoon had this to say about them:

> 'Good morning; good morning!' the General said
> When we met him last week on our way to the line.
> Now the soldiers smiled at are most of 'em dead,
> And we're curing his staff for incompetent swine.
> 'He's a cheery old card,' grunted Harry to Jack
> As they slogged up to Arras with rifle and pack.
> But he did for them both by his plan of attack.

The 7-mile distance between the British starting and finishing lines in the Somme offensive is easily covered nowadays. You can drive it in ten minutes and never be out of sight of a war memorial. It was the bloodiest 7 miles in military history. And for all that suffering, the cruel irony is that in the end Germany simply abandoned the Somme, in early 1917, to a more easily defendable line. Sixteen months after the battle ended, the Germans launched their Spring Offensive and took back the accursed Somme battlefield in a matter of days.

The Somme was a catastrophe for families all over the Empire. There are multiple memorials to English, Scottish, Welsh and Irish soldiers, but also memorials to the Canadians (Courcelette), Australians (Pozières) and New Zealanders (Longueval). Perhaps most poignant of all is the Caribou Memorial to the Newfoundlanders at Beaumont Hamel.

In 1914, Newfoundland was a British dominion. Its residents were drawn from the British Isles, emigrants who eschewed more hospitable climes to make their homes among the caribou and the cod. This isolated island, bigger than Ireland, but with a population of a few hundred thousand, was so imperturbable before the First World War that it had had no army since 1870. When war was declared, it quickly raised a regiment numbering 801 men and fought alongside the British and the Irish in the 29th Division during the Gallipoli campaign.

An hour and a half after the Battle of the Somme started, the men were ordered forward but never even got to the front line. Of the 752 men who attempted to go over the top, some 684 would end the day dead, wounded or missing. Most did not even reach their own front lines. The Newfoundlanders hardly fired a shot. The effect on this sparsely populated island was profound. 'Newfoundland is different from other countries,' the *Western Star*, its main paper, observed, 'here we seem to know each other. This makes the grief more widely felt.'[66]

One hundred years on and counting, the Somme continues to haunt the psyche of British people in particular. 'Idealism perished on the Somme,' wrote the historian A.J.P. Taylor in the 1960s. 'The enthusiastic volunteers were enthusiastic no longer. They had lost faith in their cause, in their leaders, in everything except loyalty to their fighting comrades. The war ceased to have a purpose. The Somme set the picture by which future generations saw the First World War: brave helpless soldiers, blundering obstinate generals, nothing achieved.'[67]

Others, such as the respected war historian Professor Gary Sheffield, have taken issue with this perspective. The Somme was not a victory, he has argued, but it was a tactical success, leaving the German army so weakened that it could not resume the offensive for two years.

Fundamentally, the British had only one strategy for the Somme. They were so sure that the expenditure of more than 1.6 million shells on the German lines would be enough to quell all resistance that they had no back-up plan.

'Nothing could exist at the conclusion of the bombardment in the area covered by it,' the British Fourth Army General Sir Henry Rawlinson cheerily told his men.[68] British generals believed what they wanted to believe. Multiple reports that the Germans had dug deep into the chalky soil of the Somme and created bunkers impervious to bombardment were ignored. As for an alternative, a Plan B if the artillery campaign did not work, there was none.

The Battle of the Somme resonated far beyond its time and place. Terrible slaughter occurred before the Somme and terrible slaughter occurred after it, yet, for many people, it seems to be the one First World War battle that stands out. Its first twenty-four hours have entered the public psyche as the day when the glory of the British Empire died in the blood and mud of that cataclysm. For many, the war will be forever seen through the prism of that first day on the Somme. Not even eventual victory could alter that perception.

The realisation that nearly 20,000 men died in a single day prompts a fundamental question: was it worth it? Was the threat to the British Empire so great that so many would have to die defending it? The official language of war frequently refers to death on the battlefield as a 'sacrifice'. Douglas Haig invoked it on a regular basis. But even this word is loaded. A good soldier does not sacrifice his life. The point is to stay alive. They do not give their lives. Their lives are taken from them by the enemy. But if their own commanders have colluded in their destruction, through ineptitude or hubris or negligence, then the word 'sacrifice' might be considered a benevolent euphemism for betrayal.

—

Life in this region returned to normal in the decades after the war. Stripped of its historical pall, the Somme is just another great swathe of fertile farmland. Here, they grow corn, maize, sugar beet, potatoes, green beans and all kinds of flowers. In the summer, the walls of the 400 military cemeteries are surrounded by wheat and corn fields as far as the eye can see. In the winter, the Crosses of Sacrifice protruding from each cemetery stand out against the bare earth. The seasons change; nature's cycle of growth, decay and renewal continues.

It was the fate of this blameless land to be the graveyard for a generation of young men from all over the world. It is now its fate to epitomise in its name – a single word – one of the greatest humanitarian catastrophes in military history. It remains the crucible out of which so much change came, in Europe, in France and in the Empire. The Somme signifies for many British historians the end of innocence, the end of blind faith, the end of communal trust in Britain's governing social class – the so-called betters who got it so badly wrong. A huge, working-class body of men, both rural and urban, had been lost. Society would never be the same again.

'These were the best of the nation's volunteer manhood,' the military historian Richard Holmes observed, 'and the merest glance at its casualty roll shows what the Somme did to the old world of brass bands and cricket fields, pit-head cottages and broad acres.'[69]

13

THE MONUMENT TO THE TYNESIDE IRISH AND TYNESIDE SCOTTISH AT LA BOISSELLE

Struggling for numbers in Ireland, the Irish Parliamentary Party leader John Redmond suggested the 16th should be filled up with men from the Irish diaspora in Britain. Neither Lieutenant General Sir Lawrence Parsons, the commanding officer of the 16th (Irish) Division, nor the War Office would countenance it.

In 1914, across the United Kingdom, which then included Ireland, hundreds of thousands of men responded to Lord Kitchener's call for volunteers. The response in Ireland had been mixed: good in the cities, but poor in the countryside, a pattern which was also apparent in rural parts of England.[1] Young men could not be persuaded to abandon the land. Ireland, unlike England, was overwhelmingly rural, especially in Connacht and Munster, where recruitment was slowest.

There were dark threats of filling up Redmond's 16th (Irish) Division with Englishmen. Redmond's promise that nationalist Ireland would stay loyal to the Empire if the Empire stayed loyal to home rule would be questioned if such a scenario arose. Faced with the possibility that the 16th (Irish) Division would become Irish only in name, Redmond turned to the Irish in Britain.

The Great Famine between 1845 and 1851 brought a tide of Irish emigration to Britain, which has ebbed and flowed ever since as economic circumstances have ebbed and flowed.

There were more than half a million Irish-born people living in Britain at the outbreak of war, mostly concentrated in the major population centres.[2]

There was such a high concentration of first- and second-generation Irish emigrants in Liverpool that the city returned a nationalist MP to the House of Commons. He was the Westmeath-born T.P. (Thomas Power) O'Connor, from 1885 to 1929.[3] O'Connor was elected as an MP even after the foundation of the Irish Free State.[4]

The Irish in Britain were assiduous in answering the call from Lord Kitchener for volunteers. The nationalist MP turned British army officer Stephen Gwynn observed in his book *John Redmond's Last Years*:

> The Irish in Great Britain, always outdoing all others in the keenness of their nationalism, were nearer the main current of the war, and were more in touch with the truth about English feeling. They had a double impulse, as Redmond had; they saw how to serve their own cause in serving Europe's freedom; and their response was magnificent. Mr TP O'Connor probably raised more recruits by his personal appeal than any other man in England.[5]

The Liverpool Irish raised two battalions by October 1914, the London Irish Rifles three battalions, but nowhere was the response more forthcoming than in the north-east of England. O'Connor had gone on a recruitment drive around

Britain and found greatest success in Newcastle upon Tyne. Four battalions were raised there.

At the beginning of 1915, Redmond suggested that the Tyneside Irish should join the 16th (Irish) Division. His deputy, John Dillon, referred to the Tyneside Irish as 'our men', many of whom would channel 'the old fighting Fenian element' into a new cause. Gwynn explained the rationale behind Redmond's thinking in *Last Years*:

> Redmond held that to bring over this brigade to train in Ireland, and to incorporate it bodily in the 16th Division, would please the Tyneside men for a tremendous welcome would have greeted them in their own country and would have an excellent effect on Irish opinion generally.[6]

However, the proposal was rigorously opposed by the War Office, as Gwynn explained, 'It was argued that these men had enlisted technically as Northumberland Fusiliers and Northumberland Fusiliers they must remain. In reality, as far as one can judge, the War Office was penny wise and pound foolish. "We have got these men," they said, "and we have a promise from Redmond to fill a Division. Why relieve him of one-third of his task?"'[7]

Parsons was also against incorporating the Irish in British into the 16th (Irish) Division. He wanted no 'slum birds' in his division, an appalling statement from an incorrigible snob. He wanted only 'the clean, fine, strong, temperate, hurley-playing country fellows'. [8]

Instead of being incorporated into the 16th Division, the Tyneside Irish would become 103rd Brigade of 34th Division. The 1st, 2nd, 3rd and 4th battalions of the Tyneside Irish were also known in the British army list as the 24th, 25th, 26th and 27th battalions of the Northumberland Fusiliers.

The Tyneside Irish were recruited among Irish-born or their descendants who had left Ireland after the famine for the railways pits, steelworks and chemical plants of the north-east of England, the cradle of the industrial revolution.

Many arrived in Newcastle upon Tyne from Gaeltacht areas unable to speak English. The weakest became labourers and rubbish-tippers in mines; the strong ones served in the shipyards, the mines and the brass foundries.

'Where there was a call for a pick, shovel, sledge hammer or more physical energy, the newcomers were engaged,' wrote Joseph Keating in his book about the Tyneside Irish brigade, *Irish Heroes in the War*.[9]

Most retained their sense of Irishness, which was transmitted down the generations through the Catholic Church and the Irish clubs. To be Catholic in the north-east of England was to be regarded as Irish, even if one was a third-generation emigrant.

Major William Davey from Carrickfergus, a former newspaper editor who joined the 4th Battalion of the Tyneside Irish, believed the Tyneside Irishman combined the best traits of his old homeland and his adopted home. It was nonsense, he believed, to talk of enmity between England and Ireland when both countries were so mixed up with each other:[10]

> It has been said that the Tyneside Irishman is an Irishman improved by residence in England. However, that may be, I, for my part, can aver, having lived with him under very trying circumstances, that the English north country miner is a man any Irishman might be proud to have as his neighbour. He is a stout worker, a bonny fighter, and a staunch comrade. The Tyneside Irish combined all their own good racial properties with the good points of the people in whose midst they or their fathers had made their new abode. They are, alas!, in so many cases were men of whom Ireland has every right to be proud; and it would be well for some Irishmen to recollect that the vengeance they are so fond of wishing to see exacted from England must include the million odd fellow Irishmen and women whose lot has been cast in England.[11]

In the social pyramid of the industrial North East, the Irish started out as the lowest of the low. They endured sub-standard housing and were often cramped together in tenements where disease spread quickly. A typhus outbreak in Gateshead became known as the 'Irish disease'. The Act of Union had made the Irish equal subjects in the United Kingdom, but they were treated as something other. Their poverty and Catholicism made them suspect.[12]

'It is perhaps a sad reflection on the state of things in Ireland that so many left and came to live in England where they would be despised and treated with contempt,' observed John Sheen in his regimental history *Tyneside Irish*.

The Newcastle area also attracted Protestants from the north of Ireland, many of whom went on to establish Orange Lodges. At the outbreak of war, the Irish, Protestant and Catholic alike, were targeted as a major source of manpower in the North East.

Once despised as blackleggers, because of an incident when the Irish replaced striking Geordie miners in 1850, and also as Fenians, advertisements appeared in local newspapers appealing to the Irish sense of patriotic pride.[13]

'Irishmen, to Arms!' the advertisement in the *Newcastle Evening Chronicle* exclaimed. 'The greatest fighting men of our time are Irishmen – [Lord] Kitchener, [John] French, [Horace] Smith-Dorrien and [Lord] Roberts'.[14]

Kitchener was the War Secretary, French the head of the British army, Smith-Dorrien the commander of I Corps, and Roberts, who had retired, had been a former commander-in-chief. Inadvertently, the poster demonstrated the prominent position the Anglo-Irish had in the British armed services before the First World War.

The advertisement continued, 'Those who are inspired by that love of freedom dominant in the Irish race, and which is threatened by Germany's lust for power, should enrol themselves in the TYNESIDE IRISH BATTALION and preserve for themselves and their children that glorious liberty so dear to the heart of every Irishman.'[15]

Later advertisements would appear with personal messages from the men. Kitchener, who at the time was resisting John Redmond's attempts to create a wholly Irish corps and was generally suspicious of Irish nationalism, wrote, 'For every Irishman the path of duty is clear. If you would preserve your nationality, you must fight for it. Germany, the bully of the nations, must be defeated if free nations are to exist.'

The recruitment process was aided by successive mayors of Newcastle, who were both Irish, albeit from different traditions. Johnstone Wallace, an Orangeman from County Derry, was mayor in 1913/1914. He was succeeded by John Fitzgerald, a millionaire brewer from County Tipperary who came to Newcastle Upon Tyne to settle in 1888. Fitzgerald called a public meeting in September 1914 at the Irish National Club in Clayton Street, Newcastle, to raise a Pals battalion among the city's Tyneside Irish community.[16]

This club had strong nationalist leanings. It had hosted Michael Davitt, Charles Stewart Parnell and the old Fenian Jeremiah O'Donovan Rossa in the past. In 1898, it staged a centenary banquet to mark the 1798 Rebellion, but, now, in the name of Ireland, the club would hear calls for Irishmen to fight for the cause of Britain.[17] A committee was set up, encompassing all strands of Irish opinion in the North East, including the Ancient Order of Hibernians. The response was overwhelming. Within three days, 1,052 recruits had signed up, more than the number needed for a whole battalion.

Captain Jack Arnold, one of the first recruits, described the original recruits as being a 'motley throng very reminiscent of the types that used to file along the road to annual militia musters in Ireland. They had no uniforms, no collars, boots that had toes peeping through them and trousers that were more patch than piece, there were old and young, some born in Ireland, some in England of Irish parentage, some having no connection with Ireland beyond the same church or the fact they worked in the same pit with an Irishman … Many were no stranger to an empty belly.'[18]

By 14 January 1915, all four Tyneside Irish battalions had been raised, constituting a brigade. In a bout of competitive recruitment, the Irish had beaten the Tyneside Scottish by a couple of days. The local press had given daily recruitment figures; bookmakers took bets on the result, with both expatriate communities seeking to outdo the other in what would become a roll call of cannon fodder.

Irish-born officers were drafted into the Tyneside Irish battalions. Among them was the great-grandson of Daniel O'Connell, Lieutenant Maurice O'Connell.

Kerry-born O'Connell was a member of the Irish Volunteers before the war and sided with Redmond during the split. He would go on to be wounded at the Battle of the Somme. He joined the National Army after the First World War and lived until 1972.

Another officer was Lieutenant Gerald Neilan from Ballygalda, County Roscommon, who was posted to the 1st Tyneside Irish (24th Northumberland Fusiliers) and later transferred to the Royal Dublin Fusiliers. As was noted in a previous chapter, he became the first British officer fatality of the Easter Rising. He was posted to the 1st Tyneside Irish (24th Northumberland Fusiliers) and then transferred to the Royal Dublin Fusiliers in February 1916. Coincidentally, his brothers John Alexander and Charles, who both served as doctors in the First

TYNESIDE IRISH AND SCOTTISH JULY 1ST, 1916

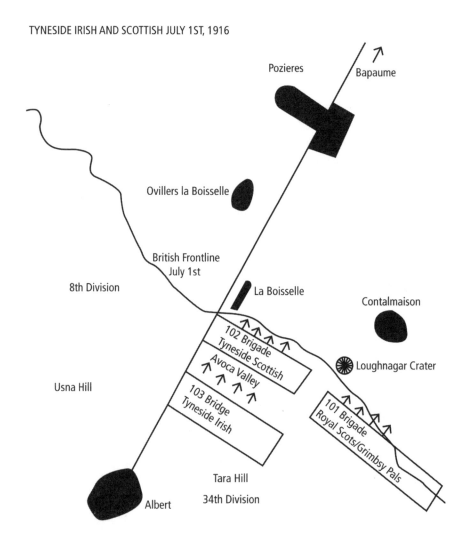

'Listed for the Connaught Rangers' by Lady Elizabeth Butler. (© Bury Art Museum, Greater Manchester, UK)

'The Angels of Mons' by Marcel Gillis. (© City of Mons, Mons Memorial Museum)

Edward Thomas.
(Courtesy of Ben Thomas)

Tom Kettle.

Robert Armstrong.
(From the Commonwealth
War Graves Commission file)

Private Michael
Ryan, to whom this
book is dedicated,
and his family.

The mayors of Guillemont and Ginchy at the unveiling of the Ireland–France Memorial in Glasnevin Cemetery, 2016.

The Malone brothers. (Courtesy of An Post and Mercier Press, Cork)

The new message board at Hulluch, 2016. (Courtesy of Anne-Sophie Douchin)

In Loving Memory
OF
No. 22689 Private Thady Dockery
3RD BATTALION ROYAL DUBLIN FUSILIERS,
Killed in action July 1st 1916,
AGED 20 YEARS.

"LORD HAVE MERCY ON HIS SOUL."
R.I.P.

BRIDGE STREET
CARRICK-ON-SHANNON,
LEITRIM, IRELAND.

A mass card for Thady Dockery.

The placard erected
by the German army
following the Easter
Rising. It was seized
by Lieutenant Francis
Joseph Biggane and
Private Timothy Kemp
of the Royal Munster
Fusiliers.

Franck Gil, the owner of the railway station at Le Pilly, pointing out the bullet holes in his
house.

Irish President Mary McAleese, Queen Elizabeth II and the Belgian King Albert II at the opening of the Island of Ireland Peace Park in Messines Ridge in 1998.
(© Frank Miller: *The Irish Times*)

Tom Kettle's name inscribed on the Thiepval Memorial to the Missing.

PORTER T.
POTTER A.

WOODS J. I.
YATES R. B.

ROYAL DUBLIN FUSILIERS

LIEUTENANT   LCE CORPORAL

KETTLE T. M.
KILLINGLEY
        H. G.

SECOND LIEUT.

BOYD W. H.
CLARKE W. J.
COONEY C. R.
NAN G. A.
DRAN L. G.
ADWELL G. F.
EEN H.
ONEY F.

BARRY P.
BOOTHMAN H.
BRADLEY T.
BYRNE J. 20346
BYRNE J. 23331
BYRNE T.
BYRNE W.
CASSIDY P. M.
CORRIGAN J.
COUGHLAN P.
COULTER P.
DONNELLY M.
DRIVER W. C.

The First Shot Memorial at Casteau.

GREATER LOVE HATH NO MAN THAN THIS THAT HE
LAY DOWN HIS LIFE FOR HIS FRIENDS

IN FRONT OF THIS MONUMENT ON THE 1ST JULY 1916
THE "TYNESIDE SCOTTISH" AND THE "TYNESIDE IRISH" BRIGADES
ATTACKED THE ENEMY. FOR MANY HOURS THE FORTUNES
OF ARMS FLUCTUATED, BUT ERE NIGHT HAD FALLEN
THE TWO TYNESIDE BRIGADES WITH THE AID OF OTHER
UNITS OF THE 34TH DIVISION ATTAINED THEIR OBJECTIVE

THINK NOT THAT THE STRUGGLE AND THE SACRIFICE WERE IN VAIN

The inscription on the Tyneside Irish monument. (© Somme Association)

World War, set up a GP practice in Seaham, Durham, in the north-east of England. Both brothers shunned Arthur who had joined the Irish Volunteers.

Lieutenant-Colonel Miles Emmet Byrne, descendant of 1798 rebel, Miles Byrne, commanded the Tyneside Irish Brigade. When it arrived in France, he reminded his men how the Irish Brigade in France 'lightened the darkness of the 17th century and changed the history of Europe'.[19] One wonders if he also told his troops that that Irish Brigade had been fighting against and not for Britain.[20]

A total of 7,325 men would serve in the Tyneside Irish in the war – 1,949 were killed, which is more than one in four.[21] The average rate of fatality of those who served in the British army during the First World War was one in seven.

More than a quarter of those killed fighting for the Tyneside Irish in the First World War were killed on one day – the first day of the Battle of the Somme.

—

The old Roman road between Albert and Bapaume marks the axis of attack of the Tyneside Irish Brigade, which was part of the 34th Division of the British army. It almost marks the centre point of the Somme battlefield.

The division's front line was either side of the road about 2 miles north of Albert. The Tyneside Scottish (102nd Brigade) trenches were on the left, facing the village of La Boisselle; the 101st Brigade (Royal Scots and the Lincolnshires, better known as the Grimsby Chums) were on the right, facing a shallow valley known as Sausage Valley.

The Tyneside Scottish was tasked with leading the assault on La Boisselle, the first village after Albert. It had been turned into a fortress by the Germans.

The Tyneside Scottish wished to capture it with a pincer movement, surrounding the village from left and right. The 101st Brigade would secure its flanks and the German strongpoint in the area, the Schwaben Höhe (not to be confused with the Schwaben Redoubt).

A mile behind both brigades, the Tyneside Irish Brigade was held in reserve, ready to exploit any breakthrough. The presumption was made, as it was made all along the line, that the attacks would face little resistance.

The bombardment of German strong points in the area was particularly severe.

The 34th Division felt confident of success. The British had dug their deepest and most powerful mine in front of the Grimsby Chums with the intention of blowing the Germans away.

The mine consisted of 60,000lbs of explosives. It was detonated at 7.28 a.m. on 1 July 1916, two minutes before zero hour. The Grimsby Chums watched awestruck as great pieces of earth 'as big as coal wagons were blasted skywards to hurtle and roll and then start to scream back all around us'.

The Lochnagar Crater is one of the most terrifying and awe-inspiring sights on the Somme battlefield. Visitors gasp at its huge circumference. It is nearly 300ft wide and 70ft deep.

The debris fell for so long that the Chums waited a full five minutes before leaving their front-line positions to cross no man's land. The delay proved to be fatal. Most likely hundreds of Germans were killed when the mines were blown, but enough survived to have the presence of mind to direct machine gun fire at the Pals as they crossed Sausage Valley.[22]

The Tyneside Scottish were doomed before they had even started. A listening post had picked up a telephone message at 2.45 a.m. from one indiscreet Tyneside Scottish officer to brigade headquarters, indicating that the attack was imminent. This would have dire consequences for the Tyneside Irish too.[23]

The area in which the Tyneside Irish assembled for the attack, a mile behind the front lines, had names redolent of the ancestral homeland. One side was named the Tara Hills; the other the Usna Hills. The open ground they crossed as they moved forward was the Avoca Valley.

The German machine guns in the village that were to be silenced by the Tyneside Scottish kept up their deadly chatter when the Scots fell back.

Having repulsed the Scottish, the Germans then trained their machine guns on the Tyneside Irish. The Irish regimental piper played 'The Minstrel Boy' as the men rose from their trenches and moved towards the front-line trenches vacated by the Tyneside Scottish.

The Tyneside Irish were ordered to advance on a two-company front with each company in a column of platoons (approximately fifty). There would be 150 paces between each company. They marched line abreast, each man about an arm's length away from the next. They presented an easy target.[24]

Most of the Tyneside Irish never even got to their own front line, which was across open country. The ones that did, though, walked onwards through a hurricane of shot and shell.

'The fighting was of the fiercest description, unsurpassed during this or any other campaign. The Irish advance never ceased, in spite of all the unadulterated hell they were going through,' an unnamed Tyneside Irish officer told the *Northern Echo*.[25]

Sergeant John Galloway of the 3rd Tyneside Irish recalled, 'I could see, away to my left and right, long lines of men. Then I heard the "patter, patter" of machine guns in the distance. By the time I'd gone another ten yards there seemed to be only a few men left around me, by the time I had gone twenty yards, I seemed to be on my own. Then I was hit myself.'

A few men heroically reached the village of Contalmaison, the ultimate objective of the 34th Division, 2½ miles from the front-line positions, but they were taken prisoner. The Tyneside Irish had advanced further than any other brigade that day, but their losses were catastrophic.

The brigade sustained 2,171 casualties with at least 599 deaths, amounting to a 70 per cent casualty rate. Others would succumb to their wounds later.[26]

Sheen estimates that 514 men of the Tyneside Irish, who died between 1 July and 4 July, are on the Thiepval Memorial to the Missing. They have no known grave.[27]

The 34th Division was the worst affected of all the fourteen British divisions involved on the first day of the Battle of the Somme. It suffered 6,380 casualties, most either killed or wounded. It was said of the men of the division that it took two years to train them and ten minutes to kill them.[28, 29]

Their losses were particularly severe because commanders insisted on all battalions attacking at once, instead of waiting to see how the situation was developing before committing more men. Battalion commanders also advanced with their men. When they were shot down, the men were leaderless.

Among those who died on 1 July was Second Lieutenant Gerald Fitzgerald, the son of the mayor of Newcastle.[30]

—

The grey memorial to the Tyneside Irish and Scottish is the first you encounter on leaving Albert. It is on the old front line where it was closest to the German positions on the right-hand side of the road. Visitors are encouraged to sit on the stone bench to 'think not that the struggle and the sacrifice were in vain'.

When one considers the appalling and unnecessary waste of life on 1 July 1916, one finds it hard to concur with that sentiment.

The inscription in English and French reads, 'Greater love hath no man than this that he lay down his life for his friend'. In front of this monument on 1/7/16 the 'Tyneside Scottish' and the 'Tyneside Irish' brigades attacked the enemy. For many hours the fortunes of arms fluctuated but ere night had fallen the two Tyneside Brigades with the aid of other units of the 34th Division attained their objective.'

This is a dubious claim. The 34th Division had succeeded in taking some trenches opposite Lochnagar crater, but were so weakened as a fighting force that the 19th Division were the ones who eventually took La Boisselle on 4 July.

The monument was one of the first on the Western Front and was unveiled by Field Marshall Ferdinand Foch in 1922. It was financed by the Colonel Joseph Cowen Fund. Joseph Cowen was the wealthy grandson of a Liberal MP of the same name who was heavily involved in Irish affairs in the nineteenth century.

14

THE ULSTER TOWER

The Ulster Tower is an incongruity among war memorials. It has a form which is untypical of the traditional masculine solemnity of most Western Front memorials. With its high tower and narrow slit window at the top, it is akin to something out of a fairytale, an edifice in which one might imagine a princess asleep for 100 years.

The Ulster Tower is located on what was the German front line on 1 July 1916. It marks roughly the midpoint of the assault by the 36th (Ulster) Division on that day. It commands clear views of the surrounding valley of death, which still bore the scars of war when it was opened in November 1921. 'Its awful surroundings strike one at once. It reigns, graceful and majestic, over a realm of hideousness and death,' *The Irish Times* reported at its opening.[1]

Near the left gate of the tower are the remains of a German machine gun observation post, obscured when the grass is high during the summer, but clearly visible in the stubble of fallow fields during winter.

The Ulster Tower is a replica of Helen's Tower, a Victorian folly built in famine times by Lord Dufferin in honour of his mother Lady Helen Blackwood, a well-known writer and poet of the first half of the nineteenth century and a granddaughter of the playwright Richard Brinsley Sheridan. It stands sentinel on the Clandeboye estate, still owned by the Dufferin family, who settled in County Down in 1674. During the First World War, the men of the 36th (Ulster) Division camped around Helen's Tower and trained on the grounds before leaving for England and then for France.[2]

Helen's Tower is situated on the highest part of the estate, overlooking the Ards Peninsula, with views across to Scotland on a clear day. As the men left Belfast in their troop ships, Helen's Tower could be glimpsed above the headland. It was one of the last sights of home many of these men would see.

The Ulster Tower was the first large-scale memorial on the Western Front. Captain James Craig, one of the founders of the Ulster Volunteer Force and Northern Ireland's first prime minister, proposed the idea of a memorial to the men of the 36th less than a week after the war ended in November 1918.[3]

He and Sir Edward Carson, the Dublin-born lawyer turned crusader for Protestant Ulster, were unanimous that the location 'should be secured and the monument erected on a suitable plot to the spot where so many gallant men laid down their lives and where the Division began its glorious career.'[4] It was opened in 1921, just five years after these gallant men had been killed in their thousands on the first day of the Battle of the Somme.

It had a political imperative too. Northern Ireland had been created in 1920, when the British government brought in the Government of Ireland Act, thus partitioning Ireland into separate political entities. It granted home rule to the South, but this was rejected by the abstentionist Dáil and was replaced by the Anglo-Irish Treaty of December 1921.

The British government made good on its pre-war promise not to include six of the nine Ulster counties in the post-war settlement. The new polity of Northern Ireland, with its majority Protestant population, would remain securely within the bosom of Empire. Craig, Carson and their unionist supporters believed they had sealed their righteous place with the blood of thousands of their compatriots during the Great War. The Ulster Tower would be a visible reminder for all eternity of that imperishable sacrifice. It would stand, too, as a rebuke to any future British government that might contemplate abandoning this corner of the United Kingdom.

The foundation of the Ulster Volunteer Force in 1912, the Ulster Covenant the same year and the Larne gun-running incident in 1914 could not have made it plainer to the British government that Ulster Protestant loyalty to the Crown was conditional on Ulster's exclusion from any legislation concerning the baleful prospect of home rule. The men, formerly of the Ulster Volunteer Force and now the British army, pledged to resist if home rule was forced on them. They went to war on the presumption that the temporary exclusion of six counties from home rule would be made permanent at the war's end.

Northern Ireland did not exist in 1916. It was not on the agenda when the Ulster Volunteer Force was created in 1912. The Protestants of Ulster wanted to retain the status quo of direct rule within the United Kingdom. Instead, they got home rule, but not of the type they envisaged. Northern Ireland, with its own Protestant-dominated parliament, was created. It needed a foundation myth.

As Philip Orr, the author of *The Road to the Somme*, has observed:

The death of the men of the 36th was ready made for political symbolism in the new Northern Ireland that emerged in the aftermath of the Great War. The sudden destruction of so many young men all across Ulster on an ironically sunny day on the bloody anniversary of the original date of the Battle of the Boyne was bound to be a potent emblem of Protestant loyalty especially given the powerful image of the rebellion launched by Pearse and Connolly which became a founding story for the Free State. It was also an act of reassurance to Britain that though the UVF might have been prepared to launch a coup d'état during the Home Rule crisis, its members were, at heart, loyal to the Empire. The urgent need to generate a powerful founding story for a Northern Ireland that Irish unionism had never expressly intended to create back in the pre-war years was important. Northern Ireland lacked the intense cultural underpinning of the long Irish national project with its century-long array of heroes and martyrs. The dead of the Somme could fill that gap and Northern Ireland, newly prized from its nine county host province, suddenly had to assert its geopolitical identity, create its own territoriality and homogeneity and do it on the hoof. The narrative of an Ulster Division which embodied 'Northernness' suited that task.[5]

No British division involved in the Battle of the Somme had more difficult terrain to cross than the 36th. The Ulster Tower commands perfect views of the 1,600 yards of front which the men had to negotiate to breach German lines.

As one faces the tower, the land on the left-hand side falls away down to the marshy River Ancre, which is more stream than river. On the right of the tower, the land rises steeply until, at the top, one can see the outlines of Mill Road Cemetery and the reverse slopes of the hill where the Schwaben Redoubt was located. Everywhere the Ulstermen were overlooked by enemy positions; everywhere the Germans had the advantage of the higher ground.

An Ulster soldier would have to struggle uphill with his 66lbs on his back while facing machine gun fire from three sides. In the case of the unfortunate men on the right flank at the end of Thiepval Wood, fire would come from behind too. They were mown down while attacking and were equally vulnerable while retreating. The men resembled 'human corn-stalks, falling before the Reaper', Lieutenant-Colonel Frank Crozier of the 9th Royal Irish Rifles remembered.[6]

Many stories have since flourished about that fateful day: that the men rejoiced when they realised that 1 July was the day by the old calendar of the Battle of the Boyne in 1690; that they went into battle wearing their orange sashes; that they shouted 'no surrender' as they bayoneted and shot the enemy. There is precious little evidence that any of this occurred. Pitched into a hell beyond comprehension, the men were probably too preoccupied with their own survival to indulge in tribal gestures.

'Boys, you have been given an impossible task,' Lieutenant-Colonel William Hessey told his men in the 11th Royal Inniskilling Fusiliers, a battalion which was part of 108th Brigade.[7] His warning was prescient. 'Whole waves of men just seemed to melt away as the following waves poured into the gaps,' remembered Private John Moffatt from that battalion. The 11th was mostly raised in Donegal and Derry. 'Men staggered on in full fighting kit, all loaded up with extra ammunition, extra bombs in sandbags and extra rations, up that hellish 95 yards, unable to run. Half way up between the two lines of a sunken road – our first halt. As we lay there panting with fear and lack of breath, the soldier immediately on my right jerked up suddenly and fell forward with blood spidering out of his forehead.'[8]

Of the 250 men from Moffatt's D Company, just five were left uninjured after the attack. Everywhere the casualties lay dead and dying on the battlefield. The tragedy for the 36th (Ulster) Division is not that it failed, but that it almost succeeded. The war correspondent Philip Gibbs described the division's attack on 1 July as 'one of the finest displays of human courage in the world'.[9]

Despite the carnage, the men actually succeeded in their first-day objectives, a feat of unparalleled heroism and good organisation; they just could not hold on to them. It emerged some time later that Major-General Edward Perceval, the general officer commanding the 49th (West Riding) Division, which was in

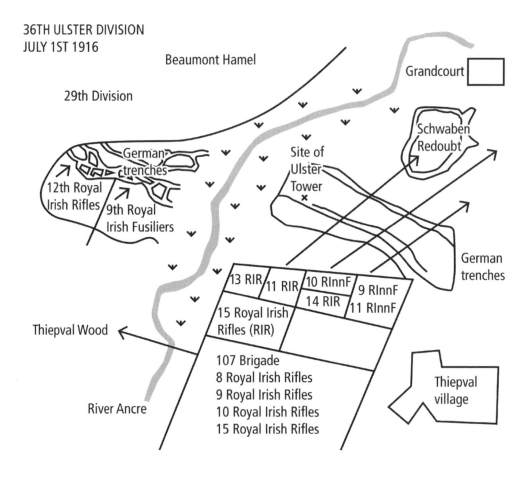

**36TH ULSTER DIVISION
JULY 1ST 1916**

reserve, had pressed for his division to be sent to support the early breakthroughs by the 36th, but was refused.[10] It was just one of innumerable missed opportunities on this most terrible of days. The 36th will forever be associated with the Battle of the Somme. Yet it only spent two days fighting during the battle. In those two days – really a day fighting and a morning retreating – it suffered 2,061 deaths, nearly all focused on the old nine counties of Ulster, and 5,500 casualties in total. That was more deaths in two days than were sustained in the first decade of the Troubles.

—

When war broke out, Carson and Craig switched their considerable energy and resources from defending Ulster against home rule to fight a greater foe.

The 36th (Ulster) Division was assembled with patriotic enthusiasm. But it also involved a tense stand-off between the Secretary of War Lord Kitchener on the one hand and Carson and Craig on the other. Kitchener, who was Irish-born of

English parents, had unionist sympathies, but none at all for meddling politicians. He alone among senior British Cabinet members grasped that this would be a long and bloody war. Britain would have to raise a vast new army of volunteers for service. Faced with such a colossal task, he was in no mood for regional quarrels. 'Surely you are not going to hold out for Tyrone and Fermanagh?' he asked the pair as his opening gambit in August 1914, a few days after war broke out. Carson was irked. 'You're a damned clever fellow telling me what I ought to be doing'.[11]

The war had barely begun when Asquith reported receiving a 'rather threatening' letter from Carson. Asquith was not the first British politician to be exasperated by the ways of Irish politicians and remarked to his mistress Venetia Stanley he would like to 'submerge the whole lot of them and their island, for say ten years, under the waves of the Atlantic'.[12] Carson made noises in his letter about Ulster Volunteer Force support for the British war effort being conditional on a guarantee that home rule would not be introduced while the men were away at the front. He told Asquith that he was prepared to 'throw in my lot with my people there in any action they may feel bound to undertake'.[13] He promised Asquith two divisions if the situation could be resolved and none at all if it was not. Asquith sought a compromise.

Carson's stance caused unease among many Ulster Volunteer Force men who thought the delay was unconscionable when the British Empire faced its greatest ever threat. Many enlisted anyway and were included in the 10th (Irish) Division. The British army's early reverses at Mons and during the retreat from Mons made Carson's conditional support for the British war effort both disreputable and untenable. Carson gave in. In early September 1914, he told the Ulster Unionist Council, 'England's difficulty is our difficulty … We are not fighting to get away from England: we are fighting to stay in England … I say to our Volunteers without hesitation to go and help save our country'.[14]

The Ulster Volunteer Force was 80,000 strong and well armed. Though it lacked artillery, it was a formidable fighting force if it could be harnessed for the war effort. Once Kitchener approved the raising of the division, Craig went straight to Moss Brothers in London and ordered 10,000 British uniforms for the would-be volunteers. Ordered in haste, he worried how he was going to pay for them all. Conservative MP Oliver Locker-Lampson, an ardent unionist, intervened to tell him not to worry. He would provide £1,000 and a further £9,000 would be found presently to make up the shortfall. This early organisation paid off. Enthusiastic men enlisted through one door in Belfast's Old Town Hall and emerged from the other side in a khaki uniform.[15]

The division was quickly raised and trained at Clandeboye, Ballykinlar, Newtownards and Finner on the Donegal coast. The division's headquarters were in Wellington Place, Belfast. The 36th (Ulster) Division was eventually composed of:

107th (Belfast) Brigade

8th Bn, the Royal Irish Rifles
9th Bn, the Royal Irish Rifles
10th Bn, the Royal Irish Rifles
15th Bn, the Royal Irish Rifles

108th (East Ulster) Brigade

11th Bn, the Royal Irish Rifles
12th Bn, the Royal Irish Rifles
13th Bn, the Royal Irish Rifles
9th Bn, the Royal Irish Fusiliers

109th (West Ulster) Brigade

9th Bn. The Royal Inniskilling Fusiliers
10th Bn, the Royal Inniskilling Fusiliers
11th Bn, the Royal Inniskilling Fusiliers
14th Bn, the Royal Irish Rifles

Only the artillery, which came from London, was raised elsewhere.

Protestant Ulstermen, no less than their Catholic counterparts in other regions of Ireland, had a long tradition of overseas adventure and emigration, especially to the United States and Canada. This would be another adventure. 'The old rowel that had driven Ulstermen over the seas, making them colonists and administrators, was sharpened again by the war,' wrote Cyril Falls, the divisional historian who also fought with the 36th. 'It pricked on these young men, the flower of their country.'[16]

The task of commanding the 36th (Ulster) Division in France was given to Cavan man Major General Sir Oliver Nugent, who had already seen service in Ypres. A hard-bitten Boer War veteran, Nugent was ruthless and sarcastic. His bile was not helped by an old war wound, which caused him constant pain. But he was also a humane man who cared about his troops. He was one of the few generals to command the same division for the duration of the war. Despite this apparent bond, he looked on his fellow Ulstermen with a cold eye. He was, according to his biographer Nicholas Perry, an 'Irish rather than an Ulster Unionist and had little in common with the largely Belfast-based leadership of Irish Unionism. Personally he found the more extreme manifestation of Ulster loyalism uncongenial and, while no supporter of home rule, nor an especial admirer of Irish Catholicism, he tried hard to discourage overt displays of party political affiliation and sectarianism in the Division.'[17]

Nugent had joined the Cavan Volunteer Force but was never comfortable with the gun being introduced into Irish constitutional issues. He loathed politicians, particularly of the Ulster variety. He was a unionist, but far enough away from the unionist heartland to resist its tribal mindset. 'How I hate the sordid outlook of the politician,' he would later lament:

I think the Irish brand is worse than any other ... I do wish we were not the
Ulster Division but just the 36th ... They are the most self-centred people
I have ever met. If you are not Ulster and if you don't subscribe to every Ulster
prejudice and if you are not as intolerant as they are, they will have nothing to
do with you. They simply won't accept you. I have found that for 10 months and
I feel no nearer to them and no more in touch with them than when I came.[18]

The division sailed from England and arrived in France in October 1915. It was
autumn and the apple trees were heavy with their fruits which were presented in
baskets to the men as they marched through the countryside. The 36th was part of
X Corps, which also comprised the 32nd Division, with the 49th (West Riding)
Division in reserve. X Corps in turn was part of the Fourth Army, which would
bear the brunt of the attack on the Somme.

The division was initially dispersed among the other divisions and brigades to
get them used to trench conditions. They were moved to the Somme sector in late
1915 and finally took over a section of front north and south of the River Ancre in
the spring of 1916. In the quiet weeks before the storm, the men took to fishing
and swimming in the Ancre, though it was just 600 yards from the German lines.
Contemporary photographs show them laughing and joking while bathing in the
river. Occasionally they would take pot shots at the odd wild duck or widgeon.

Lieutenant-Colonel Crozier observed, 'I think as I watch them ducking each
other in the water, and playing like young seals I have so often seen up North,
"what a pity they are not married in order that they might plant their seed."
Mankind has ordained that they shall shortly die. Alas! the weaklings and shirkers
escape and breed like rabbits, while the strong suffer and are wiped out.'[19]

These men, overwhelmingly Protestant, found themselves trying to liberate a
country that was nominally secular but still in 1914 a Catholic country.

'The Calvinistic Ulsterman was sometimes a little startled and pained at first
on finding a countryside so liberally besprinkled with shrines and crucifixes,'
wrote Falls in his *History of the 36th (Ulster) Division,* 'but, if he were a country-
man, especially, he made the surprising discovery that these countrymen of the
Somme were very like himself. They thought twice before speaking once; they
had a certain dourness; they did not wear their hearts on their sleeves, though they
were furnished with those organs in the proper places.'[20]

The peace of these early months was frequently broken by sporadic and sometimes deadly shelling. On 10 March, thirty Inniskillings were killed or injured in
a German shell attack on Thiepval Wood. One shell on 22 April killed a Private
William McBride, aged 21, from Lislea, County Armagh. He is buried in the
beautifully appointed Authuile Military Cemetery which slopes down to a wood.
McBride served with the 9th Battalion of the Inniskillings, known as the Tyrones.
There are sixty-six Inniskilling Fusiliers buried in Authuile, most of whom died

before the Battle of the Somme began. William McBride is not the Willie McBride immortalised in Eric Bogle's great war song 'The Green Fields of France'. Willie McBride is a fictional everyman dreamed up by the songwriter as a tragic embodiment of all the fallen.[21] The song was inspired by a visit to the Western Front by Bogle and his wife in 1975. He never visited Authuile and did not know of any soldier named Willie McBride. 'He was a generic name I coined to represent all the boys, from all the combatant nations who are buried out there in France and Flanders,' says Bogle. 'Years after I wrote the song I discovered that there are about 11 soldiers called Willie McBride who died in WW1, a melancholy if unsurprising coincidence given the millions who died in that bloody conflict.'[22]

The song's hero doesn't have a nationality, although Bogle is Scottish and the lyrics include a reference to a well-known Scottish song 'Flowers of the Forest'. Bogle did, however, have an Irish soldier in mind when he wrote 'The Green Fields of France'. 'I was touring the folk clubs in the UK in 1975 and found, because of the IRA bombing campaign on the UK mainland which was going on at the time, that there was a strong anti-Irish sentiment prevailing. Using the name McBride was a small reminder to those who heard the song that many Irish soldiers died in WW1 too, too small a reminder perhaps, and missed by most, but it gave me a jolt of self-justification.'

The men of the division brought their intense religiosity to the front line, where death was ever-present. In this regard, they had much in common with their Catholic counterparts.

'It was not uncommon to find a man sitting on the fire-step of a frontline trench reading one of the small copies of the New Testament which were issued to the troops by the people at home,' Falls wrote. 'The explanation was that, on the one hand, religion was near and real to them: on the other that they were simple men. They saw no reason to hide or disguise that which was a part of their daily lives.'[23]

The men suffered many trials in the weeks leading up to the assault on 1 July. They spent weeks assaulting dummy trenches in preparation for the real thing. When they were not on manoeuvres they were laying tramways, roads and gun-pits, cutting trenches, laying wire and bringing up a non-stop arsenal of shells, trench mortars, mills bombs and millions of rounds of ammunition.[24] Two causeways had to be built across the River Ancre to facilitate the movement of troops. The men were alternatively soaked or left sweltering from the changeable French weather, but none of these privations compared to the constant risk of injury or death.

The Ulstermen were overlooked by a series of German machine-gun emplacements encircling them. To the left were Beaumont Hamel and Beaucourt, in the centre was St Pierre Divion and to the right, Thiepval village, all heavily fortified with German machine guns, which had a range of 2,000 yards. The 36th's front was effectively two sections divided by the Ancre. On the left, two battalions of 108th Brigade faced the railway terminus of Beaucourt across a steep ravine. No man's land in this sector was approximately 400 yards across. On the other side of the river, 109th Brigade held the line from the Mill Road to the end of Thiepval Wood. Then the front turned sharply southward around the village of Thiepval, which was held by the Germans.

German defences centred on the Schwaben Redoubt, a dense warren of deep dugouts and machine-gun emplacements manned by men from the Schwaben region of south-west Germany. Despite the daunting and deadly obstacles that the 36th would face, the men were anxious to get going. Their mood was not helped when the attack was postponed because of bad weather.

On the evening of what would be many of the men's final night alive, the chaplain of the 14th Rifles told them, 'Boys, you all know as well as I do that some of you will not see tomorrow night. I wish every one of you the best of luck and may God bless you all.'[25] The night was spent watching and waiting. 'All sorts of ideas and questions slip through one's mind, the main one being, will I be here tomorrow or even in a half an hour?' Moffatt remembered. He noticed field postcards were being passed along the line. The men were encouraged to simply write 'I am quite well' on them, but he recognised that the same postcards would give families false hope if they arrived before the dreaded telegrams. Private Bell of the Derry Volunteers had more pastoral thoughts as the summer evening gathered in. 'At this particular time it would be milking time. The cows would be coming in from the meadows and everything would be lovely and peaceful at my father's farm in the little village [Moneymore] at the foot of the Sperrin Mountain.'[26]

Some men slept or stayed up smoking and chatting in whispers. Others prayed or read the bible. Others wrote a letter home. None had been over the top before. None knew what to expect.

The 36th was awarded four Victoria Crosses for its actions on 1 July, the most famous of which was won even before the men left the trenches. Bomber Private Billy McFadzean (20) from Lurgan, County Armagh, opened a box of grenades to distribute to the men. To his horror several fell out of the box and on to the floor of the trench. The safety pin on two became dislodged. McFadzean had only four seconds to act before the grenades detonated, potentially killing scores of men packed into the concentration trench in Thiepval Wood. In an act of suicidal courage, McFadzean dived on the grenades and was blown to pieces. Such extreme self-sacrifice was typical of the men who went over the top that day. The citation for his VC read, 'He well knew his danger, being himself a bomber, but without a moment's hesitation he gave his life for his comrades.'[27]

Unable to sleep himself, Crozier walked among his men. He went to admonish a young soldier who was writing a letter home by candlelight, despite a strict lights-out policy:

'Do you want to give the whole show away?' I indignantly ask. 'I am writing a letter home, Sir, it will be my last, and I just feel like it,' says an apologetic voice, adding, 'I am very sorry, Sir, I shouldn't have done it.' It's young Campbell, a stout lad. 'All right,' I say, 'no harm's done'.

Dawn broke at around 5 a.m. It was a perfect summer's morning with a slight mist which would burn off as soon as the sun appeared. The final bombardment before going over the top was a thing of awe. Shell after shell screamed over the heads of the men and into the opposing trenches. The bombardment lasted just over an hour. The division was greatly assisted by the accuracy of borrowed French artillery, which also cleared much of the barbed-wire emplacements in front of the German trenches.

At 7.15 a.m. in Thiepval Wood the men of the 9th and 10th Inniskilling Fusiliers of 109th Brigade on the right and the 11th and 13th Royal Irish Rifles of 108th Brigade on the left climbed out of their front-line trenches and crept, under cover of the bombardment, towards the German lines.

Lieutenant-Colonel Ambrose Ricardo, the commander of the 9th Inniskillings, stood on the parapet and cheered the men as they left their trenches, as if they were going to a football match. 'They got going without delay, no fuss, no shouting, no running, everything solid and thorough – just like the men themselves,' he said. The battalion diary recorded, 'Every officer and man was eager for the fray and determined to do their utmost that day. All ranks realised that the great test had arrived, that the honour of Ulster and the reputation of the regiment was at stake.'[28]

On the far side of the River Ancre, the 9th Royal Irish Fusiliers on the right and 12th Royal Irish Rifles on the left attacked in the direction of Beaucourt.

South of the Ancre, the early attackers had great success. They crossed the sunken road and seized the first two lines of German trenches, known as A and B. C line was taken at 8.48 p.m. and the men gathered to attack the Schwaben Redoubt.

The fight for the Schwaben Redoubt was hand-to-hand. 'We were being fired at by a sniper; he got five or six of us before we found him,' remembered Private J. Grange of the 14th Rifles (Belfast Young Citizens). 'My boy-oh was wounded and sheltering behind a rolled-up stretcher. Our sergeant major took Jerry's rifle away from him and smashed it across his head.'

The second Ulster VC of the day was won by Captain Eric Bell of the 9th Inniskillings. He was in charge of a trench mortar battery and advanced with the infantry in the attack. He shot a machine-gunner in the Schwaben Redoubt and threw trench-mortar bombs among the enemy. When no other bombs were available, he stood on the parapet and shot some advancing Germans with his rifle. Having taken the lives of so many of the enemy, he lost his own. 'He gave his life in his supreme devotion to duty,' his VC citation stated.

The 9th Inniskillings reached the German second line and started to send back prisoners. On their immediate left, the 11th and 13th Royal Irish Rifles of 108th Brigade seized the Thiepval-Grandcourt Road.

The Schwaben Redoubt was taken and consolidated. The men from the two battalions of the Rifles pressed on in the direction of the German second line, but their luck ran out. The wire on the German second line remained intact. A frustrating scenario then turned disastrous: they had taken their targets ahead of schedule. The artillery, which was firing to a timetable, began to shell the German second line. In doing so, it shelled the advance parties of 109th Brigade.

'We were pinned down in the open just outside the German wire which was covering their second line,' Corporal G.A. Lloyd of the 9th Rifles (West Belfast Volunteers) remembered.[29] 'It was just Hell; the British artillery were at us, the German artillery were at us and rifle and machine-gun fire as well.' As each line of infantry leaving the shelter of Thiepval Wood ventured into no man's land, the shelling and machine gun fire became increasingly fierce. The follow-up battalions of 109th Brigade, the 11th Inniskillings and the 14th Irish Rifles, suffered terrible losses from enfilade fire coming from Thiepval village, but they passed through the first two lines of captured German trenches and headed for the third line.

North of the Ancre, the 12th Royal Irish Rifles and 9th Royal Irish Fusiliers had a torrid time. They, too, suffered when the attack on their left by the 29th Division failed, leaving them exposed to enfilade fire. Both battalions attacked out of a gully and were faced with three German defensive trenches and five lines of trenches in total. To reach their objective, they would have to pass through the fortified village of Beaucourt. Still the battalions pressed on and got almost as far as Grandcourt only to be repulsed.

Worse was to follow for 107th Brigade, which had been waiting in reserve in Thiepval Wood. When Nugent saw that the attack had broken down on either side, he requested from Corps Command that 107th Brigade be stopped, but was refused.

They moved off, 'Woodbines in mouth', according to Private Davie Starrett, only to emerge into the maelstrom of a battle at full roar. They advanced the furthest, passing through the captured German trenches to approach D line, the last line of German trenches, 1,000 yards from where they had started. Some of the worst casualties were taken by the battalions of 107th Brigade in reserve. They were enfiladed from St Pierre Divion, a Somme village which had been incorporated into the German frontline.

Realising the gravity of the situation, Corps commanders changed their minds and ordered 107th Brigade to return, but it was too late. Near a spot called 'The Crucifix' the men were mown down. No man's land was now littered with dead and dying men. The 15th Rifles, part of 107th Brigade, found themselves in hand-to-hand combat with the Germans who had emerged from their deep dugouts to put up tremendous resistance.

Still, the men from 107th Brigade continued on and eventually reached Mouquet Farm. Some could see open country. This was an achievement of the utmost bravery but it couldn't be sustained. Now the men faced a terrible dilemma. They were far from safety. Advancing would leave them isolated and exposed to waves of German reserves rushing to fill the gaps; going back would take them into a maelstrom of shot and shell.

The Ulstermen clung on while Corps Command sought to get a message through to call off the attack. There was no way of getting it through except with a runner. The perils of traversing the battlefield were so obvious. The 9th Inniskillings, who had been in the first wave of attack, held out for ten hours before retreating back to the old German front line and then back to their own front lines, bleeding and bedraggled, having left the majority of their men behind them; 532 were either dead, wounded or missing.[30]

Meanwhile, the men furthest forward could see through their field glasses that trainloads of German reinforcements were disembarking at Grandcourt. A counter-attack at dusk drove 109th Brigade back and they forfeited all the territory they had fought so bravely to achieve. The last act was carried out the following day when a party of 146th Brigade from 49th Division was sent out into no man's land to bring back the stragglers who were still occupying German trenches. On the evening of 2 July, the 36th (Ulster) Division was relieved by the 49th Division. Their ordeal was over. The division had lost 5,500 of 8,500 effective fighting men. It was finished as a fighting force for the time being. Within a week, the 36th left the Somme.

The casualties were beyond anything anyone believed possible. The 13th Rifle (County Down Volunteers), who were on the extreme left of Thiepval Wood, suffered 595 casualties; the 11th Inniskillings, who had been in the vanguard of the earlier attack, 589; the 9th Royal Irish Fusiliers, who had attacked north of the Ancre, 532. Two battalions, the 9th and the 12th Royal Irish Rifles, had 500 dead men between them.[31]

Virtually every village and town and city street in Ulster had lost someone. Nearly 200 men from the Loyalist Shankill Road were killed; thirty-three died from Lisburn and Banbridge; eight from Raphoe and three from Burt in Donegal (population 153).[32]

News slowly filtered back to Ireland about the calamity. General Sir George Richardson, the officer commanding the Ulster Volunteer Force, urged the public to take an 'unfathomable and unforgettable pride in everyone of them. Their hero-ism and self-sacrifice continue to be the theme of mournful praise among their comrades in arms'.[33]

In Dublin, *The Irish Times* contrasted the loyalty of the Ulstermen with the rebels of Easter Week. 'The blood of Irishmen shed by Irishmen is hardly dry upon the streets of Dublin. Out there, in the forefront of Ireland's and the Empire's battle, the men of all our parties, all our creeds, all our social classes, are fighting side by side.'[34]

Carson responded, 'They have made the supreme sacrifice for the Empire of which they were so proud with a courage, coolness and determination in the face of the most trying difficulties … our feelings are, of course, mingled with sorrow and sadness at the loss of so many men who were to us personal friends and comrades.'[35]

The following Sunday was a sombre one in Ulster's churches. Belfast Cathedral was full of sorrowing families. Charles Grierson told mourners to be 'strong and calm and truthful'. A collection was taken up for the families.

Publicly, General Nugent paid tribute to the men and to their courage. Privately, he was furious. He believed his men had been left exposed by unforgivable bungling among the high command. Specifically, he blamed General Sir Henry Rawlinson, the commander of the Fourth Corps. Nugent wrote to his wife, 'The man I loathe is Harry Rawlinson, the army commander whose senseless optimism is responsible for the practical wiping out of the Division. He is the only man too who has never sent the Division one word of acknowledgement, thanks or praise for what they did for him.' Nugent protested that he did all he could to prepare the men for battle. 'The faults committed were those of the higher authorities in underestimating the difficulties and in giving us an impossible task. I know that unless everything went like clockwork on all sides of us, there was certain to be a failure.' He had attempted to stop his men going forward when the attacks on his flanks broke down. 'I wired at once that in my opinion any advance beyond a certain line would leave us dangerously exposed. The answer was, "carry out the programme". I could have stopped it then.'[36]

Nugent lamented the failure of messengers to get through. The First World War was the only conflict during which generals could not communicate directly with their front-line troops. In previous conflicts, they usually gave instructions from horseback. In future conflicts, they would have radio but in this war telephone wires were shattered by shellfire and messengers shot down. 'Nearly every messenger sent forward was either killed or wounded. We were really almost surrounded by the Germans owing to the failure of the Divisions on either side of us.'[37]

In his 1918 book *The Irish on the Somme*, the second part of his series, *The Irish at the Front*, Michael MacDonagh spelled out the tsunami of grief which washed over the province and could not be ameliorated by empty talk of glory and pride:

This glory was gained at a heavy cost. There was cause for bitter grief as well as the thrill of pride in Ulster. Nothing has brought home more poignantly to the inhabitants of a small area of the kingdom the grim sacrifices and the unutterable pathos of the war than the many pages of names and addresses of the dead and wounded – relatives, friends and acquaintances – which appeared in the Belfast newspapers for days before the Twelfth (of July) and after. So blinds were drawn in business and private houses; flags were flown at half-mast; and bells were mournfully tolling for Ulster's irremediable losses when, at the stroke of twelve o'clock, traffic came instantaneously to a standstill, and for five minutes the citizens solemnly stood with bared heads in the teeming rain thinking of the gallant dead.[38]

The words 'pride', 'sacrifice', 'heroism' and 'bravery' appeared time and again in tributes. The Bishop of Down Revd Charles D'Arcy believed 'the 1st of July will for all the future be remembered as the most glorious in the annals of the history in Ulster'. Such wilful self-delusion was typical of British and Irish society trying to rationalise and explain the tragedy of the First World War. In reality, it was a terrible, bloody slaughter – not the best, but the worst day in Ulster's history, and there were many bad days.

For all their undoubted bravery and sacrifice, the men of the 36th (Ulster) Division had ultimately failed in their objective. 'The Ulster Volunteers ended their participation in the Somme with a fine reputation,' wrote the historian Philip Orr, whose 1988 book *The Road to the Somme* contains interviews with the last survivors of the 36th. 'But of what use was a fine reputation? In terms of a contribution to winning the war, the Ulster Division had done virtually nothing. The ground they had won had been lost again and, not until October was the Schwaben Redoubt retaken and consolidated.'[39]

At the end of the war, some £5,000 was raised within a couple of months after Craig announced his plan to erect a suitable memorial to the men of the 36th. A Hammersmith-based firm was contracted to do the work and local tradesmen were hired. It was a difficult project to undertake in the context of a devastated local economy and landscape.[40] The tower was finally opened on Sunday, 19 November 1921. A party of some 150 people, half from Ireland, half from Britain, arrived by boat-train from Victoria Station and were taken to Amiens and from there to Thiepval for the memorial service.

The Somme region was still ruined three years after the war ended. The countryside would take generations to repair. 'To right and left, before, behind, everywhere so far as the eye can see, there is a vast sea of black despair,' wrote the unnamed *Irish Times* reporter who attended the unveiling. 'A few gaunt skeletons that once were trees stick crazily out of the pock-marked earth. The earth is littered with barbed wire, old helmets, bits of broken tanks, old helmets, even bones obstruct the feet, and a frosted November sun smiles on this withered land as if to enhance its heart rending misery.'[41]

Conspicuous by their absences were both Carson and Craig. The latter was ill with influenza; the former was just ill. Carson was a hypochondriac whose public resolution was matched by a private obsessiveness with his health.[42] Only a dozen people could fit into the room where the memorial tablet was unveiled by General Maxine Weygand, the French general who had read out the Armistice terms to the Germans, and by General Henry Wilson. Wilson, like Carson, was a southern unionist. Born in County Longford, he was a staunch opponent of both home rule and the Anglo-Irish Treaty which followed it. He became a Unionist MP in 1922 but was assassinated in June of that year by the IRA.

A service was held at the foot of the tower by Charles D'Arcy, now the Anglican Primate of All-Ireland. Dozens of wreaths were laid at the bottom of the tower, including one from the locality, which read simply, 'Authuile Reconnaissant' (Authuile, the local village, remembers).

An unnamed mother, who lost three sons on 1 July 1916, was present. After the ceremony, the parties toured the trenches. It was a melancholy group which returned to a still-ruined Albert that evening. 'We drove back to Albert in pregnant silence. Women were sobbing, men were trying to look unconcerned, but as the motor cars bumped and jolted along that ruined road that leads through Beaumont-Hamel hearts were heavy and eyes were dim,' *The Irish Times* reporter observed. The news-paper's editorial remarked that during the war 'there was no partition between the soldiers of the six counties and those of the twenty-six. Many good Irishmen, among them, John Redmond and his brave brother hoped and prayed that the common sacrifice, the common heroism would heal the discord of centuries and the via dolorosa of Messines and Thiepval would lead us to the gateway of a united Ireland.'

The Ulster Tower went through many vicissitudes over the years. It was taken over by the Germans in 1940 and used for observation of the surrounding coun-tryside. By the time the Troubles broke out in 1969, it had fallen into a state of despair. No caretaker was employed to look after it. Philip Orr recalled visiting it in 1988. He had to hunt for a key in the local village. One regular visitor stated that just forty people turned up to a 1 July service during the 1980s.

Increasingly forgotten and neglected, the campaign to rescue it from obscurity began with a rededication ceremony in 1989. The Somme Association, set up the year before, was given the task of managing it. In 1993, an obelisk memorial to members of the Orange Order who had died with the 36th (Ulster) Division was opened in a little garden to the right of the tower. It overlooks the slopes where the men of 108th and 109th brigades attacked the Schwaben Redoubt.

If the memorial to the Orange Order was exclusive, the adjacent museum, which opened in 1994, is more inclusive in sentiment. It pays tribute to all the Irish regiments, north and south, that fought at the Somme. In 2005, a section of trench in Thiepval Wood which had been occupied by the 36th was excavated and is now a major attraction in its own right. The wood itself is owned by the Somme Association. Unexploded munitions were found during the excavations; it remains dangerous terrain to this day.

The highlight of any visit to the Ulster Tower is its memorial room. It houses a painting by J.P. Beadle called 'The Attack of the Ulster Division'. But the cen-trepiece of the memorial room is the plaque which was unveiled when the tower was opened in 1921:

> To the Glory of God in grateful memory of the officers, non-commissioned officers and men of the 36th (Ulster) Division and of the sons of Ulster in other forces who laid down their lives in the Great War and of all their comrades in arms who by divine grace were spared to testify to their glorious deeds.

When the original Helen's Tower was built, the poet laureate Alfred J. Tennyson was commissioned to write a few lines. 'Helen's Tower, here I stand, dominant over sea and land, son's love built me and I hold, mother's love in lettered gold'.

The lines have been changed. 'Helen's Tower, here I stand, dominant over sea and land, son's love built me and I hold Ulster's love in lettered gold.'

That love remained conditional though. In absentia, Carson sent a tribute that the tower would remind future generations of Ulstermen to 'maintain the freedom from aggression whether at home or abroad which they won at such a heavy cost'.

The Ulster Tower is now a confident memorial, one of the most impressive on the Western Front, just as Craig and his followers had intended. The memories of the Ulster men who died on 1 July are commemorated, memorialised and respected. But what of those from nationalist Ireland who fought and died on the Somme?

15

THE CROSS AT GUILLEMONT

Not since the great home rule rally of March 1912 had the streets of Dublin seen anything like it. The huge crowd assembled in College Green spilled over into the streets and lanes surrounding Dublin's great gathering point. It was the middle of November, yet extraordinarily mild. Such were the numbers that people complained of the heat. Many fainted. Children had to be extricated from the crush.[1]

It was a day of pageantry and sorrow. Crowds clapped and cheered as ex-British servicemen marched from two directions to converge on College Green. One group left from, of all places, the General Post Office (GPO), now being rebuilt after having been the birthplace of the Irish Republic in 1916. The other contingent came from Dame Street. The Union flag flew from Trinity College Dublin, the traditional bastion of British intellectual life in Ireland, and from other buildings, though this contentious symbol was no longer the national flag of the newly independent state.

The veterans marched proudly or limped if carrying old war wounds. All wore their medals from the First World War. One old veteran wore his from the 1882 Nile Campaign. Others were just children wearing their fathers' medals. Mercifully, some were too young at the time to remember the psychic shock of knowing their father had been killed in the war. People clambered on to every vantage point overlooking College Green.

Big crowds had turned out for a victory parade in Dublin in 1919, but that was before independence. The enormous gathering that descended on the centre of Dublin for Armistice Day 1924 took everyone by surprise, not least the Dublin Metropolitan Police (DMP), which had no traffic contingency plan in place. It anticipated a small crowd that would form up around 11 a.m., observe a two-minute silence and then disperse from whence it had come. Nobody anticipated this.

A crowd estimated at 50,000 turned up on a normal working day. Neither did they disperse. Many stayed until late that night. They had kept their grief to themselves, but now seized of the opportunity to make a public display of their sorrow, they did not want to go home.

The war had left a terrible legacy of suffering in Irish households. A.P. Connolly, the head of the British Legion in Ireland, estimated that 165,000 Irish children had lost a parent, mostly a father, during the war period, 35,000 men had lost a leg or arm, 6,450 men had gone insane and were detained in 'lunatic asylums' and 3,150 were suffering from epilepsy.[2]

It was eight years after the Easter Rising and six years after the 1918 general election in which nationalist Ireland had embraced the abstentionist Sinn Féin party, precipitating the War of Independence. It was less than three years after the foundation of the Irish Free State and fifteen months after the end of the Civil War. Yet here was nationalist Ireland paying tribute to the men who had fought in British uniform during the First World War.

So many things had happened since the innocent optimism of the home rule rally when, in March 1912, the Irish nationalist leader John Redmond told an exultant crowd, estimated at 100,000 and composed of all strands of nationalist opinion, that 'this meeting is Ireland … Believe me, Home Rule is winning. We will have a parliament sitting in College Green sooner than the most sanguine and enthusiastic man in this crowd believes.'[3]

Another who spoke on one of four platforms that day was a relatively unknown schoolteacher and writer named Pádraig Pearse, who joined in the general excitement about the prospect of home rule. 'Let us unite and win a good Act from the British'.[4]

Now, twelve years on, the world and Ireland had changed beyond all recognition. Europe had fallen into an abyss of savagery; violence had trumped human progress. 'The ceremony of innocence is drowned,' the poet W.B. Yeats wrote in 'The Second Coming', published in 1919.

Redmond was dead, a broken-hearted man whose dreams of home rule foundered in the mud of Flanders and the rubble of the GPO. Pearse was dead, executed by the British along with fifteen others. Also dead were tens of thousands of their fellow Irishmen, who had fallen in the khaki of the British army or the olive green of the Irish Volunteers, later to be the IRA. For many countries, Armistice Day 1918 had been the end of Europe's nightmare. For Ireland it was only the beginning of conflict, enmity and hatred which would last for generations.

Ireland had achieved greater constitutional freedom at the point of a gun than was on offer through the constitutional settlement in 1912 that made the home rule parliament subservient to Westminster Parliament.

Many in nationalist Ireland were apt to remind those who had fought in British uniform of what had been achieved by fighting against and not for the British.

Previous Remembrance Day services had been the subject of clashes between republicans and unionists, but on this day, 11 November 1924, all was respectful. It was an altogether more sombre, subdued crowd that gathered in their tens of thousands in College Green on this Armistice Day 1924. The object that had prompted this national outpouring of grief and remembrance was a large Celtic cross, 13ft 6in high, made of solid granite and weighing 3 tons. It was enclosed by a metal railing, measuring 15ft square. At its base was an inscription in Irish and English. 'Do chum Glóire Dé agus Onóra na hÉireann' (To the Glory of God and Honour of Ireland). 'In commemoration of the victories of Guillemont and Ginchy Sept 3rd and 9th 1916 in memory of those who fell therein and of all the Irishmen who gave their lives in the Great War RIP'.

At 11 a.m., the bell of Trinity College sounded and the whole crowd fell silent, save for the quiet sobbings of a number of women and children and a siren from the docks calling on the men to down tools for the two-minute silence.[5] Then Major General William Hickie, the man who first proposed the idea of a series of memorial Celtic crosses to remember the Irish who died in the First World War, stepped forward. He pulled the cord and the black draping covering the monument fell. He placed a wreath on the head of the cross where the inscription '16th (Irish) Division' was carved into the granite.

The inscription on the wreath read, 'I place this wreath on our temporary cenotaph in commemoration of the Irishmen who gave their lives in the Great War. We will not break with ye.' He was followed by Lady Headford on behalf of General Bryan Mahon of the 10th (Irish) Division, who was representing the Free State government at the cenotaph in London. Lady Nugent represented her husband Major-General Sir Oliver Nugent and the 36th (Ulster) Division. She too laid a wreath.

Then it was the turn of the Irish Free State, founded as it had been by men who had fought against and not for the British army (in fact, in some cases both for and against). Yet, a degree of tolerance and understanding was apparent in the Cumann na nGaedheal government. It had reason to be grateful for the expertise of ex-British servicemen who joined the national army after the war and helped secure the new state against anti-Treaty forces. In addition, hundreds of thousands of citizens in the new state had a direct connection with the war. They could not be ignored.

A wreath was laid by Senator Colonel Maurice Moore, formerly of the Connaught Rangers. It read, 'O Rialtas Saorstát Éireann i gcuimhne na nÉireannach uile a fuair bás son choga mór (From the Government of Saorstat Eireann in memory of all the Irishmen who died in the Great War)'.[6]

One by one the wreaths piled up on the cross. The crowd clamoured ever closer. Wreaths were passed over the heads of the crowd, such was the crush. One came from Mary Kettle, the wife of Tom Kettle, who had been killed at the Battle of Ginchy on 9 September 1916. The inscription included lines from Kettle's famous poem written for his daughter Betty. 'Died not for flag, nor King, nor Emperor, / But for a dream born in a herdsman's shed, / And for the secret scripture of the poor.' An 80-year-old woman who had lost two sons in the war was helped to the front, as was a child whose wreath read, 'I want to see my Daddy'.[7]

For hours afterwards, the public filed passed the Guillemont cross. It was all respectful and solemn. The *Irish Independent* noted afterwards, 'In the whole ceremony there was no thought of politics, no thought of party, no thought even of the justice on one side or the other of the European War. The thousands who met yesterday at College Green went to honour our dead, to give token of their reverence to men who risked and lost life in a cause which they thought was right.'[8]

The editorial stated there should be no distinction in remembrance between both polities in Ireland. 'Some comparisons, unfortunately, have been made, but the lists of our Southern dead and the glory of the 16th and the 10th Divisions are sufficient answer to those who have sought to discriminate between north and south.'[9]

In its editorial, *The Irish Times* alluded to previous difficulties with Remembrance Day commemorations when it wrote that the 'years that have elapsed since the 11th of November 1918 were not favourable to any but the most unobtrusive memorial celebration. The brave have now been honoured in their native land.' For this it thanked the Free State government. 'Loyalty to the Empire is seen to be consistent with perfect loyalty to the Free State. The Government's tolerant and moderate policy is largely responsible for the better conditions of things.'[10]

It was the high-water mark of Free State remembrance commemorations. In 1925, Republicans, angered by the Border Commission's decision to confirm the borders of the Free State, threw smoke bombs into the crowd. Within two years, it was moved to the relatively peripheral Phoenix Park, though huge crowds still attended. The League of ex-Servicemen wanted to place a permanent Irish war memorial in Merrion Square, opposite Government Buildings, but the Free State was vehemently against such a memorial so close to the seat of power.

The president of the executive council (effectively the state's first Taoiseach) William T. Cosgrave commented, 'A large section of nationalist opinion regards the scheme as part of a political movement of an imperialist nature and view it with the same resentment as they view the exploitation of Poppy Day in Dublin by the most hostile elements of the old Unionist classes.'[11]

The Minister for Justice Kevin O'Higgins, whose brother was killed in the war, was disposed to remembering Ireland's war dead, but not in Merrion Square. Such a prominent memorial suggested the new state was founded on the sacrifice of the men who died in the First World War 'and I have no desire to see it suggested that it is'.[12] A beautiful, if peripheral, location was eventually found for the Irish National War Memorial in Islandbridge.[13]

Major-General Hickie had commanded the 16th (Irish) Division for the duration of the war. A Catholic from Tipperary, he understood the realities of the new Irish Free State well, but sought to work within the sensitivities of the time period.

—

The 16th (Irish) Division spent almost three years in France from the autumn of 1915 to the autumn of 1918, only being out of the line for three weeks in all that time. Its involvement in the attacks on Guillemont and Ginchy were its first operations in the Somme and its first major offensive operation. These two unremarkable villages are just a mile apart, but the road between them is all uphill and soaked in the blood of friend and foe.

The 16th arrived on the Somme in late August 1916. The battle, was nearly two months old and went on despite the horrors of its first day. Haig and Rawlinson, the prime architects of the first-day debacle, had invested too much time, hope and matériel not to continue irrespective of the frightful cost. To admit defeat at such an early stage after the first day rebuffs would be unthinkable.

Haig and Rawlinson survived the first day of the Somme, though their posthumous reputations would never survive the catastrophic mistakes they made when they failed to heed the warnings about the depth of German dugouts and uncut barbed wire. Both men flung their willing volunteers forward time after time in a vain attempt to achieve breakthroughs which they had sought to achieve on the first day.

The attack north of the Albert–Bapaume road, which included the assault of the 36th (Ulster) Division on the first day, was a complete disaster, but Haig saw enough progress south of the road for the battle to resume. This sector would consume most of the energies of the British Fourth Army for the summer.

The woods in this area, in particular, would cost the lives of thousands of men. The names resonate with dread across the British Empire – High Wood, Delville Wood (known as Devil's Wood), Mametz Wood, a place of sorrow for the Welsh, and High Wood.

It took two months of attritional warfare for the British to eventually take High Wood, once described by the eminent military historian Richard Holmes as 'ghastly by day, ghostly by night, the rottenest place on the Somme'.[14]

This deadly slogging match in July and August 1916 would suck in all parts of the Empire. On the road between Albert and Bapaume is the village of Pozières, now rebuilt after the war. The little village, which is home to Le Tommy cáfe, marks the spot where the Australians were thrown into the mincing machine of the Somme. Le Tommy cafe is a popular stopping-off point for tourists with its own small museum of military debris accumulated over many years from the annual iron harvest.

On 23 July 1916, the 1st Australian Division made an attack on the fortified village and captured it, but this was the beginning and not the end of their ordeal. The Germans shelled it day and night. The division suffered 5,000 casualties in five days of shelling. The 2nd Australian Division fared even worse with 7,000 casualties, followed by the 4th Australian Division, which attempted to break out of the village in the direction of Mouquet Farm, a strongpoint which they hoped could lead to an assault on Thiepval. The Australians sustained 23,000 casualties during the Battle of Pozières.

It was into this maelstrom of slaughter that the 16th (Irish) Division arrived in late August 1916. They were relieved to be leaving Loos and as yet undaunted about being sent to the Somme. 'Everyone was really pleased at the news as all had been reading of the wonderful successes of our arms in that [Somme] sector and it was feared that hostilities would cease before we got a chance to prove what we could do,' the Leinster Regiment's historian Frederick Whitton remembered.[15]

The 16th had spent months recovering from the three days of horror in late April when they were subjected to the gas attacks at Hulluch. But they were not permitted much respite. The men were constantly involved in raiding enemy trenches, dangerous work which was of dubious military value. But British commanders believed it imperative that the Germans be constantly harassed, lest they be able to further reinforce their defensive lines. The divisional war diary recorded that the 'Hun had been reduced to almost complete quiet'.[16] Such raids were carried out at a heavy cost, with some 380 killed and 2,670 injured in the time between the Hulluch gas attacks and moving to the Somme.[17]

The 16th Irish Division was withdrawn from the Hulluch sector on 24 August 1916. They were transported in cattle trucks to Amiens and then marched the 22 miles from Amiens to Bray-sur-Somme. Many bathed in the River Somme, which gave its name to the battle, though many Tommies never saw it as they never ventured that far south.

The 16th was allocated to XIV Corps, part of the Fourth Army.

The division was needed for the attack on Guillemont and Ginchy located on to the extreme right of the British line. These two villages were on a hilltop overlooking both the British and French lines. The ultimate goal was Ginchy, but Guillemont blocked the way to it. It had to be taken. Neither village stands on a great elevation (Guillemont is at 469ft and Ginchy 505ft), but they were high enough to command panoramas of the eastern end of the British section of battlefield. The previous captures of Delville and High Wood at such a colossal loss, mostly to Welsh, Australian and South African forces, would ultimately be in vain if German machine guns and artillery could still use the heights of Guillemont and Ginchy to block any further British advance.

To the west of Guillemont lay the cone-shaped Trones Wood, another deadly abode. The official British history records, 'The wood was commanded at close range both from the north and the east, and there was little chance of holding it while the enemy sat in Longueval and Guillemont. Captured it might be, at a price, but only by permission of the Germans could it be held.'[18]

Repeated attempts to take it cost thousands of lives. The wood was eventually captured on 14 July by the 12th Middlesex led by Lieutenant-Colonel Frank Maxwell, who ordered his men to shoot indiscriminately into both the undergrowth and into the tangled jumble of felled trees to ensure there were no Germans left.[19]

The taking of Trones Wood opened the way for an assault on Guillemont. But, once again, the village would not be surrendered by the Germans without a bloody struggle. The 2nd Royal Scots Fusiliers entered Guillemont on 30 July but were all killed or taken prisoner. The battalion suffered a horrendous 650 casualties. The next attempt, on 8 August, was by the 55th (West Lancashire) Division, which included the Liverpool Irish of 164th Brigade. This attack failed. The village was ruined but the Germans were carrying on a deadly underground battle.[20]

'[The village] was simply a very strongly defended position,' explains Michael Stedman in his book *Guillemont*.[21] 'The depth of dugouts and the many interconnected tunnels meant that any limited British infantry advance into the village could then be isolated and dealt with as the German defenders emerged to take these units in the rear.'

The 164th Brigade diary records, 'As soon as they had got into the village it appears that the enemy came up out of the ground below them and cut them off entirely by means of machine gun.'[22]

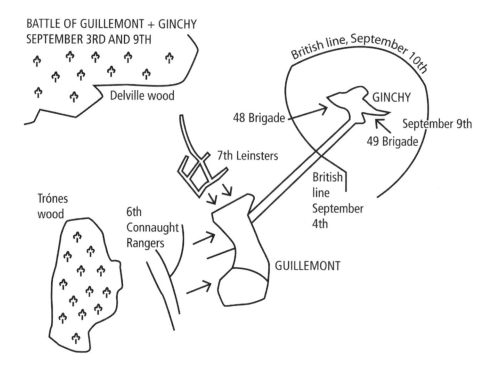

The attempt to take Guillemont cost the 55th Division 4,100 casualties. The 55th Division was replaced by the 3rd Division. It and the 24th Division renewed the assault on 18 August.[23]

The 3rd Division included the 2nd Leinster Regiment. In his brilliant memoir *Stand To!*, Colonel Francis Hitchcock wrote of the bombardment of Guillemont:

> Shell-fire was hellish all afternoon. Box barrages were put down all round and the earth was going up like volcanoes completely smothering us. During a bombardment one developed a craze for two things: water and cigarettes. Few could ever eat under an intense bombardment especially on the Somme, when every now and then a shell would blow pieces of mortality, or complete bodies which had been putrefying in no man's land and slap into one's trench.[24]

On 23 August, Guillemont Station, a light-gauge railway stop immediately to the east of the village, was captured. By then the British were surrounding Guillemont from the west and south, but the Germans still blocked the advance to Ginchy.[25] The assault was repeatedly delayed by bad weather but it was agreed to go ahead on 3 September with the 20th (Light) Division and the 16th (Irish) Division, attempting what had been beyond previous attempts.[26]

The 16th arrived in the Somme in good heart. The 8th Munsters carried a beautiful banner of the Sacred Heart made for it by local Limerick women and the nuns of the Good Shepherd Convent in Limerick. The men were assured that those who carried the banner 'would have victory with them'.[27]

The gesture earned the most effusive thanks of the battalion's chaplain Fr John Rafter SJ. He wrote to Alice Doyle, one of the women involved in making the banner:

> We had a little service in the church last evening, where I presented the banner to the Battalion, and told them that their friends and well-wishers in Limerick had sent it to them in hopes that it would bring that blessing on the regiment which Our Divine Lord promised Blessed Mother Mary would be the special portion of those families in which a picture of the Sacred Heart was exposed and venerated. The men are delighted to have the banner, they will love it, and I have no doubt it will bring a blessing on us all, and will help us to love God more, and will inspire us with courage and confidence to do our duty under the difficulties and dangers we live in.[28]

In the trenches that evening, the men prepared for battle. Rafter went around talking and consoling them. Despite the murderous carnage of more than two years of war, he had not wavered in his belief that the men were fighting a just cause. 'They came to him without orders – they came gladly and willingly, and they hailed his visit with plain delight,' Major Willie Redmond told the author Michael MacDonagh, who recorded his words in *The Irish on the Somme*. Major Redmond, brother of John, was with the 6th Battalion of the Royal Irish Regiment. He told MacDonagh:

> He [Rafter] spoke to them in the simple, homely language which they liked. He spoke of the sacrifice which they had made in freely and promptly leaving their homes to fight for a cause which was the cause of religion, freedom and civilisation. He reminded them that in this struggle they were most certainly defending the homes and the relations and friends they had left behind them in Ireland. He then gave them general absolution.[29]

These men were now hardened soldiers and not the innocent enthusiasts who had arrived in France less than a year previously. They had seen so many of their comrades cut down. On the night before the attack, Major General Hickie sent them a message that was probably both ominous and reassuring. 'The divisional commander sends his best wishes to the officers and men of the Brigades and knows that their actions tomorrow will go down in history'.[30]

The men lay down in their shallow trenches from 4 a.m., waiting for the assault. According to MacDonagh, the regimental pipers were busy from early morning. They played 'Brian Boru's March', 'The White Cockade', 'The Wearin' o' the Green' and 'A Nation Once Again'. 'The pipers strode up and down, green ribbons streaming from their pipes,' MacDonagh continued, 'sending forth these piercing invocations to ancient Irish heroes, to venerable saints of the land, to the glories and sorrows of Ireland, to the love of home, to the faith and aspirations of the race, to come to the support of the men in the fight. And what of the men as they waited in the assembly trenches for the word? The passage from Shakespeare's Henry V best conveys their mood: "I see ye stand like grey-hounds in the leash straining upon the start".[31]

At this stage, Guillemont was a village in name only. Months of shelling had reduced it to a spectral shell. Photographs taken at the time show only houses levelled to rubble and the bare stumps of stripped trees. The ghastly spectacle chilled every soldier who fought there. The woods nearby had been stripped of everything except the sturdiest tree trunks. Everywhere the work of man and nature had been confounded by pure destruction.

German soldier Ernst Jünger, whose book *Storm and Steel* is a classic of war literature, knew he had arrived in what had once been a village because of the colour of the earth:

> The shell-holes there were of a whiter colour by reason of the houses which had been ground to powder. Guillemont railway station lay in front of us. It was smashed to bits like a child's plaything. Delville Wood, reduced to matchwood, was farther behind. You could search in vain for one wretched blade of grass. This churned-up battlefield was ghastly. Among the living lay the dead. As we dug ourselves in we found them in layers stacked one upon the top of another. One company after another had been shoved into the drum-fire and steadily annihilated. The corpses were covered with the masses of soil turned up by the shells, and the next company advanced in the place of the fallen.[32]

The desolation hid a deadly secret. The Germans had turned the cellars of bombed-out houses into death traps for attackers. Yet this abyss had to be taken. The men of 47th Brigade from the 16th (Irish) Division had to wait eight hours for the bombardment to begin at midday. The delay was to give the Germans less time for a counter-attack. On the northern side of Guillemont village, the 7th Leinsters lay down in trenches so shallow that if they even sat up they could be fired upon. The men squatted motionless as time dragged on. They lay 'lying like lions in their lairs thirsting for blood,' according to Whitton.[33]

The Irish battalions involved in the Battle of Guillemont were the 7th Leinsters, the 6th Connaught Rangers, the 8th Royal Munster Fusiliers and the 6th Royal Irish Regiment.

The assault was to be made by carrying out a creeping barrage, with the infantry following at precise intervals. The 10th King's Royal Rifle Corps from the 20th Division led the attack, followed by the 6th Connaught Rangers. The Connaught Rangers suffered 200 casualties from friendly fire alone before they joined in the attack. Their commanding officer Lieutenant-Colonel John Lenox-Conyngham was killed as soon as he stood on the parapet to wave his troops on. Undaunted, the men pressed ahead. Within minutes the German's front positions in the village were overrun.

The 7th Leinsters dashed for the enemy lines as soon as the artillery barrage was lifted and surprised the Germans. 'They bombed, captured, bayoneted or brained with the butts of their rifles all the Germans in the first trench,' wrote Whitton.[34]

The men of the 20th (Light) Infantry 59th Brigade, reinforced by the 6th Oxford and Bucks Light Infantry and the 7th Somerset Light Infantry, took their second positions on time. The soldiers of the 6th Connaught Rangers were 'leapfrogged' by the 8th Royal Munsters. These soldiers then advanced eastwards along Mount Street and began to consolidate along the line of North Street and South Street, which defined the eastern perimeter of the village. These were not streets anymore but lines on a map that marked the advance.

At 2.50 p.m., the advance to the third objective, the Maurepas to Ginchy Road outside the village, was made by the 6th Royal Irish Regiment, which moved forward to the sound of their battalion pipes.[35] The British captured more than 700 wounded and unwounded Germans. At last Guillemont was in British hands.

The battle, though, had left a hideous aftermath. Fr Willie Doyle, who passed through the battlefield on 5 September, recalled:

> The first part of our journey lay through a narrow trench, the floor of which consisted of deep thick mud, and the bodies of dead men trodden underfoot. It was horrible beyond description, but there was no help for it, and on the half rotten corpses of our own brave men we marched in silence, everyone busy with his own thoughts … Half an hour of this brought us out on the open into the middle of the battlefield of some days previous. The wounded, at least I hope so, had all been removed, but the dead lay there stiff and stark, with open staring eyes, just as they had fallen. Good God, such a sight! I had tried to prepare myself for this, but all I had read or pictured gave me little idea of the reality.[36]

—

To the right of the 20th (Light) Division, the 5th Division had secured Falfemont Farm. This allowed for preparations to begin for the assault on Ginchy.[37]

The first attempt to take Ginchy occurred on 6 September, but was beaten back. The attack was rescheduled for 9 September, preceded by a long preliminary bombardment lasting from 7 a.m. The 48th Brigade of 16th (Irish) Division would lead the assault with the much depleted 47th Brigade guarding its right flank.

The brigade moved forward at 4.45 p.m. precisely. The attack of 47th Brigade was held up by fire from the enemy trenches south-east of Ginchy. A trench that the Connaught Rangers hoped was empty was full of Germans manning machine guns.[38]

The 8th Munsters and the 6th Royal Irish Regiment were met with withering fire. Of the 1,328 men the brigade could muster for the attack, 448, a third, became casualties. The 7th Leinsters following on behind advanced over the broken bodies and dismembered corpses of their comrades.[39]

The 48th Brigade, however, had a much better outcome. The brigade's lead battalions were the 1st Munsters and the 7th Royal Irish Rifles who were so depleted from friendly shelling that they needed the 7th Royal Irish Fusiliers as support. The 1st Munsters were already severely depleted from the battle of Bernafay Wood on 4 September and had an effective fighting force of just 408 men. Together the two battalions assaulted the enemy front lines. The shelling had shaken the Germans so badly that they surrendered en masse.

The follow-on battalions, the 8th and 9th Dublins, consolidated the hold on Ginchy. The Germans attempted a counter-attack but 48th Brigade stood firm. When night came, the Germans opened up an artillery barrage on the men occupying Ginchy. The attackers dug in as best they could. The men found the village well stocked with provisions, including cold coffee, bread and sacks of apples. They also augmented their food supplies with the rations from dead enemy soldiers.

Early on 10 September, the 16th (Irish) Division was relieved by the 3rd Guards Brigade. The 16th had suffered the worst that the Somme could offer. And Ginchy had been all but wiped off the face of the earth. 'There was no village there now, only a hole in the ground,' one private stated.

The men of the 16th (Irish) Division had proven to be redoubtable fighters even though the British commanders had begun to mistrust their intentions in the aftermath of the Easter Rising. The division was praised for its battlefield exploits by English newspapers that were not always well disposed to Irishmen. *Daily Express* reporter Percival Phillips spoke of how the Irish 'simply swarmed over the rubbish heap, once a brick and plaster village built around a crossroads in a dip between two wooded ridges, driving the Boches eastward in dire confusion. Between noon and mid-afternoon the 2,000 Prussians who had been ordered to hold the ground at all costs were dispersed, captured or killed.'[40] W. Beach Thomas of the *Daily Mail* likened the Irish charge to the way they played rugby. 'Their forwards who managed to get at the back of the chief German defences charged with such impetus that everything but the zest of the rush was forgotten.'[41]

Two Victoria Crosses were awarded to Irishmen at Guillemont. Private Thomas Hughes from Castleblayney, County Monaghan, was with the Connaught Rangers. He was initially injured, but had his wound dressed and returned to battle. He singlehandedly disabled a German machine gun post. He recalled, 'I noticed a machine gun firing in the German lines. So I rushed up, shot both the chaps on the guns and brought it back. I remember no more until I found myself down in the dressing station. PS: I forgot to mention I brought four German prisoners with the gun.'[42]

The other Victoria Cross went to Lieutenant John Holland of the 7th Leinsters, the son of a vet from Model Farm, Athy, County Kildare. He showed extraordinary dash in leading his men on a bombing party which cleared German trenches and captured some fifty prisoners. Of the twenty-five men who participated in this bombing raid, two were awarded the Distinguished Cross of Merit and six the Military Medal. Five were killed and all but five who participated in the raid were uninjured.[43]

Holland went on to live an extraordinary life. He emigrated to England and enlisted in the Second World War along with his two sons, Niall Vincent and Norman. Niall was killed in India in June 1944. In 1956, John and his wife Frances emigrated to Tasmania. When he died in February 1975, at the age of 84, he was awarded a state funeral with full military honours. His coffin was carried through the streets of Hobart on a gun carriage.[44]

The 16th (Irish) Division paid a terrible price for its heroics when capturing two ruined villages. Of the nearly 11,000 officers and men who arrived on 1 September, more than 4,300 were casualties. The number of dead amounted to 1,067.[45]

Throughout the 16th (Irish) Division's travails on the Western Front, the 11th Hampshire had been its faithful pioneer (engineering) battalion, building roads, repairing trenches and generally making life bearable for the men at the front. After the Battle of Ginchy, the pioneers came across oak beams from a ruined farmhouse. They fashioned the timber into an impressive cross approximately 20ft tall in memory of the death of the 16th. The cross stood forlorn in a field between Guillemont and Ginchy, anchored by a base of stones and concrete. On its base was inscribed the words, 'To those who fell at the capture of Guillemont and Ginchy, September 1916, RIP.'

In 1923, Major-General Hickie and General Bryan Mahon, both senators in the new Free State, made a public appeal through the newspapers for money to provide permanent memorials to the fallen Irish. 'Every nation whose sons took part in the war has erected on the scene of their victories and sacrifices some monument to commemorate their share in the great effort and testify to its remembrance,' the men wrote. They promised the memorials would be 'simple and unassuming in design which will for all time stand evidence of the deeds of the South Irish Divisions and keep fresh the memory of Irishmen who gave their lives in this achievement'.[46]

In correspondence with the Imperial War Graves Commission, Hickie wrote, 'Owing to political considerations in Ireland the question of a permanent memorial in France to the 16th (Irish) Division has remained in abeyance until the present time. We are, however, now in a position to carry our proposed scheme.'[47]

There were three crosses in total, the first for Guillemont, the second remembered the 16th (Irish) Division's liberation of the Flanders villages of Wytschaete (the subject of another chapter) and a third was erected in the mountains of Macedonia to remember the 10th (Irish) Division and their involvement in the Salonika campaign on the Eastern Front.

In the meantime, the original cross at Ginchy was brought to Ireland. The land on which it had been erected by the Hampshires was owned by a local farmer who wanted the cross removed so he could plough the soil around it. The Ginchy cross is now housed, and only available by appointment to see, at the War Memorial Gardens in Islandbridge.

—

The memorial party that arrived in Guillemont on 23 August 1926 had been moved and upset by a tour of the old battlefields, starting with the cross that was unveiled at Wytschaete, near Ypres. They arrived in Albert to find the little town had been substantially rebuilt save for the cathedral, which no longer had its golden Virgin on top. Corn meadows and fields full of poppies had replaced the trenches and the shell holes.[48]

The locals of Guillemont had prepared a banner across the main street that proclaimed 'Viva l'Irlande'. The local fire brigade turned out in uniform; children picked wild flowers from the fields and placed them at the base of the Celtic cross located next to the rebuilt Catholic church. The strict separation of Church and State in France meant that a religious symbol could only be permanently erected in church grounds.

The principal guest was Marshall Joseph Joffre, the acclaimed saviour of France and the victor of the Battle of the Marne in September 1914. Joffre, the '*grandpére de la Victoire*', had aged considerably since the war ended. Now 74, his gait was bent with age and his moustache had turned a snowy white. Mounted gendarmes lined both sides of the road.[49] The Irish Guards band attended. Joffre and Major General Hickie pulled down the drapes that covered the cross. The Bishop of Amiens was the principal speaker. He spoke of the long service of Irishmen in the armies of France stretching back three centuries. '*La belle Irlande*' and '*la douce France*' were now 'sisters in sorrow' but rejoiced in a freedom that had been won at a bitter cost, he said.

The church at Guillemont itself is paradoxically dedicated to both peace and to the 16th (Irish) Division. A plaque on the wall lists all the battalions of the division. There is also a plaque to the men from the 16th (Irish) Division who won the Victoria Cross – Hughes and Holland. Sergeant David Jones of the 12th Battalion of the King's (Liverpool) Regiment, who won a VC at Ginchy and was killed a month later, is also remembered in the church. A statue of St Patrick was presented to the Mayor of Guillemont by the Combined Irish Regiments Association to mark the ninetieth anniversary of the battle in 2006.[50] There is both a Rue de la 16e Div Irlandaise in the village, and a Rue Ernst Jünger.

The Battle of the Somme continued for two months after the Battle of Ginchy. Having secured Ginchy, the Guards Division then assaulted Lesboeufs, a village over the next hill in the German third line of defence.

The Irish Guards were involved in an assault which gained them 800 yards of ground or the 'extreme range of a service rifle', according to Rudyard Kipling in his book *The Irish Guards in the Great War*. They paid for the advance with 300 casualties including Clarke and many other Irishmen who were buried in

Lesboeufs Cemetery. Among the Irish Guards who died in this attack was Private John Clarke (21), who is buried in Lesboeufs. The cemetery overlooks Bapaume, the original objective of the Battle of the Somme, which was never reached. From the cemetery, one can discern the water tower of Bapaume a notable landmark that was so near and yet so far away for the British.

Clarke was the son of Kate Clarke and the late colour sergeant John Clarke of the 9th King's Royal Rifles. He had enlisted in Mallow, County Cork, in April 1915 and was killed on 13 September 1916.

Every year on the anniversary of his death, his mother put a notice in the *Cork Examiner*. The years did not seem to diminish the intensity of his family's grief. In 1925, the memoriam notice read:

> Sadly missed and deeply mourned by his loving mother, aunt and cousins.
> May he rest in peace.
> His warfare o'er, his battle fought,
> His victory won though dearly bought;
> His fresh young life could not be saved,
> He slumbers now in a soldier's grave.[51]

The inscription on Clarke's grave reads, 'An only child sadly missed and deeply mourned by his loving mother R.I.P.'

On Remembrance Sunday 2016 the French Government unveiled a replica of the Ginchy Cross in blue limestone in Glasnevin cemetery, Dublin. The France-Ireland memorial pays tribute to the Irish who fought with the French during the Franco-Prussian War, the First World War and the Second World War.

In the programme for the event, the French President Francoise Hollande paid tribute to the Irish who had died in France during the First World War. 'By recalling this shared history of the blood we shed together, we will help others understand the purpose of the joint commitment we French and Irish have to the Middle East and Africa, to people under threat, so that peace, freedom and human rights triumph.'

The memorial was designed by students from the École des Beaux-Arts in Paris, some of whom had lost their classmates in the Bataclan massacre in November 2015. The inscriptions on the monument are a tribute from the Allied Supreme Commander during the First World War, Field Marshal Ferdinand Foch, and were first published in *The Irish Times* in November 1928:

> Some of the flower of Irish chivalry rests in the cemeteries that have been reserved in France, and the French people will always have these reminders of the debt that France owes to Irish valour. We shall always see that the graves of these heroes from across the sea are lovingly tended, and we shall try to ensure that the generations that come after us shall never forget the heroic dead of Ireland.

16

THE THIEPVAL MEMORIAL TO THE MISSING

You proved by death as true as they,
In mightier conflicts played your part,
Equal your sacrifice may weigh,
Dear Kettle, of the generous heart

George Russell (AE)

The knock on the door that Mary Kettle had been dreading finally came in September 1916. Her husband Tom was fighting in France and she had felt for a long time that he would not be coming home. The telegram boy stood at the front door of their house in Rathmines bearing the ominous communiqué that would confirm her abiding fear. The message was terse and devastating. 'To Mrs Kettle, University College Dublin: Deeply regret to inform you, Lieut T.M. Kettle, Dublin Fusiliers was killed in action, September 9th. The Army Council expresses their sympathy. Secretary War Office.'[1]

Mary Kettle, at the age of 32, was now a widow. The couple's 3-year-old daughter Elizabeth (Betty) was left without a father.

Tom Kettle had foreseen his own death. Five days before he died, he wrote a poem for Betty that would become one of the best-known Irish poems of the war. If he ended up with the 'foolish dead', he wrote, she should know why he died:

And oh! they'll give you rhyme
And reason: some will call the thing sublime,
And some decry it in a knowing tone.
So here, while the mad guns curse overhead,
And tired men sigh with mud for couch and floor,
Know that we fools, now with the foolish dead,
Died not for flag, nor King, nor Emperor,
But for a dream, born in a herdsman's shed,
And for the secret Scripture of the poor.

Tom and Mary Kettle were paragons of a new type of confident, outward-looking Irish nationalism in a country preparing itself for greater autonomy from Britain.

Kettle had been the Irish Parliamentary Party MP for the East Tyrone constituency from 1906 and 1910. His career in politics had been cut short because of money problems but many spoke of him as a future nationalist leader. He had been a barrister, a journalist and a Professor of National Economics at University College Dublin.

Tom Kettle and Mary Sheehy had known each other from childhood. They began dating at University College Dublin, where they were both students. Both were from prominent and prosperous nationalist families. He was the son of Andrew Kettle, a north Dublin farmer and a founder of the Land League. Tom had gone to secondary school at the Jesuit-governed Clongowes Wood in Kildare.

In the early twentieth century, UCD was becoming a Catholic, intellectual counterweight to the Protestant Trinity College Dublin. Mary Sheehy was the daughter
of nationalist MP David Sheehy. She was a student activist and suffragist, as was
her sister Hanna Sheehy Skeffington.[2]

Tom Kettle was an Irish nationalist with a European sensibility. Mary Kettle
described him as an 'internationalist nationalist' in *The Ways of War*, a book they
had co-authored that was published, posthumously in Tom's case, in 1917. Tom
was a multi-linguist who, unusually for men of his generation, had travelled widely
abroad. He believed an independent Ireland should look with an open mind to
influences and relationships well beyond its own shores. 'While a strong people
has its own self for centre, it has the universe for circumference.'[3]

The author and government adviser Ronan O'Brien has noted in the Jesuit
journal *Studies* that 'Kettle's Europeanism endures, Redmond's imperialism does
not'.[4] It was Kettle that President Michael D. Higgins referenced in his speech to
the joint houses of parliament during his 2014 state visit to Britain, not Redmond:

> Kettle died as an Irish patriot, a British soldier and a true European. He under-
> stood that to be authentically Irish we must also embrace our European identity.
> It is an identification we proudly claim today, an identification we share with
> the United Kingdom, with whom we have sat around the negotiating table
> in Europe for over 40 years. We recognise that it has been in that European
> context of mutuality and interdependence that we took the most significant
> steps towards each other.[5]

Kettle was in Belgium when the war broke out, trying to smuggle arms back
to Ireland. He chartered a boat, the *l'Avenir*, on behalf of John Redmond, who,
despite his reputation as a constitutionalist, was determined the Irish Volunteers
would be fully armed for any contingency. Kettle sent half the consignment of
arms back to Ireland via land and sea in late August 1914; the other half was
requisitioned by the Belgians for their war effort.[6]

Instead of returning to Ireland, Kettle decided to stay and work in Belgium
as a correspondent with the *Daily News*, a now defunct UK national newspaper.

He witnessed the indiscriminate shooting of civilians and the state of terror
that Germany had imposed upon a neutral country. This convinced him that the
future of civilisation was at stake. He returned to Ireland and threw his considerable intellectual weight behind the British war effort, making speech after speech.
The England of 1914 was 'on the side of the ten commandments' and her sins
towards Ireland were in the past; Prussian militarism was on the side of barbarism.

But Kettle was no Germanophobe. On the contrary, he was passionately
engaged with the country and could speak the language fluently. He was appalled
by Germany's ultra vires conduct and believed the Allies had just cause in opposing

the annexation of the country. 'It is impossible not to be with Belgium in this struggle,' he wrote. 'It is impossible any longer to be passive. Germany has thrown down a well-considered challenge to all, the forces of our civilisation. War is hell, but it is only a hell of suffering, not of dishonour, and through it, over its flaming coals, justice must walk, were it on bare feet.'[7]

Tom Kettle willingly enlisted in the British army. He was 36, old for enlistment at the time. He also had a secure job as an economics professor in UCD and of course his beloved wife and daughter. He felt, however, that he had a duty to serve. He would prefer to do his bit as a 'sixth-rate soldier than as a first-rate man of letters'.[8]

His attempts to gain a commission proved to be traumatic. He was given the rank of lieutenant but only for recruiting purposes. He was neither physically nor mentally up to the strain of command. Popular and sociable, Kettle also had a streak of melancholia that was doubtless deepened by an ongoing drink problem. His background, education and public reputation made him an automatic choice for the officer ranks. But in reality he neither had the temperament or discipline for the task – he was known to turn up drunk in uniform.

Kettle had spent time in a private hospital for 'dipsomania' – or what he called his 'old sin' – an early-twentieth-century euphemism for a drink problem. At one stage, he sought to be discharged on medical grounds, but was turned down by the army. He feared disgrace if his discharge was gazetted, having accumulated a mountain of debt. When the army finally relented and pushed for him to leave, he decided to stay, believing service at the front would give him a chance at redemption, which would amount in essence to a cure for his alcoholism. He took to the new regime with resolution. 'The dominion of drink has fallen off me like an enchantment,' he wrote to his wife. He took a total abstinence pledge.

Kettle's wish to serve overseas was eventually granted.

He was given command of B Company in the 9th Royal Dublin Fusiliers even though, by his own admission, he was no battlefield leader. He was dismayed by the Easter Rising, but presciently wrote of the leaders, including his friend Thomas MacDonagh, 'these men will go down in history as heroes and martyrs; and I will go down – if I go down at all – as a bloody British officer'.[9]

The 9th were brought to the Somme, in preparation for the Battle of Ginchy. 'The long-expected is now close to hand,' he wrote days before the battle to his wife back in Dublin in tones which were foreboding:

I was at Mass and Communion this morning at 6 o'Clock, the camp is broken up, and the column is about to move. It is no longer indiscreet to say that we are to take part in one of the biggest attacks of the war. Many will not come back. Should that be God's design for me you will not receive this letter until afterwards. I want to thank you for the love and kindness you spent and all but wasted on me. There was never, in all the world, a dearer woman or a more perfect wife and adorable mother. My heart cries for you and Betty whom I may never see again. I think even that it is perhaps better that I should not see you again. God bless and keep you! If the last sacrifice is ordained think that in the end I wiped out all the old stains. Tell Betty her daddy was a soldier and died as one. My love, now at last clean, will find a way to you…[10]

The private torments and self-recrimination hinted at here were very much at odds with his accomplished public persona.

His death was witnessed by Second Lieutenant Emmet Dalton, a man who would go on to become a general in the Irish Free State and the founder of the film production company Ardmore Studios. Though just 18, Dalton was already a leader of men. He joined the Royal Dublin Fusiliers in January 1916 against the wishes of his father and was decorated for his actions at Ginchy.

Kettle and Dalton spent a couple of days together preparing for the battle. Four days before Ginchy, they slogged through driving rain before taking up positions outside Trones Wood. Constant shelling thinned their numbers. The men marched to the battlefield through the horrible detritus left by the Battle of Guillemont.

'I was with Tom when he advanced to the position that night and the stench of the dead that covered our road was so awful that we both used some foot powder on our faces,' Dalton remembered. 'When we reached our objective we dug ourselves in and then at 5pm on the 9th we attacked Ginchy. I was just behind Tom when he went over the top. He was in a bent position and a bullet got over a steel waistcoast that he wore and entered his heart. Well he only lasted about one minute and he had my crucifix in his hands.' He concluded with some scant words of consolation to Kettle's wife. 'Tom's death has been a blow to the regiment and I am afraid that I could not put into words my feeling on the subject. Mr Kettle died a grand and holy death, the death of a soldier and a Christian.'[11]

Despite his tender years, Dalton took control of the company after Kettle was killed and was subsequently awarded the Military Cross at Ginchy, an award he would later receive from King George V at Buckingham Palace.

He was promoted to Major of the 9th Dublins after the battle and served out the war in the Middle East. On his return home, he joined the IRA and fought against the same army he had served with for three years. In 1922, he would witness the tragic and premature death of another leader: Michael Collins at Béal na Bláth during the Irish Civil War.

It was customary to reassure grieving relatives that their soldier boy had died quickly and had suffered no pain. The information was usually couched in euphemism and amounted to a white lie to spare the trauma of grieving relatives. Dalton would appear to have conformed to those sensitivities in his account of Kettle's death.

Another account of Kettle's death told a slightly different story. Lieutenant-Colonel F.S. Thackeray, the commanding officer of the battalion, wrote to Mrs Kettle in October 1916, explaining the circumstances of his death. Tom had been sheltering in a shell hole when he was struck over the heart with a bullet. 'The only words he said were, "oh my God, I'm struck". He died within ten minutes.' Thackeray based his letter to Mary Kettle on eyewitness accounts.[12]

Both Dalton and Thackeray agreed that Kettle's papers and effects were taken from him by another officer, Lieutenant William Boyd, who was subsequently blown to pieces by a shell.

Kettle's death meant a second Sheehy sister had been left widowed and grief-stricken. Five months earlier, Hanna Sheehy-Skeffington had also lost her husband in violent circumstances. Francis Sheehy-Skeffington was a pacifist who had been imprisoned for his opposition to the war in Europe. During the Easter Rising, he went out on to the streets of Dublin in a bid to stop the looting and chaos. A deranged British officer, Captain J.C. Bowen-Colthurst, later found guilty of insanity, had him and two others shot. For four days Hanna wandered across the city searching for her husband before eventually discovering his fate. His body was recovered and buried in Glasnevin Cemetery.

Tom Kettle was buried where he had fallen, Thackeray told her in his letter. It raised her hopes that his body could be found and repatriated. Sadly, it never was. However, Mary Kettle would not give up looking for her husband's body and wrote a voluminous correspondence to those who might help.

In March 1917, Lieutenant William Browne from the Royal Dublin Fusiliers, Royal Naval Divisional School of Instruction, wrote home about the search for Tom's body. He did not have good news. The ghastly business of recovering and identifying bodies was proving to be a hopeless task in the vast ossuary that the Somme had become. 'There are hundreds of graveyards all around,' Browne informed his family. 'It would take you a day to look through one of them, 10 or 12 being sometimes buried in one grave. Some of the graves are being constantly blown up and the remains scattered all over the place so you could never tell where to find them. Besides a larger number are buried along the roadside. You could see the arms and legs sticking out of the bushes and a lot are never buried at all.'[13]

Captain Maurice F. Healy was, like Kettle, a lawyer and Clongowes Wood alumnus. He did not always agree politically with Kettle but they had been friends and Healy was determined to locate his remains.

'I have read of Tom's gallant death with a sorrow not so much for him as for you and for the country that he died for. There was nobody who as well expressed the voice of young Ireland,' he wrote to Mary Kettle two weeks after the Battle of Ginchy. 'During the 11 years I knew him, we were separated by all the things that make men bitter in Ireland and yet I am happy to say we remained good friends.'[14]

Healy's battalion had been posted to the Ginchy area in early October 1916 for the Battle of the Le Transloy Ridges, which is about 2.5 miles north of where Kettle had been killed. He made what inquiries he could about Tom's last possible resting place. In April 1917, he wrote again to Mary. He had contacted the Director of Grave Registrations (DGR) only to be told that Tom Kettle's grave had not been found:

> I meant to write to you immediately, but we have been on the move and now are once again in the heart of things. The lack of information will be all the more galling when you learn that for three weeks, my corps was just east of Bernafay Wood and I think I searched every graveyard between my camp and the Ginchy-Longueval-Combles line without ever thinking of looking behind me.

He reassured her that her husband's body was buried in the earth and not lying out in the open somewhere as she feared, but he was careful not to give her false hope. Many bodies like Kettle's were buried late at night with an anonymous cross on top, but battles move on and the men have to move on too.

Healy continued, 'There are hundreds such [bodies]. I myself have buried men under shell fire and in the confusion have found it impossible to find the identity disc or any other identification. This is often done in the hope of almost instant re-internment. But it often proves impossible through moves etc to return to the same place and then the graves remain anonymous.'[15]

On the night of 9 September, the exhausted 48th Brigade of the 16th (Irish) Division was relieved by the 1st Battalion of the Welsh Guards. The Welsh Guards were engaged in a fierce battle to hold Ginchy from counter-attacks. Identifying dead bodies was not a priority.

Healy sought to ameliorate Mary Kettle's pain by praising her husband's virtues. Healy compared Kettle to Robert Emmet, the Irish patriot executed in 1803 for staging an ill-thought-out rebellion against the British. His body was never found. Healy remembered that Tom Kettle had alluded to the search for Emmet's body in the past:

> As he proclaimed Emmet still to live, immortal in the hearts of the Irish people, so do I think that a later generation of Irishmen, blest in peace and heart free from political bitterness will find Tom's spirit in their company, eloquent as in life and a constant guide to the principles for which he died.[16]

At some stage in 1917, Mrs Kettle had received information that her husband's body might have been located in Carnoy. What was it doing there, some 7 miles from Ginchy and well behind the British lines? In the absence of the original correspondence from Mary Kettle, the answer is uncertain.

Healy wrote to her:

I was delighted to hear your good news about Tom's grave. I do not know if you are aware that Major WB Dunne of the 4th Dublins is area commandant at Maricourt which is only about two miles from Carnoy. I have written to him giving him the particulars you have sent me and I will have him know that it will give you great pleasure to see that the grave is properly tended. Strangely enough just a fortnight ago I had given him all the particulars I then had in the hope that he would find some clues near Bernafay Wood. A number of our battalion are buried in the same cemetery so poor Tom has company.

But again it amounted to false hope. In November 1916, a building contractor wrote to Mary Kettle about attempts to find Tom Kettle's grave. K.M. McLaughlin told her the graves of Raymond Asquith, the son of the British Prime Minister Herbert Asquith, and the poet Edward Wyndham Tennant had been located but not Kettle's.

Both Asquith and Wyndham Tennant were with the Grenadier Guards, who, in turn, had been part of the Guards Division that followed up the assault on Ginchy.

When the battlefield areas were secured, divisional salvage companies went in to recover bodies from the battlefield.

In his next correspondence with Mrs Kettle, McLaughlin had no good news:

I am now divisional salvage officer and my area includes just where Tom Kettle was killed. I have made a diligent search for his grave and am continuing to do so, although so far unsuccessful. Found Raymond Asquith's and young Tennant's almost side by side, but so far have not found the grave of a single Dublin Fusilier. If by any chance you happen to know the exactly locality please let me know as I would like to build an Irish cairn above him with a Celtic Cross over it. I wrote in reply to this after having tried to find out from several officers if they knew the exact spot but no one seemed to know where the grave was.[17]

Maurice Healy's frustration was apparent in a letter he wrote to McLaughlin on behalf of Mary Kettle, 'You may note that I recently learned that her husband was supposed to be buried east of Bernafay Wood a point where I actually lived three of the weeks I was searching vainly for his grave expecting to find it near Guillemont or Ginchy. I was disappointed that I did not receive this news sooner when I might have put it to some useful purpose but after all we don't know where Emmet's grave is other than in the heart and memory of all his country.'

Hope of finding Kettle's grave continued to recede when the whole area of the Somme was fought over twice again in 1918, once during the German Spring Offensive and then during the last 100 days, when the Allies pushed the Germans back and finally defeated them in November 1918.

Mary Kettle still harboured hopes that her husband's body could be found. In 1924, she wrote to the Imperial War Graves Commission (IWGC) seeking information.[18]

The correspondence, held in the UCD archives, does not include her letters but it suggests that she had information her husband's body lay somewhere east of Bernafay Wood. Bernafay Wood lies near Trones Wood, south of Guillemont. It is a considerable distance from Ginchy.

The Imperial War Graves Commission wrote back to her:

Madam, with reference to your letter of the 30th, I regret to inform you that although the neighbourhood east of Bernafay Wood, where the late Mr Kettle was reported to have been buried has been searched and the remains of all those soldiers buried in isolation or scattered graves reverently reburied in cemeteries in order that the graves may be permanently and suitably maintained, the graves of this soldier has not been yet identified. As you will understand, in many areas military operations caused the destruction of crosses and grave registration marks and completely changed the surface of the ground so that the work of identifying even those graves of which the position was accurately known has often been difficult. It is the intention of the commission to erect memorials to those officers and men whose graves cannot be found. You may rest assured that the dead who have no know resting place will be honoured equally.

Tom Kettle is listed among the 72,255 names of UK and South African soldiers on the Thiepval Memorial to the Missing in the Somme. The number decreases slightly every year as more bodies are found and identified. Originally the number stood at 73,367. The Somme was like no other battle in British military history. It surpassed even the horrors of Ypres, Passchendaele, Arras, Gallipoli, Cambrai, Loos or any of the other lamentable bloodbaths that destroyed a generation of young men. Nothing in the Second World War was comparable in terms of bloodiness for the British army.

The monumental numbers left missing at the Somme therefore required a monumental statement of commemoration. The Thiepval Memorial is that magnificent monument. It was designed by the great British architect Sir Edwin Lutyens, who had both German and Irish antecedents. His mother Margaret Theresa Gallwey, known as Mary, was from Ballincollig, County Cork.

Initially there were difficulties acquiring the Thiepval site because the whole area was devastated. Eventually, in January 1928, the design for Thiepval was submitted to the French government. Approval was given in April 1928 and a year later permission was granted to starting building.

Construction of the Thiepval Memorial took three years. The design borrows from the pyramids and the ziggurats of ancient civilisations, which had a great influence on the art deco movement of the post-war period. Some 10 million bricks were used. It consists of a series of elliptical arches, big and small. The main arch is orientated east to west. Imported Portland stone was used for the wall panels upon which the names were inscribed. The land around it was planted with silver birches, Cornish elms, holly bushes and pyramid oaks.[19]

The memorial stands at the highest point of the Thipeval plateau and is itself 140ft high – a diplomatic 13ft lower than the Arc de Triomphe in Paris. Arches are traditionally associated with victory, but there is nothing victorious about the Thiepval Memorial. It is a British creation, yet a monument of co-operation between France and Britain. The Union flag and French tricolore fly from the top of the monument.

The dedication is in French, not English. '*Aux armées Française et Britannique L'Empire Britannique Reconnaissant*' (To the French and British armies, from the grateful British Empire). In the adjacent field, there are both British and French graves for unknown soldiers, the British graves made of Portland stone, the French crosses arranged in diagonal rows. The French crosses have one simple word, '*inconnu*' (unknown); the British graves the traditional 'A soldier of the Great War – known unto God'.

Tom Kettle's name is listed first of the 428 men of the Royal Dublin Fusiliers who are commemorated on the Thiepval Memorial. The only other RDF lieutenant on Thiepval is Lieutenant Hastings Killingley, the 21-year-old son of a Church of Ireland clergyman from Rathfarnham, County Dublin. Directly underneath him on the list of missing Royal Dublin Fusiliers second lieutenants is Boyd, the 29-year-old son of a Methodist clergyman from the North Circular Road in Dublin, who took possession of Kettle's personal effects after Kettle died, only to be 'blown to atoms' himself a short time afterwards.

Another Irishman who died at the Battle of Ginchy and is remembered on the Thiepval Memorial was Private William 'Willie' McDowell of the 7th Leinsters. He was an orphan who had been taken in by his grandfather Jack McDowell, a prominent member of the Irish Parliamentary Party. Willie McDowell joined the Leinsters at the age of 18 in 1915. In May 1916, he sent a letter home to his stepfather, whom he knew as his 'Uncle Jack', inquiring as to when the authorities were going to start rebuilding Dublin after the Easter Rising.

On 9 September 1916, Jack McDowell wrote to Willie, 'My dear Willie, just a line to know how you are doing?' The letter was returned marked 'killed'. Willie McDowell was a relation of Michael McDowell, the former Irish Minister for Justice. McDowell's maternal grandfather was the founder of the Irish Volunteers, Eoin MacNeill, who in 1914 defied Redmond's call that volunteers should serve in the British army.

In the list of privates from the Royal Dublin Fusiliers on the Thiepval Memorial is a young man from my home town of Carrick-on-Shannon in County Leitrim.

Thomas Dockery and his family lived next door to my family home. His brother Thady Dockery was killed on the first day of the Battle of the Somme with the 1st Royal Dublin Fusiliers. Both the 1st and 2nd battalions of the Royal Dublin Fusiliers were involved on the first day. The 1st was with the 29th Division, not far from where the spectacular Hawthorn Crater was gouged out of the earth by a massive dynamite explosion at 7.20 a.m. that morning. The same battalion had also been involved in the first day of Gallipoli, another battle which began in bloodshed. The 1st Royal Dublin Fusiliers sustained 147 casualties, including 22 dead, on the first day of the Somme.

Thady Dockery was just 21. A keen boxer, one of six children to Michael and Maria Dockery, he'd worked in a local shop before enlisting. In 1915, he went to Boyle and signed up with the Royal Dublin Fusiliers, a regiment desperate to replenish its ranks after the bloody slaughters at Gallipoli and Ypres. The *Leitrim Observer* reported his death in August 1916. 'He was only a comparatively young man and, prior to joining the colours, was a prominent member of the local football club. He was highly respected and esteemed by those who knew him in his native town and now regret his death. The sympathy of the public go out to his parents and relatives in their affliction – R.I.P'.[20]

Another Carrick-on-Shannon native also died on that first day of the Battle of the Somme: Private Bernard Morahan of the Hampshire Regiment. Both are among the 3,779 men from Irish regiments who died during the Battle of the Somme and are remembered on the Thiepval Memorial. The 3,779 comprises:

> 1,199 Royal Irish Rifles
> 842 Royal Inniskilling Fusiliers
> 428 Royal Dublin Fusiliers
> 342 Royal Irish Fusiliers
> 280 Royal Irish Regiment
> 230 Royal Munster Fusiliers
> 212 Irish Guards
> 112 Leinster Regiment
> 71 Connaught Rangers
> 63 London Irish Rifles[21]

Not all of those who served in Irish regiments were Irish-born. Equally, there were hundreds, if not thousands, of Irishmen lost to official Irish records because they had enlisted in non-Irish regiments. In any event, they are all remembered on the walls of Thiepval, if scarcely anywhere else.

Among the ranks of the missing Inniskillings is Private Anthony Gallagher from Donegal. Like many from his county, he had emigrated to Scotland. He was recruited into the 1st Royal Inniskilling Fusiliers and was killed on the first day of the Somme. The 1st Royal Inniskillings was attached to 29th Division and suffered 568 casualties on that terrible day, adding to the already lamentable roll call of suffering endured by their fellow Ulstermen in the 36th (Ulster) Division.

His great-nephew Gerry Moore, a history teacher in Donegal, knew nothing about him until he came across a crumpled old photograph in the early 1990s. He wrote to the Commonwealth War Graves Commission inquiring as to the location of his great-uncle's grave only to be told there was no grave.

Moore recalls:

Like many others his body was never identified, which means he was either found in such bad condition that he couldn't be recognised or he was ripped apart till nothing was left of him to find. If his body was found it would have been buried in one of the many graves of unknown soldiers in the Somme battlefields. Written on his headstone would be the words 'Known unto God'. We can never know what happened to Anthony Gallagher on that day in 1916 but his name will forever be etched into the Thiepval Memorial in the Somme.[22]

Moore resolved that the current generation of Irish schoolchildren would not be allowed to forget, as his generation had been allowed to forget, the Irish war dead. He began a project with Irish transition year students and their Northern Irish equivalents. A pupil from each of the thirty-two counties was encouraged to 'adopt' a soldier who had died in the Battle of the Somme from his or her county and find out all they could about them. The research can be accessed at www.myadoptedsoldier.com. It was also the subject of a two-part documentary on RTÉ.

As one crosses the expansive plaza and ascends the central staircase leading up to the Thiepval Monument, the battlefield where the 36th (Ulster) Division were slaughtered on the first day of the Somme is framed by the monument. In previous memorials, the names of kings, queens, generals and other assorted grandees would be remembered; the men who did the fighting were usually an afterthought. This kind of instinctive deference for establishment figures was no longer appropriate in a world where trust in authority had been irrevocably shaken.

There are forty-eight wall panels on the Thiepval Memorial, each of them inscribed with long, harrowing roll calls of the ordinary fallen, those everymen of the villages, fields, factories and cities.

Also listed on oval-shaped panels around the monument are the various battles which in aggregate amounted to the great conflagration of the Somme. Each had a casualty list which in other circumstances would have made them major military engagements in their own right – Beaumont Hamel, Morval, Guillemont, Ginchy, Pozières, Flers, Delville Wood, Mametz. Some 90 per cent of the men named on the Thiepval Memorial died between July and November 1916.

Lutyens also designed the Irish National War Memorial Gardens at Islandbridge in Dublin and the Cenotaph in London. The Cenotaph was a simple and brilliant idea: an empty tomb that would symbolise the sacrifice of every soldier. There was nothing vainglorious, triumphant or even religious about it. Unveiled in 1920 as a temporary memorial, it became the permanent and perhaps definitive monument of the war in Britain because it expressed, as Lutyens said, the 'human sentiments of millions'.[23]

By the mid-1920s, some 970 different war grave cemeteries had been built by Britain on the Western Front. It was a suitably colossal achievement in honour of such colossal losses. The Thiepval Memorial was finally finished in 1932 and officially opened in July of that year by Edward Prince of Wales and the French President, Albert Lebrun. Prince Edward, who was later to abdicate as King Edward VIII, referenced the 'myriad of names':

> a mass multitude of silent witnesses to the desolation of war. They must be, and I believe, they are, the opening chapter in a new book of life, the foundation and guide to a better civilisation, from which war, with all the horrors which our generation has added to it, shall be banished, and in which national bitterness and hate, selfishness and greed, shall flee abashed before the spirits of the dead.[24]

No Irish representative was present at the opening of the Thiepval Memorial. A syndicated article appeared in Irish newspapers pointing out that more than 4,000 Irishmen were remembered at Thiepval and on the Arras Memorial, which was opened on the same weekend.

The Irish Times, which in the 1930s frequently lamented the lack of interest in the Irish war dead, remarked that the opening ceremony for the Thiepval Memorial had 'pathetic Irish interest'. The paper concluded, 'Every Irish soldier, officer and man who was lost and not found is now remembered by a name on the memorial to the missing. None has been forgotten and left out. They trod the paths of war and found the fork marked death. Their road was not our road; their ways not our ways.'[25]

Tom Kettle was one of those lost and not found. Mary Kettle lived in the hope that one day his body might be recovered and repatriated. The permanent engraving of his name at Thiepval was presumably a thin consolation. A memorial committee was set up shortly after his death. A bust was commissioned and the sculpture was completed by Albert Power by March 1921. Yet it was not erected in St Stephen's Green until 1937 because of multiple objections from the Commission of Public Works and it did not have an unveiling ceremony. The inscription read, 'Thomas M Kettle 1880-1916, born County Dublin. Killed at Ginchy 9th September 1916. Poet, Essayist, Patriot'.[26] Why he died or what he died fighting for is not mentioned.

Mary Kettle dedicated herself to her husband's memory. She produced a calendar and selected an epigram or aphorism from her husband's prodigious writings to go with it.[27] She never did have the comfort of a grave at which she could pray and mourn. The ongoing absence of his mortal remains meant she could never close the circle, never heal the wound.

Mary Kettle quickly turned against the country for which her husband had given his life. In 1919 she urged Irish ex-servicemen to boycott the victory parade because the British had not honoured the mandate given to Sinn Féin in the 1918 general election which sought independence for Ireland.

She questioned why 'soldiers were asked to march past College Green, their own House of Parliament, where their rights were bartered away, to salute Lord French, not as an Irish soldier, but as Lord Lieutenant and head of the Irish Executive, which was responsible for the rule of coercion in this country and for the betrayal of every Irish Nationalist soldier who fought and fell in the war. Did any Irish Nationalist fight for any country except the country of his birth? If they went on the side of England it was because they thought for the first time in her history the grace of God was operating in her, and she was at last about to take the side of honour in the world's conflict.'

Mary Kettle went on to become a Dublin city councillor and a tireless campaigner for education rights. She also founded the Joint Committee of Women's Societies.

She died in December 1967. An Obiturist in *The Irish Times*, who went by the name of M.M., wrote that Mary Kettle 'worked with one end in view, the welfare of others, absolutely regardless of self. We are happy to know too, that there are many who join us, though silently, in the praise of this great woman.'

Her last public appearance was at a Mass the year before to mark the fiftieth anniversary of her husband's death.[28] The couple's only child, Betty, to whom Kettle had dedicated his famous poem, died in 1996.[29]

17

THE CROSS AT WYTSCHAETE

The time was 3.10 a.m., the date 7 June 1917. In Ronssoy Wood, the nightingales could be heard completing their night-time chorus. An unnatural calm had settled over the hills to the south and east of the ruined Belgium town of Ypres. The clouds had passed over and the waning moon, just off full, shone from a clear sky. It was approaching the summer solstice. There was just enough light in the sky to play bridge at midnight, as some officers had done a few nights before.

The shelling of the German lines died down at 2 a.m. For the next hour and ten minutes, all was quiet in this battle-tormented Flanders landscape. In their shallow front-line trenches, the Irish, British, New Zealand and Australian infantry waited for the fateful moment to arrive. They had been preparing for the approaching hour for many months.

'By midnight, our lines were packed with tense young men from the cities and towns and farms of Ireland. In all, some 16,000 Irishmen were to go into action at Messines before the day was out,' Lieutenant Michael Fitzgerald of the 6th Royal Irish Regiment would remember years later.[1]

The British high command had decided the 16th (Irish) Division and 36th (Ulster) Division should fight alongside each other at Messines Ridge in IX Corps of the Second Army. This would be the biggest joint effort by the Irish in the war. Unlike the Somme, the British had sound tactical reasons for fighting this battle. It was where British commander-in-chief Field Marshal Douglas Haig had wanted to fight before his plans were rudely pre-empted by the Somme offensive the previous year. The resumption of unrestricted submarine warfare in early 1917 by the Germans was taking a fearsome toll on British merchant shipping. The situation became critical in the summer of 1917. The First Sea Lord Admiral Jellicoe startled the British War Cabinet with this admission, as Haig remembered in his diary, 'Jellicoe stated that owing to the great shortage of shipping due to German submarines, it would be impossible for Great Britain to continue the war in 1918. This was a bombshell for the Cabinet and for all present … Jellicoe's words were, "there is no good discussing plans for next spring – we cannot go on".'[2]

Haig wished to seize back the Belgian ports of Ostend and Zeebrugge, which were being used as German U-boat bases. Thereafter, he planned to push on to Brussels. The British also wanted to seize the critical German railway junction of Roulers, a tantalising prize just 17 miles north-east of Ypres.

Messines Ridge, though a huge operation in itself, was a preliminary to the big offensive of 1917, which would become known as the Battle of Passchendaele. In order to break out of the Ypres salient, the British needed to secure the ridges that allowed the Germans to observe and shell the British positions at Ypres. These were some of the darkest days of the war for the Allies. The Second Battle of the Aisne, also known as the Nivelle Offensive, in April 1917 was supposed to end the war in forty-eight hours, but the foolish French commander-in-chief Robert Nivelle, who promised the breakthrough, only precipitated a mutiny by French soldiers. They had had enough of incompetent bungling, useless sacrifice and a war that had cost them a million men dead since 1914. In the east, Tsar Nicholas II had abdicated and a provisional government had taken over. The Russians were on the brink of collapse. Only the entry of the United States into the war in April 1917 offered any hope of a decisive breakthrough, but they would not be ready for at least another year.

Messines had been seized by the Germans in November 1914. Adolf Hitler was involved in the fighting around Messines and Wytschaete[3] with the 16th Bavarian Reserve Infantry Regiment. With nobody else to correspond with, he wrote to his landlord, 'We were all proud of having licked the Britishers. Since then we have been in the front lines the whole time. I was proposed for the Iron Cross, the first time in Messines, the second time in Wytschaete. On 2 December I finally got it.'[4]

It was near Messines that the Germans and British fraternised during the Christmas Day truce of 1914, but that sort of friendship was now a distant memory. In this attack three years on from the original fighting, nothing would be left to chance. The British would bring the entire weight of its matériel against the enemy to maximise their casualties and minimise their own. They had learned from the debacle of the Somme. They had better maps, better guns and better gunners. The shells too were of superior quality. Day and night every calibre of shell rained down on the defenders. The British specialised in hurricane half-hour bombardments designed to both demoralise and disorientate the Germans and to make them believe the attack was imminent. Every morning, reconnaissance planes flew over German lines taking photographs. Those places left sufficiently undamaged would be revisited again and again.

Between 26 May and 6 June, 1917, the British fired 3,561,530 shells into the German lines at Messines Ridge, yet even that was regarded as insufficient to ensure victory.[5] The British had an even more devastating weapon, the result of a colossal endeavour involving 20,000 skilled men who worked in the most difficult conditions.

'Gentlemen, we may not make history tomorrow, but we will certainly change the geography,' the chief of staff of the Second Army, General Sir Charles Harington, told the press in advance of the Battle of Messines Ridge.[6]

The British intended to remove the Germans from Messines Ridge not just with a risky frontal assault but from beneath. Nineteen mines and a million pounds of high explosives were levered into place inch by inch and yard by yard under the German lines.

The work was done by the best miners the British Empire could find. When war was declared, no group of men enlisted with more alacrity. Mining was dirty work, badly paid and often unreliable. Anything, even war, was preferable. Many of these men were enlisted into tunnelling companies. By 1916, the British alone had eight tunnelling companies. New Zealand, Australia and Canada had their own tunnelling companies. The British dug deep into the Flanders soil using vertical metal tubes to get under the wet sands to the solid clay beneath.

The men engaged in this work were no strangers to hardship or cramped conditions. The earth was removed by a process known as clay kicking, a technique first perfected in the Manchester sewers.[7] Men lay on their backs, propped up against an underground trolley, and levered the clay away with a sharpened spade known as a grafting tool. The work was carried out silently and stealthily. Canaries or candles signalled if subterranean air was poisonous. The men wore felt slippers and the trolleys were fitted with rubber wheels to quiten the noise. They brought the distinctive blue clay of Flanders away and returned with the timber supports for the mine shafts. The work was extraordinarily dangerous. The men risked entombment, suffocation, but mostly they feared camouflets, small but deadly charges the Germans used to collapse enemy tunnels. The Germans, too, were digging.

The British tunnels were disguised as water wells. They were as deep as 40 yards and as long as 750 yards. Into these underground mazes, the British transported some 400 tons of ammonium nitrate and aluminium powder for the explosives, along with wire fuses and detonators.[8]

The Germans had prepared themselves for a Flanders assault. Since the Second Battle of Ypres in 1915, they had secured the high ground. As the soil was unsuitable for deep dugouts, they built up rather than down; massive pillboxes of reinforced concrete and steel were constructed. These were camouflaged with sods of earth, grass and sometimes dung, but the constant shelling dislodged these attempts to conceal the emplacements and the camouflage fell away. The British official history stated, 'On those bright summer evenings, when the sun began to sink in the west behind the observer, they stood out in whitish nakedness as perfect targets.'[9]

The attack was planned with the greatest precision. Lessons had been learned by British commanders from previous battles, albeit at the cost of tens of thousands of lives. A scale model of Messines Ridge was made and officers were ordered to remember it. It was an acre in size, so big that it could only be seen properly from a viewing platform. Every contour, trench, village, wood, railway line and German machine gun emplacement was detailed. The model was carefully constructed by German prisoners of war. 'It looked like a huge toy village, and would have delighted the children,' Captain Rowland Feilding of the 6th Connaughts wrote in a letter to his wife.[10]

It was big enough for a company of 250 officers and men to see at the same time. Officers attended the briefings of neighbouring battalions so they could be familiar not only with their own plan but also with the overall plan.

Stores were brought up to the front line and allocated at divisional, brigade and battalion level. Communications were improved. Forward stations were selected in the captured enemy positions for sending back cable lines for field telephones. Back-up signal operations using pigeons, runners, lucas lamps and rockets for SOS distress signals were also introduced.

The assault at Messines Ridge was to be carried out by the British Second Army commanded by Field Marshal Herbert Plumer. Plumer's preparations reassured men who had witnessed the horrors of the Somme and other egregious examples of bad British military planning. Known as 'Daddy Plumer' because of his benevolent attitude to his men, his thoroughness filtered down through the ranks. 'The sympathy and understanding which existed between the staff of the Second Army and the man in the fighting line created a moral tone of incalculable value to the Army's efficiency as a fighting force,' Cyril Falls, the 36th (Ulster) Division historian wrote. 'They had watched the stage prepared for the triumphant dénouement prepared with matchless industry and forethought, and they were ready to play their part fitly when the curtain raised.'[11]

Trench raids were carried out on a nightly basis to capture prisoners and elicit valuable intelligence information. These were substantial operations in their own right, often involving hundreds of men. In one attack on 27 May, the 2nd Royal Dublin Fusiliers took fifty prisoners. The constant harassment was having an effect on the enemy. 'The morale of the prisoners seems to be distinctly poor,' a raid from the 8th Royal Inniskilling Fusiliers concluded.

The two Irish divisions (16th and 36th) retained their separate identities, though they came close to amalgamating in early 1917 following the dreadful losses of the Somme and the precipitous reduction in recruitment numbers in Ireland. Nothing came of this, mostly because no political compromise could be found which would make it acceptable at home. The aftermath of the Easter Rising and the new militant nationalism sentiment had contributed to an even more febrile atmosphere back in Ireland. Nationalists and unionists were even further apart. But, in this uncharacteristically hilly part of Flanders, both divisions had a common cause, even if they had diametrically different views of Ireland's place within the British Empire.

The divisions fraternised with each other behind the lines in Bailleul and played football matches against other. 'The battalion (6th Connaughts) has twice played football lately again battalions of Carson's (36th) Division and I'm sorry to say got beaten both times,' Feilding wrote.[12] One match was watched by between 2,000 and 3,000 spectators, making it a tempting target for the Germans had they known about it. Feilding worried about so many men in such close proximity to the German lines, but concluded, 'To stop a match in process between the two great opposing factions of Ireland, in a spirit of friendliness which, so far as I'm aware, seems unattainable on Ireland's native soil – even though in sight (or almost in sight) of the enemy, was a serious matter: and I decided to let the game go on.'

The Revd John Redmond, a Church of Ireland chaplain with the 9th Royal Inniskilling Fusiliers, also commented on the friendly relations between the two divisions. 'It was impressive to see what a feeling of security before the battle the Ulster Division had in having the 16th Irish on our left flank and that the 16th Division had in having the Ulster Division on their right flank. This feeling of goodwill and confidence between the two divisions had been growing for some time. I wish the entire north and south that they represent, could participate in the same spirit.'[13]

Now, as zero hour approached, these men pondered their fate, but also that of their enemies. They knew what awaited those opposite, who were already severely shaken and unnerved by the terrifying bombardment.

Fr Willie Doyle realised that the faceless enemy cowering in their trenches on the other side of no man's land would shortly be no longer of this world. 'One felt inclined to scream out and send them warning. But all I could do was to stand on top of the trench and give them absolution, trusting to God's mercy.'[14]

The 16th (Irish) Division had changed the words of 'The Wearing of the Green' to reflect a doom-laden note:

Oh! Paddy dear an' have you heard the news that's going round?
Our guns are hid, just where we're bid, by diggin' underground.[15]

The attack on Messines Ridge was a huge operation on a semi-circular front from Hill 60 in the north to Ploegstreet Wood in the south, a front 10 miles long and heavily defended by the Germans, who occupied the higher ground. The attack involved two British army corps, IX and X, and one Australian/New Zealand corps, II Anzac Corps. The Anzacs were under the command of Lieutenant General Sir Alexander Godley, a man whose family seat was in Carrigallen, County Leitrim.

On the eve of battle, the 16th (Irish) Division's commander Major General William Hickie sent out a message which was resolute in its optimism:

The big day is very near. All our preparations are complete, and the divisional commander wishes to express his appreciation and his thanks to all the officers and men who have worked so cheerfully and so well. The 16th Division is fortunate in having had assigned to it the capture of the stronghold of Wytschaete. Every officer and man – gunners, sappers, pioneers, RAMC, ASC and infantry of historic Irish regiments knows what to do. Let all do their best as they have always done, continuing to show the same courage and devotion to duty which has characterised the 16th (Irish) Division since it landed in France and it will be our proud privilege to restore to little Belgium, the 'White Village' which has been in German hands for nearly three years.[16]

The explosions were timed for dawn. As it was almost mid-summer, that would be 3.10 a.m. At the appointed hour, the mines were detonated simultaneously under the German lines. They created the loudest man-made noise in history, the loudest until the detonation of the atomic bombs at Hiroshima and Nagasaki. A student is reported to have heard it in Dublin. The explosion was heard by the British Prime Minister David Lloyd George, who was working late in his Downing Street study. It registered on the seismograph at Lille University 15 miles away.

In an instant, thousands of German soldiers were likely vaporised or killed where they lay. Four German officers were discovered later propped up at a table. They had died of shock.

An officer with the 12th Royal Irish Rifles wrote in his diary of the unspeakable carnage he witnessed, 'They were all packed into the Spanbroekmolen woods … I never saw carnage like it in such a short space. There wasn't a human body intact lying around the place … just bits and pieces, arms, heads, feet, legs. Terrible mess.'[17]

Feilding's men found one dead German machine-gunner chained to his gun and a last note which read:

> A terrible firing has driven us all under cover. To the right and left of me my friends are all drenched in blood. A drum fire which no one could ever describe. I pray the Lord will get me out of this sap. I swear to it I will be the next. I have prayed to God. He might save me, not for my sake, but for my poor parents. I feel as if I could cry out, my thoughts are all the time with them. I have already had 12 months of the Western Front, have been through hard fighting, but never such slaughter.[18]

Many British soldiers were pinned to the back of their trenches by the blast wave. Eyewitnesses compared the explosions to giant Cyprus trees ascending thousands of feet into the air before falling back to earth.

Fr Edmund Kelly, the chaplain to the 6th Royal Irish Regiment, watched the explosions with a mixture of awe and horror. He compared it to an 'overflow of hell itself. You can form no true idea of the diabolic beauty and fury of the whole scene'.[19] Lieutenant Fitzgerald felt that 'all hell was let loose. Thousands of tons of earth were flung into the sky. I felt like a helpless being clinging to a boulder on the side of a hill when the mine was fired.'[20]

Lance Corporal P. White told his mother in a letter home, 'I felt very much frightened when the earth shook violently beneath me. I thought every minute the bowels of the earth were opening to swallow me and burn me within that sheet of flames that spread across no man's Land to the German trenches.'

Four mines had been exploded opposite the 16th (Irish) Division and three in front of the 36th (Ulster) Division.

The British official history likened the explosions to a 'huge volcano' while the Germans saw a magnificent horror to the whole thing comparing the explosions to '19 gigantic roses with carmine petals or as enormous mushrooms which rose up slowly and majestically out of the ground'.[21]

Then every gun in the Second Army opened fire on the German front-line positions until it the 'whole western horizon seemed to be ablaze'.

Once the explosion had died down, nine divisions of the British army, including, side-by-side, the 16th (Irish) Division and the 36th (Ulster) Division, arose from their trenches. The men from the 16th (Irish) Division moved forward swiftly, fortified by the sacraments they had received that morning. Doyle recalled:

Even a stolid English Colonel standing near was moved to enthusiasm: 'My God!' he said, 'what soldiers! They fear neither man nor devil!' Why should they? They had made their peace with God. He had given them His own Sacred Body to eat that morning, and they were going out now to face death, as only Irish Catholic lads can do, confident of victory and cheered by the thought that the reward of Heaven was theirs.[22]

In front of the 16th Division was Wytschaete, known to the Tommies as White Sheet. It occupied one of the highest points in the area and was suitably occupied and fortified by the German defenders. For weeks it had been pounded by some of the biggest guns the British could muster, mostly 15- and 18-inch howitzers. The section of front occupied by IX Corps resembled the contours of a face. The 19th Division sector, which rested on a wood, was the forehead, the nose was the 16th Division sector and, in the south, the mouth and chin was the 36th (Ulster) Division sector. IX Corps goal was to seize Wytschaete and push the Germans off the ridge, retiring once they had reach Oosttaverne about a mile beyond.

The 36th (Ulster) Division had one of the most difficult points on the front to negotiate, a fortified German position known as Spanbroekmolen. This was the site of the largest underground mine, which had a shaft measuring almost 600 yards long. Twice construction was stopped by German countermines and it was a race against time to have it finished before zero hour.

It nearly did not explode. The Ulstermen were out of their trenches before it finally detonated fifteen seconds after zero hour. This short but deadly delay killed several of them. Spanbroekmolen was to be held at all costs by the Germans, but the shock of the underground mine explosion killed all the defenders.

Spanbroekmolen is now the site of the biggest mine crater left by the explosion, known with a mixture of irony and regret as the Pool of Peace. Water lilies grow and frogs spawn. It is home to perch and other small fish. Visitors comment on how something so beautiful could come from something so ugly.

'The most moving place I visited was the Pool of Peace near Ypres,' former Irish President Mary McAleese recalls. She visited it in 2004. 'It was a deep lake created by a WWI crater. Many men lost their lives in the creation of that crater and what was worse thanks to poor leadership and planning higher up they knew they were going to their certain deaths and yet went nonetheless.'[23]

The 25th Division on the right and the 36th on the left surrounded and captured Lumm Farm and took its garrison prisoner.[24]

Four mines were detonated in front of the 16th (Irish). A year previously, eleven miners were killed when the Germans blew two camoflets, which smashed in 250ft of gallery in front of the Irish lines.[25]

That mine was rebuilt. One at Maedelstede Farm was successful, but enough attackers remained to cause casualties to the lead battalion, the 6th Royal Irish Regiment, including Major Willie Redmond who tragically died from his wounds.

Wytschaete occupied the summit of the ridge and the road to it is steep and exposed. It had been converted into a fortress with an outer line and an inner line of trenches. Vaulted cellars were turned into fortresses and machine guns were strategically placed, but the bombardment of 3 June reduced what remained of the village to rubble.[26]

The capture of Wytschaete village was an all-Ireland affair. The 1st Royal Munster Fusiliers, advancing behind a tank, stormed the village and the 2nd Royal Irish Fusiliers followed. By 8 a.m., the objective had been taken.[27] The men of the 16th (Irish) Division also had to negotiate Wytschaete Wood, which had been reduced to ashes by incendiary drums and shelling. Despite days of incessant shelling, one redoubtable concrete pillbox of Germans inflicted heavy casualties on the advancing Irish before they were rushed. The same pillbox, now almost swallowed by undergrowth, can be seen today. The wood at Petit Bois was taken by the 7th Leinsters and 7th/8th Irish Fusiliers with few losses. The defenders were stupefied into paralysis by the mine explosions in front of them and surrendered straight away.

The attack was a complete success. In the south, the Australian and New Zealanders took all their objectives, including the village of Messines.

There were fewer casualties than expected and the ground gained was in excess of expectations. The two German lines on the brow and crest of Messines Ridge were taken. Some 7,500 German prisoners surrendered immediately. Contemporary film footage of them shows shaken and shell-shocked men who had witnessed terrors beyond the imaginings of most people. Feilding saw Germans waving handkerchiefs. 'The ordeal through which they have been passing the last fortnight must have surpassed the torments of hell itself.'[28]

The 7th Inniskillings in the 16th (Irish) Division reached their first objective within twenty minutes but could find no trace of the German front line. They reached their final objectives by 4.45 a.m. with German opposition still light.

The 36th (Ulster) Division, assisted by two tanks, captured the German battalion headquarters near Wytschaete. By 9 a.m., the British and Commonwealth forces had won an incontestable victory. The victorious troops expected a counter-attack but it had been 'more like a picnic than a battle', according to one Australian officer.[29]

The goals had been achieved with relatively light casualties: 3,500 dead among 24,562 casualties, the majority of those in II Anzac Corps. The Germans suffered at least 19,923 casualties, this included 7,548 missing, thousands of whom were most likely killed in the mine explosions on 7 June.[30]

The casualties for the 16th (Irish) Division from 6 June to 9 June were 134 dead, 900 wounded and 149 missing, mostly taken prisoner. The 36th (Ulster) Division's casualties were 164 dead, 910 wounded and 45 missing. By the standards of the carnage of the Western Front, these casualty figures were unexceptional.[31]

'The outstanding feature, I think, was the astounding smallness of our casualties,' Feilding told his wife. 'The contrast in this respect with Loos and the Somme was most remarkable.'[32]

The battle of Messines Ridge was hailed as a complete military success. The newspapers in both Britain and Ireland were jubilant. The co-operation between the two traditions in Ireland was noted. The special correspondent for the *Morning Post* wrote:

> There was a particular appropriateness in the manner of their taking Wytschaete and the ground around it. I can tell you, for example, that the Dublin men were going with the barrage, touching shoulders with their comrades of an Orange Lodge in North Ulster. There were Munster lads raking through the brick piles and shivered concrete cellars of Wytschaete and Irish riflemen pinning down stubborn 'no surrender' Prussians among the stumps of Wytschaete Wood.[33]

A *Times* correspondent was quoted in the *Cork Examiner*, contrasting the political squabbling back in Ireland with the efforts of Catholics and Protestants in Flanders, 'It is well to know that the feeling between the two bodies here is most convivial. How ashamed these Ulster soldiers will feel when they hear of the ignoble conduct of those who profess to speak in their names at home, and what a reckoning they will demand some day.'

The British official history recorded that a 'great victory had been won by General Plumer's Second Army and with a swift completeness beyond that of any previous major operation of the British Armies in France and Flanders'.[34]

The Battle of Messines Ridge was one of the few successful offences undertaken by both the 16th (Irish) Division and the 36th (Ulster) Division. The two divisions would fight together at the Battle of Passchendaele in August of that year, but both were confounded by the dreadful conditions and suffered some 8,000 casualties between them.

The British Battle Exploits Memorial Committee was set up after the war to decide on the merits of the hundreds of proposed monuments to be erected on the Western Front. In 1923, Wytschaete was identified along with Guillemont as the two locations on the Western Front where memorials should be erected to the men of the 16th (Irish) Division.

Major General Hickie, now a senator in the new Irish Free State, wrote to them to explain his reasons for picking Wytschaete:

> The front of our attack extended from the point where our front trench crossed the Vierstraat-Wytschaete road on the north to Maedelstede Farm on the south. Our objectives included Unnamed Wood, the Hospice, the Bois de Wytschaete and the village itself, the attack being everywhere successful. We brought in 1,100 prisoners and 11 guns. The casualties of the division were 89 officers and 1,376 other ranks.[35]

The cross at Wytschaete was supposed to be erected in the centre of the rebuilt village, but the Burgomaster (mayor) objected, believing, wrongly, that it would be a pretentious object rather than a simple granite cross.[36] When that site was excluded, the alternative on the road out of Wytschaete was chosen instead. The cross was unveiled on Sunday, 22 August 1926. A party of approximately 150 people from Ireland and Britain, a large number by the standards of the time, travelled to Belgium for the event.

A further fifty came from the Channel Islands, which had been part of the 16th (Irish) Division during the war. When war broke out, the Guernsey militia opted to join the 6th Royal Irish Regiment because the regiment had been stationed on the island between 1910 and 1913. It made up D Company in the battalion.

The travelling party arrived in Ypres, which had been destroyed in the war. To their astonishment, the old town, that Verdun of the British army, had been completely rebuilt in just eight years and showed few scars of battle. 'It is hardly an exaggeration to say that it does not show many more signs of devastation than Dublin,' a correspondent in *The Irish Times* reported, alluding to how the scars of the Easter Rising and Civil War were still present in the Irish capital:

> Men with a breast full of medals stood aghast when they saw Ypres today. Was this pleasant countryside, the anguished wilderness they had known? Nobody would dream that a few years ago, that stretch of highway was trodden by hundreds of thousands of feet on the march to the grave. Then it was raced by shells, its surface pockmarked by countless craters. Now it is as smooth as the road from Dublin to Bray and Minerva cars skim along its silky length at hair raising speeds.[37]

The Irish Free State was represented by Count Gerald O'Kelly, its trade agent in Brussels, the equivalent of an ambassador. The new Irish Free State was in a quandary as what to do in such circumstances. It had no control over the unveiling of a memorial to its fellow countrymen. These had been British soldiers and this would be a British monument, despite appearances to the contrary.

Count O'Kelly wrote to Joseph P. Walshe, the secretary-general of the Department of External Affairs:

So far as I can see we are on the horns of a dilemma, because you may be perfectly assured that if there is no Irish representation the British Embassy's publicity services will see that quite a lot of publicity is given to the fact that they still run Irish manifestations overseas. If on the other hand there is an Irish representation and the British Embassy are allowed to run the ceremony, my position here will obviously have been completely undermined whether the representative be myself or somebody from home.[38]

O'Kelly was instructed to attend on the basis that it was considered natural the British ambassador would be involved in the unveiling ceremony, given that the men involved had fought in British uniforms. However, a communication from the Department of External Affairs instructed him, 'Your presence cannot in any sense be interpreted as bestowing the blessing of the Saorstát Government on the details of the ceremony.'[39]

The British had their way. The British and Belgian national anthems were played. The Union flag was placed across the arms of the Celtic cross. A banner was carried by one of the official Irish delegation. It was a replica of that presented by King Louis XV to the Irish Brigade after the Battle of Fontenoy in 1745. The buglers of the Irish Guards sounded the Last Post and Revd Maurice O'Connell, the senior chaplain of the 16th (Irish) Division blessed the cross.

Also present at the memorial unveiling was the Reverend Mother of Locre Convent. The Catholic soldiers had regularly attended Mass there.

When the service was over, Major General Hickie presented her with a copy of the eight-volume Irish National War Memorial Records, which had been compiled in 1923.

The Irish tricolour was not flown though it was later flown at a separate event in Belgium.

The Irish Times editorial lamented how the vast Irish expenditure of blood and sacrifice during the war had not led to the reconciliation between Catholic and Protestants in Ireland, nor to the respect those who fought could expect to receive when they returned home:

For the young fighters of the Sinn Féin movement any cause that England championed was alien. Many a time, during the years between 1920 and 1923, Irishmen who fought in the Great War must have asked themselves, 'Why did we answer the call?' They had suffered loss of blood, of health, and often of wealth; they were without honour in their own country. Their comrades had paid a toll that must depress the national vitality until the 20th century is far spent.[40]

The cross at Wytschaete stands alone beside the British military cemetery outside the village. It is similar in size and design to the cross at Guillemont, but it has a much greater presence and is surrounded by a 15ft square border. In 2007, to mark the ninetieth anniversary of the battle, the municipality of Heuvelland, which contains the village of Wytschaete, erected two memorial stones nearby, one to the 16th (Irish) Division and another to the 36th (Ulster) Division. The inscription on both stones reads simply, 'Comrades in arms'.

18

THE GRAVE OF MAJOR WILLIAM REDMOND MP

On the road between Locre and Kemmel in south-west Flanders, where the land gently rises, there stands a solitary war grave. Major Willie Redmond is one of the few British soldiers who died on the Western Front to have a marked grave that is not located in a Commonwealth War Graves Commission cemetery.

His grave is simple, consisting of a limestone cross, paid for by his widow Eleanor, flanked in a triangular fashion by two stones from the old convent. Evergreen shrubs surround it. Above his grave, suspended in a glass case, is a statue of the Virgin Mary, a symbol of Redmond's personal piety and fidelity to the Catholic faith. The inscription on the cross reads, 'Major W.H.K. Redmond 6th Batt Royal Irish Regt, Killed in Action 7-6-1917 R.I.P.'

The grave is accessed via a 100-yard-long grass path which passes by one of the smallest war grave cemeteries on the Western Front. The Locre Hospice Cemetery contains 244 graves, including twelve from the Second World War.

There are many reasons why Willie Redmond has a solitary grave but none have anything to do with him. He did not, as has been reported several times in the Irish media, make a request that, in the event of his death, he be buried apart from his fellow British soldiers in protest at the execution of the leaders of the Easter Rising. Such a request would never have been countenanced by the War Office; nor would Redmond ever have contemplated such an idea. He regarded the Easter Rising as a violation of the principle of solidarity between Britain and Ireland in a time of war. In 1918, his friends put together a memoriam souvenir booklet for him. The anonymous author of the character sketch made clear Redmond's feelings towards the Easter Rising:

> It would be hard to imagine with what an agony of soul he read of the events of Easter Week which to Major Redmond appeared to undo in a single week every-thing which he and his colleagues had striven to build up in a lifetime – nay, more, to close forever the vista of hope which seemed to be opening up into friendship. To him it meant more than treason to the Empire in which Ireland had been at last conceded her just and proper place, it meant treason to herself. For was not France, Catholic, democratic France, the national and traditional ally of Ireland?[1]

Redmond died because he did not want to be treated any differently. He was alone in that wish. His senior commanders, knowing his age and profile, wanted him nowhere near the front line. His death would serve no purpose, they believed, yet Redmond insisted on putting himself in harm's way. The War Office refused to allow private burials or the repatriation of bodies, yet Willie Redmond was an exceptional case. He was one of the oldest battle casualties of the war, but also one of the most famous. His death caused universal grief, even among erstwhile political foes.

With his death, the dream of peaceful reconciliation between Ireland and Britain within the British Empire also died. Four months later, Commandant

Éamon de Valera, the most senior surviving leader of the Easter Rising, as far apart as any Irishman could be in temper and outlook to Redmond, won the East Clare by-election for Sinn Féin in the seat vacated in the wake of Redmond's death.

Unlike the austere and insular de Valera, Willie Redmond had a cosmopolitan sensibility with a great sense of fun. He was personally popular, 'one of the most loveable and most distinguished Irishmen in public life', according to Denis Gwynn, like his father Stephen, biographer of his brother John Redmond.[2]

Redmond's is a lonely grave, but in life he was never a lonely man. 'He had constant good humour and integrity and his sense of fair play nobody ever questioned,' Gwynn explained. 'It is strange now to think that his forgotten grave, beside the convent, where he used to pray in those harrowing times, should have become known as the lonely Irish hero's grave. No man was ever less lonely in fact and had had so many devoted friends.'[3]

At 56, he was much too old for the vigours and privations of the trenches and his age was a critical factor in his succumbing to wounds that a younger man might have survived when he was wounded and died on the first day of the Battle of Messines Ridge on 7 June 1917.

Colonel Dr Brendan O'Shea of the Irish Defence Forces, an admirer of Willie Redmond, made these succinct observations about his death at a conference in Cork on the First World War:

> He did not have to join the army. He did not have to go to the front. He did not have to serve in the forward lines. He certainly did not have to go over the top on June 7th [1917]. You can say that it doesn't make any sense, that it is absolutely mad. To most people who are not in the military, there is a madness to it. There's no question about it. There's a willingness to complete the job and, in a sense, to believe in your own invincibility. I'm absolutely certain he had all of that. There is no way it could be otherwise.[4]

His death deprived Ireland of a big-hearted, generous-minded politician who had travelled from nationalist firebrand to a conciliatory internationalist who saw the big picture.

Willie Redmond lived and died by his principles, but was willing to modify his views when circumstances changed. He was born into privilege, part of a long line of Catholic merchant princes of Anglo-Norman descent, yet he took the side of the poor and dispossessed throughout most of his life. It was axiomatic to him and to most Irish nationalists at the time that British misrule in Ireland was the cause of all of Ireland's ills.

His family embodied many of the competing loyalties of Irish history. The Redmonds were wealthy Catholics whose family home was at Ballytrent House near Rosslare in County Wexford. His father, William Archer Redmond, married Mary Hoey of the Protestant Hoey family from County Wicklow.

Yet it was the Catholic side of the family who helped put down the 1798 Rebellion. Willie Redmond's Catholic grandfather Walter Redmond was a yeoman, the part-time British army militia at the time. His Protestant mother's descendant William Kearney was hanged for being on the side of the rebels.[5]

Redmond was born in Liverpool in 1861. He went to Clongowes Wood College. He was destined for a life of privilege, but his father, who became one of the first home rule MPs, ensured that his sons John and Willie would know the real state of the country.

There were never two more different brothers, the older John 'silent, reserved, calculating and consistent', the other (Willie) being 'conversational, spontaneous and impulsive in policy', according to Stephen Gwynn, John Redmond's first biographer, who was an Irish Parliamentary Party MP and a British officer.[6]

William Archer Redmond introduced his sons to Michael Davitt, the founder of the Land League. Land agitation and land hunger was the abiding issue in Ireland during the 1870s. Willie Redmond threw himself into the cause as fervently as he would answer another call during the First World War.

He joined the part-time Wexford militia as a young man and obtained a commission as a second lieutenant. He had no time for the professional British army, which he regarded as an instrument of oppression, but justified his involvement in the militia on the basis that it was run by and on behalf of Irish nationalists. He spent his twenty-first birthday in Kilmainham Jail. He was jailed for his land reform agitation in February 1882 and shared a cell with Charles Stewart Parnell, the great hope of nationalist Ireland.

The Redmond brothers stood by Parnell when most of the Irish Parliamentary Party turned against him over his affair with Katharine O'Shea. The respect between Parnell and Willie Redmond was reciprocated. 'I have always justly relied upon you as one of the most single-minded and attached of my colleagues,' Parnell told him.[7]

Willie Redmond was first elected to the House of Commons in 1883 for Wexford. In 1885, he switched constituencies to Fermanagh North. He was noted for the intemperate nature of many of his House of Commons speeches, which were invariably on the theme of perfidious Albion and her treacherous ways.[8]

Despite his loyalty to Parnell and his status as an MP, he was not always wedded to constitutional politics. On the contrary, Willie Redmond was noted for many incendiary pronouncements, saying in Boston, USA, in 1884, 'We will work to make Ireland a nation and give her a harp without a crown. Nationalists will be the enemies of English power in Ireland so long as England refuses to grant her a parliament. The bulk of Irish people are in a state of rebellion which is merely tempered by the absence of firearms. England's difficult under the provenance of God, is Ireland's opportunity.'[9]

Afer he died, the author Wilfred Meynell, writing in *The Tablet* newspaper, referenced that speech but spoke of how Redmond had learned the 'heart's most difficult lesson, namely, to forgive. Ardent nationalist as he was, he disdained to make England's difficulty Ireland's opportunity.'[10]

In 1888, he was jailed again, this time for opposing the eviction of a man called Summers from his property in Coolrae, County Wexford. It took 200 police and soldiers to remove him and his supporters. He spent three months in jail. 'I undoubtedly cheered those men,' he said afterwards, 'when they were defending their homes against unjust eviction and I shall always continue to cheer every man who does so'.[11]

When the Boer War broke out in 1899, Willie Redmond, like many Irish nationalists, took the side of the Boers in their struggle against the British. He even met with the deposed Boer president Paul Kruger when he came to Britain.

He was jailed once again in November 1902 for land agitation.

His brother John took control of the Irish Parliamentary Party in 1900 and brought a discipline and purpose to it after the bitterness of the split over support for Parnell.

In the years of relative quietude before the Third Home Rule Bill of 1912, Willie Redmond championed a number of causes relating to education, third-level education in Ireland being a particularly pressing issue in these years. He also promoted the Irish language and sought greater temperance (like his father, he was a non-drinker), though he championed tobacco growing in Ireland.[12]

The Home Rule Bill brought the gun back into Irish politics. When the Irish Volunteers was formed in November 1913, Eoin MacNeill invited Willie Redmond to join the central committee, but he declined out of deference to his brother, who was suspicious of an organisation he could not control. Eventually John Redmond's party would take control of it, much to the chagrin of those such as Patrick Pearse and Tom Clarke who wanted to use the Irish Volunteers to stage a rebellion while Britain was occupied by the war.

In June 1914, Willie Redmond went to Belgium to acquire 500,000 rounds of ammunition for the Volunteers. These were to be used only in the event of the home rule settlement not being implemented, yet at heart Willie Redmond, like his brother, was a constitutional nationalist.[13]

When war broke out in August 1914, there were no greater Irish advocates for the Allied war effort than John and Willie Redmond. It was an extraordinary journey for both brothers, but especially for Willie Redmond, who had morphed from firebrand nationalist who held England responsible for all the ills of Ireland into a champion of the British Empire in wartime. His memorium obituary records:

> The day that the Home Rule Bill was introduced into the House of Commons William Redmond became a changed man and when at last it was placed upon the Statute Book he told England that since she had proven true to her word he would show that Ireland could also keep to hers. There were not wanting, however,

critics who still doubted his sincerity, and who were only too willing to discount his assurances by memories of past bitterness, but such men were soon put to shame by the example of William Redmond, who though well over the age limit, prepared to don the uniform of a country which he had spent all his life in fighting. In this great matter he might well be compared to the great South African General, General Smuts, once fighting against now fighting for England.[14]

John Redmond encouraged the Irish Volunteers to join the British army during his Woodenbridge speech in September 1914. His brother went one step further. In November 1914, he made a recruitment speech in Cork. Willie Redmond set out his nationalist credentials to the crowd. He had been jailed three times; an ancestor of his had been hanged during the 1798 Rebellion. Nobody cared more about the freedom of Ireland than he did. Nobody could question his patriotism. Then he added, 'And when it comes to the question, as it may come, of asking young Irishmen to go abroad and fight this battle, when I am personally convinced that the battle of Ireland is to be fought where many Irishmen now are, in Flanders and France, old as I am, and grey as are my hairs, I will say, "Don't go, but come with me".'[15]

He meant what he said. In February 1915, at the age of 53, overweight and out of shape, William Redmond was commissioned into the 6th Battalion of the Royal Irish Regiment. He was given command of B Company, which included in its ranks some 200 men from Derry and a contingent from the Channel Islands.[16]

It was the manifestation of what he believed in, this group of people, Catholic and Protestant, nationalist and unionist, who put their differences aside and co-ordinated themselves for a common purpose.

Redmond was shipped to France with the rest of 16th (Irish) Division in December 1915 and was deployed to the front line near Loos.

The early months were relatively quiet though shelling terrified him. 'The destruction, havoc and suffering I have encountered is truly appalling,' he wrote in a letter to a friend.[17] Unionist MP Walter Long tried to persuade Lord Kitchener to send Willie Redmond home, but Kitchener would not countenance it. Long, like so many others, thought it daft that a man as old as Redmond should be in the front line. In February 1916, forty-eight men from the battalion were sent home because they were deemed medically unfit. Redmond was not one of them.[18]

Redmond was on leave at home in Ireland when the Easter Rising broke out and might have been better employed using his authority to stay the hand of a British military intent on executing the Rising's leaders. Instead, he insisted on returning to his men. In June 1916, he was invalided home, but promoted to major in July 1916. His commanding officers gave him a post at divisional headquarters to keep him out of harm's way.

He was not in the front line when his battalion was involved in the attack on Ginchy on 9 September, though he saw the casualties the battle had wrought on his beloved battalion: 500 men killed, wounded or missing.

On 17 September 1916, Major Redmond wrote to his friend Una Taylor expressing his admiration for his fellow Irish soldiers who had taken Guillemont and Ginchy during the latter stages of the Battle of the Somme.

'The Irish captured Guillemont and Ginchy in most glorious fashion,' he wrote in a letter which is now in the Foynes Flying Boat Museum in County Limerick. 'Nothing could be more splendid. I saw enough of it though at head-quarters to be lost in admiration at the bravery of these Irish soldiers and they never forgot Ireland but sang her songs all the time … Everyone agrees that the Irish troops could not have done better. The losses were of course comparatively heavy. So many dear young boys dead. I never regretted feeling old before. I wish I could have done more.'[19]

In December 1916, he made preparations for his possible death by depositing his will with O'Keeffe and Lynch solicitors in Dublin. He wrote, 'If I should die abroad I will give my wife my last thought and love and ask her to pray that we meet hereafter. I should like all my friends in Ireland to know that in joining the Irish Brigade and going to France I sincerely believed, as all the Irish soldiers do, that I was doing my best for the welfare of Ireland in every way.'[20]

By this point, Willie Redmond was sick of the war and anxious for the fate of Ireland. The Easter Rising and its aftermath was sapping the morale of the men at the front. Protestants and Catholics were getting on well in the trenches, yet, at home, the tensions were growing.

He told the House of Commons in December 1916, 'It is miserable to see men who went out with high hearts and hopes, who have acquitted themselves so well, filled with wretchedness because their country is in an unhappy position.'

After the Somme, both the 16th (Irish) Division and 36th (Ulster) Division moved to Flanders to await the next offensive. Throughout early 1917, both divisions prepared for the 'big push' that followed the failed offensive on the Somme.

In March, William Redmond made his last speech in the House of Commons. Dressed in his major's uniform, he made a powerful plea for fairness and reconciliation in Ireland. He began by assuring the house that, despite all that had gone on in Ireland, 'the great, generous heart of the Irish race beats in sympathy with the Allies' cause'. He then went on to make a last impassioned and ultimately doomed plea for reconciliation between Britain and Ireland. Many were moved to tears by the power of his oratory:

Mistakes, dark, black, and bitter mistakes, have been made. A people denied justice, a people with many admitted grievances, the redress of which has been long delayed, on our side, perhaps, in the conflict, and in the bitterness of contest, there may have been things said and done, offensive if you will, irritating if you will, to the people of this country; but what I want to ask, in all simplicity, is this, whether, in face of the tremendous conflict which is now raging, whether, in view of the fact that, apart from every other consideration, the Irish people, South as well as North, are upon, the side of the Allies and against the German pretension today, it is not possible, from this war to make a new start.

T.P. O'Connor, the only Irish party MP to represent an English constituency (Liverpool Scotland), recalled, 'You could hear the heavy breathing of men around you, and I was told by one who was in the gallery that men around him sobbed and wept unabashed.'[21] Redmond returned to Belgium for the 'big push', soon to be the Battle of Messines Ridge. He was determined to join in the attack. He had been ordered by Hickie not to move any further forward than the first battlefield clearance station at the Battle of Ginchy and he resented it. By his own admission, Redmond had 'besieged that wretched War Office until they were sick to death of the sight of me'.[22]

In the days before the Battle of Messines Ridge, he was billeted in quarters outside the village of Locre, close to the convent where a field hospital had been established. Redmond's own niece, Dora Howard (Dame Teresa), had been a nun in the Benedictine Convent in Ypres and was forced to flee during the fighting in late 1914.[23] He regularly attended Mass with the nuns in Ypres. The nuns provided baths and wholesome food for the forces.

For three days prior to the battle, he and Fr Edmund Kelly, the chaplain to the Irish forces, slept in the cellar under the chapel at the hospice, which was also a field hospital.[24] Redmond felt 'absolutely miserable at the idea of being left behind,' Kelly remembered, and he tried to influence Hickie to allow him to go over the top. 'He spoke in the most telling manner of what awaited the poor fellows, and longed to share their suffering and their fate. He brought up the subject saying that unless the General [Hickie] allowed him to mount the parapet with his regiment, he would resign.'[25]

For reasons that are not clear in Kelly's account, Hickie seems to have changed his mind. He allowed Redmond to go over the top, but only in the third wave, presumably after the first two waves had secured the objectives and eliminated the opposition. Redmond was 'bubbling over with joy' at the prospect, Kelly recalled, and he laughed while putting his uniform on.

After the massive explosions that blew the Germans off the hillsides in Messines, Redmond charged out of his trench. An (unnamed) comrade told *The Tablet* that Redmond 'had a joke and a smile for every man and, as we flew over the parapet to shouts of "Up the County Clare", Major Willie showed us a clean pair of heels'. He was soon hit by bullets in the wrist and legs.[26]

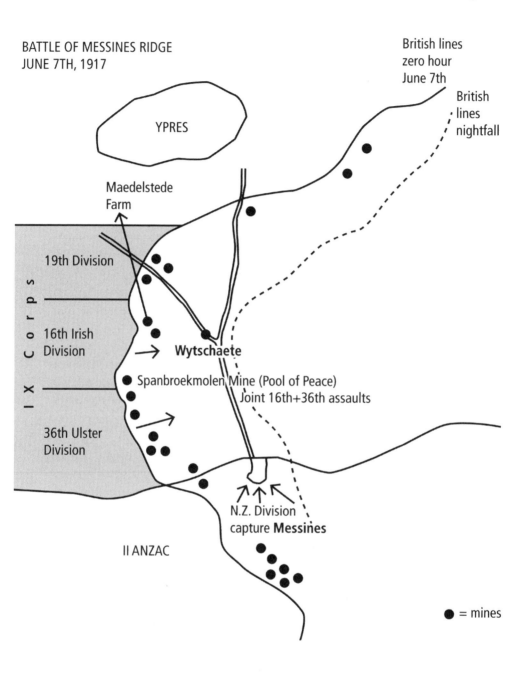

BATTLE OF MESSINES RIDGE
JUNE 7TH, 1917

British lines
zero hour
June 7th

British
lines
nightfall

YPRES

Maedelstede
Farm

19th Division

IX Corps

16th Irish
Division

→ **Wytschaete**

Spanbroekmolen Mine (Pool of Peace)
Joint 16th+36th assaults

36th Ulster
Division

N.Z. Division
capture **Messines**

II ANZAC

● = mines

Redmond was rescued from the battlefield by Private John Meeke, a stretcher-bearer with the 11th Royal Inniskilling Fusiliers. Meeke dodged machine gun fire to attend to Redmond's wounds. He himself was hit by shrapnel before the pair were rescued by a Royal Inniskilling Fusiliers patrol.

Meeke received the Military Medal for his actions on the battlefield that day.[27]

Redmond was carried to the safety of a field dressing station. His injuries were bad, but not life-threatening, or so it was believed. But he had been much too old for the vigours and privations of the trenches, which had left him physically weakened and prey to toxic shock.[28]

Before he passed away, Willie Redmond told the Anglican clergyman Revd John Redmond (no relation) to tell his wife to 'please thank her for all she has done for me and tell her that if we do not meet again in this world, I hope we shall meet again in the next'.

He died later that evening. 'His wounds were not grave, but he had overtaxed himself and in a few hours he succumbed to shock,' Stephen Gwynn wrote. 'It was the death that he had foreseen, that he had always desired – a death that many might have envied him. He had said more than once since the rebellion that he thought he could best serve Ireland by dying.'[29]

Many have speculated over the years that Willie Redmond had a death wish, the mirror image of that of the leaders of the Easter Rising, but, in Redmond's case, he hoped his death would become a symbol for reconciliation, not division.

Hickie ordered a coffin and Redmond was taken to the convent chapel in Locre. Coffins were a luxury on the Western Front. A guard of honour was performed by troops from the 10th Royal Inniskilling Fusiliers of the 36th (Ulster) Division and the 2nd Royal Irish Regiment of the 16th (Irish) Division, Catholics and Protestants together just as Redmond would have desired. He was buried in the convent grounds, probably with a view to moving him to a war cemetery at a later date.

His death profoundly affected public opinion in Ireland and beyond. Tributes came from those on all sides in Ireland and elsewhere. The Pope sent a message of condolence, as did King George V and Queen Mary, Lord Carson and General Botha of South Africa. Poor, good-hearted, generous-minded Willie Redmond was gone. His fellow nationalist MP, Sir Walter Nugent, put it succinctly, 'He was too good for politics'.

Willie's death was a hammer blow for his sibling. John Redmond had lost a brother, a like-minded soul and a wise advisor – and this at a time when he was striving desperately to salvage a home rule solution through the ill-fated Irish Convention, which was boycotted by Sinn Féin. The bereavement was the second grievous family sorrow of the year. His beloved daughter Esther Redmond Power had died in New York in January, leaving behind four young children. John Redmond was losing heart and, unknown to himself, was physically sick and depressed. He was isolated and deeply unpopular even with his colleagues. Gwynn observed of his ailing leader, 'Sorrow gave a strong grip to depression on a brooding mind which had always a proneness to melancholy, which was now linked with a sick body, and which lived among disappointments and grief and the sense of rancorous dislike in men who once thought it a privilege to cheer him on his passing.'[30]

John Redmond would die just nine months after his brother, following a rou-
tine operation for an intestinal blockage in a London hospital. Nationalist Ireland's
leader succumbed to heart failure. In death, he and his brother were at least spared
the trauma of the destruction of the Irish Parliamentary Party by Sinn Féin at the
general election held in December 1918.

—

A memorial fund for Willie Redmond was set up shortly after his death and was
heavily subscribed to by his division, but also by the 36th (Ulster) Division and
the Tyneside Irish Brigade.

Willie Redmond's grave was already a place of pilgrimage when a delegation from the memorial committee compromising of the Mayor of Wexford,
the High Sheriff of Dublin Myles Keogh and Dr James Ashe, the secretary of
the committee, visited it in November 1917, an event which attracted a great
deal of publicity.

Willie Redmond's grave could have been moved on many occasions over the
next century. The relative tranquillity of this part of Flanders was shattered in
April 1918 when the Germans launched an assault on the Ypres salient, known as
the Fourth Battle of Ypres or the Battle of Lys. Locre was fought over many times
in April 1918 and the convent was badly damaged by shells, yet Redmond's grave
remained intact. After the war, many of the soldiers buried where they fell were
removed and put into concentration cemeteries. Redmond's would have been
moved, but for the opposition of a number of key people.

The founder of the Imperial War Graves Commission, Sir Fabian Ware, found it
intolerable that Redmond's grave could remain in situ while those of other men
buried in the grounds of the hospice were moved into war cemeteries, but Willie
Redmond's widow Eleanor Redmond would not countenance it.[31]

She wrote to the Imperial War Graves Commission in 1919, 'I should only wish
to have my husband's grave left untouched … I just want it left where it is in the
good care of the nuns.'[32] In November 1920, she wrote to the commission again,
'I have just returned from Locre and having seen the grave as tenderly cared for
by the nuns, the thought of any removal seems more dreadful'.

After the war, it was tended to by the nuns. There it remained, but a visiting party in
the summer of 1956 was not impressed with its upkeep, judging by a letter published
in the *Irish Independent* that year, written by a J.F. McCarthy of Tramore, County
Waterford. He had visited it with a party of ex-members of the 36th (Ulster) Division:

> The object of this letter is to draw the attention of the people of Waterford to
> the sadly neglected state of the grave at Locre. It is in sad contrast to the beauti-
> fully kept graves in the military cemeteries I visited. It is now lost in a jungle

of wild grass, scrub and fallen timber, and were it not for the rough-hewn cross at the head, there is no semblance of a grave whatever. The North of Ireland contingent, which was composed of nationalists and orangemen, unionists and republicans, asked me to write to some of the Southern papers about this matter when I got back. I am doing so now, and; I trust you will find the subject of sufficient importance to the people of Wexford to warrant its publication.[33]

In 1958, the convent finally closed and maintenance of the grave passed to the Locre commune. The state of the grave did not improve. In 1964, the Cork Choral Society visited the area and inquired from the burgomaster (the local mayor) about the location of Redmond's grave. He was unable to help and were it not for the intervention of an elderly missionary priest who was living locally, they would not have found it. When they did locate the grave, it was 'completely overgrown with weeds and climbing plants', which the Irish visitors cleared away.

Eighteen months later, a member of the Royal Irish Regiment Old Comrades Association visited the grave and was shocked by what he saw. He reported back to the chairman of the association P.J. Boyce. 'He had been horrified to find that the grave was in ruins, overgrown with weeds and totally uncared for,' Boyce told *The Irish Times* in June 1967. 'In fact it was no more than a wilderness, furthermore the grave was situated in unconsecrated ground.'

The state of Redmond's grave irked the Commonwealth War Graves Commission. It complained that it was taking the blame for something that was not its responsibility as the local commune had agreed to maintain it. In March 1967, the commission made the decision to move Redmond's grave into the nearly Hospice Cemetery.

It did so after getting the support of Willie Redmond's closest relative, his great-nephew John Redmond Green, who wrote to the commission saying he was 'fully in agreement' with the proposals. The commission also wrote to Mr Boyce and got the Old Comrade's Association wholehearted support.

Boyce wrote back to the commission, jubilant at the thought that the grave would be moved. 'This wonderful news will be a cause of much satisfaction and a great relief to a considerable number of our members who join me in thanking you most sincerely.'

The commission suggested leaving a plaque at the location of Redmond's grave and offered to ship the cross back to the Redmond family in Ireland. The memorial would read, 'In memory of Major W.H.K. Redmond buried in the adjoining Loker Hospice Cemetery'.[34]

The commission would have exhumed Redmond's grave were it not for the imminent fiftieth-anniversary commemoration of his death, which was to due to take place in Locre in June 1967. However, it and the Redmond family had not reckoned on the righteous anger of an elderly local priest named Fr Rafaël-Augustinus Debevere. Debevere had been ordained before the First World

War and remembered the German occupation of Belgium well. He regarded Redmond as a great man and had been the driving force behind a conference and booklet he had compiled to mark the fiftieth anniversary of his death.

The example of Redmond's life had a particular resonance in Flanders, which had its own aspirations to nationhood within Belgium, a country where tensions between French-speaking Walloons and Dutch-speaking Flemish have persisted since the creation of the Belgian state in 1830.

Debevere, the director of St Anthony Hospice, was dismayed by any attempt to move the grave. It would be against the 'explicit wishes' of Redmond's wife, he told the commission. Redmond had been a great friend of the nuns in the convent and had a special devotion to Our Lady. He was buried with the full approval of the British army and that of his comrades-in-arms. His grave was listed as a 'place of pilgrimage' in the *Irish Dictionary of National Biography*. Debevere conceded that in the past the grave had been unkempt, but 'through my intervention the grave was cleaned from weeds and superfluous bushes and trees. Now it stands in a peaceful neighbourhood before seven maples. It can be seen from very far away and it is kept clean by the population of Locre who also planted some flowers on the grave.'

The local commune was equally animated about the commission's proposals. The burgomaster and secretary wrote to the commission asking why it intended to act when the issue of the municipality maintaining it had been resolved and it was now being cared for properly.

'Therefore we request you in our name as well as in the name of Rev. Debevere: DO NOT DO IT! [their emphasis] Take care that the grave of Major Redmond may be seen by everybody where it is at present and you will satisfy a lot of people.'

Some members of the commission believed locals might have had an ulterior motive. Redmond's grave was part of a popular remembrance tourism trail. 'I think it is not uncharitable to suppose that they are mainly concerned at the prospect of losing a potential tourist attraction,' the commission's external affairs manager P.N. Dolan wrote to the military attaché Brigadier F.G. MacMullen at the British embassy in Dublin. Nevertheless, Dolan conceded that it would be 'tactful' to wait until after the fiftieth-anniversary commemorations in June to move the grave. The commission was adamant that 'we do not intend to allow considerations of local interest to deflect us from implementing the removal of the grave as soon as it is practical to do so'.

Debevere took his campaign to the Irish newspapers, writing to both *The Irish Times* and the *Sunday Independent*. The publicity generated by his campaign made newspapers in Britain and the United States too. The commission now had a public relations headache, which spread far beyond the little commune of Locre.

Debevere's opposition to the move grew more intense. What would be left of the remains of Willie Redmond if they decided to move them? Willie Redmond was not a British soldier, but an Irishman fighting as an ally of the British forces, he maintained.

He wrote again to the commission, 'The grave is a place of pilgrimage. Exhumation would seem a profanation and would be a pity for the population of Loker and the region. I beseech [you]: can you obtain that the grave remains untouched and the body not exhumed? It would give me and the people of Loker a [*sic*] great satisfaction.'[35]

The cause was taken up by Denis Gwynn. 'It will be a national disgrace if some sensible decision is not found for the custody and the upkeep of his grave: though he would have cared so little himself where he should lie in peace.'

The commission changed its mind and decided to keep a watching brief on the grave. When it was satisfied after six monthly inspections that it was well cared for, it dropped its proposal to exhume Redmond's remains.

Those agitating for the perpetuation of the status quo might have concluded that that was the end of the matter, but the commission had not given up. After Debevere died in 1977 at the age of 93, it reopened the case. An internal memo from September 1979 read, 'It is felt that it would be difficult to justify the relatively high cost of maintaining this isolated burial, but before going firm, we should look to hear if there is likely to be any local reaction to the proposed move.'

The proposal got short shrift from the local authority, which decided in January 1980 that 'no authority can be granted for the exhumation of the remains of Major W H K Redmond.'

In the early 1990s, the land was acquired by the Openbaar Centrum voor Maatschappelijk Welzijn, the Belgian national health and welfare authority. In 2006, Willie Redmond's closest surviving relatives, John and Mary Green, his great-grand-nephew and great-grand-niece, wrote to the commission to state they had been upset with repeated suggestions that they objected to his grave being moved to the hospice cemetery. 'We have the greatest respect for the work of the commission and we were anxious that Major Redmond's grave should be placed under your care in perpetuity.'

In 2009, Peter Houlton, the records supervisor at the Commonwealth War Graves Commission, could find no evidence that Redmond's widow had ever suggested that he remain outside a British cemetery by way of a protest against British policy in Ireland. 'There is no implication from the correspondence with the family in the 1960s that the siting of the grave outside the main cemetery was a political statement. In my opinion the opposite is true as they wanted it moved.'[36]

In 1931, his home town of Wexford unveiled a bust in his honour, but the memory of Redmond, like that of thousands of other Irishmen who fought and died in the First World War, went into abeyance.

The former British officer turned leader of the National Volunteers Maurice Moore had forecast at the time of Redmond's death that 'Ireland will grieve over his loss as sorrowfully as she does over [Pádraig] Pearse and [the] O'Rahilly' but Willie Redmond's first biographer Terence Denman concluded, 'Ireland did, and does, nothing of the sort. Willie Redmond's lonely grave stands as mute testimony to that'.[37]

In 1995, Denman published a biography of Redmond, which was appropriately entitled *A Lonely Grave*. He had cause to lament. 'Willie Redmond, like all the nationalist Irish who fought in the Great War, has been pushed to the margins of Irish history. Realistically, his life may be seen as a tragic failure.'[38]

Yet, since Denman's book was published in 1995, there has been a sea change in southern Irish attitudes to the Irishmen who served in the First World War. Redmond's message of peace and reconciliation between Britain and Ireland was an idea whose time had come. Willie Redmond's name became popular again. In his famous speech on 7 March 1917, Redmond asked a series of rhetorical questions:

> Is there an Englishman representing any party who does not yearn for a better future between Ireland and Great Britain? There is no Irishman who is not anxious for it also. Why cannot there be a settlement? Why must it be that, when British soldiers and Irish soldiers are suffering and dying side by side, this eternal old quarrel should go on?

On 19 December 2013, Taoiseach Enda Kenny and the British Prime Minister David Cameron visited Willie Redmond's grave. Kenny left a laurel wreath on one ceremonial stone; Cameron left a wreath of poppies on the other.

An Irish Guardsman from the British army and an Irish soldier stood by his grave.

Both men signed the visitors' book. Enda Kenny wrote, 'To honour a soldier who lived and died for his beliefs, and whose faith in the power of unity still resonates powerfully'. Later he would reveal that his thoughts at Willie Redmond's grave were bound up with the aspirations of the European Union:

> I thought it was symbolically very important. The thought crossed my mind standing at the grave of Willie Redmond: that was why we have a European Union and why I'm attending a European Council. I think it was the first time that an Irish Taoiseach actually had the opportunity to pay tribute to British soldiers and Irish soldiers who fought in World War I. So for me, personally, this was something very important, I have to say. And it was also a great privilege being able to lay a wreath on behalf of the Irish people at the grave of Willie Redmond.[39]

In the visitors' book, Cameron wrote, 'It is an honour to visit with the Irish PM to commemorate all those who gave their lives in the cause of freedom, including this historic site.'

Willie Redmond, who gave his life for a free and confident Ireland at peace with Britain, would surely have approved.

19

THE ISLAND OF IRELAND PEACE PARK

On the morning of 11 November 1998, eighty years to the day after the Armistice was signed, three heads of state travelled to the Belgian village of Messines, known today by its Flemish name Mesen.

Locals had hung out the Belgian, British and Irish flags from lamp posts and balcony windows. In one car, the talk between Queen Elizabeth II and President of Ireland Mary McAleese ranged from the difference between shinty and hurling to the Good Friday Agreement, then less than six months old.

This was also the first anniversary of Mrs McAleese's inauguration as Irish president. A Catholic from Belfast, she and her family had been burned out of their home during the 1970s, yet she never succumbed to hate. 'Building bridges' would be the theme of her presidency.

Their destination on this morning was a new memorial ground to be known as the Island of Ireland Peace Park. As the convoy of cars drew closer, through a gathering crowd, the park's centrepiece, its round tower, heaved into view. The guests of honour fell silent. McAleese remembers:

> Our first sight of the tower produced a reverential silence, a realisation that in this place sharp shards of bitter memory were about to be reconciled and the narrative of the past would no longer be told in a way that divided the people of today. The snippet of a poem from Tom Kettle immortalised in a plaque was haunting, the 'secret scripture of the poor'. Best of all was the solemn solidarity of the very mixed audience representing so many diverse and argument-prone elements of Irish and British life, united in respect for the Irish who died in British uniform. You could feel a rubicon was being crossed.[1]

The two men most responsible for this landmark day, Donegal politician Paddy Harte and veteran unionist representative Glen Barr, welcomed all those present. The rush to ensure that the park would be completed on time prompted Harte to acknowledge an 'invisible hand that we could not understand that has been at work through all of this'.[2]

The war dead of Irish unionism had become an integral part of the unionist story in the twentieth century. The fallen of 1914–18 had been elevated into the pantheon; they have been staunchly commemorated and celebrated in the decades since. Now Glen Barr appealed to Catholic Ireland to remember its own fallen, in order 'that the spirits of those young heroes who have haunted these battlefields for 80 years can be laid to rest'.[3]

The two men read a peace pledge in honour of the Irish who had died in 'shockingly uncountable numbers'. The pledge, cast in bronze, reads:

> As Protestants and Catholics, we apologise for the terrible deeds we have done to each other and ask forgiveness. From this sacred shrine of remembrance, where soldiers of all nationalities, creeds and political allegiances were united in death,

we appeal to all people in Ireland to help build a peaceful and tolerant society. Let us remember the solidarity and trust that developed between Protestant and Catholic soldiers when they served together in these trenches. As we jointly thank the Armistice of 11 November 1918 – when the guns fell silent along this Western Front – we affirm that a fitting tribute to the principles for which men and women from the Island of Ireland died in both World Wars would be permanent peace.

President McAleese, Queen Elizabeth II and the King of Belgium, Albert II, paused with bowed heads before the round tower, built from the stones of an Irish workhouse. The President placed a black wreath with a tricolour ribbon, the Queen followed with a wreath of poppies and King Albert laid down a wreath of autumn leaves.

Some 1,500 people attended the ceremony at Messines. These were, for the most part, the children and grandchildren of Irishmen who had fought in the First World War, many compelled by the uniqueness of the occasion to visit the battlefields for the first time. The Irish Army No. 1 Band and the Royal Irish Regiment band from Northern Ireland played the 'Reveille' and a hush descended on the crowd. As a minute's silence was observed, the sun disappeared behind a cloud and an autumnal chill was felt.[4]

The Island of Ireland Peace Park is a war memorial which repudiates war. As the name suggests, it is there to remember those from all over the land who died in the First World War. But it also remembers all those who died closer to home during the war between the nationalist and unionist traditions.

The Armistice had ended one global conflict. The formal partition of Ireland four years later served to harden a divide that pre-dated the First World War by hundreds of years. By comparison, this was clearly a micro-conflict, a local contagion that simmered beneath the surface for decades on the western margins of Europe. But it was no less tragic for its many victims when it erupted into the sectarian war that would become known as 'the Troubles'. The common cause that unionist and nationalist, Protestant and Catholic, had found in the trenches was long forgotten by the 1970s and '80s when Ulster was inflamed with enmity between the two traditions.

Poignantly, even the act of remembering the war dead became another instrument of division. It should have been a case of unity through history; instead it mutated into the politics of the tribe. The Ulster Protestant dead were venerated by their side. Down south, the Irish nationalist dead were gradually forgotten and denied, their memory confined to what McAleese described as a 'shoe box of medals and memories'.

Therefore, 11 November 1998 was as much about the present as the past. There could hardly be a more potent symbol for contemporary reconciliation than that of the Irish and British heads of state walking together in a foreign field to remember all the Irish dead of the First World War. Though it was coincidental, the timing of the opening of the Island of Ireland Peace Park was perfect. In April of that year, the Good Friday Agreement had been signed. An imperfect peace though it may have been, it has nevertheless endured. Two months later, it was overwhelmingly endorsed by the majority of people, both North and South. The presence of the Queen and the President at Messines that day was the sovereign embodiment of hope for a new and peaceful era in Irish society.

In a very palpable sense, the Irishmen who had sacrificed their lives in the First World War were once again being summoned to the cause of a noble ideal.

Reflecting on the opening of the park, Sir Kenneth Bloomfield, the former head of the Northern Ireland civil service, who had once been targeted by the IRA, understood both the historical and contemporary import of the event. Speaking following the opening, he said, 'The significance of the two heads of state appearing together in public in this particular setting is that it retrospectively brings those people back into the generous embrace of the Irish nation.'

—

Between conception and opening, the development of the Island of Ireland Peace Park progressed with dizzying speed. Its opening took place two years to the day after a visit to the Somme that so profoundly moved the co-founders of the initiative that they resolved to do something once and for all to remember the Irish war dead.

Paddy Harte was a Fine Gael TD (member of the Irish parliament), the Father of the Dáil, having represented the Donegal North-East constituency for thirty-six years. His home in Lifford, County Donegal, abuts the border with Northern Ireland. As a young man, he knew the local war veterans whose service was only spoken about in whispers. His mother was from Derry. She had a devotion to Fr Willie Doyle, the Irish chaplain killed at the Battle of Passchendaele in 1917, and believed he should be a candidate for sainthood. Doyle's piety and the internationally successful biography by Professor Alfred O'Rahilly had made the Jesuit priest an individual who was venerated in many Irish households.[5] It was a common sentiment in nationalist Ireland at the time.[6]

Harte held unorthodox views. He unapologetically wore the poppy, a divisive symbol in the Republic. He believed that James Dillon, the only national politician to oppose Irish neutrality in the Second World War, was Ireland's lost leader. In 1996, at the promptings of his wife Rosaleen, he fulfilled a long-standing wish to visit the war graves on the Western Front. He was stunned by what he found: row after row of familiar Irish names, so many and yet they had all been so forgotten. 'It seemed to me that the list of Irish names was endless,' he recalled in his 2005 memoir *Young Tigers and Mongrel Foxes*:

> I was very emotional as I came face to face with the evidence of the slaughter of
> young men and women in a war that should never have happened. As a Catholic,
> I had been taught to pray for the dead and here were many thousands killed in a

most cruel and savage way and for whom I had never been asked to say a prayer. They had been conveniently forgotten. The Catholics and Protestant Irish who died in two world wars as comrades fighting tyranny and a common enemy would not have envisaged returning to an Ireland in which they would hate and kill each other.

Harte resolved to assemble a delegation, comprised of unionists and nationalists, to visit the Western Front. In November 1996, a party of fifty left Dublin for the Somme. They were struck by the imposing edifice that is the Ulster Tower and by how well-maintained it was by comparison with the cross at Guillemont – the monument to 16th (Irish) Division – which was in a sorry state of disrepair. Harte remembered, 'A comparison of the monuments clearly showed how one tradition was properly remembered on the battlefield and the other was not. It seemed unfair.'

Glen Barr was part of that delegation. Barr was a former trade unionist who was prominent in the Ulster Defence Association, a paramilitary organisation responsible for more than 250 deaths during the Troubles. Barr had been involved in the workers' strike of 1974, which brought down the Sunningdale power-sharing agreement. But, like many in the North, his long journey had brought him from sectarian conflict to the principle of reconciliation. Barr's father Robert and four of his uncles had fought at the Somme. All survived. He was struck by his own ignorance. He knew nothing of the involvement of the 16th (Irish) Division at the Somme, their exploits as much ignored as those of the 36th (Ulster) Division had been commemorated.

One time, he was visiting the New Menin Gate with a few former Ulster Defence Association comrades when a party of Irishmen came marching down the street carrying the Irish tricolour. 'What are those Fenian bastards doing here?' his friend asked. He replied, 'Those Fenian bastards are remembering their dead like we remember ours.'

Barr was also moved by the decrepit state of the Guillemont cross. It looked weather-beaten and neglected. The iron railings around it were rusting. He remembered:

> That hit me the worst after having left the Ulster Tower. This was the treatment being meted out to the nationalists who fought in the war. That still remains with me to this day. RTÉ radio came out with us, but nobody could talk to them. Everyone was overcome with emotion. I could not speak, I was confused, I was angry at the difference between the two memorials and I was full of guilt that my educational system had not taught me anything about this part of history and angry at myself for not making the effort to find out.[7]

One member of the delegation suggested that a suitable gesture of recompense for the Irish dead would be the restoration of the Guillemont cross. Harte had another idea. 'No, we will build a Round Tower,' he declared. The proposal was not received with any great enthusiasm by the travelling party. 'We cannot build a Round Tower,' came one response. Harte had made his mind up. 'Well we can always try.'[8]

On returning to Ireland, Harte and Barr set up the Journey of Reconciliation Trust. Messines was chosen as the site because of the battle of 1917 in which the 16th (Irish) Division and 36th (Ulster) Divisions fought side by side, though the site of the peace park was actually captured by the New Zealanders on 7 June 1917.

Messines town council identified a vacant site and the Belgian prime minister intervened to speed up the necessary planning permissions. A round tower was an inspired choice. It symbolised Ireland's brief tenure as the keeper of Western civilisation when the barbarians overran Europe after the fall of the Roman Empire in the fifth and sixth centuries and long before Ireland became the last battleground of the Reformation.

Harte's idea was not met with universal approval. At a meeting in the Somme Centre in Newtownards, County Down, one loyalist told Harte it was a 'Fenian tower'. It was no such thing and Harte had little difficulty persuading interested parties that a round tower was an appropriate, non-sectarian symbol.

In addition, by virtue of their height, they can dominate a landscape and command attention for miles around. His ambition was to build the round tower to a height of 100ft, as high as the one in Glendalough in County Wicklow, the best-known round tower of them all. Harte wanted a memorial that would 'last for centuries and be as meaningful in 500 years as when it was built'.[9]

It needed the right type of stone, which proved to be a challenge. The trust was on the verge of commissioning a quarry in Carlow when it had a lucky break. An old workhouse in Mullingar, built during the famine, was about to be demolished. The demolition provided 200 tons of weathered stone, which would give the new tower a suitably antique look from the start. The stones were packed and transported to Dublin on trains. Irish Ferries provided free transportation to mainland Europe and the stones arrived in Messines in August 1998.[10]

Funding the £IR500,000 (€635,000) cost was a daunting challenge. FÁS, the Irish training agency for trades, and the Training and Employment Agency in Belfast were invited to participate and accepted. The banking federation in Dublin chipped in £50,000, but the trust was still short of funds.

Harte went to the then Taoiseach John Bruton, a greater admirer of John Redmond. But Harte had a difficult relationship with Bruton and had resigned the whip in April 1995 over the issue of abortion, though he was subsequently readmitted to the party.[11]

Harte requested £IR150,000 (€190,000) from the Irish government and promised a similar figure from the Northern Ireland Office. Bruton baulked at the figure, offered £50,000 (€63,000) instead and suggested Harte build a smaller tower. Harte responded:

Yes, John. We could build it sixty feet, fifty feet or even forty feet, but we are not. We are going to build it the same height as Glendalough – 100 feet high. This is to remember the dead of the First World War who our tradition has forgotten and if it is the last thing I do, it will be done right.[12]

The Northern Ireland Office provided the cost of a project director and ancillary support services. Still short of the required money, Harte's fundraising efforts were interrupted by the Irish general election of the summer of 1997 in the Republic, which saw a change of government. After thirty-six years as a Dáil deputy for Donegal North-East, Harte lost his seat.

He was now out of office, but his idea was not out of favour. Help came from an unexpected source. Previous Fianna Fáil Taoisigh had been ambivalent about commemorating the Irish dead of the First World War, but Bertie Ahern had no such compunction. When he became Taoiseach in 1997, he placed the peace process at the top of his political agenda. He understood immediately the symbolic importance of the peace tower. To Harte's surprise, he turned up at a meeting, which was only supposed to be between Harte and Ahern's personal secretary. As Minister for Finance in the early 1990s, he earmarked money for the Irish National War Memorial Gardens in Islandbridge, now part of his re-shaped constituency.

He remembered, 'I went for a look around my new constituency in 1990 and I came across this derelict place. It was a disaster. The place was a disgrace. The whole front was blocked up. In three years I got it cleaned up, the graffiti off the monuments and got the drug pushers out along with the cats and dogs and the rats. I turned into a decent enough place.'[13]

As a leader of the Fianna Fáil opposition in 1996, he had met with the Royal Dublin Fusiliers Association and knew that the continued neglect of the Irish dead was unconscionable. He promised if he was ever Taoiseach to do something to remember the Irish dead of the First World War. 'That Dublin Fusiliers [meeting] really opened up for me how important it was to all those people. Out of all of this, Paddy Harte and Glen Barr came to me. They told me about Messines. They needed a few hundred grand and would I help them. I went with them.'

The two men suggested that President McAleese might attend the opening. Ahern agreed to ask her. Then they upped the ante. Barr suggested they ask Queen Elizabeth II too. Ahern interceded with the British Prime Minister Tony Blair. Blair asked and the Queen accepted. Barr insists that Ahern's active support made a huge difference to the project. 'A big lot of thanks goes to Bertie Ahern. He supported us 110 per cent. He was a statesman.'[14]

The invisible hand Mr Harte alluded to in his welcoming speech was working stealthily to get the park finished on time. Harte requested the Army No. 1 Band. The Irish Department of Defence demurred at the cost, but CIÉ stepped in and provided two coaches for the journey.

It rained incessantly in the days before the unveiling, but the day itself was dry. Everything came together just in time and the event was a triumph. Harte was justifiably proud of their work, as he recalled in his memoirs:

> It was a memorable day and a great historical occasion. It must rate as one of the most significant moments of true reconciliation between the peoples of Ireland and Great Britain in the last 80 years. Stories of people throughout Ireland, North and South, nationalist, unionist, loyalist and republican, who had watched the events with tears in their eyes were received by men and my family for months afterwards. People were overjoyed that at last the State had acknowledged the wrong and put it right. Many explained that they had a grandfather, an uncle or granduncle who fought and died. Some were getting to know for the first time about relatives who had died in the battle.[15]

The opening garnered universal praise. David Trimble, the then first minister of the Northern Ireland power-sharing executive, believed it would 'help to get rid of the anti-British element in Irish culture'.[16]

The Irish Times editorial observed:

> It is now 80 years since the guns fell silent. Yet it is only in the latter part of this, the last decade of the century, that it has been possible for the two great traditions of this island to recognise each other's sacrifice and pain in the terrible bloodletting of that war. The mythology of Protestant Ulster refused to recognise the contribution of those outside its own ethnic boundaries. And the ascendant spirit of Irish nationalism consigned to oblivion the tens of thousands of young men – its sons, brothers, fathers, uncles – who freely went to fight in Europe.[17]

John Downing wrote in the *Irish Independent* that, 'The round tower dedicated in Messines yesterday is more than a nostalgic mirror of a golden Celtic past. It is a strong pointer to the future, to an Ireland becoming more at ease with itself and its history, pluralist, tolerant, capable of accommodation and rejoicing in diversity. The whole exercise is a benign variety of recovered memory, of acknowledgement and repatriation.'[18]

Looking back on the fateful day, Bertie Ahern is convinced it would not have happened had the Good Friday Agreement not been signed. 'There was no possibility. If you are going to have a shared history and share our tradition and share our peace, you have to share the whole history of the war dead.'[19]

The opening of the tower had been a triumph over time, but corners had been cut to have it ready in time. Tree bark was placed on the ground where a lawn was supposed to be and small wooden boards were sunk into the ground to separate the gravel paths from the grass.

After the crowds left, the garlands of flowers withered and the park took on a dishevelled appearance. Kevin Myers feared it would become what the War Memorial Gardens at Islandbridge had been for many decades, a monument to forgetting, not remembering.

In June 2001, the Office of Public Works in the Republic and the Northern Ireland Construction Service agreed to take over the maintenance and landscaping of the park. It is now maintained on their behalf by the Commonwealth War Graves Commission with its usual dedication and professionalism. In 2005, the Messines Peace Village nearby was opened and thousands of schoolchildren from Northern Ireland have since spent time learning about conflict transformation and community relations.

The Island of Ireland Peace Park is stunning both in scale and beauty. It is not only the pre-eminent Irish war memorial, but one of the pre-eminent memorials on the entire Western Front. It commands views of the surrounding countryside, which resembles in places a typical Irish landscape.

The visitor is greeted firstly by the bronze plaque and granite stones recalling the opening of the park by President Mary McAleese. (It was not a joint opening with Queen Elizabeth II; she was a guest.) Another plaque remembers the Battle of Messines and reminds us that the terrain on which the park is built was seized not by the British or Irish but by the II Anzac Corps. Nine stone tables evoke the experience of the Irishmen involved in the war. One recalls Fr Francis Gleeson's appalled recollection of the aftermath of the Battle of Aubers Ridge:

> Spent all night trying to console, aid and remove the wounded. It was ghastly to see them lying there in the cold, cheerless outhouses, on bare stretchers with no blankets to cover their freezing limbs.

The last stanzas of Tom Kettle's poem 'To My Daughter Betty, The Gift of God' are also engraved on one of the tables. It also includes the words of the soldiers and writers Francis Ledwidge and Patrick MacGill.

Three upright edged slabs (monuments) represent each of the three Irish divisions and the casualties they suffered: the 36th (Ulster) Division (32,186 killed, wounded or missing), the 16th (Irish) Division (28,398) and the 10th (Irish) Division (9,363). Another granite slab lists all of the counties of Ireland in alphabetical order. Symbolically, they all run together. The tower opens out into a circular room in which there are copies of the eight-volume Irish National War Memorial Records. The room is topped with a conical roof that resembles an all-seeing eye. The tower is configured in such a way that the light only shines in through the upper window on 11 November every year.

McAleese believes the event had a 'cathartic' impact on remembrance of the Irish war dead. Though it took another thirteen years, she believes it was also a milestone that helped pave the way for the visit of Queen Elizabeth II to the Republic in 2011, the first such visit by a British monarch:

> There is an undoubted link between the two. The first presaged a new emerging form of mutuality between Ireland and Britain in which the contested elements of the past could be dealt with without jeopardising the present. The Queen's visit to Ireland indicated just how solid the foundations of this era of neighbourliness have become, how they rest on honesty about the past, generosity about the future, on shared stewardship of the peace process and a determination to keep the momentum moving in the direction of a respectful partnership between good neighbours. It has helped to create a platform of shared memory and shared commemoration in place of what was previously a contested zone. Wreath laying ceremonies at cenotaphs and memorials which were once symbolic of division and unresolved conflict have become the opposite. A new generosity and willingness to listen to one another's perspective became evident thanks to the persistence of those who brought the Island of Ireland peace park into existence. All over Ireland neglected stories of family members who had fought in the Great War were taken from attics and conscientiously used to help forge healthier bonds between those who in the present are crafting the pathway to a stable and peaceful future.[20]

Although the park symbolised all this hope and harmony, its two prime movers, in a blackly comic twist of irony, eventually fell out over some financial complications connected to the project. Barr and Harte did not speak for many years afterwards.

Barr says with some regret, 'It could only happen in Ireland that two men were friends for 20 years, started a journey of reconciliation trust and they haven't spoken since. Paddy was driving it all along. He was totally committed to it. Pulling him back at times was the problem. Unfortunately, there was a major disagreement over it. Our families were close together and unfortunately Paddy took one side of it and I took the other.'[21]

In his otherwise forthright autobiography, Harte never refers to Barr by name, but just calls him the 'Northern chairman', a curious omission. The dispute was over 'financial and ethical issues', he wrote, 'the details of which I do not feel it proper to record here'.[22]

The roots of the falling out was over money, Barr explained. He was running a young people's outreach programme at the time and had secured £84,000 in funding from the International Fund for Ireland to bring out teenagers from both sides of the border to carry out maintenance on the park at a time when Harte was still raising the money to finish the tower:

> Paddy felt that £84,000 should have gone towards the tower. Civil servants talked to him about it and told him that even if Glen Barr didn't get the £84,000,

he wouldn't have got it either because it was not for that programme. This money has been set aside for young people. We decided that this was the end. We've done the work in building the tower. My job was not finished because the tower only represents for me, anyway, that if we don't sit down and solve our problems through dialogue, this is how it ends up with memorials all over the place. That's not what we wanted. It is certainly a source of regret for me. We have lost so much and the story has lost so much because Paddy Harte and Glen Barr were driving this whole thing forward. We could have achieved so much more. Now others are jumping on the bandwagon and claiming credit for work that we had done, but Paddy and I have a lot to be proud of together. It was just an unfortunate situation.[23]

However, they did speak by phone in 2015, though Harte has not been well for many years. Both men were given a joint award in Donegal in the autumn of 2015, one of multiple awards the pair have won for their work on the peace park. Paddy Harte Jr picked up the prize on his father's behalf.

Perhaps the greatest praise accorded to Harte came from the man who demoted him as a junior minister in 1982, the former Taoiseach Garret FitzGerald. Both of his parents had fought in the GPO, but FitzGerald had similarly devoted his career to reconciliation between Protestant and Catholic Ireland. In *The Irish Times* on the morning after the unveiling of the Island of Ireland Peace Park, FitzGerald wrote:

In no way would I diminish the role of Glen Barr as Paddy Harte's generous partner in this project, but it was Paddy who tackled and transmuted into something more open and generous the single-track mind-set which had gripped nationalist public opinion between 1916 and 1918, wiping out the memory of all that had gone before. Since I came to know him a third of century ago Paddy Harte has had one agenda: the reconciliation of nationalist and unionist. And he has pursued it so undeviatingly that he ruled himself out of mainstream politics. For politics is a stormy sea, traversed by frail vessels under sail, which must constantly tack to and fro to reach its destination. And Paddy's vision has been so fixed on that far shore that he has had no time for tacking. Nationalist Ireland now has the capacity to understand and accept the points of view of both the majority and the minority of nationalists in August 1914. We don't have to take sides any longer, to identify with either Redmond or Pearse. Both played valid roles and can now be accepted side by side in our Irish Pantheon. As this climactic century approaches its close, our State has reached maturity.[24]

On this spot was killed
the Irish poet and soldier

Op deze plek sneuvelde
de Ierse dichter-soldaat

FRANCIS LEDWIDGE

° Slane 19 august 1887 / † Boezinge 31 july 1917

He shall not hear
the bittern cry
In the wild sky,
where he is lain

Hij zal de roerdomp
niet horen roepen
in de wilde lucht,
waar hij ligt

20

THE MONUMENT TO FRANCIS LEDWIDGE

There is only one standalone monument on the Western Front to an Irishman who died fighting in the First World War. Appropriately, it is dedicated to Francis Ledwidge, the poet and soldier from a family of poets and soldiers who was killed during the first day of the Battle of Passchendaele on 31 July 1917.

His memorial, made of the distinctive yellow Ypres brick, marks the exact spot where he fell, near the village of Boezinge, directly north of Ypres. His grave is a further 200 yards down a cycle track in Artillery Road Cemetery.

Ledwidge was not killed in the line of fire, but by a German shell that blew him to pieces while his battalion, the 1st Royal Inniskilling Fusiliers, was laying duckboards for the 29th Division.

Duckboards, wooden paths to keep soldiers from floundering in the mud, would become the leitmotif of the Battle of Passchendaele. When the battle started, so did the rain and it continued to pour down day after day. Australian photographer Frank Hurley captured the best-known image of the battle – perhaps of the whole war – at Chateau Wood near Ypres during the Battle of Passchendaele. It depicts Australian soldiers traversing a ghostly moonscape of flooded craters and blasted trees on duckboards. It is a scene of utter desolation.[1]

In his short life, Ledwidge had sought to rise above his status as the son of a farm labourer. He might have been fated for an anonymous life of manual toil but for a modicum of education and the intervention of his aristocratic patron Lord Dunsany. Ledwidge instead became a poet of no little renown during his lifetime. It remains a poignant irony that he died doing the sort of labouring work that was the duty of the unschooled army private. Five comrades in his battalion died with him.

The inscription on his memorial at Ypres is the first verse of his own poem, 'Lament for Thomas MacDonagh'. Written in the aftermath of the Easter Rising executions, it became Ledwidge's most famous poem. Before the war, he had befriended MacDonagh, one of the seven signatories of the Proclamation. MacDonagh was killed by firing squad on 3 May 1916. Ledwidge subsequently penned the poem, which contains these immortal opening lines:

> He shall not hear the bittern cry
> In the wild sky where he is lain
> Nor voices of the sweeter birds
> Above the wailing of the rain.

This poem became familiar to later generations of Irish schoolchildren as part of the official curriculum. It chimed perfectly with the new state's glorification of nationalist revolutionaries. Ledwidge's own death in a British uniform was overlooked, lest it complicate the narrative.[2]

The bittern is a shy bird with a loud, booming voice that once haunted the bogs of Ireland. The choice of bird was deliberate. Thomas MacDonagh had translated the old Gaelic poem '*An Bonnán Buí*' ('The Yellow Bittern') from Irish into English. The original is a lament for a bittern which, unable to penetrate a frozen lake to get a drink, dies of thirst.

As much as Ledwidge's poem was a tribute to a lost friend, it was also an elegy for all those young lives cut short in those violent times. 'Lament for Thomas MacDonagh' could also be read as a foretelling of his own demise. He had seen so many other Irishmen who would no longer hear the bittern cry and he knew he might soon be among them. The Nobel Laureate Seamus Heaney observed, 'It is a poem in which his displaced hankering for the place beyond confusion and his own peculiar melancholy voice finds a subject which exercises them entirely, no doubt because in lamenting MacDonagh he was to a large extent lamenting himself.'[3]

Ledwidge is buried near the poet Hedd Wyn, a Welsh nationalist who railed against the war at its beginning, but signed up, as Ledwidge had done. He too was killed on the first day of the Battle of Passchendaele.[4]

Francis Ledwidge embodied all the contemporary contradictions in Irish politics and Irish identity. He was an Irish nationalist and a supporter of the GAA and the Gaelic League who had joined the Irish Volunteers. He initially publicly opposed John Redmond's call for Irishmen to join the British army and yet signed up six days later.

But the Easter Rising and its savage aftermath left Ledwidge feeling utterly conflicted by his status as a British soldier. Heaney alluded to this turmoil of identity and loyalty in his 1979 poem 'In Memoriam Francis Ledwidge':

> In you, our dead enigma, all the strains
> Criss-cross in useless equilibrium
> And as the wind tunes through this vigilant bronze
> I hear again the sure confusing drum
>
> You followed from Boyne water to the Balkans
> But miss the twilit note your flute should sound.
> You were not keyed or pitched like these true-blue ones
> Though all of you consort now underground.[5]

Francis Edward Ledwidge was born into poverty in Slane, County Meath, on 19 August 1887. In his heart and mind, he never left this beautifully situated village overlooking the Boyne Valley, though he was compelled by force of circumstance to travel further than most British soldiers in the First World War. 'I am always homesick,' he wrote to the novelist Katharine Tynan in 1917. 'I hear the roads calling, and the hills, and the rivers wondering where I am. It is terrible to be always homesick.'[6]

Ledwidge was the second youngest of nine children. His younger brother Joe recalled in a 1959 Radio Éireann documentary, 'We grew up together and we were always very close to each other. He was very intelligent and he learned very easily. When he was only in the junior grade at school, he was writing poetry. He was helped in this by the oldest member of the family Pat who was a monitor in the school.'[7]

The children grew up with ancestral memories of a proud family who once upon a time had owned substantial lands around Meath. 'I have heard my mother say many times,' he recalled, 'that the Ledwidges were once a great people in the land and she has shown me, with a sweep of her hand, green hills and wide valleys where sheep are folded … and this was all ours.'[8]

His father Patrick was a respectable labourer who worked hard to provide for his family. In the late nineteenth century, they moved into a sturdy little labourer's cottage in Janesville, outside Slane on the main road to Drogheda, which stands to this day and has been converted into a museum. The Ledwidges valued education more than anything else.[9]

Francis's oldest brother Patrick Jr was the first autodidact in the family. He was a monitor in the local national school, the equivalent of a teaching assistant, and had plans to become a teacher. His poems were published in local newspapers. He helped Francis in his reading and writing, fostering a love of language and a love of nature and place.

The family was convulsed by the death of Patrick Snr at the age of 52. Francis was 4 at the time. While their material circumstances had always been precarious, they were now frighteningly exposed to want and penury. Patrick's widow Anne was left to bring up their family alone. Her options were severely limited. She could have put her family in a workhouse but instead took what work she could find, in the fields or in the home, to support her children. 'My mother laboured day and night as none of us were strong enough to provide for our own wants,' Francis Ledwidge recalled. 'She never complained and even when my eldest brother advanced in strength she persisted in his regular attendance at school until he qualified at book-keeping and left home for Dublin.'[10]

Patrick became the main breadwinner, but another devastating tragedy occurred three years later when he died from tuberculosis, a widespread killer in Ireland at the time. It was a desperate time for the family. 'Oh, those four years,' Francis stated years later. 'It was as though God forgot us.' Only the local doctor saved the family from eviction when the bailiff and police attempted to eject them for non-payment of rent.

Francis Ledwidge had to leave school at 13, his bright career in formal education over. He worked as a farm labourer, a shop assistant and then as a miner in the local copper mines. He was already composing verse. His poems were first published in the *Drogheda Independent* when he was 14.[11]

At 16, he got a job as a grocer's assistant in Rathfarnham in south County Dublin. He did not last long. Though only 30 miles from Slane, he was so homesick that he lifted the latch on his lodgings and walked all the way home to get away from the 'city's strife and din'. A job in the Beauparc copper mine near Navan accelerated the development of a growing social conscience. He was appalled by the conditions they were obliged to endure. He was fired in 1911 for trying to organise the workers. He also held the position of general secretary of the Slane branch of the Meath Labour Union Approved Society. This would lead to his co-option on to the Navan Board of Guardians and Navan Rural District Council.[12]

All the while, Ledwidge was pursuing his poetic vocation. In 1912, he wrote to Lord Dunsany, himself a publisher of fantasy novels, seeking encouragement for his verse. Dunsany was a member of the prominent Plunkett family which included St Oliver Plunkett and Joseph Mary Plunkett, another of the seven signatories of the Proclamation. The family was both Catholic and Church of Ireland. Dunsany was from the Anglican side. He was a prolific writer – the author of some eighty books – and the heir to Dunsany Castle in County Meath. He had the money to indulge his art. Ledwidge's writings were in a series of copy books. There were elemental errors of spelling and grammar and plentiful examples of a nascent poetic talent trying too hard, such as 'thwart the rolling foam' and 'waiting for my true love on the lea'.

Nevertheless, Dunsany recognised the makings of a substantial talent. Ledwidge had that 'easy fluency of shapely lines which is now so noticeable in all he writes; that and sudden glimpses of the fields that he seems at time to bring so near to one that one exclaims. I was astonished by the brilliance of that eye that had looked at the fields of Meath and seen there all the simple birds and flowers, with a vividness that made those pages like a magnifying glass, through which one looked at familiar things seen thus for the first time. I wrote to him greeting him as a true poet, which indeed he was.'[13]

Dunsany gave him the run of his extensive library; he introduced him to the work of Keats and Shelley, among many others. Keats, in particular, would become a big influence on Ledwidge's later work. Dunsany also used his contacts to further Ledwidge's career. Dunsany ensured that Ledwidge's poem 'Low Moon Land' was published in the London-based *Saturday Review*, thus finding him a new and much bigger audience. Ledwidge was pleasantly startled by the fee he received.

Dunsany's enthusiasm for Ledwidge never wavered. His praise of the young poet was published in the *Freeman's Journal*: 'England today has hardly anyone to beat him and few to equal him'.[14] A syndicated profile of him was published in twenty-seven English newspapers in March 1914. 'All this helps to make one famous, and fame is a fulcrum upon which a man may rest and overturn worlds,' Ledwidge wrote to a female admirer, Alice Curtayne.[15]

An English publisher, Herbert Jenkins, agreed to publish his first volume of verse *Songs of the Fields*, with a preface by Dunsany. In August 1914, the Cork-based *Southern Star* reported a conversation with Ledwidge's unnamed brother in

Manchester. Francis Ledwidge, according to his brother, was a 'mastermind' and a 'fine natural genius'. Francis was beginning to believe it himself. His head was turned. He grew his hair long. He developed affectations.

However, poetry still could not give him a living. But his profile probably helped get him a job as a full-time union official with the Meath branch of the county labour unions, implementing the State Insurance Act.[16]

The more promising things looked for Ledwidge, the more the wider world intervened. In the summer of 1914, Ledwidge responded to the call for Irish Volunteers. He and his brother Joe set up the Slane corps. Weeknights and weekends were spent drilling and training with what weapons were available. Poet, union organiser, Irish Volunteer, Ledwidge had escaped his impoverished roots to become a man of some importance. His love life, though, was much more problematic.

The Ledwidges and the Vaugheys were family friends. The Vaughey children were from a well-off family by the standards of the time – they owned much of the Hill of Slane – but had been left orphans at a young age. Ellie Vaughey worked in Drogheda and would take Ledwidge's poems with her and bring them to the *Drogheda Independent* to be published. She became the love of his life. He would not be the first nor the last poet to find unrequited love a greater muse than the requited version.[17]

Ellie Vaughey indulged his attentions, but marriage was a different matter. She came from a propertied family. Ledwidge, despite his growing public reputation, had only his art. She instead began to court another local man, John O'Neill. Ledwidge wrote to a friend in January 1914, 'A maiden's heart is the same: you may think it is a jewel but touch it with the tender words of love, and immediately the reptile burst forth, and you are lost, lost.'

Heartbroken and in turmoil, he turned his romantic attentions to 20-year-old Lizzie Healy, the sister of Paddy Healy, the school teacher in Slane.

Professionally in the ascendant, with his personal life in turmoil. This was how Francis Ledwidge's life looked on the brink of the great cataclysm.

———

Like millions of others, Ledwidge's life was changed and significantly shortened the day war broke out. Ledwidge accepted the exhortation by John Redmond for the volunteers to 'defend the shores of Ireland from a foreign invasion'. It was their own country after all. But Redmond's call for the Irish Volunteers to go overseas and fight for the British was too much.

Ledwidge sided against Redmond in his call for the Irish to go overseas. At the Navan Rural District Council meeting of October 1914, he was unmoved by calls that the 'young men of Meath would be better fighting on the fields of France for the future of Ireland'. He accused the British army of duplicity, of saying one thing to unionists and another to nationalists. Irishmen were being asked to defend

Belgium, but Belgium was an anti-clerical country and had treated German prisoners badly. He responded bitterly to allegations that he was pro-German. 'I *am* an anti-German and an Irishman'.

In October 1914, he was reported by the *Irish Independent* to have voted against Redmond and sided with Eoin MacNeill, the founder of the Irish Volunteers, who had split from Redmond. 'Mr Ledwidge thought the proper men to follow at present are those who started the movement and not Mr Redmond. They had to think how uncertain they were still of getting Home Rule'.[18]

Five days later, Ledwidge walked into Richmond Barracks in Dublin and joined Dunsany's regiment. This quite astonishing *volte-face* has perplexed Ledwidge scholars for the last century. Why would he enlist when only days before he had been publicly against the British war effort? In the month before he died, Ledwidge wrote a letter to Professor Lewis Chase of the University of Wisconsin explaining his decision:

> I joined the British army because she stood between Ireland and an enemy common to our civilisation and I would not have her say that she defended us while we did nothing at home, but pass resolutions.[19]

But this *post-facto* justification was made almost three years later. Could it be that Ledwidge gave political reasons for a decision that was fundamentally personal? Ledwidge's biographer Alice Curtayne believes a broken heart may have been just as compelling a reason because Ledwidge wrote in June 1914:

> I'm wild for wandering to the far-off places.
> Since one forsook me whom I held most dear.[20]

His pre-war existence was precarious. His position as an insurance agent was only temporary and was not being renewed. His attempt to get a job as a journalist had failed. There was no vacancy at the *Drogheda Independent*. He was stung when he was labelled pro-German, a singular insult in the context of the time.

Another theory for his U-turn is that he had been persuaded by his great mentor to enlist. Curtayne was the first to address the myth that Dunsany had anything to do it. Dunsany himself, far from attempting to recruit his friend, Dunsany had offered Ledwidge a stipend to stay behind and work on his poetry. Dunsany was a veteran of the Boer War. He knew what war was like. Seamus Heaney observed, 'To see him [Ledwidge] as the dupe of a socially superior and politically insidious West British toff is to underrate his intelligence, his independence and the consciously fatal nature of his decision to enlist.'[21]

Ledwidge joined the 5th Inniskillings but, whatever the confluence of reasons that brought him to his fateful decision, Lord Dunsany does not appear to have been a contributing influence.

Ledwidge enjoyed a period of contentment during his first few months of training in Ireland. He was well fed and enjoyed the comradeship of the army. He handed
over half of his private's pay to his dear mother. Later letters home would note
that the war was not going to be over quickly and, even while still based in Ireland,
he was 'drifting far away from Slane, far, far'.[22] Ledwidge was quickly appointed to
lance corporal, the lowest level of non-commissioned officer.

In November 1914, Ellie Vaughey married John O'Neill in the local church at
Slane. Ledwidge was disconsolate. He again turned his attentions to Lizzie Healy.
'I am always too lonesome. I can think of nothing but Slane and the quiet peace
of the homeways, and you.'[23]

Like most of those who signed up in 1914, Ledwidge assumed he would be
fighting in France or Belgium, yet his battalion left Ireland in April 1915 bound
for Gallipoli. Successive battalions marched down the quays in Dublin and were
cheered with every step until the naval ships sailed out to sea. As the 10th (Irish)
Division to which Ledwidge's battalion was attached headed for the shores of
Gallipoli, the first reports appeared in the Irish newspapers about the initial landings. These reports gave only scant indication of the bloody disaster that had
ensued and of the disproportionate toll on Irish troops. The 1st battalions of the
Royal Dublin, Royal Munster and Royal Inniskilling Fusiliers all took heavy casualties, but no reports surfaced in the newspapers. Ledwidge's battalion was shipped
first to England and then to Gallipoli with the rest of the 10th (Irish) Division.

Ledwidge was still dreaming of Ireland as his ship, the SS *Novian*, made its slow
way to Gallipoli. The initial journey was pleasant, but the temperature rose as the ship
headed southwards and the summer sun grew stronger. Ledwidge's homesickness
grew with every nautical mile. Before he left, he received news that Ellie, his first
love, had died in childbirth in 1915 after emigrating with her husband to Manchester.
He missed Slane like a sharp pain and wrote the poem 'The Heights of Crocknaharna'
for his mother. Guilt assailed his conscience. How could he leave his mother who
had already suffered an ocean of grief over the deaths of her husband and eldest son?

> On an evening dim and misty
> Of a cold November day,
> There I heard a woman weeping
> In the brown rocks and the grey.
> Oh, the pearl of Crocknaharna
> (Crocknaharna, Crocknaharna),
> Black with grief is Crocknaharna
> Twenty hundred miles away.

Ledwidge's spirits lifted as the ship sailed into the eastern Mediterranean and his
ship turned north, passing by the ancient site of Troy. On the island of Lesbos, his

battalion transferred from the *Novian* to the cruiser HMS *Heroic* and began their journey to Suvla Bay.

Off Suvla Bay, the men waited for hours in sweltering heat to board the black-coloured motorised lighters known as 'beetles' that would bring them to shore. This semi-circular bay with promontories like a cow's horns was the embarkation point for the division. It fronted a dried-out salt lake and, behind that, in the heights above, thousands of Turkish soldiers lay in wait. The 5th Inniskillings was part of 31th Brigade, which was tasked with taking Chocolate Hill, a low hill of 'rocks and shrub, resembling the lower slopes of Ticknock'.[24]

Ledwidge's first experiences of war were both terrifying and exhilarating. His regiment was constantly repulsed but continued rallying. 'It was a horrible and great day. I would not have missed it for the world.' His exhilaration would not survive the first major assault by the 10th (Irish) Division on Turkish positions. Lady Day, the Feast of the Assumption of the Blessed Virgin into Heaven was on 15 August. Slane would be looking its best, the houses limewashed for the visitors who would come for miles around to the holy well in the village.

Ledwidge, however, did not have time to dwell on thoughts of home. His D Company was involved in the assault on Kiretch Tepe Ridge. Soon he was immersed in outright carnage. Some 170 of D Company's 250 men were casualties. The company had captured its position but 'when we handed it over to our reinforcements and retired for a rest we were a jaded and sorry few'. Ledwidge survived Gallipoli. It had been an inferno of death and hideous injury, unending thirst, flies, dead bodies putrefying in the summer heat and atrocious setbacks. The smell of the putrefying bodies would linger in their nostrils long afterwards.

The failure of the Suvla Bay offensive was the effective end of the Gallipoli campaign, but it took three months to wind down, by which time Ledwidge and the rest of the 10th (Irish) Division were long gone. Now they were converging on a place that had figured in nobody's calculations as a battleground – Salonika. The British sent the 10th (Irish) Division as a diplomatic sop to the French who had landed in modern-day Thessaloniki in Greece to assist the Serbians. The entry of Bulgaria on the side of the Central Powers had created a new front. All the British had to offer was a broken division commanded by a querulous senior officer, General Sir Bryan Mahon, who had abandoned his men at one stage and was heartily detested by his senior commander General Sir Ian Hamilton.

This strange landscape of minarets and snowy mountains was the antithesis of the heat and intensity of Gallipoli. The men found themselves separated from civilisation in the high mountains on the border between modern-day Greece and Macedonia. The weather turned cold; the men had only their summer uniforms and slept under greatcoats at night. The big Irish engagement of the Salonika campaign was fought at the Battle of Kosturino on 7 December 1915.[25] Ledwidge recalled, 'God only knows how I escaped the fields of the Bulgars. I saw horrors there that must have made the soul of Dante envious.'[26]

The men were deprived of many necessities in this isolated wilderness but their mail still got through. The only solace in this ordeal for Ledwidge was the day he received a copy of his first collection of poetry, *Songs of the Fields*, which was finally published in 1915, after a year's delay.

He was understandably delighted, but his pleasure was tempered by the realisation that many of these poems were years old and he had evolved as a poet in the meantime. They also harkened back to a more innocent time before the war. 'I wish the damn war would end,' he wrote to Dunsany. 'We are all sick for the old countries.' He signed off to Dunsany, 'You know how grateful I am.'[27]

Salonika was a trial for him. Too hot in summer, too cold in winter, the extremes of the Balkan climate were a hell for the Tommies in comparison with the familiar temperate climates of Flanders and northern France. Ledwidge suffered rheumatism as a result of exposure. 'The nights when not raining are freezing and one wonders which is the worst for the pains.'[28]

The great retreat of the 10th (Irish) Division was a six-day ordeal in the winter of 1915 from Macedonia back over the mountainous border into neutral Greece. It was the end of Ledwidge's Eastern campaign. His back gave in and he was evacuated to Cairo. Ledwidge spent four months in a hospital bed in Egypt. All the time he was thinking about home and his mother:

> She came unto the hills and saw the change
> That brings the swallow and the geese in turns.
> But there was not a grief she deeméd strange,
> For there is that in her which always mourns.
>
> Kind heart she has for all on hill or wave
> Whose hopes grew wings like ants to fly away.
> I bless the God who such a mother gave
> This poor bird-hearted singer of a day.[29]

Ledwidge was finally transferred to Manchester in April 1916, the most fateful month in modern Irish history. He was discharged from hospital the day the Easter Rising broke out in Dublin and was prevented from returning home. He had not been back to Ireland in twelve months, a year he described succinctly as 'hell, hell, hell'.[30]

Ledwidge was stunned by the Rising. The actions of the leaders, in an initially unpopular rebellion, had recast the whole relationship between Ireland and Britain. Long before history would deliver its varied verdicts, Ledwidge understood deeply and presciently the significance of the Rising. His friends Thomas

MacDonagh and Joseph Plunkett had been executed by the British army. In his poem 'O'Connell Street', he wrote:

> A noble failure is not vain
> But hath a victory of its own.
> A bright delectance from the slain
> Is down the generations thrown.
> And, more than Beauty understands
> Has made her lovelier here, it seems;
> I see white ships that crowd her strands,
> For mine are all the dead men's dreams.

Such sentiments from a serving British soldier could have seen him court-martialled had they been published. Ledwidge was utterly depressed by the situation in Ireland, confiding to his brother Joe, 'If I heard the Germans were coming in over our back wall, I wouldn't go out now to stop them. They could come.'[31]

He was therefore in a disconsolate mood when he answered back to a commanding officer after overstaying his leave. He lost his lance-corporal's stripe. 'The present is a dream I see of horror and loud sufferings,' he wrote in the poem 'After Court Martial'. Ledwidge was heartily sick of the war at this stage and regretting his decision to join.

He had some respite from the front line after the Rising when he was posted to Ebrington Barracks in Derry, where Dunsany was based for most of the rest of 1916. There he assembled the poems for his second collection, sadly published posthumously, entitled *Songs of Peace*. Four poems in the collection dealt with the Easter Rising. The event and its aftermath would obsess Ledwidge.

In late 1916, he transferred from the 5th Royal Inniskilling Fusiliers to the 1st Inniskilling Fusiliers and so to the 29th Division. The 'Incomparables', as the men of the division called themselves, had been to Gallipoli and to the Somme. It was an experienced outfit. In December, he joined his regiment north of Amiens. That summer, Ledwidge's unit had been ordered north for the Battle of Passchendaele. The 29th Division was located in Boezinge in full view of the enemy. Shelling was frequent and deadly. The months and weeks advanced towards the 'big push'. The men were cheered by the success of the Battle of Messines Ridge and believed a breakthrough could be made with minimal effort.

As the days closed in on the battle, Ledwidge wrote his last poems home. In one of these, 'To A German Officer', he acknowledges the common humanity he shares with his enemy:

> And greater peace than swords have fought
> Flashing in emprises divine

Shuts up their memories in one thought
That hears the quiet waves of the Rhine.

The Battle of Passchendaele began at 3.30 a.m. on 31 July 1917. The 29th Division was in the reserve of XIV Corps, commanded by the Earl of Cavan. All along the 11-mile front the British made considerable early progress. The main attack was led by Sir Hubert Gough's Fifth Army. Early gains were encouraging but then the rains came and did not relent for weeks on end. The ground had been ploughed by shellfire, the water table disturbed, the drainage system destroyed. All the British preparations were confounded by the one variable that could never be controlled – the weather. Passchendaele became a muddy abyss. Soldiers drowned in mudholes. Guns became lodged in the bottomless sludge. Further progress was impossible.

Francis Ledwidge and the rest of his crew were laying duckboards towards the captured heights of Pilckem Ridge when they were killed by a shell early in the afternoon of 31 July. The Jesuit chaplain Fr Francis Devas was quickly on the scene. He wrote in his diary, 'Crowds at Holy Communion. Arrange for services but washed out by rain and fatigues. Walk in rains and dogs. Ledwidge killed, blown to bits.'[32]

Ledwidge's death was an unmitigated tragedy, which, along with those of Tom Kettle and Major Willie Redmond, deprived Ireland of three generously spirited men of vision. Devas wrote to Ledwidge's mother. He told a shattered Anne Ledwidge that her son had died 'before the world had been able to spoil him with its praise and he has found far greater joy and beauty then ever he would have found on Earth'.[33] His mother saw her son in a vision a short time afterwards. She leaned over to place his hand on her shoulder but his shade disappeared before she could touch him.

His old friend Matty McGoona also thought he saw Francis strolling down the streets of Navan a few days after he died.[34]

Dunsany was disconsolate. Loyal and supportive of Ledwidge to the end, he wrote of his death:

He nearly always wrote of the fields and lanes of his own beloved home, and even when in Serbia or Salonika, Gallipoli, Egypt, France or Belgium, up to the end some happy inspiration guided homeward his dreams, so that even in those far lands, even at war, he wrote of his wild birds and wild roses, and equally wayward loves, as truly as when leaning out at evening to watch the chaffinches from the window he loved. The enemy that laid the gun that killed Ledwidge, if it were not aimed by Fate before the beginning of things, did more for Kaiserism, the antithesis of all things beautiful, than any shell they fired at Rheims Cathedral.[35]

What if Ledwidge had survived the war? Dunsany believed his fame would have 'surpassed even Burns and Ireland would have lawfully claimed, as she may do even yet, the greatest of peasant singers'.[36]

A contemporary English poet, John Drinkwater, observed, 'His poetry exults me, while not so his death … to those who know what poetry is, the untimely death of a man like Ledwidge is nothing but calamity.'[37]

Some time in the early 1990s, a visitor to Artillery Wood Cemetery wrote Ledwidge's 'Crocknaharna' into the visitor's book and signed it 'F.E. Ledwidge'. The cemetery caretaker brought it to the attention of Piet Chielens, a writer and First World War historian. Intrigued, Chielens bought a copy of *The Ledwidge Treasury*. 'That was the first I ever heard of Francis Ledwidge. I was pleasantly surprised. Little by little I got to know the story historically.'

Chielens became the head of In Flanders Fields in 1996, the permanent exhibition on the First World War, in Ypres' architectural masterpiece, the Cloth Hall. So many men of stature died in Ypres over the four years that an individual memorial to each of them would have been logistically unfeasible and politically unsustainable. Individual memorials were not encouraged by the authorities, but there were rare exceptions.

A memorial was erected in 1997 to Dr Noel Chavasse, the only double Victoria Cross winner of the war. He died during the Battle of Passchendaele just five days after Ledwidge. There is a memorial also to the composer and poet Ivor Gurney, who was gassed at Ypres but survived the war only to die of tuberculosis in 1937. That memorial was erected in 2007.

The local community would make an exception for Francis Ledwidge too. The people of Flanders have a particular affinity with Ireland. Chielens explains, 'In Flanders, we've always had an eye on Ireland and how things develop there. There is a real sensitivity over that. From my personal background, I knew Redmond's grave already as a kid. I lived only four kilometres from there.'

Ledwidge was chosen because of his reputation as a poet and because of his conflicted identity as an Irish nationalist and British soldier.

Chielens contacted the Irish novelist Dermot Bolger, who had compiled the *Selected Poems of Francis Ledwidge* (introduced by Seamus Heaney in 1993). Bolger had made the journey to Slane as a 20-year-old, long-haired devotee of the poet. It was a short journey for the Dubliner, but a personal pilgrimage nonetheless. Bolger was haunted by the memory of Ledwidge then and remains in thrall to his story.

Bolger wrote in *A Tree for Francis Ledwidge*:

To me he represents the thousands of unremembered Irish ghosts from that war walking home to every corner of Ireland – men whose experiences were not spoken about in Ireland, even among their families. As I get older I often think about Ledwidge, of the futures he missed, how he never owned a house or had a wife or children. After he died his face became trapped in time. Like other War poets he stares out from a few photographs, condemned to the limbo of being forever young. But like thousands of fellow Irishmen who fought in the war he was condemned to another limbo. Rupert Brooke's death immortalised him, just like the Canadian poet, John

McCrea, is immortalized by his poem, In Flanders Fields, featuring on the Canadian $10 bill. Their posthumous reputation is simple, with no legacy of divided loyalties. They were never viewed as traitors, their stories never blotted from their country's collective memory. But only in recent years is the Irish experience of the Great War being fully explored and viewed as part of a healing process where Irishmen from different political convictions who shared the same fate are jointly remembered.[38]

The monument to Ledwidge was unveiled on 31 July 1998. The guest of honour was Joe Ledwidge, the poet's nephew, who spoke afterwards at a ceremony in Boezinge. He brought some soil from the family home at Janeville, Slane, and brought back some of the soil of Flanders. The Slane museum to Ledwidge now includes an exact replica of the memorial in Ypres.

On the monument, beneath the lines from the 'Lament for Thomas MacDonagh', are verses from another of his poems, 'Soliloquy'. Here too Ledwidge writes in anticipation of his young death and the thwarted life that would not be lived. In his letter to Lewis Chase, Ledwidge pleaded for understanding of the dilemma being called 'a British soldier while my own country has no place among the nations but the place of Cinderella'.

In writing of his own fate, he was speaking on behalf, too, of all the millions of other men who would never return to their beloved homelands:

> It is too late now to retrieve
> A fallen dream, too late to grieve
> A name unmade, but not too late
> To thank the gods for what is great;
> A keen-edged sword, a soldier's heart,
> Is greater than a poet's art.
> And greater than a poet's fame
> A little grave that has no name
> Whence honour turns away in shame.

In July 2016 the then Deputy First Minister of Northern Ireland Martin McGuinness unveiled a bronze bust to Ledwidge at Richmond Barracks in Dublin. Ledwidge had trained at the barracks before going to the front and it was also the location where the leaders of the Easter Rising were sentenced to death. McGuinness said Ledwidge was part of the complicated narrative of Irish history and that his story and that of many thousands of Irishmen had been the subject of a 'national amnesia'. McGuinness paid a visit to Ledwidge's grave during a visit to the Western Front in 2016. He described it as a 'very emotional occasion'.

This chapter is dedicated to my mother, Chris McGreevy, who passed away during its writing.

THE STONE MEMORIAL AT FREZENBERG RIDGE

More even than the Somme, the Battle of Passchendaele would leave a lingering bitterness that has never dissipated. The images of man and beast floundering in suffocating mud would define not just this battle, but the First World War in the popular imagination. Tens of thousands of men died because British generals lacked the moral courage to call off the whole doomed enterprise. As the military historian John Keegan observed of the British commander-in-chief Field Marshal Sir Douglas Haig:

> In his public manner and private diaries no concern for human suffering was or is discernible. At the Somme he had sent the flower of British youth to death or mutilation; at Passchendaele he had tipped the survivors into the slough of despond.[1]

Passchendaele was originally known as the Flanders northern operation to distinguish it from Messines Ridge (southern operation). Once Messines Ridge was secured, it was planned to break out of the 15-mile salient surrounding Ypres which had been a giant gaol for the British army. The Fifth Army would then capture the critical railway junction of Roulers, the supply centre for the Germans in Flanders. Haig had anticipated this operation would take about a week to be followed by an amphibious landing off the Belgian coast by the Fourth Army to catch the high tides of 7 and 8 August 1917.[2]

Even if the plan did not succeed, Haig reasoned it would still be worthwhile. Because of manpower shortages, the Germans had abandoned much of their own frontline positions in France to establish the Hindenburg Line, a new series of fortifications built well behind the original front line that were easier to defend. They surrendered territory which had no strategic value, but they could not take a step back in Flanders. Any retreat from Flanders would see them surrender the advantageous ground that had kept the British pinned into the Ypres salient. If the British pressed the assault, the Germans would have to fight.

Prime Minister David Lloyd George believed Haig had a cavalier disregard for the lives of the men under his command. Haig only cared about casualties so far as they hindered his plans. He was single-minded to the point of being indifferent to the fate of his men so long as they served the greater end. Victory could only be won, he emphasised again and again, by engaging the main enemy in the main theatre of battle. In his *War Memoirs*, published in 1931, which eviscerated Haig's posthumous reputation (he died in 1928), Lloyd George bitterly recounted not following his own judgment on the matter of Passchendaele.

> Ought I to have vetoed it? Ought I not to have resigned than acquiesce in this slaughter of brave men? I have always felt there are solid grounds for criticism in that respect. My sole justification is that Haig promised not to press the attack if it became clear that he could not attain his objectives by continuing the offensive.[3]

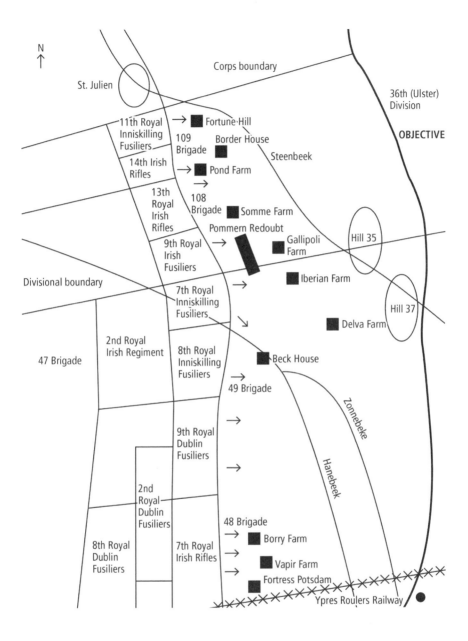

The land to be seized was a semi-circle series of mounds around Ypres. To call them hills would be stretching it. 'The minor ridges, so-called, are really no more than "rises" and the valleys shallow depression,' the British official history of the war concluded. At its highest elevation it was just 260ft.[4] The village of Passchendaele stood at the top of a ridge 8 miles from the centre of Ypres. It marked the furthest point of the German defence in depth. After that it was open countryside. The area contested at Passchendaele was once swamp land that had been reclaimed in the Middle Ages. It is crisscrossed by canals and rivers which are more like streams. The water table is only a few feet below the surface. The soil was a mixture of sand and clay and turned to the consistency of porridge after heavy rain.

Many factors contributed to the six-week delay between Messines Ridge and the start of Passchendaele, known then as the Third Battle of Ypres. The first was the familiar logistical difficulties of moving men and materiel to the front, the second was ensuring that the French were on board. Their commitment was uncertain given the mutiny after the Nivelle Offensive of May 1917 and only confirmed the week before the battle started as was the support, reluctantly given, of the British war cabinet.

———

After their triumph at Messines Ridge, the two Irish divisions, the 16th (Irish) Division and 36th (Ulster) Division, moved across the border to the French town of St Omer. Away from the cramped, unsanitary trenches and the constant deafening din of artillery, the troops took their respite. These were days remembered with fondness by the men in both divisions. The weather was beautiful, the training for the coming offensive not too taxing.

'The men were soaked in sunshine,' wrote Cyril Falls, the historian of the 36th. 'The division probably never had, during all its service in France and Flanders, a pleasanter period than these twelve days of rest and training.'[5]

The men of the predominately nationalist 16th too were in good spirits after the success of Messines Ridge. They expected the coming battle to be a repeat. John 'Max' Staniforth of the 7th Leinsters recorded in his diary that the assaulting troops would be the lucky ones. 'With such incredible artillery preparations, it's usually accounted the best job to have. With luck there may not be a Boche left alive by the time the attack is launched.'[6]

They practised the coming assault 'forwards, backwards and upside down until we could do it in our sleep with infantry glorifying in their new status as stormtroopers,' the Jesuit chaplain Fr Willie Doyle SJ recalled. 'We were withdrawn from the line and given three weeks special training. The whole Division was in splendid order.'[7]

The 16th held a mass in the cathedral in St Omer on 20 July. In his sermon, Doyle reminded them that Daniel O'Connell, the revered Irish 'Liberator' of the previous century, had spent time there as a young student. He compared them to the Irish brigades who had distinguished themselves in battle on the fields of continental Europe in the sixteenth and seventeenth centuries. This acquired a feat of Jesuitical reasoning as the former fought against and the latter fought for the British.

The men were an impressive sight, remembered his fellow Jesuit, the world-renowned photographer Fr Francis Browne, the chaplain to the Irish Guards.

'Every button, every badge shone and shone again; their belts were scrubbed till not even the strictest inspection could reveal the slightest stain; and their fixed bayonets only wanted the sun to show how they could flash.'[8]

Both divisions were part of XIX Corps, which consisted of four divisions: the 15th (Scottish) Division, the 55th Division, the 16th and the 36th.[9]

After their success at Messines Ridge, the Irish divisions left the Second Army for the Fifth Army, commanded by General Hubert Gough. This would be the second time the 16th was under his command. Previously it had been when Gough commanded I Corps at Hulluch. Gough had been promoted shortly before the Battle of the Somme to command the Fifth Army.[10] The Irish divisions had displayed sufficient élan at Messines to be a part of the vanguard for the coming assault.

The men of both divisions, however, had their reservations about him. They had come to respect General Sir Herbert Plumer, the general commanding the Second Army. These were contrasting leaders. Where Plumer was slow and methodical; Gough was regarded as impetuous and indifferent to his men's welfare. He would not be a success and his command would have tragic consequences for both Irish divisions.

Passchendaele, then known as the Third Battle of Ypres, was preceded by the biggest bombardment of the war to date. It was of a magnitude many times greater than either the Somme or Messines. Between 15 July and 2 August, the British expended 4,283,550 shells in the Ypres salient.[11] Day and night the guns roared. The Germans answered with a ferocious counter-battery of their own. Fr Doyle observed: 'Though there was not very much infantry fighting owing to the state of the ground, not for a moment during the week did the artillery duel cease, reaching at times a pitch of unimaginable intensity.'[12]

Even before the battle began, there were thousands of casualties on both sides.

After the Somme, the Germans adopted a new system of defence in depth comprising of three lines: a forward zone, battle zone and a rearward zone. The forward zone was for observation purposes and was lightly held. The battle zone consisted of fortified farmhouses and reinforced concrete steel pillboxes bristling with men and machine guns. These were impregnable to shellfire and their presence would have terrible consequences for assaulting infantry.

Behind the battle zone, the Germans kept their counter-attacking divisions (*eingrief* divisions) and counter-battery artillery. These were kept out of the range of British artillery and readied for attack when the British infantry assaults exhausted themselves.[13] The Germans had thus created a giant spider's web into which the enemy would steadily enmesh itself with terrible consequences.

—

The day of 30 July had been hot. The 16th (Irish) Division moved off in the cool of night at 10 p.m from south of Ypres. As they did, Fr Doyle noted the following day, 31 July, would be the feast of St Ignatius of Loyola, the soldier-saint who had founded his order. As he watched the men march towards the flash of the guns, he was filled with foreboding that not even his adamantine faith could dispel.

> Success is certain our generals tell us, but I cannot help wondering what are the plans of the Great Leader and what the result will be when He has issued his orders. This much is certain: the fight will be a desperate one, for our foe is not only brave, but clever and cunning, as we have learned to our cost.[14]

The 16th tramped past gun battery after gun battery, now thundering in unison as a prelude to the start of the battle. As dawn broke and the first men went over the top, the motorised ambulances streamed past Doyle bringing the first casualties, Doyle wondered to himself if his men too would be soon among the wounded or were destined for the 'final roll call on the great review day'.[15]

The 16th was directed to proceed through Ypres. Doyle was shocked. 'Ruin and desolation, desolation and ruin, is the only description I can give of a spot once the pride and glory of Belgium.' Bone-weary from marching, the men found what shelter they could. Doyle fell asleep in the ruins of a house.[16]

The battlefield for the initial assault was divided in three. The British sector began with the Second Army on the right near Wytschaete, the village captured by the Irish in June, the Fifth Army, which would bear the brunt of the attack occupied the centre ground, with the French First Army on its left.

Zero hour for the big push was set for 3.50 a.m. on the morning of 31 July.

The British and French had some initial successes. In the first days of the battle the British captured Pilckem Ridge, the low ridge north-east of Ypres, but the Germans still held most of the high ground. The French made good progress on the left.[17]

The rain began to fall on the afternoon of 31 July and did not stop for days. During the month of August 127mms of rain (6ins) fell in Flanders. Rainfall in the area was five times what it had been in August 1915 and 1916.

All the preparations for Passchendaele had been confounded by the one thing no general could legislate for – rain. It was rotten luck for the poor bloody British infantry and their German adversaries. Each of the millions of shells burrowing into the cloying earth sent up fountains of mud and left huge craters.

The rain made it impossible for tanks to traverse the ruined waterlogged bog, negating a potentially important advantage for the British. Men, fully laden with pack, found even the approaches to the trenches to be exhausting. In some cases, the only way of moving forward was across duckboards, providing an easy target for German machine-gunners. Shell holes filled with water. Men fell into them and drowned. Some, wounded and immobilised, sheltered in them only to find the water rising around them.

The initial attack was suspended on 3 August because of the weather. The next day, Haig briefed the British cabinet. The allies had taken back 18 square miles of territory and 6,000 German prisoners-of-war. Casualties, he ventured, had been low for such a big battle, 31,850 men (7,500 dead) from 31 July to 3 August, compared to 57,540 casualties on the first day of the Battle of the Somme.[18]

The two Irish divisions moved to the left of the British attack near Langemarck, best known today for its spectral German graveyard and its etching in wood of the name of every pre-war German university from which the young and the patriotic marched off to certain slaughter during the First Battle of Ypres in 1914.

In the territory held by XIX Corps, the assault on the first day was carried out by the 55th and the 15th (Scottish) Division on the first day of Passchendaele. Both divisions had initial successes. The village of Frezenberg was captured, but, typically – and this would become a pattern throughout the battle – they reached their initial objectives only to be subjected to counter-battery fire by the Germans followed by a devastating counter-attack.[19]

Nevertheless, they managed to hold on to the German trenches opposite Frezenberg village. On 4 August, the Irish divisions relieved them and moved into these trenches. They would not leave them for nearly two weeks.[20]

Even in reserve the men from the 16th and 36th were not spared the horrors of Passchendaele. They were pressed into the battlefield to evacuate the wounded, dig forward trenches and bury communication cables which were, as often as not, destroyed a short time afterwards by shellfire.

They dwelt in horrendous conditions marooned in a shallow valley flooded by the overflow of the two streams that crossed the battlefield, the Hanebeek and Steenbeek. The enemy had the range and shelled their frontline positions incessantly. Moving meant the risk of certain death. 'If you stand up you're shot if you stoop down you're drowned,' Private Herbie Andrew from the 10th Inniskillings remembered. Similarly, the 7th Royal Inniskilling Fusiliers battalion diary noted: 'Men had to sit tight and not move or show themselves or they were promptly sniped at and the trenches or shell holes they were in were all waterlogged.'

Even the 47th Brigade, in reserve some way back, was not spared the relentless shelling with its commanding officer Brigadier General George Pereira lamenting, 'Up to your first relief in the early hours of August 6th you have to stand or lie in the open without overhead protection with everything soaked and sore feet, while the continuous bombardment banished all chance of sleep for four days.'

The 16th occupied trenches from the Ypres-Roulers Railway to the rear of the now ruined village of Frezenberg and to a point a half mile further on, opposite a German strongpoint called Iberian Farm. In front of the Irish was the occupied Frezenberg Ridge, taken by the Germans in May 1915 during the Second Battle of Ypres.

The 36th (Ulster) Division moved up at the end of July to the back area of XIX Corps but within range of German shelling. Major General Oliver Nugent, the commanding officer of the 36th, realised early that his men were being subjected to terrible risks to no obvious end:

> It is always the most unsatisfactory way of all that one can lose men, because it goes on day after day gradually frittering the men away and shaking their morale with no tangible results in the shape of ground gained or visible dead Boche ... where our front line is now is very much overlooked, in fact no one can show a nose on it by day and we shall continue to be overlooked until we gain more ground.[21]

Years of shelling had reduced the whole landscape to a dun-coloured wasteland of bombed-out buildings and trees reduced to withered stumps. There were no discernible landmarks left, nothing to relieve this pitiless vista.

Lieutenant Arthur Glanville of the 2nd Royal Dublin Fusiliers recalled:

> In and out of the line on Frezenberg sector. Hell all the time! Mud awful, no trenches, no shelters, no landmarks. All movement by night all the time and everywhere casualties enormous! Several killed every day and wounded every hour.[22]

The rain was so relentless that operations were postponed until 10 August, when the British made another assault on the Gheluvelt Plateau, the slab of high ground on the right of the British front which had not been captured on 31 July. Without its capture, the infantry advancing on the left could be targeted by German artillery from territory which was supposed to have been seized the first day. Again the assault was thwarted.

The next phase of the attack was scheduled for 14 August, but the rain was unrelenting and it was postponed for two days. This phase would become known as the Battle of Langemarck. Gough's Fifth Army was tasked with the assault assisted by the French First Army on the left.

By the time the 16th and 36th were readied to go over the top, they were down a third on their strength and even those men available to go over the top were so weakened by their ordeal that many were not fit for combat. Most had not slept except in stolen moments between the shelling. Their nerves were frayed and many were suffering from trench foot because of the waterlogged conditions. Food could only be brought up at night. They were malnourished, filthy and depressed.

The Battle of Langemarck, which began on 16 August, was unfinished business. Gough intended to take the terrain that had not been captured on the first day of the battle.

He had three corps at his disposal with six divisions going over the top at zero hour, scheduled for 4.45 a.m.

The goal was the green line, an unbroken series of German defences on high ground that stretched from Gheluvelt in the south to Langemarck in the north.

The portents were not good. An inch of rain fell on the battlefield on 14 and 15 August. Major Noel Holmes, the deputy assistant adjutant general of the 16th, went to look for himself at the terrain the men were supposed to attack.

He was aghast and told Major General William Hickie, the man commanding the 16th, that the men could not be expected to advance in such conditions. Hickie responded knowingly. 'I'm not going to mention your name, else they'll say, "what does this young pup know".' [23]

This was exceedingly dangerous territory. The two divisions between them held a front of 2,700 yards (a mile and a half) from the Ypres-Roulers railway line to outside the village of St Julien. The German frontline opposing them was a series of blockhouses, pillboxes and ruined farms turned into fortifications on the slopes of Frezenberg Ridge, a gentle rise which overlooked the Irish trenches.

In the 16th sector, these were Fortress Potsdam, Vampir Farm, Borry Farm, Delva Farm, Beck House and Iberian Farm. Vampir Farm was a ruined Flemish farmhouse that concealed a deep bunker the Germans had captured from the British in 1915.

The divisional boundary was a low ridge perpendicular to the German lines known as Gallipoli Copse. It was overlooked by the Pommern Redoubt, one of the most impressive fortifications in the area. The 36th was billeted slightly forward of the 16th, overlooking German redoubts with names redolent of previous military disasters, Somme Farm and Gallipoli Farm.

On the left flank of the division were three fortified bunkers, Fort Hill, Pond Farm and Corn Hill, designed together to provide an arc of fire directed at the advancing enemy.

In order to have any chance of success, the British artillery had to accurately target the German strongholds, there had to be an element of surprise, preferably with poison gas to stun the defenders, and the attackers had to have overwhelming force. None of these conditions were present for the Irish at Passchendaele.

Four brigades were deployed in the initial assault, 48th and 49th brigades from the 16th with 108th and 109th brigades from the 36th. Preparations began badly. 49th Brigade lost its commanding officer, Brigadier General Hugh Leveson-Gower, and much of his support staff to a gas attack on the night before the assault. [24]

At zero hour, each brigade attacked with two battalions, but in reality most of them were only at half-strength. On the extreme right nearest the railway, the men from the 7th Royal Irish Rifles were shelled before they left their trenches.

As soon as they went over the top, they were hit by machine-gun fire coming from the Ypres-Roulers railway line and from the direction of Borry Farm, a strongpoint which was rumoured to contain 100 men and five machine guns.

The 7th Rifles advanced under a creeping barrage over the Hanebeek stream and were assailed by two machine-gun posts from Fortress Potsdam. The battalion sustained 325 casualties of whom eighty-seven were fatalities.[25]

Assisting them were the 2nd Dublins in reserve, so depleted that they were bolstered by a company from the 8th Dublins, but they too made little progress. Lieutenant Glanville recalled the horrors of the early exchanges. The battalion's advanced companies were almost 'completely wiped out' in the initial attack.

'Under hellish fire I collect as many of the company as possible and give the signal to advance but one after another is shot down. It is death to move – to raise oneself an inch out of the mud.'[26]

B Company of the 2nd Dublins was almost annihilated. Only five men emerged unscathed; the figure for C Company was twelve unwounded men.[27]

An unnamed officer from the 8th Dublins, who provided support to the operation, recalled in approaching Vampir Farm that the advance parties were 'either dead or wounded being particularly thick along the road. The ground near us was dotted with numerous dead'.[28] The 9th Dublins on the left of the 7th Royal Irish Rifles even managed to reach the green line, but the men found themselves fired on in the rear from pillboxes that had been bypassed.

On their left, the 7th and 8th Royal Inniskilling Fusiliers fared no better. Initially the 7th made strong progress, capturing Beck House and sending back German prisoners. They then crossed the Zonnebeke stream, but were held up. Like the 9th Dublins, they found themselves fired upon by machine-gunners from behind who had not been dealt with in the initial assault.

They were also targeted in the open by German planes which strafed them as they lay crouched in shell holes. Most of the officers of the battalions were killed or wounded before they retreated to their starting positions. Out of 492 men in the 7th, just 121 were left standing at the end of the day. The 8th Inniskillings on their right were slaughtered by the machine guns from Borry Farm.[29]

The 7th and 8th battalions were amalgamated a week after Langemarck; the 8th and 9th Dublins a short time after that.[30] The 9th Dublins lost fifteen of its seventeen officers and two-thirds of its men.

A similar pattern was apparent with the 36th. On the right the leading waves of the 108th Brigade were attacked by machine-gun fire from Gallipoli and Somme Farms and corralled by rows of barbed wire strung across the battlefield, the better to funnel the attackers into lines where they could be mown down at will.

On the left, the men of 109th Brigade waded across the flooded Steenbeek and quickly came under machine-gun fire from Pond Farm and Border House, which marked the extreme edge of the division and corps boundary.

The left managed to occupy Fortuin Hill, a slight rise 400ft from the start and hold it, the only ground gained on this terrible day.[31]

In his otherwise exhaustive account of the 36th during the First World War, Cyril Fall deals with Langemarck succinctly:

> The story of the attack, alas! is not a long one. Enemy machine guns all along the front opened fire almost simultaneously with our barrage. The concrete pill boxes contained in some cases half a dozen separate compartments and seemed to be entirely unaffected by the pounding of many weeks. The lanes cut by artillery fire were covered by machine-guns. The ground was a veritable quagmire. The 'mopping up' system was found to be impossible. The strength of the attacking force had become inadequate to its frontage of 1,500 yards. So heavily had the battalions lost since the division took over the line, and particularly during the last 24 hours in the trenches, that 70 men were about the average size of the company. There were assuredly not 2,000 infantrymen in the force which went over the top. The foremost wave must have consisted of less than 300 men, probably reduced to a third within half a minute.[32]

About 9 a.m. waves of German infantry came over the crest of the Zonnebeke-St Julien ridge and drove the men back to their original position. At 10.15 a.m. the corps commanders decided to bring all the men back to the starting line. That afternoon, a request was made by them for the two divisions to renew the attack. It was not acted upon. Neither division was in any state to go further.

At some point in this pitiless maelstrom, Fr Doyle was killed by a shell. His luck ran out. In the days leading up to the assault Doyle had repeatedly dodged shellfire, scurrying from one waterlogged, shell-torn trench to another to minster to the dead and dying. As the only chaplain available for 48th Brigade, he was always in demand.

On 12 August, a shell exploded so close to him that it singed his hair and left him temporarily deaf. He felt assured. 'Is it not proof that He can protect you no matter what the danger?'[33] he wrote to his father, concluding that his 'old armchair up in heaven' was not ready yet.[34]

According to his biographer, Professor Alfred O'Rahilly, Fr Doyle died on the afternoon of 16 August, doing what he always did — attending to the men lying wounded out in no man's land, waiting for the end. He went to the assistance of two officers of the 8th Dublins who were dying, Second Lieutenant Arthur Green and Second Lieutenant Charles Marlow.[35]

According to one account, Fr Doyle was anointing one of the men when a shell burst among them killing them all and Private John Meehan, who had taken refuge in the same shellhole. There was little time while fighting a desperate retreat to bury them so a few survivors hurriedly covered them with sods and stones and left them there. Their bodies were never recovered from the battlefield.[36]

Doyle's death shocked men, who thought of him as invincible and omnipresent despite all the attendant dangers. 'How grieved they are at their sad loss nobody can tell unless they speak to them personally. He seemed to have gripped them all, individually as well as collectively,' observed his fellow Jesuit priest Fr John Delaney.[37]

Major General Hickie said even in a division of brave men, 'Fr Doyle stood out. He appeared to know no fatigue, he never knew fear.'[38] Hickie nominated him for the Victoria Cross; it was turned down. O'Rahilly, was sure he would have been awarded the VC was it not for the 'triple disqualification of being an Irishman, a Catholic and a Jesuit'.[39] He advanced no evidence in support of this contention. O'Rahilly's 1920 biography *Fr William Doyle SJ* was a hagiography which became a publishing sensation and was translated into six languages. It remains in print to this day. A devotion to Fr Doyle became popular in the 1920s and 1930s. Thousands of people attested to his divine intervention in some difficult aspect of their lives. The Jesuits themselves decided to canvass their own members as to his suitability for sainthood. The reaction was mixed. All thought him a courageous man; but many doubted his judgment. On reflection, the Jesuits did not refer his case to the Congregation for the Causes of Saints at Rome instead concluding that 'the matter should be left to Providence'.[40]

The Battle of Langemarck carried away many other Irishmen who had distinguished themselves earlier in the war. Lieutenant Francis Biggane, one of the two men who crawled into no man's land to retrieve an offending German placard after the Battle of Hulluch (see Chapter 12), was killed on Frezenberg Ridge with the 1st Munsters who were pressed into the attacks late in the day. He was a medical student and just 22 years of age. After he was reported missing, his parents clung to the belief that he had been captured. It was another five months before his death was confirmed. The Cork Constitution reported: 'The official intimation of his death comes as a sad ending to a period of suspense on the part of his parents, to whom the utmost sympathy of the citizens goes out in their great affliction.'[41]

Captain Jim Shine was the third of the Shine brothers to die in the war. Lieutenant John Denys Shine, was killed at the Battle of Mons on 23 August (see chapter 2) and 2nd Lieutenant Hugh Patrick Shinen was killed during the Battle of Mouse Trap Farm.

Jim Shine joined the 9th Royal Dublin Fusiliers in October 1916 to take command of 'C' Company. He and seven officers from the battalion were killed in the assault on Fortress Potsdam and Vampir and Borry Farms. He is remembered on the Tyne Cot memorial to the missing.[42]

Many of the 36th's finest officers were killed in the battle, including Lieutenant Colonel Audley Charles (AC) Pratt from Enniscore, Crossmolina, County Mayo, the commanding officer of the 11th Inniskillings and Lieutenant Colonel Stafford James Somerville, the commanding officer of the 9th Royal Irish Fusiliers who was from Devon. Somerville's son, also called Stafford, was killed during the Battle of the Somme a year previously.

The Pratt family, in their grief, managed to convey their condolences to the family of Sergeant Richard John Wolfe from Portadown who had survived the first day of the Battle of the Somme but was one of hundreds of casualties from the 9th Royal Irish Fusiliers who had attacked the Pommern Redoubt at Langemarck. Pratt's father Joseph wrote to Wolfe's mother.

> I cannot tell you with what sorrow I saw in yesterday's Irish Times the name of your son Dick in the roll of honour. It went to my heart and grieved me as much as if he had been a near and dear relation. Colonel Audley was so attached to him and held him in such high esteem. He was indeed such a gallant soldier.

John Dwyer O'Brien from Skibbereen, County Cork, was a lieutenant in the Irish Volunteers before the war. He was commissioned as an officer in the Royal Munster Fusiliers. After the Battle of the Somme, the ranks of officers in the 36th were so depleted that he was transferred to the 14th Royal Irish Rifles (Young Citizen' Volunteers), evidence that the sectarian boundaries were becoming blurred as the war progressed.

O'Brien was awarded the Military Cross for his actions at the Battle of Messines Ridge when his platoon captured two German machine guns. He was seriously injured during the Battle of Langemarck. One Jesuit army chaplain witnessed his arrival at a casualty clearing station. He wrote to his father, reassuring him that his son had received the sacraments on the previous Sunday. 'I have every hope that he will pull through all right; he has a splendid constitution, and every care is being taken of him.'[43]

O'Brien died shortly afterwards. Another letter from another chaplain Fr W.N. Close arrived some days later.

> It will be a source of strength to you in that sorrow to call to mind the splendid Catholic example that your boy gave out here. He has done his duty nobly to King and country; he has made his great sacrifice for the women and children, for the poor and defenceless, and he died a good soldier and a splendid Catholic, strengthened with the Church sacraments, and I am sure he went to his Judge to receive his reward.[44]

The *Skibbereen Eagle* expressed similar sentiments:

> He fell fighting; that the submarines of Germany may not starve those at home he loved; that the poor workingmen from the City of Cork, whom the Germans sent to a sudden death in the 'Bandon,' may be avenged; and that we all at home in Ireland may go to our work and our rest, despite what the Germans can do

on sea or land. These things we owe to this brave Irishman, and the thousands of his race who are winning renown for us where today alone it can be won. This can never be too often repeated.[45]

After Langemarck the British press were full of tales of doomed Irish heroism. Percival Phillips, of the *Daily Express*, concluded that the men's sacrifice had not been in vain. 'There are incidents of courage and devotion that will live as long as there are men of Ulster and men of Clare. The battalions of the North and South are proud of each other.'[46]

But they had died in vain. 16 August 1917 was an unmitigated disaster. There was no glory, only death, misery and mud. 'It has been a truly terrible day,' Oliver Nugent wrote to his wife. 'Worse than the 1st July [1916, first day of the Battle of the Somme] I am afraid. Our losses have been very heavy indeed and we have failed all along the line, so far as this division is concerned and the whole division has been driven back with terrible losses.'[47] Nugent knew who to blame for the failure of the attack:

> I went to see Gough this afternoon. He was very pleasant and is a charming man as he always is, but my dearest, no one can talk to him and come away thinking that he is mentally or intellectually fit to command a big army. He isn't and it is wrong that the lives of thousands of good men should be sacrificed through want of forethought and higher leading.[48]

Philip Gibbs, of the *Daily Chronicle*, chaffed under the restrictions of war time censorship. He waited until after the war to deliver his withering verdict on Langemarck:

> The two Irish divisions were broken to bits and their brigadiers called it murder. They were violent in their denunciation of the Fifth Army for having put their men into the attack after those 13 days of heavy shelling ... I found a general opinion among officers and men, not only of the Irish division under the command of the Fifth Army, that they have been the victims of atrocious staff-work, tragic in its consequences. From what I saw of some of the Fifth Army staff-officers, I was of the same opinion. Some of these young gentlemen, and some of the elderly officers, were arrogant and supercilious without revealing any symptoms of intelligence.[49]

Gough instead blamed both divisions. Haig's diary records:

> He was not pleased with the action of the Irish Divisions of the XIX Corps (36th and 16th). They seemed to have gone forward, but failed to keep what they had won. These 2 divisions were in the Messines battle and had an easy victory. The men are Irish and did not like the shelling, so Gough said.[50]

But Haig, not a man known to be overly concerned about the welfare of the troops, was having none of it.

> I gather that the attacking troops had a long march up the evening before the battle through Ypres to the front line and then had to fight from zero 4.45am until nightfall. The men could have had no sleep and must have been dead tired. Here also a number of concrete buildings and dugouts were never really destroyed by artillery fire and do not appear to have been taken.[51]

Haig would later inform Gough of the unpopularity of the Fifth Army with the troops. Judging by his surprised reaction, Gough appears to have been the last to know.

The 7th Inniskillings war diary enumerated the many reasons why the August 16th attack failed among them insufficient artillery preparation and depth in the attack, bad communication to the rear and lack of leadership on the part of non-commissioned officers (NCOs) when their officers had fallen.[52]

Between 1 August and 20 August, the 16th sustained 4,265 casualties, including 2,157 on 16 August. The equivalent figures for the 36th were 3,585 casualties with 2,036 from 16 August.[53]

It had been a terrible time for both divisions who had nothing to show for the horrors they endured and for the almost 8,000 casualties they had suffered in less than two weeks.

Yet, even those figures as recounted in the British official history do not tell the whole story. It has taken 100 years to determine the full extent of the tragedy on Frezenberg Ridge. In Flanders Fields, the organisation which runs the Cloth Hall museum in Ypres, has determined that on 16 August 1917, 1,175 men from the two Irish divisions died, 595 from the 16th and 580 from the 36th. This makes it the worst day for the Irish in the First World War with the exception of the first day of the Battle of the Somme.[54]

In total from 1 June to 1 September in the Ypres salient, 2,608 men were killed from both divisions.[55] Of the 99,253 soldiers from the UK (which then included Ireland) who were killed from June to November 1917 in Ypres, 4,901 are listed in the Irish National War Memorial records.[56]

—

Frezenberg Ridge was not a success to be remembered like Messines Ridge, Guillemont or Ginchy. It was not a disaster to be analysed and commemorated like the first day of the Battle of the Somme or the landings at Gallipoli. It was not remembered for good or ill. It was simply forgotten about.

It was just a terrible incident in a terrible stage (the Battle of Langemarck) of a terrible battle (Passchendaele) that should never have been prosecuted past its initial stages.

Nor were the Irish uniquely afflicted. Passchendaele smothered all its combatant nations in mud and gore. The men from the UK who died at the Somme were mostly volunteers; those who died at Passchendaele were the remnants of the volunteers and the conscripts.

Having tipped the flower of British and Irish manhood into a muddy grave, Haig turned to the soldiers of Empire.

At nearby Poelcappelle, New Zealand had its worst day in military history with 846 deaths alone on 12 October. A total of 12,387 Australians were killed during the Battle of Passchendaele. The Canadians who finally took the ruined village that gave the battle its name on 10 November lost 4,834 men.[57]

The Irish debacle at Langemarck came by accident to the attention of a Belgian army officer Erwin Ureel. He knew of the story of Major Willie Redmond and in 1997 organised a remembrance weekend on the 80th anniversary of Redmond's death. He also instigated the corten steel silhouette to remember both Willie Redmond and John Meeke, the man who attended to him on the battlefield.

In 2014 he assisted the Royal Welsh Fusiliers Association in the creation of the Welsh National Memorial Park in Langemarck. The monument was made with Welsh blue pennant stones transported from the Craig yr Hesg quarry in Pontypridd.[58]

Ureel had the foresight to order an extra stone with a view to erecting a memorial to the Irish who died at Langemarck. In the years since the unveiling of the Island of Ireland Peace Park, much attention had been given to Messines Ridge but none to Langemarck.

> For 10 years I tried to promote the story, but to no avail. Nobody seemed to be interested in Langemarck … There is a perception that the Battle of Messines Ridge has become quite popular. Regrettably the Irish interest never went further than the successful 7th June Wytschaete story and even that took a long time to recognise. That distracts a bit from the fact that the two divisions fought twice together and only twice and those two times were in Flanders. It is a story of triumph and disaster. The triumph was Messines; the disaster was Langemarck. I am sure that is why Langemarck was forgotten.[59]

—

In late 2016 a crane trundled down the Haezeweidestraat, a single-track road between Zonnebeke and St Julien, and deposited the memorial stone at a site opposite what was once the Pommern Redoubt.

> In memory of the men of the 16th (Irish) Division and 36th (Ulster) Division who fought alongside each other near this spot during the Battle of Langemarck

16–18 August 1917.[60] It was the last battle in which these two Irish Divisions fought together in the First World War. Also remembered are all Irish soldiers who fought in Irish and non-Irish regiments and their non- Irish comrades who fought in Irish formations during the Third Battle of Ypres (Passchendaele) 31 July – 10 November 1917.

A Soldier's Grave
By Irish poet Francis Ledwidge 1st Royal Inniskilling Fusiliers, killed by a German shell near Boezinghe on 31 July 1917.

Then in the lull of midnight, gentle arms
Lifted him slowly down the slopes of death
Lest he should hear again the mad alarms
Of battle, dying moans, and painful breath.

And where the earth was soft for flowers we made
A grave for him that he might better rest.
So, Spring shall come and leave it sweet arrayed,
And there the lark shall turn her dewy nest.

Erected by members and friends of the Royal Dublin Fusiliers Association

From this vantage point, the high ground which cost the blood of so many brave Irish sons is barely discernible against the broad horizon. Somewhere beyond lie the bodies of men who were every bit as much victims of British military obduracy as they were of German bullets and bombs. Fr Doyle wrote of those lost men shortly before he would join them, all of them asleep forever somewhere in a Flanders field.

My poor brave boys. They are lying now out on the battlefield: some in a little grave dug and blessed by their chaplain, who loved them all as if they were his own children; others stiff and stark with staring eyes, hidden in a shell-hole where they had crept to die; while perhaps in some far-off thatched cabin an anxious mother sits listening for the well-known step and voice which will never gladden her heart again.[61]

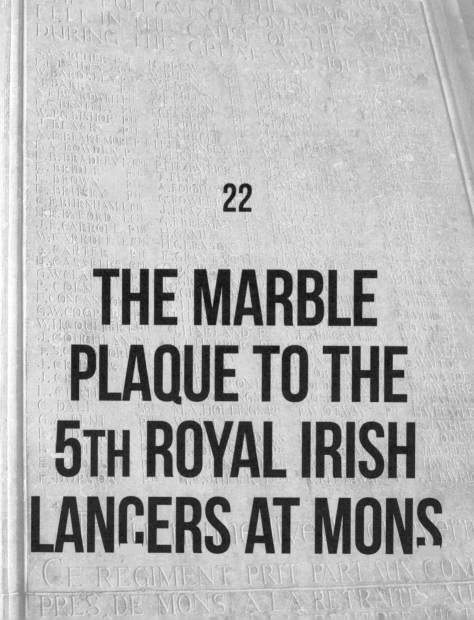

THE MARBLE PLAQUE TO THE 5th ROYAL IRISH LANCERS AT MONS

At 5 a.m. on 11 November, in a railway carriage at the forest of Compiègne outside Paris, the armistice was signed between Allied forces and Germany.

The Great War was at an end, a proposition which would have seemed unthinkable when Germany came close to breaking the Allies during her Spring Offensive of March 1918. For Germany, it was a harsh peace that stopped short of outright surrender, but made it abundantly clear who was the victor and who was the vanquished.

Hostilities were scheduled to cease at 11 a.m., a time chosen so all the units across the scattered battlefields could get the news. The timing chosen was also symbolic – the eleventh hour of the eleventh day of the eleventh month.

By that hour, Canadian forces had already occupied the centre of the Belgian town of Mons. There had been bitter fighting the night before. 'The Canadian Infantry had made it a point of honour, notwithstanding the cautions against casualties to drive the enemy from Mons before the ceasefire sounded,' wrote Major General Edward Morrison, the commander officer of the Canadian Artillery.[1] 'The entry of the Corps commanding [General Arthur Currie] with his staff mounted proceeded by an escort of cavalry and followed by his battle standard, was a magnificent climax to the day of rejoicing. He literally rode into the captured city along the streets garnished with the enemy dead.'[2]

The Canadian dead of that last day were laid out on the Grand Place in front of the Hôtel de Ville.

For the 5th Royal Irish Lancers, the symmetry was perfect. Mons was the place where the British Empire had begun the First World War and also the place where the war ended. By coincidence, it was the place where the 5th Lancers had begun and ended its war. It was also the last British regiment to leave Mons during the retreat in August 1914 and the first to enter the town at the end of hostilities. As we saw in the first chapter, on 11 November 1918, Canadian troops pushed on north of Mons until they found themselves on the same road and in the same place where Corporal Edward Thomas from the 4th Royal Irish Dragoon Guards had fired the first shot for the British on 22 August 1914. Thus, the war began and ended for the British with Irish cavalry regiments.

The 5th Lancers was the regiment chosen to lead the victory parade in Mons on 11 November. The Canadian commander, General Arthur Currie, widely regarded as one of the most capable Allied commanders, understood the symbolism well. He remembered the 'contemptible little British army that they were at Mons that day … the place of honour should be taken by them'.[3]

The men from the 5th Lancers proudly paraded on horseback, wearing their Mons Stars, the medal given to that tiny band of warriors that had been part of the British Expeditionary Force at the start of the war.[4] The British had mobilised nearly 8 million men for the war; just 160,000 had been present at the very beginning (2 per cent). These were the 'Old Contemptibles' and many of them were now dead, wounded or in German prison camps.

In this war, the traditional role of the cavalry as the ultimate instrument of war, the highly trained elite designed to give the coup de grâce once the infantry had done its work, had been rendered obsolete by the power of the machine gun. The men and their horses were made for charging. Instead, they found themselves mostly on scouting duties or, worse still, they had to dismount and serve with the infantry.

By 7 a.m., the Canadian troops filled the Grand Place in Mons. Slowly, French and Belgian civilians joined them, hardly able to believe that the cataclysm was over. Locals came to pay homage to the 'most feared troops on the Western Front, masters of war', according to the Canadian military historian Norm Christie.[5] The Canadians had been outstanding soldiers, distinguishing themselves at Kitcheners' Wood, Vimy Ridge, Passchendaele, Amiens and now Mons.

Yet, in deference to the 5th Lancers who had endured the whole war, Currie asked Second Lieutenant Archibald Allison of the regiment to join him on the step of the Hôtel de Ville (town hall) in Mons. When the ceremony was over, he allowed thirty-four men from the ranks of the Lancers to lead the parade, the pennons on their lances fluttering in a light breeze.

—

Not only was the 5th Royal Irish Lancers present at the beginning and end of the First World War, they were also present at critical moments in Irish history too, the two great rebellions of modern Irish history (1798 and 1916) and the Curragh crisis of 1914.

The officers of the 5th (Royal) Irish Lancers were as one – they would not obey orders or carry out their duties in the north of Ireland.

Twenty men were asked if they wished to do their duty or resign. Seventeen offered to resign, two cited family connections in Ulster and another was unavoidably absent.

The Curragh crisis – it was not a mutiny, just the threat of one – marked a sinister turn in the politicisation of the British army. The 5th Lancers would once again find itself accused of subverting the will of the British government.

The regiment was founded in Enniskillen in 1688 by James Wynne as the Enniskillen Dragoons. Wynne was a Protestant of Welsh origin who had raised the regiment to fight on the side of King William III at the Battle of the Boyne. During the 1798 Rebellion, it would earn a degree of censure unprecedented in the history of Irish regiments.[6]

The 5th Dragoons, as the regiment became known, had done its duty in helping to put down the rebellion in Wexford in June 1798. Faced, though, with an invading French army aided by a rebel Irish force, many of its number fled in a celebrated but, unfortunately for the Irish, short-lived victory known as the Races of Castlebar in August of that year. Though by no means the only regiment to have turned tail, the 5th Dragoons was singled out for the ultimate sanction.[7]

It was found to have been infiltrated by rebels, namely two Feney brothers from Drogheda and a man named Michael D'Nasser, who turned King's evidence and isent the brothers to the gallows. D'Nasser was transported to Australia.[8]

King George III was determined to make an example of the 5th Dragoons, though the overwhelming majority of the regiment stayed loyal. He had it disbanded. It was, according to the *British Military Library* of April 1800, 'one of the most singular instances of censure and disgrace that has occurred in the military history of Great Britain'.

The number 5 was retired from the army list. It went from the 4th Dragoon Guards to the 6th. The omission was meant to convey the disgrace. It was not until 1858 that the regiment was reconstituted to deal with the threat of the Indian Mutiny. It became the 5th Royal Irish Lancers.

In 1914, fifty-six years after from its re-commissioning, the officers of the regiment would once again be accused of disloyalty, though they would protest that, if they were guilty of anything, it was an excess of loyalty to the British Empire. They would not be party to any attempt by the British government to impose home rule on Ulster. The 5th Lancers was part of the 3rd Cavalry Brigade based in the Curragh. The cavalry was no meritocracy among its officers. A cavalry officer needed an independent income on top of his meagre salary.[9] They came from the public schools, the aristocracy and the landed estates. If they were Irish, they were nearly all Anglo-Irish. They were not inclined to move on Ulster.

Field Marshal Sir William Robertson, the army's director of military training, warned that to put 'down those with whose ideals and religion they are in sympathy is to expect a great deal'.[10]

The 3rd Cavalry Brigade was commanded by Brigadier-General Hubert Gough, whose family had an estate in Gurteen, County Waterford. As was noted in the previous chapter, Gough would go to command the Fifth Army during the war. Gough described himself as 'Irish by blood and upbringing' though he was born in England and raised in both India and England, where his father General Sir Charles Gough moved around.

It was a misfortune for Ireland that when cool heads were needed, at this critical time, the British army had as its head in Ireland General Sir Arthur Paget, a blustering, figure given to long-winded pronouncements. Paget was 'a stupid, arrogant, quick-tempered man', according to the author Victor Bonham-Carter.[11]

In March 1914, there was a real fear that the Ulster Volunteer Force would attempt to seize weapons from armouries in the north of Ireland. The Cabinet agreed to move troops to the north of Ireland as a precaution. Paget was summoned to London. All the politicians left the Cabinet briefing, except the Secretary of War, John Seely, the head of the British army, Sir John French, and Paget.

What happened is unclear, but it appears as if Seely told Paget that men based in the Irish Command who had families in Ulster could 'disappear' for the duration of any conflict in the north of Ireland. Those without family connections who wished not to take part in any military operations in the province would have to resign.

Paget went back to Dublin and called together seven senior officers, including Gough. Gough told him 'on account of birth and upbringing, and many friendships, he did not see how he could bear arms against Ulster loyalists'.[12] Also present was Major-General Sir Charles Fergusson, the commanding officer of the 5th Division. Despite being an Orangeman, he immediately pledged the infantry's loyalty. Clearly the infantry and cavalry had distinctive cultures.

Gough went to Marlborough Barracks (now McKee Barracks) in Dublin, where the 5th Lancers was based, and put the ultimatum to its commanding officer Lieutenant-Colonel Arthur Parker, who had connections in Fermanagh. Parker flopped down on the sofa and exclaimed, 'It's monstrous, it's monstrous. I won't go. I won't go'.[13] A 5th Lancers officer wrote to his father, 'Can you imagine a subaltern of 22-26 making up his mind in an hour as to whether he should shoot down Loyalists in Ulster or try to start a civil job without a bob? … Imagine anything more criminal than making us decide a matter which might affect our whole careers, without giving us time to think or get advice from anyone.'[14]

Gough played for time and sent a letter to Paget. He sought clarification. His men were prepared to go north to maintain law and order. They were not prepared to take offensive action against loyalists. In that case, he gave a list of officers who would 'respectfully, and under protest, prefer to be dismissed'.[15] King George V did not know what was really going on until he opened his morning papers on 21 March 1914. As the titular head of the armed forces, a role he took seriously, he could hardly believe that his own officers would go so far as to subvert the will of the government. He requested lists of telegrams from all the 3rd Cavalry Brigade. King George V wrote to British Prime Minister Herbert Asquith, 'I was grieved beyond words at this disastrous and irreparable catastrophe which has befallen my army'.[16]

Attention was focused on the 5th Lancers. The regiment was 'in a very undisciplined state and drastic steps might have to be taken with them', Seely told the King. Gough and three colonels were summoned to the War Office to be told that the situation was most grave.[17] As usual, Asquith's dithering made a bad situation worse. He told the King that Paget was not acting under authority. The government had never intended to coerce Ulster. The incident ended with Asquith giving a written statement that it had all been a 'misunderstanding'. Seely and French both resigned, though French would later be reinstated.

The effect of this sorry incident on opinion in Ireland was immediate. The cavalry officers proved to be the best recruiting sergeants the Irish Volunteers ever had. Thousands of nationalists joined up on the basis that if the British army could not be trusted to defend home rule, they would have to do so themselves. Fortunately and unfortunately for the officers involved, the Curragh crisis was superseded by the outbreak of war, giving the same officers an unlikely chance at redemption.

'I often wonder if General Seely and Mr Churchill ever offer little candles to the memory of William Hohenzollern,' the author and British general Sir George MacMunn observed years later, 'for restoring the officer cadre of the British army and navy for them, even though it died in the process'.[18]

The 5th Lancers regimental historian noted, 'No sooner was the Regiment relieved from the worries of the historic Ulster episode, than they became aware that more glorious orders were to be issued to them, than the preceding ones they had received in the early part of the war.'[19]

The British army mobilised with astonishing rapidity and none more so than the cavalry. Some 165,000 horses were requisitioned within twelve days. The 3rd Cavalry Brigade, including the 5th Lancers, marched through the streets of Dublin to Dublin Port. They were 'greeted the whole way down the Liffey by sirens and steam whistles … also enthusiastic crowds. Rather a change to the feeling three weeks ago when the sight of a soldier drove them mad.'[20]

This was a reference to the Bachelors Walk massacre of three civilians on 26 July 1914 by a party of the King's Own Scottish Borderers. The 5th Lancers saw action at the Battle of Mons on 23 August 1914. While the British infantry was engaged in a desperate fight for survival, the Cavalry Division was largely helpless to intervene.

When the French Fifth Army was forced to fall back, the British were left isolated and were forced to retreat. The 5th Lancers operations began at 1.30 a.m. on the morning of 24 August, when its transport column moved southwards. It was to provide a cavalry screen for the retreating British infantry. It was the last British formation to leave Mons. This would have symbolic significance many years later.[21] Lieutenant-Colonel Parker, one of the *agents provocateurs* of the Curragh crisis, was hit by a ricochet bullet at Mons and had to be evacuated.

—

On Easter Monday, 24 April 1916, the bulk of the regiment were holding a horse show at St Pierre in France. There was a high standard in the turnout of 'horses, saddlers, and wagons', but, elsewhere, the 5th Lancers was involved in events that would change Ireland forever.[22]

Another contingent was attached to the 6th Reserve Regiment of Cavalry at Marlborough Barracks in Dublin. It was the training reserve for both the 5th and 12th Lancers.

The timing was terrible for its commanding officer, Lieutenant-Colonel Cyril Kirk, and the regimental sergeant-major, who were away at Fairyhouse Races on this most significant of days.[23] The Lancers were ambushed by rebels in the GPO garrison as they proceeded down Sackville Street on the way to Dublin Castle. Three Lancers were killed immediately; a fourth, 22-year-old Patrick Leen from Abbeyfeale, County Limerick, died of wounds on 1 May, two days after the Rising ended. He had been a boarder at Rockwell College in County Tipperary, the same school that Thomas MacDonagh, a signatory of the Proclamation, had attended.[24] He was one of seven men from the 5th Lancers who were killed in the Easter Rising. A horse was also killed. Its putrefying body lay in O'Connell Street until the end of the Rising.[25]

On the Western Front, meanwhile, their comrades found themselves largely superfluous to the action. They patrolled, scouted, operated as working parties and occasionally in the trenches as dismounted cavalry, but the big breakthrough, the return to open warfare, as envisaged by the British commander-in-chief Field Marshal Sir Douglas Haig, a cavalryman, came very late.

In June 1917, the 5th Lancers sustained some of its heaviest casualties to date in the defence of Gillemont Farm, an isolated outpost near the Hindenburg Line, losing sixteen men dead and a further sixteen wounded. Gillemont Farm, often confused with Guillemont, which is nearby, was the same place where James Bond creator Ian Fleming's father, Major Valentine Fleming, was killed while serving with the Queen's Own Oxfordshire Hussars.

Few imagined at this point that 1918 would be the last year of the war. The Americans had entered the war in April 1917 in response to unrestricted submarine warfare and maladroit attempts by the Germans to encourage a Mexican invasion of the United States.

The Allies believed American resources would eventually prevail, but most likely in 1919. The Germans too had reason for optimism. The Russians surrendered in late 1917, freeing the Germans to concentrate all her resources on the Western Front. On 11 November 1917, one year to the day before the Armistice, the German high command met at Mons. General Erich Ludendorff drew up an attack for the spring of 1918, which would bear his name, the Ludendorff Offensive, better known as the German Spring Offensive.[26]

Ludendorff no longer believed Germany could win an outright victory. Instead, he hoped to force a peace on favourable terms for his country.

Time was not on the German side. Germany had to strike before the Americans could deploy their men. Ludendorff set March 1918 as the date for the offensive. His goal was to separate the British and French armies physically on a battleground where the Allies were weakest. He chose well. The Ludendorff Offensive took place on a 50-mile front opposite the town of St Quentin.

March 1918 would be one of the worst months of the war both for the British army and the Irish formations within it. It was the same month that the Irish Parliamentary Party leader John Redmond had died, ostensibly of complications after an intestinal operation, but just as likely from a broken heart. He was beset in his last year by personal and professional tragedy (see also Chapter 18).

In March 1918, the 16th (Irish) Division suffered reverses as bad as any it had suffered previously in the war. The 36th (Ulster) Division would also be reduced to a rump. The 16th held a 2-mile line of front from the villages of Ronssoy to Épehy, two forlorn-looking villages 10 miles north of St Quentin.[27]

The Allies knew a German offensive would come, but they did not know where or when. The Irish were engaged in back-breaking work, digging a trench system. With reduced numbers, there were simply not enough of them to do it. They had to dig new trenches, cruciform posts and lay barbed wire.

At 4.40 a.m. on 21 March 1918, the Germans fired 1.16 million high explosive and gas shells in a five-hour barrage. As dawn broke, a thick mist reduced visibility to 25 yards. At 9.35 a.m., 500,000 German soldiers advanced through the mist.

The 16th (Irish) Division bore the full fury of the German attack and none more so than Royal Dublin Fusiliers.

By midnight on 21 March, the 1st Battalion of the Royal Dublin Fusiliers had lost 600 men killed, wounded or missing. There were only five officers and ninety other ranks left. Between them, the 1st and 2nd Battalions of the Royal Dublin Fusiliers lost more than 300 men dead in the German Spring Offensive. In the first few days of the German offensive, the 16th Division had a total of 1,085 killed and 3,255 wounded, casualties as bad as those suffered at the Somme.[28] By the time it was relieved on 3 April, it had suffered 7,149 casualties and was done as a fighting force.[29]

During these critical days, the 5th Lancers found themselves operating as dismounted cavalry in conjunction with the infantry in a failed attempt to hold a bridge on the Crozat Canal near St Quentin.[30]

Ten days after the offensive began, the Germans reached the outskirts of Amiens, the hub of Allied transport in the Somme region. At this critical juncture in the war, when the Allies were hard-pressed in every theatre of war, the usually undemonstrative Haig made his famous speech on 12 April 1918:

> There is no other course open to us but to fight it out. Every position must be held to the last man: there must be no retirement. With our backs to the wall and believing in the justice of our cause each one of us must fight on to the end. The safety of our homes and the freedom of mankind alike depend upon the conduct of each one of us at this critical moment.

Fortunately for the Allies, the Germans had extended themselves too far. Their forward divisions had outrun their supplies and had taken enormous casualties. The Spring Offensive was predicated on a quick victory. After nearly four years of war, Germany simply did not have the manpower for another protracted battle of attrition.

The Spring Offensive would have serious implications for Ireland and mark the final demise of the Irish Parliamentary Party. The British government needed men and the only place where substantial numbers were still available was the one part of the United Kingdom where conscription was never introduced – Ireland.

The Conscription Bill of April 1918 united all shades of Irish nationalist opin-ion against it. The bill was introduced but never acted upon. Though the Irish Parliamentary Party was vehemently against it, Sinn Féin would be the beneficiar-ies in the December 1918 election.

The Allies stopped the Germans outside Amiens. The German 18th Division had pushed so far forward that it became isolated and its men half starved. The German infantry were amazed at the provisions that Allied soldiers enjoyed – not only the basic necessities, but wine, cigars and tobacco. Looting became widespread, discipline broke down.

By July, the Germans had made their last desperate attempt to force a settlement, but once again they were stopped on the Marne and pushed back. The Second Battle of the Marne had the same effect on French morale as the first, but a more decisive impact tactically. The Allies had taken 29,000 prisoners and 800 guns. 'The impetus had gone. Defeat now inevitable,' Ludendorff concluded. 'The attempt to make the nations of the Entente inclined to peace before the arrival of the American reinforcements by means of German victories had failed. It was quite clear to me that our general situation had thus become very serious.'[31]

The Allies began their great offensive in August 1918. The 100-day offensive would finally break the Germans, drive them out of France and end the most destructive war in history to that date.

On 7 August, the Cavalry Corps, including the 5th Lancers, was put at the dis-posal of the Canadian Corps. On Thursday, 8 August, the Cavalry Corps advanced 13 miles in a single day across the old Somme battlefield, where progress two years earlier had been measured in blood not miles.[32]

This was the 'black day of the German Army', according to General Ludendorff, a blow so bad that it would never recover. A total of 400 Allied tanks were used in an offensive which was both massive and a surprise to the waiting Germans.

The Allies captured 15,000 troops. Many German units just gave up.

Ludendorff concluded, 'The fate of the German people was too high a stake. The war must be ended.' In late September, the 5th Lancers was involved in the taking of the last major obstacle in northern France, the Canal du Nord.[33]

For much of September and October, the regiment remained in billets at the ruined village of Sains-lès-Marquion and then, on 8 November, in the final days of the war, it was placed under the command of the Canadian Corps.

The Germans had been almost completely left French soil and now the Allies crossed the old Belgian border and advanced upon Mons. One last obstacle remained – the same obstacle the British defended on the very first day of the war – the Mons-Condé Canal.

The 5th Lancers was sent out to reconnoitre a crossing of the canal. The Germans had blown all the bridges so a temporary bridge was built across the canal due west of Mons.

One squadron of the Lancers went with the Canadian 2nd Division and the remainder came under the direct orders of the Canadian 3rd Division.

The crossing took place on the morning of 9 November under the cover of darkness, with C Squadron leading the way. There was no opposition, but when they reached a railway embankment, they found the bridge had been blown. The Lancers faced high explosive shells and a nasty surprise. Gas was used for the last time in the war, surprising the men who were not prepared for the attack.

On 10 November, the 5th Lancers was engaged in clearing the Bois de Ghlin to the west of Mons, where they faced machine gun fire from the wood. It was the last significant opposition before the regiment became the symbolic liberators of Mons on Armistice Day.[34]

—

The First World War had demonstrated that the old-fashioned cavalry was now obsolete and to be replaced by tanks. Originally the decision was taken to disband the 5th Lancers, but eventually it was decided to amalgamate it with the 16th (Queens) Lancers in 1922. Even then, a century-old disgrace had not been forgotten. The formation would be known by the inelegant title 16th/5th Lancers rather than the 5th/16th Lancers as, in theory, the 5th Lancers was the more senior regiment.

—

In November 1922, it was decided to unveil a monument to the now disbanded 5th Royal Irish Lancers at the Hôtel de Ville in Mons central square. This large, marble plaque displays in relief figurines of both St Patrick and St George, reflecting the dual identity of the regiment. It states, 'Erected by the 5th Royal Irish Lancers to the memory of the following comrades who fell in the cause of the Allies during the Great War 1914-1918'. Underneath, in bas relief, is the representation of the painting showing the 5th Lancers being greeted by young and old as they enter Mons. It conveys how the 5th Lancers left Mons at the start of the war and returned to it at the end.

The chief guests at the unveiling ceremony were Hubert Gough and Arthur Parker, their reputations redeemed after the Curragh crisis, which must have seemed like ancient history given everything that had happened since March 1914. The provocateurs of the Curragh crisis survived the war, unlike so many millions of others.

The plaque includes the names of 144 Lancers who died in the war in four columns. Curiously, the names of the dead of the Easter Rising are not included, though the British regard the Rising as an episode of the First World War.

The last British soldier to die in the war served with the 5th Lancers. He was Private George Edwin Ellison from Leeds. He joined the army, left to become a coal miner, and was recalled at the outbreak of war. He survived the Retreat from Mons and the battles of Ypres, Armentières, La Bassée, Lens, Loos and Cambrai. What horrors he must have seen; what relief he must have felt if news had got to him that the Armistice had been signed. Tragically, he was killed by a concealed German machine gun placed in a wood on the outskirts of Mons at 9.30 a.m., an hour and a half before the end of the war.

He had one son, James, who was five days short of his fifth birthday. As part of a documentary broadcast in 2008 to mark the ninetieth anniversary of the Armistice, George Edwin Ellison's granddaughters Catherine and Marie visited Ellison's grave in St Symphorien Cemetery outside Mons. They were the first relatives to visit. Ellison is buried opposite Private John Parr, the first British soldier to die in the war.[35]

One of the last Irishmen to die was Private Thomas Farrell from Navan, County Meath, who also served with the 5th Lancers. He was injured on 10 November and succumbed to his wounds two days later, a day after the war ended. Farrell is buried in Valenciennes (St Roch) Cemetery. The Irishman who would tend to his grave in the years after the war had a remarkable story to tell.

23

THE PLAQUE TO ROBERT ARMSTRONG

On the side wall of the shelter at Valenciennes (St Roch) Communal Cemetery, there is a marble plaque to a remarkable Irishman who survived the First World War only to die in a German prison camp in the Second. Robert Armstrong was the head gardener at Valenciennes (St Roch) military cemetery near the French-Belgian border between the wars. Located among the extravagant sepulchres of the local populace are the graves of 882 British and Commonwealth soldiers who died, mostly in the last months of the First World War.[1]

In the same cemetery, there are also graves to thirty-four Allied airmen who died in the Second World War. Armstrong tended to them all.[2]

Armstrong was born in October 1894 in Newbliss, County Monaghan, into a Church of Ireland family. His father James was an itinerant estates manager. The family moved around Ireland, finally settling in Currygrane outside Edgeworthstown, County Longford, the family home of Field Marshal Sir Henry Wilson.[3]

A fine soldier, but also an intriguer and a gossiper, Wilson rose to become Britain's highest-ranking soldier when he was promoted to Chief of the Imperial General Staff in 1918. He was a southern unionist, an opponent of home rule and an even more ferocious opponent of the IRA campaign of the War of Independence.

He urged the British government to impose a military fiat on Ireland, even while the same government sought a political solution. The 'rough, iron-fisted Hunnish ways', as Clementine Churchill described the activities of British forces in Ireland, only succeeded in making the country even more ungovernable and sullied Britain's reputation in the eyes of the world.[4]

Wilson opposed the Anglo-Irish Treaty signed in December 1921, which secured independence for the Irish Free State. It was a 'shameful and cowardly surrender to the pistol. We must clear out or govern.' He resigned shortly afterwards and became a Unionist MP.

Wilson was assassinated in London by Reginald Dunne and Joseph O'Sullivan, two British-born First World War veterans of Irish parents who became IRA volunteers. He was shot dead in London on 22 June 1922, on his way back from unveiling a monument to dead railwaymen of the Great War at Liverpool Street Station. His killers were hanged in August. The IRA retaliated by burning down the Wilson family home in Currygrane on 24 August. The Wilsons had already fled. James Armstrong was left without a livelihood.[5]

After the Civil War ended in 1923, the Land Commission broke up the Wilson estate and Armstrong was allowed to keep his working man's cottage and 60 acres of land. It was not much of a farm. Robert Armstrong's brother Edward, who inherited it after their father died in 1944, lamented that it was too small to sustain a family.[6]

Robert Armstrong would follow his father's vocation in life. He was a career gardener whose peacetime profession was interrupted by the cataclysms of two world wars. His pre-war career is covered in a series of testimonials, which are in the archives of the Commonwealth War Graves Commission. It sought references before offering him a post overseas.[7]

The Armstrongs were described by their former vicar, Revd W.R. Scully, in Blessington, County Wicklow, as among the most 'respected of my parishioners'. Robert Armstrong himself was 'sober' and honest', the vicar concluded, sentiments which appear regularly in testimonies about him.

Armstrong began his career as a gardener in Manor Kilbride, County Wicklow, in the pay of Colonel William Henry (W.H.) Daniel. He was employed for three years in stables and gardens, making up flower beds. He then went as an apprentice gardener to Plassey in County Limerick. His work made a good impression. He was always 'honest and willing'.[8]

His next posting was at the Royal Hospital Kilmainham, which was, until 1928, a home for retired British soldiers. Its garden, laid out in the French style of the late 1700s, with beautifully manicured box hedges, variegated-topiary holly bushes and classical sculptures, remains an urban haven to this day in what is now the grounds of the Irish Museum of Modern Art. Armstrong was employed as a journeyman gardener at the Royal Hospital Kilmainham. He was 'industrious, paid attention to duties … can confidently recommend, hard working and trustworthy'. His final posting as a gardener was at Fortfield House in Terenure between October 1914 and June 1915. He was, according to the caretaker, 'a most reputable man, strictly sober and honest'.

When war broke out, the Irish Guards assiduously recruited around Ireland. Though an Irish regiment, they were based, then as now, in Wellington Barracks, London. In June 1915, Armstrong enlisted.[9] Three factors may have influenced his decision. One was his nationality. The second was his height. He was 6ft, tall now, exceptionally tall then. The Guards' regiments recruited tall men. Thirdly, and possibly most significantly, his brother Private James (Henry) Armstrong was already serving in the regiment.

The 1st and 2nd battalions of the Irish Guards were incorporated into the newly created Guards Division of the British army. Robert Armstrong was posted overseas on 1 September 1915, just in time for the Battle of Loos in September-October 1915. Both Irish Guards battalions suffered terribly in a battle which cost the British almost 60,000 casualties, including 20,000 dead. Tragically, his brother was killed on 2 October in the same battle and is buried in Nœux-les-Mines Cemetery.[10]

Years later, in correspondence with the Imperial War Graves Commission, Armstrong's sister Augusta Lindsay lamented the loss of the £2 a month he had sent her while in the pay of the commission. She felt entitled to a pension in the wake of his loss. 'I miss this money very much indeed. It is a poor recompense after all my family did for England. I lost my two brothers and my husband served in the Royal Navy 1914-1918 war (he was on Arctic convoys). We live in Ireland but we served England well. I thought you would surely grant me a pension after all the lives my brother saved in France; his own he could not save.'[11]

A year after enlisting, Armstrong was appointed to lance corporal and in December 1916 to lance sergeant, the Guards equivalent rank of corporal. One report from the Imperial War Graves Commission suggested he had been the youngest Irish-born sergeant in the Irish Guards.

In January 1917, while serving in the Somme sector, two months after the dreadful battle of 1916 ended, he was badly injured. The last phase of the Battle of the Somme was the Battle of the Ancre in mid-November 1916, which was halted because of a snowstorm. This marshy valley was a killing ground for men from the 36th (Ulster) Division and the 29th Division, which included two Irish regiments, during the early stages of the Battle of the Somme.

The British resumed offensives in January 1917 when frost hardened the ground. Armstrong was wounded from a bursting shell, which shattered his hip. He was evacuated to Britain and treated at Bermondsey Hill Hospital in London. Doctors adjudged that the injury left him with a lot of pain and restricted movement. His loss of mobility was estimated at 20 per cent. His war was over. Every soldier secretly longed for a 'blighty', an injury bad enough to be sent back to Blighty (England), but not bad enough to cripple or disfigure one for life. As blighties go, Armstrong's was on the severe end of the scale.[12]

He finally left the British army in 1920. He was, according to his service record, a 'very good NCO in every respect' and 'thoroughly reliable'. The culmination of the excellent references he received from his former employees in Ireland and from the British army provided a compelling case for the job he applied for in 1920 with the Imperial War Graves Commission.

Battles that lasted days in previous campaigns lasted months. Deaths, once numbered in the hundreds, were now numbered in the tens of thousands and soon in the hundreds of thousands.

In previous campaigns, such as the Battle of Waterloo, the 'men', the rank-and-file soldiers who did the killing and dying, were tipped into unmarked graves. Only the deaths of officers and those in the higher ranks were ever marked by memorials.

Dealing with the death toll of the First World War exercised the conscience of retired general Fabian Ware, who was turned down for active service during the war. A war on this scale, in which so many of the men who died were not professional soldiers but volunteers, demanded a different response. He set up the Imperial War Graves Commission (later to be the Commonwealth War Graves Commission) in 1917. Three decisions it made were bitterly contested at the time. The commission decided not to allow the repatriation of bodies, irrespective of means. Families were not allowed to decide on the headstone design for their dead relatives. The final decision was the most controversial of all. The commission decided to give every dead serviceman the same headstone, and therefore status, in death, irrespective of rank in life.

In the hierarchical structure of post-Edwardian society, this was a concession too far for some. The issue over what to do with the dead of the First World War went on for years and culminated in a particularly heated debate in the House of Commons in 1920. Many MPs believed the commission's edicts were a form of tyranny that the men had died to prevent. What could be less British than denying a relative the right to bury their dead as they saw fit?

Then the former Prime Minister Herbert Asquith made a telling intervention. The most powerful man in Britain was not spared the grief that visited countless homes from No. 10 Downing Street to the meanest Dublin tenement. His son Raymond was killed at the Battle of Flers-Courcelette in September 1916.

Asquith silenced the house:

> There are some of us, of whom I am one, who have a direct and personal interest in this matter, and I only rise to say in a sentence what I know to be the feelings of large numbers of grieved parents and relatives, as they are my own. These men, be they officers or rank and file who fell, died with the same courage and the same devotion and for the same cause, and they should have their names and their services perpetuated by the same memorial.[13]

To facilitate the work of the commission, a new peacetime army had to be found. It needed hundreds of gardeners and landscape architects for the cemeteries being created across the old battlefields. These cemeteries would be meticulously created and kept into perpetuity. The commission moved early to ensure that the care of its soldiers who died abroad would be entrusted to the British themselves and not the host nation.

An elaborate gardening programme was drawn up for each cemetery. Graves were to be placed in rows and flattened to ensure uniformity. Carefully manicured grass was to grow between the headstones. Evergreen shrubbery would ensure a uniform look across the seasons. Where possible and climate allowing, English yew trees were to be grown to replicate the country churchyards of home. A 1918 report for the Imperial War Graves Commission concluded, 'There is no reason why cemeteries should be places of gloom; but the restfulness of grass and the brightness of flowers in fitting combination would appear to strike the proper note of brightness and life.'[14]

Some of Britain's finest architects gave their services to the commission. Sir Herbert Baker designed the cemetery layout. Sir Reginald Blomfield, who created the New Menin Gate Memorial, came up with the Cross of Sacrifice and Sir Edwin Lutyens the Stone of Remembrance, with its inscription from the Book of Ecclesiasticus chosen by Rudyard Kipling: 'Their name liveth for evermore'. Every cemetery would have a Cross of Sacrifice and a Stone of Remembrance.

The combination of his experience as a gardener and his impeccable war record made Armstrong the type of worker the commission needed. Not long after arriving in France to work for the commission, he met Claire Maricq, the sister of a Belgian commandant. Romance blossomed rapidly. Within a year of his arrival, Armstrong proposed to her.[15]

The Maricq family made inquiries through the commission as to Armstrong's bona fides. Did he have a steady job? What was his military service record like? Had he been married before? Was he a 'steady respectable man'? What kind of family did he come from? The last question was not considered of 'special significance'.

The commission's answers were enough to satisfy her family. The couple were married in 1922. They had no children. In 1929 Armstrong offered to resign from the commission to go into business with his wife in Charleroi where they lived. He also complained that he could not find a suitable house in Valenciennes. He later rescinded his offer of resignation and was accepted back into the commission without demur. The marriage was dissolved in 1932.

His supervisor Mr Grinham told the commission that Armstrong was a good gardener, a 'willing and hard worker' in company, but 'under no circumstances' should he be allowed to work unsupervised. He noted Armstrong's sociability, stating he had a 'very wide circle of friends', that his timekeeping was sometimes tardy and his work not as thorough as it could be.

This judgement would appear to be at odds with the otherwise exemplary reports that Armstrong received from those who knew him. Indeed, it would not stop him becoming head gardener of the Valenciennes group of the Imperial War Graves Commission in 1937. In the same year, he and Grinham at Valenciennes were given medals by the municipality for their work in the cemetery.

In 1939, war broke out again. Initially commission staff remained in situ. The British joked of hanging out their washing on the Siegfried Line and the French crouched behind their Maginot Line. An air of unreality pervaded the Western Front as Hitler turned his attention eastwards to wipe Poland from the map.

Armstrong took advantage of the so-called Phoney War to make a trip home. On 13 December, he left Valenciennes to visit his father in Edgeworthstown, returning on New Year's Day 1940. It would be the last time he visited Ireland.[16]

The uneasy peace that settled over northern France was shattered on 10 May 1940 when Germany invaded Belgium and France. Striking through the Ardennes Forest, using mechanised armour and the Luftwaffe, the German assault of 1940 was a generation removed from the ponderous advance of 1914, which ended in trench stalemate.

The Germans crossed the rivers Meuse, Lys, Sambre and Somme, which had prevented or stalled their advance in 1914, traversed old battlefields where millions of their antecedents had died, defeated the French in just forty-four days and forced the British back across the English Channel at Dunkirk.

The commission belatedly ordered the evacuation of all British citizens in its pay. There were 600 British and Irish gardeners in France and Belgium. Many of them were ex-soldiers like Armstrong. Some had married locally, as Armstrong had done. Others had created mini-colonies, especially in Ypres, which had its own British school. The mass evacuation broke the hearts of those involved. Its historian Philip Longworth had cause to lament, 'Within a month the organisation in France as well as Belgium had crumbled, the work of a generation abandoned to the enemy.'[17]

Old soldiers, now working with the commission, mixed with the new ones as the British presence on the Continent headed for the little ships of Dunkirk, but not Armstrong. He was an Irish citizen and therefore beyond the control of the commission.

Why Armstrong stayed is a mystery. His nephew Doug Armstrong said a family story might go some way towards explaining his situation. Robert Armstrong told his father on his last visit home to Ireland that he was returning to France because all his friends were there.[18]

His financial situation was critical as the commission was in no position to pay Armstrong once the Germans occupied France. For months, neither the commission nor Armstrong's family heard from him. Then, in early 1941, a message was transmitted home through the Irish legation in Vichy:

> Armstrong Valenciennes informs father Currygrane Edgeworthstown Longford and sister Mrs Lindsay Cambrian Churchtown Road Dundrum that very well sends love, wishes sister to send some money if possible.

Money did arrive in February 1941 via the Irish government: some £30 as part of a hardship fund for Irish nationals stranded abroad during the Nazi occupation. It would appear from the commission files that he was paid some money by the protecting power, the Swiss in this case, who sought the return of wages paid to him after the war.

A protecting power usually acts as a conduit between two countries at war that have broken off diplomatic relations. Though Armstrong was Irish, not British, the Swiss acted for him as he worked for an arm of the British government.

Armstrong could have returned to Britain and remained in the pay of the commission. Initially it had to provide charity help to its evacuated staff, but soon roles as gardeners were found for them around Britain. The men proved to be invaluable replacements for conscripted gardeners sent to the armed forces.[19]

Alternatively, he could have returned home to Ireland. His options might have been limited, but at least he would have been safe. His father wanted him back and his brother Frederick had a successful motor dealership in Dublin. Frederick Armstrong's son Reg Armstrong would go on to be a successful businessman and a Grand Prix motorcycle road racer.[20]

Robert Armstrong's wife had remarried, he was unattached. In 1941, his father James wrote to the commission seeking information about his son. They were unable to tell him anything. 'We do not know whether Armstrong is interned or free, working at his cemetery or not so working. Nor do we know whether he has asserted his Irish citizenship to the Germans or the French or what attitude they would take if he did.'[21]

Many of the commission staff did not make it back in the chaos of war. Some 159 of them were interned for the duration of the war by the Germans. Armstrong was allowed to stay free. He moved in with a friend, a Monsieur Panet in Valenciennes. Later he moved to another safe house and to the home of Marcel Maillaird, who was involved in the French Resistance.[22]

The assumption is that the Germans allowed his liberty free because of his Irish nationality. They presumed that he was a neutral. 'It may be that his popularity enabled him to do this. He was known far and wide,' one official wrote to the commission.

Armstrong expressed no gratitude towards the occupiers. On the contrary, he needled them whenever he could. It was a dangerous game. His defiance of the Germans started early.

One anonymous local observed:

An old boy who lived almost opposite the entrance to Famare Communal Cemetery Extension told me that Armstrong decided to place the tools etc from our cemetery in the custody of the Mairie [town hall], and the old boy warned him not to go. But Armstrong decided that the tools were to go to the Mairie and took them personally to the Mairie. I have heard that when recognised by the German Feld Police in Valenciennes that he resisted arrest and gave several of them an uncomfortable time.[23]

Unable to confront Germany on the ground in occupied Europe, the British took to the air to harass the Germans, bombing military and civilian targets. It was exceedingly dangerous work. Bomber Command suffered more casualties pro rata than any other branch of the British armed forces. Nearly half were killed.

Armstrong's area of Belgium and France was across the flight path of many British and American bombers. Valenciennes (St Roch) Cemetery accepted another generation of war dead. The first Allied airmen were buried there in October 1942. At first, the Germans even provided full military honours for their foes, but the burials became the focus for acts of local patriotism. On 23 August 1943, two flying officers were buried without military honours and the public were excluded from the ceremony and from subsequent burials. This provoked an extraordinary act of defiance on the part of the local populace. On Armistice Day 1943, thousands came to Valenciennes (St Roch) to pay tribute to the Allied war dead. Some seventy-two pots of chrysanthemums, along with an estimated 2,500 bouquets and crosses, were placed on Allied graves. This mass display would have put a further strain on Armstrong's relationship with the Germans.[24]

Compounding his estrangement was German suspicion, accurate as it turned out, that Armstrong was not a neutral, but a determined member of the French Resistance. Though too old to fight, Armstrong found another way to help the Allied cause. He joined the St Jacques evasion network, one of a myriad of networks set up to smuggle stranded Allied servicemen out of occupied Europe.

On the night of 9 March 1943, a Halifax bomber took off from RAF Elvington in Yorkshire on a bombing mission to Munich. On their return, the bomber was harassed by German fighters and shot down. The pilot was killed and two men captured but four escaped, including Flight Lieutenant Brian Desmond Barker.[25] A few days later, Barker met Armstrong in a café in Valenciennes. Armstrong arranged for Barker to hide for a couple of days before he took him to another safe house in Paris. From Paris, Barker made a number of failed attempts to escape. Eventually, Barker and eleven other airmen were put on a train from Paris to the Spanish border. They were met by Basques opposed to General Franco, who took them to Pamplona. They were briefly arrested by the Spanish civil guard before making their way to Madrid and from Madrid to the ultimate destination of most evaders: the British colony of Gibraltar.[26]

Finally, on 13 July 1943, four months and four days after crash landing in Belgium, Barker made it back to Britain on board a cargo plane.

These were highly trained men, resourceful, intelligent and incredibly brave. The best of them were irreplaceable. Many had spent years flying before getting to the operational standards demanded by war. The cost of training them was prohibitive. Everything had to be done to get them back.

In his memoir, Airey Neave, the first British officer to escape from Colditz, estimated that it cost £10,000 (€875,000) to train a bomber pilot and £15,000 (€1.25 million) to train a fighter pilot.

Neave had an extraordinary war. Captured by the Germans at Calais in May 1940, he escaped from Colditz in the depth of winter, crossing the Swiss border in January 1942. This made him a *cause célèbre* at home. He was made head of MI9, the agency charged with repatriating Allied servicemen caught behind enemy lines. In the 1960s, Neave wrote his memoir *Saturday at MI9* (he was known by the code name Saturday). In it, he estimated that 3,000 Allied airmen were repatriated between the fall of France in 1940 and D-Day in June 1944. This, he stated with considerable British understatement, was a 'significant renewable of manpower'.[27]

In later years, he became a Conservative politician and was appointed to the front bench by Margaret Thatcher in 1975 as her spokesman on Northern Ireland at the height of the Troubles. Neave said he understood terrorism, having been a terrorist himself during the war, when he organised clandestine acts to undermine German rule in occupied Europe. In March 1979, two months before Thatcher took power in Britain, Neave was killed by an Irish National Liberation Army bomb left under his car at the House of Commons.

Armstrong was part of a civilian army which fought the Germans by proxy. They were an extraordinary collection of individuals: men and women, professionals and farmhands, socialists, Communists, anti-clerical firebrands, devout Catholics and even Germans opposed to the Nazis. They were united by a common enemy and the desire to do the right thing by those who would be their liberators. As Neave put it, 'By the end of the war this form of clandestine service had become a popular movement in which large numbers of men and women of different backgrounds and political beliefs made their contribution to victory. Harbouring men shot down in air combat or cut off from their regiments, appealed to their humanity.'[28]

It was difficult and dangerous work. These men and women faced the Gestapo, the Vichy police, collaborators and traitors within their midst. One, an Englishman named Harold Cole, was captured by the Germans and betrayed his erstwhile comrades. Some fifty were executed by the Germans.

A myriad of resistance networks was set up. Armstrong's was known as St Jacques. Others included the Comet Line and the very Irish-sounding Pat O'Leary line. The Pat Line, as it became known, was set up by a Belgian doctor and Resistance fighter, Albert Guérisse, who assumed the *nom de guerre* of a French-Canadian airman with a distinctly Irish name.[29] These evasion networks took different routes, but mostly they led south, across the border through neutral Spain to Gibraltar.

According to the commission, Armstrong was also involved in the escape of an American airman who was in Britain for six months before the Germans knew he had escaped.

Maillard, who sheltered Armstrong for a time, informed the Irish *chargé d'affaires* in Paris that together they had helped to liberate paratroopers and to smuggle arms on behalf of the Resistance.

Armstrong was clearly a valuable link in the evasion networks. He was an Anglophone. He presumably had a working knowledge of the French language, having worked there for twenty years and having been married to a French speaker. He knew the lie of the land well. He also had a valid reason to be in France. Above all else, he was a neutral, or so the Germans assumed.

However, they were now monitoring his movements. Armstrong was already a marked man on 11 November 1943 when an incident occurred, which would have tragic consequences.

Some local women put flowers on the graves of Allied soldiers to remember Armistice Day in defiance of a ban by the German authorities. When a German officer kicked the flowers away, Armstrong reacted furiously and assaulted him. He was arrested and detained for a few days. He fled Valenciennes, but on return was recognised by the Gestapo as a Resistance worker.[30]

On 25 November 1943, his good friend Emanuelle Dossche, the manager of the cemetery, was summoned by the local German commandant and told to get rid of Armstrong. The Germans would tend to the graves of the Allied war dead. Dossche went immediately to Armstrong and warned him that he was in significant danger. Unfortunately, it was too late. He was arrested the following day.

He was taken to a prison in Loos-lez-Lille in the same vicinity where he had fought and where his brother had died nearly thirty years previously. Armstrong was detained there for six months.

He was sentenced to death by the Tribunal de l'Air, the Luftwaffe court, in May 1944. A month later, the German Under-Secretary of State informed the Irish *chargé d'affaires* that Armstrong had been condemned to death.

The fate of Armstrong came to the attention of the family's local TD in Longford, Seán MacEoin, a stalwart of the Irish revolutionary period and post-independence Ireland general. MacEoin, known in local lore as the Blacksmith of Ballinalee, made interventions to try and save Armstrong's life.[31] One might not expect a committed Irish Republican to intervene on behalf of an ex-British soldier ostensibly working for the British government, but for MacEoin, his intervention was deeply personal.

The MacEoins and the Armstrongs had been near neighbours in Longford. During the War of Independence, MacEoin was one of the most-wanted IRA men in the country. His flying column inflicted death and injury on the British forces in the midlands. He needed a safe house. James Armstrong provided him with one.

The Black and Tans came looking for MacEoin and called at the Armstrong home. James Armstrong was able to persuade them to look elsewhere. Given Armstrong's religion, his son's military service in the British army and his services in the family of one of the IRA's most indomitable enemies, Henry Wilson, the Black and Tans departed, convinced James Armstrong was on their side.

'We were a Protestant family and the British assumed we were loyal,' says Doug Armstrong. MacEoin, who went on to become a Free State army general and government minister, never forgot the gesture and did what he could to help Robert Armstrong.

Armstrong's death sentence was commuted to fifteen years in jail, but it turned out only to be a reprieve. The Germans kept moving him from prison to prison to keep one step ahead of the Allies, who had landed on the continent of Europe on D-Day. He was transferred from Brussels to a prison in Aachen and then to a prison near Cologne. While there, he was badly beaten by a German prison guard. He also developed a boil on his leg that failed to heal and sapped what energy he had left.

In October 1944, he was moved eastwards to Kassel-Wehlheiden to work outside building a new camp.[32] Armstrong and the other inmates were forced to rebuild the camp every time the Americans bombed it. At first, the conditions in early autumn were relatively clement, but, as the weather deteriorated, so did Armstrong's condition. The poor nourishment and harsh weather became intolerable. After the war, an unnamed Dutch prisoner who had been transferred with Armstrong gave this account of Armstrong's final days:

> He had a big boil on his leg which was only very poorly treated and day by day he grew thin. Because he could not work …he was shoved by guards, among whom there were some nasty individuals. On December 14 he left with us to go to Waldheim. His situation was now grave. The day before departure a guard struck him again because he was not eating his meal quickly enough. He could hardly move. As soon as he arrived in Waldheim, he was transferred to hospital. We hoped he would recover as we heard that the medical treatment in Waldheim was much better than in Kassel, but alas he was too weak. He died roughly two days after his arrival. All comrades were very moved by his deaths and prayed for him.[33]

The Dutch eyewitnesses concluded his testimony by stating that even in his terrible last days, Armstrong still exhibited 'courage and good humour' and his morale was good.

Evidence of Armstrong's mistreatment also came from Alfred Delporte, the Mayor of Montay, a small village in the Pas-de-Calais. Delport said he witnessed Armstrong being knocked to the ground by a large German warden and 'violently and repeatedly struck on the head'. He was beaten so badly that Armstrong did not appear for exercise for three to four days. When he did, his head and neck was covered in bandages from which blood constantly seeped. Delport reported, 'From this time he grew rapidly thinner and his condition deteriorated from day to day. Armstrong was a well built and upstanding man and there is very strong evidence to show that his death on or about 16.12.44 was hastened, if not actually caused, by the ill-treatment and insufficient food received from the enemy.'[34]

Armstrong's death was not confirmed until nearly two years later. His sister Augusta Lindsay wrote repeatedly to the commission, seeking information. The commission wrote back, apologising that they had no news. Waldheim was located in the Soviet sector. The Germans burned their records and chaos ensued after the war.

Eventually the British Prime Minister Clement Attlee intervened. Armstrong's death was finally confirmed by the British Consular Representative in Berlin in November 1946. The German authorities stated that he died of tuberculosis of the lungs. It was a lie.

The commission found Armstrong had died of 'ill-health and hunger'. He had been reduced to a 'mere skeleton' and 'had multiple leg wounds'. It was so enraged by his treatment that it considered treating Armstrong's death as a war crime, but nothing came of it.

In November 2015 Doug Armstrong and his son Wendell visited Waldheim, where they were cordially received by those who managed the site on which it is located. Doug left a wreath which stated: 'In loving memory of Robert Armstrong who died in this prison 18-12-1944 due to medical neglect and starvation'.

Dealing with Armstrong's financial affairs after his death also consumed much time for the commission. Between his insurance payout and accrued wages, the commission had £338 to disperse among his family. This was a considerable amount of money at the time and it was badly needed, judging by the correspondence between the commission and the Armstrong family.[35]

His sister Mrs Lindsay demanded that the £2 a month usually remitted to her by Armstrong should be paid, a sum of £108 in total. She cited letters from Field Marshal Bernard Montgomery and Air Marshall Arthur Tedder, who wrote to her praising her brother's activities. Harry Lindsay, Augusta's son, recalled there was considerable hardship in Ireland during the Second World War:

> Money was so scarce that I remember looking over the bridge into the River Dodder and day after day seeing the frame of a bicycle frame. I got it and it turned out to be a women's bicycle frame. I brought it home and cleaned it up. I brought into to a fellow in Dundrum, Joe Daly, and swapped it for a male bicycle frame. My father built a bicycle out of that over the weeks and months that followed. Eventually he had a bicycle that he would ride in and out to work. After a while some debt or otherwise arose and he had to sell the bicycle. Times were that tough.

Harry Lindsay remembers Bob Armstrong from his childhood. Money was tight, except when his beloved uncle returned from France:

> My mother worshipped him. Anything Bob wanted, Bob got. Our house was very rigorously controlled financially. When Bob came home, that went out the door. Bob always brought my mother a bottle of perfume from France and this was absolutely treasured as if it was holy water.

He remembered his uncle as a physically impressive man. Hard physical work had made him strong. He would prance around his mother's house wearing only shorts. 'He had the same physique as Jack Doyle (the boxer) and I've seen both of them in the nip believe it or not.'[36]

He also brought home bacon from a convent in Valenciennes, which had many resident Irish nuns. It gave rise to another story about Armstrong. The Mother Superior did not co-operate with the Germans. They surrounded the convent to starve them into submission. Armstrong threw food over the wall to them until he was caught by the Germans and given a hiding.

Bob Armstrong was very popular when he went home to Longford, Harry Lindsay remembered. He had a marvellous shot. He would shoot rabbits from early morning and he would return with a pair of them entwined in such a way that they would hang on the back of the door. 'Then they knew Bob Armstrong was back and they would come over to see him.'

Harry Lindsay reckons Armstrong was a 'natural rebel'. The story was passed on through the family that after he had left the British army, Armstrong would come home and help Seán MacEoin with his IRA activities. 'We heard he would chop down trees to block roads and all that carry-on.' Another story held that he was once hauled into a barracks for questioning. His interrogator hit him with a riding crop and Armstrong punched him and knocked him out. Defiance of authority was a constant theme in Armstrong's life.

The request for a permanent memorial to Robert Armstrong came from Dossche, still the manager of the cemetery. Initially the commission demurred. When it was first proposed to erect a memorial to Armstrong, the commission stated that it must wait until his death was officially confirmed. This did not come until 1946. The commission would also have to bend its own rules that only those whose military deaths are commemorated are worthy of mention in a war graves cemetery. That rule was easily circumvented. The only other issue was the inscription on the memorial. By tradition, the commission would not allow any criticism of an erstwhile foe, so, after much discussion the following dedication was approved in French and English:

> To the memory of Robert Armstrong, head gardener, Imperial War Graves Commission. Died in captivity at Waldheim Camp (Saxony), the 16th of December 1944, Homage from his friends in Valenciennes.

Dossche continued to lobby the commission to erect a plaque at the cemetery. Local people had raised 10,000 French francs for the memorial. It was a generous offering given the privations of post-war France. He even visited the commission in Britain to press his case. Finally, it was decided that the plaque would be unveiled on 11 July 1948 and then attached to the shelter at Valenciennes.

Despite all his efforts, Dossche declined to speak at the inauguration, fearing he would be overcome with emotion. The unveiling ceremony took place as planned. It was a big event. His fellow Resistance fighters processed through the streets of Valenciennes. The event got extensive coverage in the local press.

The tablet in French and English was laid out on the Cross of Sacrifice. The base of the cross was banked with scarlet geraniums. The plaque was unveiled by the Mayor of Valenciennes, who made a speech, followed by the President of the

L'Association Amicale Franco-Britannique, an association for ex-French and British servicemen who had fought together, and the British Consul.

The two medals awarded posthumously to Armstrong, *La médaille de la Résistance française* and the Franco-Britannique medal, were presented to his brother Edward Armstrong, who made it to the ceremony.[37]

There appears, from the contemporary newspaper reports at the time, to have been nobody from the Irish legation in Paris there, though they were invited. Instead, the Irish government claimed itself as a creditor of Armstrong's estate and sought the return of the £30 1s 0d it had given to him earlier in the war. The money was returned to the Irish government by the Imperial War Graves Commission in August 1948, a month after the plaque was unveiled.[38]

At every turn, Robert Armstrong, this proud, stubborn and courageous man, had chosen a path which led to his premature death. He could have evacuated to Britain or Ireland and seen out the war tending to his shrubs, trees and flowers on some English country estate. He owed nothing to anybody or any cause.

Having chosen to stay, he could have remained aloof from a global conflict, which ostensibly had nothing to do with him. What could just one man acting alone do in such an unceasing maelstrom of enmity and hate? Armstrong was not neutral. Unlike tens of millions of others, he had a choice and he chose to do his best to oppose Nazi tyranny. It cost him his life.

When the proposal was put to the commission by the townspeople of Valenciennes, the commission had no doubt that Armstrong deserved to be honoured:

> As a neutral he could probably have carried on unmolested but his patriotism compelled him to assist Allied soldiers and later an American airman to escape thus rendering himself hostile to the occupying power.[39]

A full border of red roses planted by Armstrong was laid out in front of the marble plaque. Beside it was a bunch of shamrock. He remained in death, as in life, an Irishman.

NOTES

Introduction

1 UK's National Maritime Museum and the UK National Archives, October 2013. Based on surviving records, 3,573 sailors from Ireland out of 12,000.
2 Lt Col. Harvey, *A Bloody Day: The Irish at Waterloo (2015)*. He estimates that 8,500 of the Duke of Wellington's 28,000 British soldiers, including Wellington himself were Irish.
3 Peter Karsten, 'Irish Soldiers in the British army 1792–1922: Suborned or Subordinate', *Journal of Social History*, Vol. 17, No. 1 (Autumn 1983).
4 Ibid.
5 Graham Davis, *In Search of a Better Life: British and Irish Migration* (Stroud, 2011), p.17.
6 Ibid.
7 Ibid.
8 Quoted in John Talbot, *Earl of Shrewsbury, Reasons for not Taking the Test* (London, 1828) Introduction, p. CXXX.
9 Wellington's speech to the House of Lords 1828, as reported in *The Newfoundlander*, 4 May 1880.
10 Great Britain Parliamentary Accounts and Papers, Trade Wages, 1893–1894, Vol. 34, Part II, 454–55.
11 Company Sergeant William Leeman Kent was killed at the Battle of Arras on Tuesday, 24 April 1917, a year to the day after the Easter Rising broke out. Bill, as he was known, was in the 3rd Reserve Battalion of the Royal Dublin Fusiliers. In September 1916, he was posted to the front and fought in the Battle of the Somme. His family was informed of his death on 8 May 1917, the anniversary of his brother's execution.
12 <http://www.easter1916.ie/index.php/people/a-z/michael-mallin/>
13 Seán Ó Faoláin, 'A portrait of the artist as an old man', *Irish University Review* (1976)
14 Tom Barry, *Guerilla Days in Ireland* (Dublin: 1949), p.8.
15 Peter Karsten, 'Irish Soldiers in the British army, 1792–1922: Suborned or Subordinate', *Journal of Social History*, Vol. 17, No. 1 (Autumn 1983), pp.31–64.
16 *Freeman's Journal*, 16 January 1898.
17 Peter Karsten, 'Irish Soldiers in the British Army, 1792–1922: Suborned or Subordinate', *Journal of Social History*, Vol. 17, No. 1 (Autumn 1983) pp.31–64.
18 Stephen Gwynn, *John Redmond's Last Years* (New York: Longman's Green and Co., 1919).
19 Dr Aoife Bhreatnach, 'What is a garrison town?' (2 March 2012), *Irish Garrison Towns* [website] <http://irishgarrisontowns.com/what-is-a-garrison-town/#fn-51-3>.
20 Harold E. Raugh, *The Victorians at War, 1815–1914: An Encyclopedia of British Military History* (Santa Barbara, California: ABC-CLIO, 2004).
21 David Lloyd George, the House of Commons, 30 March 1914.
22 Letter from Herbert Asquith to Venetia Stanley, 24 July 1914.

23 Winston S. Churchill, *The World Crisis* (New York: Charles Scribner's Sons, 1932), p.94.

24 Quoted in *The Fateful Year: England 1914*. Taken from a letter Asquith sent to his mistress Venetia Stanley.

25 Winston S. Churchill, *The World Crisis* (New York: Charles Scribner's Sons, 1932).

26 Quoted in Jack Beatty, *The Lost History of 1914: How the Great War Was Not Inevitable* (London: Bloomsbury, 2012).

27 Sir Edward Gray, the House of Commons, 3 August 1914.

28 *Freeman's Journal*, 21 September 1914.

29 'Statement to the Irish Volunteers, 24 September 1914', *History Hub* [website] <http://historyhub.ie/statement-to-the-irish-volunteers>.

30 Professor Keith Jeffery, *Ireland and the Great War* (Cambridge: Cambridge University Press, 2000).

31 Patrick Callan, 'Recruiting for the British army during the First World War', *The Irish Sword*, Vol. XVII, No. 66, 1987.

32 Professor Keith Jeffery, 'Ireland and the First World War: The Historical Context', *Ireland History Live* [website], Queen's University Belfast <www.qub.ac.uk/sites/irishhistorylive/IrishHistoryResources/Articlesandlecturesbyourteachingstaff/IrelandandtheFirstWorldWar/>.

33 Ronan McGreevy, 'New figures show almost 20,000 Irishmen fought for Canada in WW1', *The Irish Times* [website], 1 August 2015 <www.irishtimes.com/news/social-affairs/new-figures-show-almost-20-000-irishmen-fought-for-canada-in-ww1-1.1885044>.

34 Ronan McGreevy, 'Irish in Australia "were not shirkers" in first World War', *The Irish Times* [website], 17 October 2014 <www.irishtimes.com/news/ireland/irish-news/irish-in-australia-were-not-shirkers-in-first-world-war-1.1967446>.

35 <www.archives.gov/st-louis/military-personnel/fire-1973.html>.

36 Irish Central 7 April 2015 www.irishcentral.com/roots/history/Nearly-1000-Irish-died-serving-US-army-in-World-War-I.html

37 'Ireland's Memorial Records', In Flanders Fields Museum [website] <imr.inflandersfields.be>.

38 'Find your ancestors in Ireland's Memorial Record: World War 1: 1914–1918', *Find My Past* [website], <www.findmypast.ie/articles/world-records/full-list-of-the-irish-family-history-records/military-service-and-conflict/irelands-memorial-record-world-war-1>.

39 'Ireland's Memorial Records', In Flanders Fields Museum [website], <imr.inflandersfields.be>.

40 'Find your ancestors in Ireland's Memorial Record: World War 1: 1914–1918', *Find My Past* [website], <www.findmypast.ie/articles/world-records/full-list-of-the-irish-family-history-records/military-service-and-conflict/irelands-memorial-record-world-war-1>.

41 Ronan McGreevy, 'Irish first World War dead "may be higher than claimed"', *The Irish Times* [website], 12 June 2014 <www.irishtimes.com/culture/heritage/irish-first-world-war-dead-may-be-higher-than-claimed-1.1829795>.

42 'Mayo Great War Memorial', *Irish War Memorials* [website] <www.irishwarmemorials.ie/Memorials-Detail?memoId=679>.

43 <http://fermanaghherald.com/2014/11/fermanagh-war-memorial-book-of-honour-launched/> The Irish War Memorial Records records 498 men from Fermanagh who died in the war. The Fermanagh War Memorial in Belmore records 581, with an additional 200 names that are not listed on the memorial but are in the memorial book.

44 *The Irish Times*, 12 November 1924.

45 Fr F.X. Martin, *Studia Hibernica*, No.7, 1967, pp.7–126.

46 Ibid.

47 'History of Irish National War Memorial Gardens', *Óglaigh na hÉireann* [website] <www.military.ie/info-centre/df-ceremonial/history-of-war-memorial-garden/>.

48 Kevin Myers, *Ireland's Great War* (Dublin: Lilliput Press, 2014), <http://www.irishtimes.com/culture/books/kevin-myers-on-ireland-s-great-war-1.2060463>.

49 *The Irish Times*, 9 April 2005.

50 Paddy Harte, *Young Tigers and Mongrel Foxes* (Dublin: O'Brien Press, 2005), p.328.

Chapter 1

1 *The Great War* (TV series), BBC, 1966, Episode 1: 'The Idle Hill of Summer'.

2 Ibid.

3 Ibid.

4 T.C Blanning (ed.), *The Nineteenth Century: Europe 1789–1914* (Oxford: Oxford University Press, 2000).

5 Harold MacMillan, 'The Kingdom and a Holy Place', *The Watchtower* (magazine), 15 September 1982.

6 Francis Ledwidge, *The Complete Poems of Francis Ledwidge with introduction by*

Lord Dunsany (New York, 1919), p.12.

7 Fritz Stern, cited in David Fromkin, *Europe's Last Summer: Who Started The Great War in 1914?* (New York: Vintage, 2004).

8 'SHAPE in France', Supreme Headquarters Allied Powers Europe [website] <www.shape.nato.int/page134353332>.

9 'Mapping the Impact of the Great War', *World War I Centenary* [website] <http://ww1centenary.oucs.ox.ac.uk/space-into-place/mapping-the-impact-of-the-great-war/>.

10 Nikolas Gardner, *Command and the British Expeditionary Force in 1914* (Alberta: University of Calgary, 2000), p.1.

11 Churchill memo to British Cabinet, January 1914. Cited in John Darwin, *The Empire Project* (Cambridge: Cambridge University Press, 2010), p.268.

12 Richard Cannon, *Historical record of the Fourth or Royal Irish Regiment of Dragoon Guards* (London, 1836).

13 Ernest Edward Thomas, *I fired the first shot*, information supplied by Ben Thomas.

14 Richard van Emden, 'Benjamin Clouting', *Britain's Last Tommies* [website]

<http://britainslasttommies.wordpress.com/clouting>.

15 Revd Harold Gibb, *Record of the 4th Irish Dragoon Guards in the Great War 1914–1918* (Canterbury, 1925), p.3.

16 Ibid.

17 Ernest Edward Thomas, *I fired the first shot*, information supplied by Ben Thomas.

18 Ibid.

19 Interview with author.

20 Tom Hurley, 'In Search of E.E Thomas', *Tipp FM*, first broadcast on 20 October 2014 <http://tippfm.podomatic.com/entry/2014–10–20T03_12_06–07_00>.

21 Ibid.

22 Ibid.

23 Interview with author.

24 Tom Hurley, 'In Search of E.E Thomas', *Tipp FM*, first broadcast on 20 October 2014 <http://tippfm.podomatic.com/entry/2014–10–20T03_12_06–07_00>.

25 Sir Tom Bridges, *Alarms & Excursions: reminiscences of a soldier* (London: Longmans, Green and Co., 1938), p.88.

26 John Hutton, *August 1914: Surrender at St Quentin* (Barnsley: Pen and Sword, 2010), p.145.

27 Ibid.

Chapter 2

1 Richard Holmes, *War Walks* (BBC TV series 1, episode 3), first broadcast 9 August 1996.

2 Peter Doyle and Robin Schäfer, *Fritz and Tommy: Across the Barbed Wire* (Stroud: The History Press, 2015).

3 R.C. Riley, 'Recent Developments in the Belgian Borinage: An area of declining coal production', *Geography*, Vol. 50, No. 3 (July 1965), pp 251–273.

4 Brigadier-General Sir James E. Edmonds, *British Official History of the War Military Operations France and Belgium 1914* (London: MacMillan, 1937), p.72.

5 John Lucy, *There's a Devil in the Drum* (London: Naval and Military Press, 1938), p.109.

6 Ibid.

7 Quoted in Peter Hart, *Fire and Movement: The British Expeditionary Force and the Campaign of 1914* (Oxford: Oxford University Press, 2012), p.88.

8 Ibid.

9 'Turbotstown House, Coole, County Westmeath', *National Inventory of Architectural Heritage* [website], <www.buildingsofireland.ie/niah/search.jsp?type=record&county=WM&regno=15400330>.

10 Edmund Dease, *Complete History of the Westmeath Hunt* (Dublin: Browne and Nolan, 1898).

11 Peter Bland, interview with author.

12 <http://www.catholic-hierarchy.org/bishop/bdease.html>

13 Revd C.P. Meehan, *The rise and fall of the Irish Franciscan monasteries, and memoirs of the Irish hierarchy in the seventeeth century* (Dublin: J. Duffy, 1872).

14 Anthony Cogan, *The Ecclesiastical History of the Diocese of Meath: Ancient and Modern*, Volume 2 (Dublin, 1864), p.166.

15 Ibid.

16 'James Arthur Dease', *The Peerage* [website], <www.thepeerage.com/p7559.htm#i75586>.

17 *Kilkenny Echo*, Saturday, 11 July 1914.

18 *The Stoneyhurst Magazine*, Vol. XIII, No. 197, December 1914 <www.worldwar1schoolarchives.org/wp-content/uploads/2013/11/1914_12.pdf>.

19 Jon Robinson, 'Former Stonyhurst pupil may be ignored in First World War centenary' (28 August 2013), *Lancashire Telegraph* [website] <www.lancashiretelegraph.co.uk/news/10638198.Former_Stonyhurst_pupil_may_be_ignored_in_First_World_War_centenary/?ref=rss>.

20 Mark Ryan, *The First VCs: The Moving True Story*

of First World War Heroes Maurice Dease and Sidney Godley (Stroud: The History Press, 2014).

21 Brigadier-General Sir James E. Edmonds, *British Official History of the War Military Operations France and Belgium 1914* (London: MacMillan, 1937), p.77.

22 John Lucy, *There's a Devil in the Drum* (London: Naval and Military Press, 1938), p.114.

23 Peter Hart, *Fire and Movement: The British Expeditionary Force and the Campaign of 1914* (Oxford: Oxford University Press, 2012).

24 John Lewis-Stempel, *Six Weeks: The Short and Gallant Life of the British Officer in the First World War* (London: Orion, 2011).

25 Richard Holmes, *War Walks – Mons* (BBC TV series 1, episode 3), first broadcast August 1996.

26 *London Gazette*, Issue 28976, p.9373.

27 *The Victoria Cross* [website], <www.victoriacross.org.uk/bblucasc.htm>.

28 *London Gazette*, 24 February 1857 <https://www.thegazette.co.uk/London/issue/21971/page/659>.

29 Ronan McGreevy, 'Irishmen who won first World War VCs to get commemorative paving stones' (27 January 2014), *The Irish Times* [website] <www.irishtimes.com/news/ireland/irish-news/irishmen-who-won-first-world-war-vcs-to-get-commemorative-paving-stones-1.1668601>.

30 'For Valour – the story of Sidney Godley VC', *East Grinstead Online* [website] <www.eastgrinsteadonline.com/2014/08/14/valour-story-sidney-godley-vc/>.

31 Mark Ryan, *The First VCs: The Moving True Story of First World War Heroes Maurice Dease and Sidney Godley* (Stroud: The History Press, 2014).

32 'Major Gerald Dease', *The Peerage* [website] <www.thepeerage.com/p27780.htm#i277798>.

33 Peter Bland, interview with the author.

34 Ibid.

35 Gerald Gliddon, *VCs of the First World War 1914* (Stroud: The History Press, 2011), p.20.

36 'Memorial Plaque – Nimy Railway Bridge', *Great War Forum* [website] <http://1914-1918.invisionzone.com/forums/index.php?showtopic=159607>.

37 'Museum secures future of important portrait', *The Fusilier Museum London* [website] <www.fusiliermuseumlondon.org/uncategorized/museum-secures-future-of-important-portrait/>.

38 The British Empire suffered 1,114,914 deaths in the First World War. The United Kingdom, which included Ireland, had total deaths of 994,138, of which 885,138 were civilian deaths, comprising 2.19 per cent of the population of 45.4 million. Germany suffered 2,050,897 military deaths and 426,000 civilian deaths out of a population of 64.9 million, or some 3.82 per cent of the total population. <www.centre-robert-schuman.org/userfiles/files/reperes%20%E2%80%93%20module%201–1%20–%20explanatory%20notes%20%E2%80%93%20World%20War%20I%20casualties%20%E2%80%93%20EN.pdf>.

39 'Maud Mary Dease', *The Peerage* [website] <www.thepeerage.com/p27781.htm#i277803>.

40 *The Peerage* [website] <www.thepeerage.com/p34832.htm>.

41 <http://www.worldwar1schoolarchives.org/wp-content/uploads/2013/11/1914_10.pdf>.

42 *Glasnevin Trust* [website] <www.glasnevintrust.ie/>.

Chapter 3

1 *The Man Who Shot Liberty Vallance*, John Ford, dir. (Paramount Picture, 1962).

2 The *Evening News* was an evening paper published in London from 1881 to 1980. In 1914, it had a daily circulation of 600,000, making it London's highest-selling newspaper.

3 Arthur Machen, 'The Bowmen', *Evening News*, 29 September 1914.

4 Ibid.

5 Rudyard Kipling, 'For All That We Are', *The Times*, 2 September 1914.

6 'A Troop of Angels', *The Hereford Times*, 3 April 1915.

7 'The Angelic Guards at Mons: Comments by the Vicar of All Saints', *The Bath Society Paper*, 9 June 1915.

8 Arthur Machen, *Delphi Collected Works of Arthur Machen (Illustrated)* (Hastings: Delphi Classics, 2013).

9 Sir John Hammerton, *The True Story of the Angels of Mons, The Great War: I Was There*, Volume 2 (London, 1938).

10 The regiment was formed in 1684 by the Earl of Granard. It fought at the Siege of Namur in 1695. By coincide, Mons is only a short distance away.

11 Within two years, Drohan had become radicalised by the failure to implement home rule. He was arrested and imprisoned after the Easter Rising, went on to become a Sinn Féin TD, an anti-Treaty supporter and a passionate advocate for the Irish language.

12 *Who's Who* (A&C Black)

13 Brigadier General Stannus Geoghegan,
    *The Campaigns and History of the Royal
    Irish Regiment* (London: Naval and Military
    Press, 1927), p.76.

14 *The Old Contemptible* was a magazine published
    by the Old Contemptible Association which
    was started in 1925 and published on a
    monthly basis until the 1970s. Copies of it are
    available in the Imperial War Museum.

15 *The Old Contemptible*, March 1955.

16 Ibid.

17 Dermot Keyes, 'A fitting record of our First
    World War story' (18 November 2010),
    Munster Express [website]

<www.munster-express.ie/opinion/to-be-honest-with-you/a-
fitting-record-of-our-first-world-war-story/>.

18 Brigadier General Stannus Geoghegan,
    *The Campaigns and History of the Royal
    Irish Regiment* (London: Naval and Military
    Press, 1927), p.79.

19 Ibid.

20 *The Irish Times*, 12 November 1923.

21 Adam Hochschild, *To End All Wars:
    A Story of Loyalty and Rebellion, 1914–1918*
    (Boston: Mariner Books, 2011), p.326.

22 'John French, 1st Earl of Ypres', *Wikipedia*
    <https://en.wikipedia.org/wiki/John_French,_1st_Earl_of_
    Ypres#cite_ref-Holmes_2004.2C_p15_3-0>.

23 Interview with author.

Chapter 4

1 H.S. Jervis, *The 2nd Munsters in France*
   (Aldershot: Naval and Military Press,
   1922). Jervis was a Boer War veteran who
   commanded D Company during the
   Battle of Étreux. He was taken prisoner for
   the duration of the war. He was the last
   Lieutenant-Colonel of the battalion before it
   was disbanded in 1922.

2 Ibid.

3 Ibid.

4 British army Field Service Regulations, British
   War Office, 1909.

5 Richard Holmes, *War Walks,* (BBC TV series 1,
   Episode 3) first broadcast 9 August 1996.

6 Brigadier General Sir James Edmonds, *British
   Official History of War*, p.140.

7 H.S. Jervis, *The 2nd Munsters in France*
   (Aldershot: Naval and Military Press, 1922).

8 *Limerick Chronicle*, 27 October 1914.

9 Ibid.

10 H.S. Jervis, *The 2nd Munsters in France*
   (Aldershot: Naval and Military Press, 1922).

11 Ibid.

12 http://1914ancien.free.fr/edmoch10.htm

13 Brigadier-General Sir James Edmonds, *British
   Official History of the Great War* (London:
   Macmillan, 1922), p.223.

14 Capt. S. McCance, *The History of the Royal
   Munster Fusiliers*, 2 Vols (Aldershot: Naval and
   Military Press, 1922), p.117.

15 Ibid.

16 Brigadier-General Sir James Edmonds, *British
   Official History of the Great War* (London:
   Macmillan, 1922), p.226.

17 Capt. S. McCance, *The History of the Royal
   Munster Fusiliers*, 2 Vols (Aldershot: Naval and
   Military Press, 1922), p.119.

18 *The Irish Times*, 27 August 2015.

Chapter 5

1 *Limerick Chronicle*, 10 February 1919.

2 John Yarnall, *Barbed Wire Disease: British and
   German Prisoners of War 1914–1919* (Stroud:
   The History Press, 2011). Yarnall recounts
   that some 9 million food parcels were sent to
   British POWs during the First World War.

3 *Limerick Chronicle*, 10 February 1919.

4 Limerick Chronicle, 13 February 1919.

5 Fintan O'Toole, 'The Multiple Hero', *New
   Republic*, 2 August 2012.

6 National Library of Ireland Manuscript 8385,
   Personal statement of William Cadbury on the

death of Roger Casement 1916.

7 Casement arrived in New York on
   20 July 1914. He was delighted when he
   heard of the successful gunrunning at Howth
   on 26 July 1914.

8 John Devoy, *Recollections of an Irish Rebel*
   (New York: Chas P. Young Co., 1929), p.405.

9 *Irish Independent*, 5 October 1914.

10 Jeff Dudgeon, 'Casement's War', *Dublin Review
   of Books*, Issue 74, January 2016.

11 Reinhard Doerries, 'Casement's mission in
   the German Empire 1914–1916', *Historische*

Zeitschrift, Vol. 222, No. 3 (1976).

12 George H. Knott, *The Trial of Roger Casement* (Glasgow, 1917), p.39.

13 Ibid.

14 UK National Archives, MI5 files KV 2/6, K/V 2/7 and K/V 2/9. These files were released in April 2014 by the National Archives in Kew as part of the National Archives First World War 100 programme. It featured cases against spies and those under surveillance. It included Mata Hari and Ezra Pound, the American poet and author.

15 Ibid.

16 'Roger Casement', *Irish Brigade* [website] <www.irishbrigade.eu/other-men/casement/casement.html>.

17 Ibid.

18 G. de C. Parmiter, *Roger Casement* (London: Arthur Baker, 1936), p.362.

19 Ibid.

20 UK National Archives, MI5 files KV 2/6, K/V

2/7 and K/V 2/9.

21 Quoted in 'Harry Timothy Quinlisk', *Irish Brigade* [website] <www.irishbrigade.eu/other-men/plunkett/plunkett.html>.

22 Casement to McGarrity, 1 March and 22 March and 20 June 1915.

23 Notes by Sir Roger Casement on back of letter from Fr Raymond Crotty, dated 4 February 1916, NYPL, Maloney Collection Box 2.

24 Roger Casement to his sister, Mrs Nina Newman, from Pentonville Gaol, 25 July 1916.

25 *Mount Ida Chronicle*, 10 August 1917 (republished from *The Times*) <http://paperspast.natlib.govt.nz/cgi-bin/paperspast?a=d&d=MIC19170810.2.9>.

26 *Cork Examiner*, 17 October 1917.

27 *Limerick Chronicle*, 13 February 1919.

28 Interview with author.

29 Translated text of address delivered at restoration.

Chapter 6

1 George Le Mesurier, *The Campaigns and History of the Royal Irish Regiment 1900–1922* (Cork: Schull Books, 1997), p.20.

2 *Cork County Eagle*, Saturday, 31 October 1914.

3 'The Great War Timeline – 1914', *The Great War 1914–1918* [website] <www.greatwar.co.uk/timeline/ww1-events-1914.htm>.

4 *Cork County Eagle*, Saturday, 31 October 1914.

5 George Le Mesurier, *The Campaigns and History of the Royal Irish Regiment 1900–1922* (Cork: Schull Books, 1997), p.27.

6 *Cork County Eagle*, Saturday, 31 October 1914.

7 George Le Mesurier, *The Campaigns and History of the Royal Irish Regiment 1900–1922* (Cork: Schull Books, 1997), p.26.

8 UK National Archives, 2nd Battalion Royal Irish Regiment, August 1914–February 1915 WO95/1421/3.

9 Wilhelm Müller-Loebnitz, *Das Ehrenbuch der Westfalen* (Stuttgart, 1931).

10 Rachel Collins, 'Band of brothers: One family's story of the first World War', *The Irish Times* [website] <www.irishtimes.com/news/ireland/irish-news/band-of-brothers-one-family-s-story-of-the-first-world-war-1.1885281>.

11 *The Irish Times*, 2 August 2014.

12 Robert A. Anderson, 'With Horace Plunkett in Ireland', *The Irish Book Lover*, Vol. XXIII, September–October 1935, pp. 118–119.

13 Ibid.

14 *The Irish Times Weekly*, 7 November 1914.

15 *The Irish Times*, 13 November 1915.

16 *The Irish Times*, 10 November 1915.

17 The Le Touret Memorial commemorates over 13,400 British soldiers who were killed in the sector between October 1914 and September 1915 (the start of the Battle of Loos) and have no known grave. The memorial is about a half a mile from the site of *The Last General Absolution of the Munsters at Rue du Bois*.

18 Interview with author.

19 Ibid.

20 Maurice Meade, like many survivors of the War of Independence, gave witness statements to the Bureau of Military History. His lengthy statement was given on 23 September 1953. The archives of the Bureau of Military History were opened to the public in 2003. <www.bureauofmilitaryhistory.ie/reels/bmh/BMH.WS0891.pdf#page=1>.

21 Ibid.

22 Ibid.

Chapter 7

1 'Les Onze Anglais d'Iron', pamphlet published in Guise in the early 1920s. The authors are unknown. The pamphlet has been translated into English by Hedley Malloch and Paul Crowther
2 Ibid.
3 Ibid.
4 Herbert A. Walton, 'The Secret of the Mill', *Worldwide Magazine*, 1928.
5 Ibid.
6 Ibid.
7 Helen McPhail, *The Long Silence: The Tragedy of Occupied France in World War 1* (London: I.B. Tauris, 1999), p.29.
8 Ibid.
9 *King's County Chronicle*, January 1915.
10 Herbert A. Walton, 'The Secret of the Mill', *Worldwide Magazine*, 1928.
11 This was picked up by Reuters and published in newspapers in Ireland and Britain on 12 March 1915. See *Freeman's Journal*, 12 March 1915. It was reported without comment.
12 Angelique Chrisafis, 'France pressured to remember WW1 soldiers executed for "cowardice"' (1 October 2013), *Guardian* [website] <www.theguardian.com/world/2013/oct/01/france-first-world-war-soldiers-cowardice-executed-memorial>.
13 Ben Fenton, 'Pardoned: the 306 soldiers shot at dawn for "cowardice"' (16 August 2006), *Telegraph* [website] <www.telegraph.co.uk/news/1526437/Pardoned-the-306-soldiers-shot-at-dawn-for-cowardice.html>.
14 Jerry Chester, 'World War One: Eleven shot at dawn in Tower of London' (26 February 2014), *BBC News* [website] <www.bbc.com/news/uk-england-25654341>.
15 Helen McPhail, *The Long Silence: Civilian Life Under the German Occupation of Northern France* (London: I.B. Tauris, 2001), p.13.
16 Quoted H.F.N. Jourdain and E. Fraser, *The Connaught Rangers*, Vol. 2 (London, 1926), p.404.
17 Ibid.
18 Ibid.
19 Ibid.
20 Diana Souhami, *Edith Cavell: Nurse, Martyr, Heroine* (London: Quercus, 2010).
21 Helen McPhail, *The Long Silence: Civilian Life Under the German Occupation of Northern France* (London: I.B. Tauris, 2001), p.34.
22 Ibid.
23 'Les Onze Anglais d'Iron', pamphlet published in Guise in the early 1920s.
24 Ibid.
25 Herbert A. Walton, 'The Secret of the Mill', *Worldwide Magazine*, 1928.
26 Interview with author.
27 Ben MacIntyre, *A Foreign Field* (London, 2001)
28 'Les Onze Anglais d'Iron', pamphlet published in Guise in the early 1920s.
29 Interview with author.
30 H.F.N. Jourdain and E. Fraser, *The Connaught Rangers*, Volume 2 (London, 1926), p.417.
31 *King's County Chronicle*, June 1916.
32 Interview with author.

Chapter 8

1 Archdiocese of Dublin Diocesan Archives. The Diary of Fr Francis Gleeson <http://dx.doi.org/10.7925/drs1.ucdlib_36574>.
2 Ibid.
3 <https://en.wikipedia.org/wiki/Gorlice%E2%80%93Tarn%C3%B3w_Offensive>
4 Erich von Falkenhayn, *General headquarters, 1914-1916, and its critical decisions* (English translation) (London: Hutchinson, 1919) p.74.
5 Alan Clark, *The Donkeys* (London, 1961), p.104.
6 Adrian Bristow, *A Serious Disappointment: The Battle of Aubers Ridge 1915 and the Subsequent Munitions Scandal* (London: L. Cooper, 1995), p.48.
7 Alan Clark, *The Donkeys* (London, 1961), p.107.
8 *Cork Examiner*, 11 October 1915. Leahy was killed on the first day of the Battle of Loos on 25 September 1915.
9 Archdiocese of Dublin Diocesan Archives. The Diary of Fr Francis Gleeson.
10 Company Sergeant Major James Leahy was killed on the first day of the Battle of Loos, 25 September 1915.
11 Des Ryan, 'The Second Munsters in France', *Old Limerick Journal* <www.limerickcity.ie/media/Media,4025,en.pdf>.
12 <www.rmfa92.org/the-war-service-of-james-meehan-7460-sgt-r-m-f/>

13 H.S. Jervis, *The 2nd Munsters in France* (Aldershot: Naval and Military Press, 1922), p.27.

14 Alan Clark, *The Donkeys* (London, 1961), p.126.

15 *The Times*, 12 May 1915.

16 'Pte Robert Ackland, Royal Welsh Fusiliers', *Great War Forum* [website] <http://1914-1918.invisionzone.com/forums/index.php?showtopic=14896>.

17 Lucinda Gosling, *Goodbye, Old Man: Matania's Vision of the First World War* (Stroud:

The History Press, 2014), p.6.

18 Ibid.

19 'Last Absolution of the Munsters', *Great War Forum* [website] <http://1914-1918.invisionzone.com/forums/index.php?showtopic=36423>.

20 Interview with author.

21 Ibid.

22 'Last Absolution of the Munsters', *Great War Forum* [website] <http://1914-1918.invisionzone.com/forums/index.php?showtopic=36423>.

Chapter 9

1 'Address at the Annual Conference of the Labour History Society' (9 October 2015), *President of Ireland* [website] <www.president.ie/en/media-library/speeches/address-at-the-annual-conference-of-the-labour-history-society>.

2 The 1st Battalion of the Royal Dublin Fusiliers lost 163 men dead in the first week of the Gallipoli campaign (25 April 1915 – 30 April 1915).

3 '1st Battalion, Royal Dublin Fusiliers, in Gallipoli', *Royal Dublin Fusiliers: A Forgotten Regiment* [website] <www.dublin-fusiliers.com/battaliions/1-batt/campaigns/1915-gallipoli.html>.

4 Obituary of General Horace Smith-Dorrien, *The Times*, 13 August 1930. <http://ghgraham.org/text/horacesmithdorrien1858_obit.html>.

5 Adolf Hitler, *Mein Kampf* (Berlin, 1925), p.263.

6 'Fritz Haber', *Chemical Heritage Foundation* [website] <www.chemheritage.org/discover/online-resources/chemistry-in-history/themes/early-chemistry-and-gases/haber.aspx>.

7 Jan Willem Erisman *et al.*, 'How a century of ammonia synthesis changed the world', *Nature Geoscience*, 1 (2008), pp.636–9 <www.nature.com/ngeo/journal/v1/n10/full/ngeo325.html>.

8 John Dixon, *Magnificent But Not War* (Barnsley: Pen and Sword, 2009), p.43.

9 'Hitler - the Soldier 1914-1918', *Adolf Hitler – Mein Kampf* [website] <http://meinkampfvol1.blogspot.ie/2013/09/hitler-der-soldat-1914-1918-hitler.html>.

10 Ibid.

11 John Lee, 'Gas Attack: Ypres 1915', *The Campaign Chronicles* (Barnsley: Pen and Sword, 2009), p.7.

12 'St. Julien and Kitcheners Wood', *The Calgary Highlanders* [website] <www.calgaryhighlanders.com/history/10th/history/stjulien.htm>.

13 Colonel H.C. Wylly, *Crown and Company:*

The Historical Record of the 2nd Battalion of the Royal Dublin Fusiliers (Aldershot: Naval and Military Press, 1923).

14 UK National Archives, letter from Brigadier-General Arnold R. Burrowes, 6 February 1925.

15 Ibid.

16 Brigadier-General Sir James E. Edmonds, *British Official History of the War Military Operations France and Belgium 1914* (London: MacMillan, 1937).

17 <http://warfarehistorynetwork.com/daily/military-history/world-war-is-second-battle-of-ypres-salient-of-death/>

18 *The Irish Times*, 21 October 1924.

19 '"No surrender, no retirement and no quarter given or accepted" – The 2nd Battalion Royal Dublin Fusiliers during the Second Battle of Ypres' (2 March 2015), *Jeremy Banning* [website] <http://jeremybanning.co.uk/2015/03/02/no-surrender-no-retirement-and-no-quarter-given-or-accepted-the-2nd-battalion-royal-dublin-fusiliers-during-the-second-battle-of-ypres/>.

20 Army records retained by the Malone family.

21 Family letter given to author.

22 *Irish Independent*, 6 May 1916.

23 Taken from the military pensions archives file of the Irish government. The files for those who claimed a pension from the State for activities during the revolutionary period were released in 2014. There are files relating to Michael Malone, his mother, sisters and brother. <http://mspcsearch.militaryarchives.ie/detail.aspx?parentpriref=>.

24 Seamus Grace witness statement to the Bureau of Military History, 20 October 1949. <www.bureauofmilitaryhistory.ie/reels/bmh/BMH.WS0310.pdf#page=2>.

25 Ibid.

26 Ibid.

27 James Moran, 'Easter 1916: A British
  soldier's family reunion and death in Dublin'
  (6 April 2015), *The Irish Times* [website] <www.
  irishtimes.com/life-and-style/people/easter-1916-a-british-
  soldier-s-family-reunion-and-death-in-dublin-1.2162615>.

28 Seamus Grace witness statement to the Bureau
  of Military History, 20 October 1949.

29 Ibid.

30 *The Irish Times*, 27 December 2012.

31 Ibid.

32 As quoted in Brian Hughes, *Michael Mallin:
  16 Lives* (Dublin: O'Brien Press, 2013).

33 Taken from the military pensions archives
  file of the Irish government. <http://mspcsearch.
  militaryarchives.ie/docs/files/PDF_Admin/2/W2_4334.pdf>.

34 Irish Military Pensions Collection, Michael
  Malone: Secretary Department of Defence
  to Minister for Defence <http://mspcsearch.
  militaryarchives.ie/docs/files//pdf_pensions/r1/1d315michael
  malone(claimantmarymalonemother)/w1d315michaelmalone(cl
  aimantmarymalonemother).pdf>.

35 Interview with author.

36 Ibid.

Chapter 10

1 Commonwealth War Graves Commission.

2 Jonathan Owen, 'Tower of London to
   remember WWI dead with 880,000 ceramic
   poppies' (7 May 2014), *Independent* [website]
   <www.independent.co.uk/news/uk/home-news/tower-of-
   london-to-remember-wwi-dead-with-880000-ceramic-
   poppies-9333842.html>.

3 'John Condon', lyrics and music by Richard
   Laird, Sam Starrett and Tracey McRory,
   Boys of the Island [album], 2002 <www.
   antiwarsongs.org/canzone.php?id=35016&lang=en>.

4 'Poelcapelle British Cemetery', *Commonwealth
   War Graves Commission* [website]
   <www.cwgc.org/find-a-cemetery/cemetery/56100/
   poelcapelle%20british%20cemetery>.

5 'Age 14, the youngest soldier killed in the
   Great War? The John Condon myth explained',
   Jack Clegg [website] <www.jackclegg3.webspace.
   virginmedia.com/Condonevidence.htm>.

6 'Residents of a house 12.1 in Jenkins
   Lane (Waterford No. 1 Urban, Waterford)',
   The National Archives of Ireland [website]
   <www.census.nationalarchives.ie/pages/1901/Waterford/
   Waterford_No__1_Urban/Jenkins_Lane/1760954/>.

7 <http://www.dublin-fusiliers.com/battaliions/2-batt/
   other-ranks/condon-14.html>

8 <http://www.jackclegg3.webspace.virginmedia.com/
   Condonevidence.htm>.

9 Email from Commonwealth War Graves
   Commission to author.

10 'Some British army statistics of the Great War',
   The Long, Long Trail [website]
   <www.longlongtrail.co.uk/army/
   some-british-army-statistics-of-the-great-war/>.

11 J. McCauley, Imperial War Museum
   documents 97/10/1.

12 'Residents of a house 12.1 in Jenkins

Lane (Waterford No. 1 Urban, Waterford)',
   The National Archives of Ireland [website]
   <www.census.nationalarchives.ie/pages/1901/Waterford/
   Waterford_No__1_Urban/Jenkins_Lane/1760954/>.

13 *Waterford News*, 8 July 1938.

14 Ibid.

15 'SS Coningbeg (+1917)', *WRECK Site*
   [website] <www.wrecksite.eu/wreck.aspx?12759>.

16 Interview with Sonny Condon.

17 Geert Spillebeen, *Age 14 (An Irish Boy Soldier)*,
   translated by Terese Edelstein (Cork: Collins,
   2010), p.2.

18 Ibid.

19 Ibid.

20 Interview with author.

21 'Pte. John Condon', *Waterford Ireland* [website]
   <http://waterfordireland.tripod.com/pte__john_condon,_
   soldier.htm>.

22 Lieutenant-Colonel G. Le M. Gretton,
   *The Campaigns and History of the Royal Irish
   Regiment 1900–1922* (Edinburgh, 1927).

23 Interview with author.

24 Ibid.

25 Ibid.

26 Ibid.

27 UK National Archives, 2nd Royal Irish Rifles
   regimental diary WO 95/1415/.

28 C.N. Trueman, 'Boy Soldiers' (31 March 2015),
   The History Learning Site [website]
   <www.historylearningsite.co.uk/world-war-one/
   the-western-front-in-world-war-one/boy-soldiers/>.

Chapter 11

1   Patrick MacGill, *The Great Push: An Episode of the Great War* (London: Herbert Jenkins, 1916), p.35.

2   Nord-Pas-de-Calais Mining basin designated in 2012 <http://whc.unesco.org/en/list/1360>.

3   Interview with author.

4   Ibid.

5   Ibid.

6   This incredible piece of research gives a day-by-day breakdown of British war dead. In only two days did the daily total surpass 10,000, the first day of the Battle of the Somme on 1 July 1916 and the first day of the Battle of Loos, 25 September 1915. <http://codehesive.com/commonwealthww1/>.

7   The other two are Second Lieutenant Walter Clifford and Second Lieutenant Thomas Packenham Law from Howth, County Dublin. Their names appear on the Loos Memorial to the Missing.

8   Quoted in Tonie and Valmai Holt, *My Boy Jack* (Barnsley: Pen and Sword, 1998).

9   Tonie and Valmai Holt, *My Boy Jack* (Barnsley: Pen and Sword, 1998).

10 Ibid.

11 UK public records office, February 1998, John Kipling's application for a temporary commission.

12 <http://www.army.mod.uk/infantry/regiments/24589.aspx>.

13 Rudyard Kipling, 'The Rowers', 1899. Written about a proposal for a joint military demonstration by the UK and Germany. 'In sight of peace – from the narrow seas / o'er half the world to run / with a cheated crew, to leagues anew, with the Goth and the shameless Hun'.

14 Rodney Atwood, *The Life of Field Marshal Lord Roberts* (London: Bloomsbury, 2014), p.78. Speech made in the Free Trade Hall Manchester, 22 October 1912.

15 Thomas Pinney (ed.), *The Letters of Rudyard Kipling 1911–1919* (London: Macmillan, 1990), p.133.

16 Katharine Fullerton Gerould, *Atlantic* magazine, January 1919 <www.theatlantic.com/magazine/archive/1919/01/the-remarkable-rightness-of-rudyard-kipling/306597/>.

17 Thomas Pinney (ed.), *The Letters of Rudyard Kipling 1911–1919* (London: Macmillan, 1990), p.251.

18 Tonie and Valmai Holt, *My Boy Jack* (Barnsley: Pen and Sword, 1998).

19 Rodney Atwood, *The Life of Field Marshal Lord Roberts* (London: Bloomsbury, 2014).

20 *The Irish Times*, 16 November 1914.

21 Lord Roberts died while visiting troops at the front at St Omer, France on 14 November 1914 at the age of 82. Though not officially listed as a battle casualty, Waterford claims the distinction of having the youngest and oldest soldiers to die in the First World War.

22 Owen Dudley Edwards, 'Kipling and the Irish', *London Review of Books*, Vol. 10, No. 3, 4 February 1988, pp.22–3 [website] <www.lrb.co.uk/v10/n03/owen-dudley-edwards/kipling-and-the-irish>.

23 Rudyard Kipling, 'Cleared', printed in *Scots Observer*, 8 March 1890. 'They only took the Judas-gold from Fenians out of jail, / They only fawned for dollars on the blood-dyed Clanna-Gael. / If black is black or white is white, in black and white it's down, / They're only traitors to the Queen and rebels to the Crown.'

24 Edward Wilson, 'The Kipling That Nobody Reads', *Atlantic Monthly*, 167 (1941).

25 <https://catalog.hathitrust.org/Record/000767945>

26 C.R.L. Fletcher and Rudyard Kipling, *A History of England* <https://archive.org/details/historyofengland00flet>.

27 'Letter from the Archive: John Kipling to his father Rudyard, 1915', *The Keep* [website] <www.thekeep.info/letters-archive/>.

28 'The Battle of Loos', *The Long, Long Trails* [website] <www.longlongtrail.co.uk/battles/battles-of-the-western-front-in-france-and-flanders/the-battle-of-loos/>.

Chapter 12

1   Kipling, *The Irish Guards* (1923), p.113.

2   UK National Archives Regimental Diaries 8 Royal Munster Fusiliers, 1915 Dec–1916 Nov.

3   UK National Archives Regimental Diaries

WO95/1974/3 8 Royal Dublin Fusiliers, 1915 Dec–1916 December 1915– 31 October 1917.

4   J.F.B. O'Sullivan, 'At Rest in Philosophe', June 1916, IWM London.

5   Carole Hope, *Fr Willie Doyle, Worshipper and*

Worshipped (London: Reveille Press, 2013), p.221.

6 Ibid.

7 Professor Alfred O'Rahilly, *Father Willie Doyle* (London, 1922), p.217.

8 Ibid.

9 Ibid.

10 Ibid.

11 Frank Laird, *Personal Experiences of the Great War* (Dublin: Eason and Son, 1925), p.140.

12 '18 November 1917: General Hickie's praise for Fr Doyle', *Remembering Fr William Doyle SJ* [website] <http://fatherdoyle.com/2015/11/18/18–november-1917–general-hickies-praise-for-fr-doyle/>.

13 Irish Jesuit archives.

14 Terence Denman, *Ireland's Unknown Soldiers* (Dublin: Irish Academic Press, 1995).

15 Ibid.

16 C.A. Cooper Walker, *The Royal Inniskilling Fusiliers: From Tipperary to Ypres* (London, 1920).

17 Jane G.V. McGaughey, *Ulster's Men: Protestant Unionist Masculinities and Militarization in the north of Ireland* (Montreal: McGill-Queen's University Press, 2012).

18 Though strategically important towns with naval bases, the main reason to bombard the towns from naval ships was an attempt to entice the Royal Navy out to sea, where the German fleet were waiting for them. The plan failed. The two battlecruiser squadrons came within 50 miles of each other, but did not meet. The raid ended in twenty-five British fatalities, mostly at sea. There were three civilian fatalities.

19 Darragh Murphy, 'A blow-by-blow guide to the Easter Rising', *The Irish Times* [website] <www.irishtimes.com/culture/heritage/1916–schools/a-blow-by-blow-guide-to-the-easter-rising-1.2353931>.

20 Irish Jesuit archives.

21 UK National Archives, 8 Battalion Royal Irish Fusiliers WO 95/1978/2.

22 Brigadier-General Sir James Edmonds, *British Official History of the Great War* (London: Macmillan, 1922).

23 UK National Archives, regimental diaries, 8 Royal Dublin Fusiliers WO95/1974/3.

24 Brigadier-General Sir James Edmonds, *British Official History of the Great War* (London: Macmillan, 1922).

25 8 Royal Dublin Fusiliers regimental diary.

26 'Officers 8th Battalion Royal Dublin Fusiliers', *Dublin Fusiliers* [website] <www.dublin-fusiliers.com/battaliions/8–batt/personnel/officers/officers-8–bn.html>.

27 Ibid.

28 UK National Archives, regimental diaries, 7 Royal Inniskilling Fusiliers WO 95/1977/2.

29 Brigadier-General Sir James Edmonds, *British Official History of the Great War* (London: Macmillan, 1922).

30 'Officers 8th Battalion Royal Dublin Fusiliers', *Dublin Fusiliers* [website] <www.dublin-fusiliers.com/battaliions/8–batt/personnel/officers/officers-8–bn.html>.

31 Sir Frank Fox, *Royal Inniskilling Fusiliers in the World War (1914–1918)* (London: Naval and Military Press, 1928).

32 'Michael Ridge 1st Munsters Letter', *Great War Forum* [website] <http://1914-1918.invisionzone.com/forums/index.php?showtopic=39214&hl=%2Bmichael+%2Bridge+%2Bletter#entry320669>.

33 <http://www.irishtimes.com/culture/heritage/public-takes-wwi-treasure-trove-of-medals-letters-to-glasnevin-1.1798966>

34 Professor Alfred O'Rahilly, *Father Willie Doyle* (London, 1922), p.258.

35 Joe Duffy, *Children of the Rising* (Dublin: Hachette Books Ireland, 2015), p.107.

36 'Gas attacks at Hulluch explained', *Everything Explained Today* [website] <http://everything.explained.today/Gas_attack_at_Hulluch/>.

37 'Letter from Fr Henry Gill SJ to Fr Thomas V Nolan SJ, 3 May 1916', *Letters of 1916* [website] <http://letters1916.maynoothuniversity.ie/diyhistory/scripto/transcribe/2008/5027>.

38 Brigadier-General Sir James Edmonds, *British Official History of the Great War* (London: Macmillan, 1922), p.127.

39 UK National Archives.

40 Ibid.

41 Bureau of Military History, Seán Moylan witness statement. <www.bureauofmilitaryhistory.ie/reels/bmh/BMH.WS0838.pdf>.

42 Mainchín Seoighe, *Dromin Athlacca: The Story of a Rural Parish in Co. Limerick* (Áth Leacach: Glór na nGael, 1978), p.68.

43 Ibid.

44 *Cork Weekend Examiner*, 27 May 1916.

45 Ibid.

46 Source: Jean Prendergast, image sent to author.

47 UK National Archives, Irish Grant Committee.

48 Capt. S. McCance, *The History of the Royal Munster Fusiliers*, 2 Vols (Aldershot: Naval and Military Press, 1922), p.197-8.

49 8th Royal Munster Fusiliers Battalion Diary.

50 *Irish Examiner*, 30 May 1916.

51 *Limerick Leader*, 24 May 1916.

52 UK National Archives, Irish Distress Committee and Irish Grants Committee, Files and Minutes, Files 131–160. CO762/14/8.

53 'Nœux-les-Mines: depuis 1917, Notre Dame des Victoires ne manque pas d'Eire' (22 August 2014), *La Voix du Nord* [website] <www.lavoixdunord.fr/region/noeux-les-mines-depuis-1917-notre-dame-des-victoires-ne-ia30b53960n2337110>.

54 Carole Hope, Fr Willie Doyle, *Worshipper and Worshipped* (London: Reveille Press, 2013), p.461.

55 Charles Carrington, *Soldiers from the Wars Returning* (London: Pen and Sword, 1965), p.219.

56 Richard Holmes, *War Walks – The Somme*, (BBC TV series 1, episode 4), first boradcast August 1996.

57 The so-called Christmas Memorandum, which von Falkenhayn produced in his 1919 memoir, has been widely discredited by historians. No copy of such an important document has been found in the Reichsarchiv. Many German historians believe von Falkenhayn was simply trying to justify the failure of the Verdun offensive to achieve a breakthrough. <https://www.youtube.com/watch?v=xnwZjUrSc2k>

58 'A letter sent to the editors of the main British newspapers by Sir Douglas Haig, May 1916', *The National Archives* [website] <www.nationalarchives.gov.uk/education/greatwar/transcript/g4cs3s1t.htm>.

59 'The Somme and Normandy compared', *Great War Forum* [website] <http://1914-1918.invisionzone.com/forums/index.php?showtopic=162206>.

60 'Battle of the Somme (1916)', *McGill University* [website] <www.cs.mcgill.ca/~rwest/wikispeedia/wpcd/wp/b/Battle_of_the_Somme_%25281916%2529.htm>.

61 The British lost 21,097 men during the Crimean War, but less than 5,000 in combat operations. The rest died from disease. The number of British soldiers who died in the Boer War was around 22,000, but only a third died in combat, the rest from disease. Casualties at the Battle of Waterloo were relatively light – estimated at around 3,500 for the British.

62 According to Bernard Montgomery, the British sustained 6,010 fatalities in the Battle of Normandy from 6 June to 19 July 1944.

63 Duff Cooper, *Haig: A Biography* (London: Doubleday, 1936).

64 'The Battle of The Somme' (29 June 2006), *Independent* [website] <www.independent.co.uk/news/world/europe/the-battle-of-the-somme-6096776.html>.

65 A.J. Coates, *The Ethics of War* (Manchester: Manchester University Press, 1997).

66 Robert J. Harding, 'Glorious Tragedy: Newfoundland's Cultural Memory of the Attack at Beaumont Hamel, 1916-1925', *Newfoundland and Labrador Studies*, Vol. 21, No. 1 (2006) <https://journals.lib.unb.ca/index.php/nflds/article/view/5884/6891>.

67 Robert J Harding, 'Glorious Tragedy: Newfoundland's Cultural Memory of the Attack at Beaumont Hamel, 1916-1925', Dalhousie University <https://journals.lib.unb.ca/index.php/nflds/article/view/5884/6891>

68 'How the British artillery developed and became a war-winning factor in 1914-1918', *The Long, Long Trail* [website] <www.1914-1918.net/artillery_development.html>.

69 Richard Holmes, *War Walks – The Somme*, (BBC TV, series 1, episode 5), first broadcast August 1996.

Chapter 13

1   In November 1914, levels of recruitment in Cornwall (2.7 per cent of the male military age population 18–35), Devon (4.7 per cent) and rural North Wales (5.1 per cent) were significantly lower than the average (10.2 per cent) for England, Wales and Scotland.

2   The Irish-born population of England, Scotland and Wales in 1911 was 550,040, constituting 1.4 per cent of the population. The Irish-born population of Scotland was 174,715, constituting 3.7 per cent of the Scottish population in 1911. The Irish-born population in Britain reached a peak of 781,119 in 1881. See Donald M. MacRaild, *The Irish Diaspora in Britain, 1750–1939* (London: Palgrave, 2010).

3   The Irish-born population of Liverpool in 1911 was 34,632 or 4.6 per cent of the city's population of 746,421. The Irish population of Liverpool peaked in 1851 at 83,813 or 22.3 per cent of the population. The Irish-born, second- and third-generation Irish combined constituted a huge proportion of the Liverpool population.

4 O'Connor represented the Liverpool Scotland constituency. After 1918, he was returned unopposed and died in 1929 at a time when he was the father of the House of Commons.

5 Stephen Gwynn, *John Redmond's Last Years* (New York: Longman's Green and Co., 1919), p.190.

6 Ibid.

7 Ibid.

8 Quoted in L.W. Brady, *T.P. O'Connor and the Liverpool Irish* (London: London Royal Historical Society, 1983).

9 Joseph Keating, *The History of the Tyneside Irish Brigade: Irish Heroes in the War* (London: Naval and Military Press, 1917), p.44.

10 *Carlow Sentinel*, 10 October 1918.

11 Ibid.

12 John Sheen, *Tyneside Irish* (Barnsley: Pen and Sword, 1998), p.2.

13 Ibid.

14 Ibid., p.13.

15 Ibid.

16 Ibid.

17 Ibid.

18 Quoted in John Sheen, *Tyneside Irish* (Barnsley: Pen and Sword, 1998).

19 Thomas Bartlett and Keith Jeffery, *A Military History of Ireland* (Cambridge: Cambridge University Press, 1997), p.19.

20 Ibid.

21 Ibid.

22 Ibid.

23 John Sheen, *Tyneside Irish* (Barnsley: Pen and Sword, 1998).

24 Ibid.

25 Ibid.

26 'First Day of the Somme: La Boisselle', *John Clare* [website] <www.johndclare.net/wwi2_FirstDay_LaBoisselle.htm>.

27 John Sheen, *Tyneside Irish* (Barnsley: Pen and Sword, 1998).

28 Mike Kelly, 'How the Irish helped build the North East – and where they set up the first ever Irish Club' (4 March 2015), *Chronicle* [website] <www.chroniclelive.co.uk/news/history/how-irish-helped-build-north-8326837>.

29 'First Day of the Somme: La Boisselle', *John Clare* [website] <www.johndclare.net/wwi2_FirstDay_LaBoisselle.htm>.

30 Second Lieutenant Gerald Fitzgerald, Tyneside Irish, Northumberland Fusilers was 24 when he died <http://archive.thetablet.co.uk/article/29th-july-1916/24/second-lieut-cormac-wray-of-the-inniskillings-batt>.

Chapter 14

1 *The Irish Times*, Monday, 21 November 1921.

2 'Helen's Tower', *Clandeboye Estate and Courtyard* [website] <www.clandeboye.co.uk/helens-tower/

3 UK National Archives WO32/5868>.

4 Ibid.

5 Philip Orr, *The Great War, the Somme and the Ulster Protestant Psyche* (2012) <https://www.youtube.com/watch?v=0cDioAlXy0k>.

6 'Frank Percy Crozier', *Spartacus Educational* [website] <http://spartacus-educational.com/FWWcrozierF.htm>.

7 Private John Moffatt, *From the Menin Gate to San Quentin 1915–1918* <http://webcache.googleusercontent.com/search?q=cache:G_e8BLtcppcJ:ww1lit.nsms.ox.ac.uk/ww1lit/files/original/37f9d2630130a9aae177d7715d1d513f.pdf+&cd=1&hl=en&ct=clnk&gl=ie>

8 Ibid.

9 Quoted in Sam Allen, *To Ulster's Credit* (Belfast: Plantation Press, 1986).

10 Andrew Rawson, *The Somme Campaign* (Barnsley: Pen and Sword, 2014), p.26.

11 *The Irish Times*, 14 May 2014.

12 Quoted in Michael and Eleanor Brock, *HH Asquith, Letters to Venetia Stanley* (London, 2009).

13 Carton to Asquith, 10 August 1914, as quoted in Ian Colvin, *Carson the Statesman* (Belfast, 1935).

14 *The Irish Times*, Wednesday, 18 November 2015.

15 Cyril Fall, *The History of the 36th (Ulster) Division* (Belfast 1922), p.1.

16 Ibid.

17 Nicholas Perry, *Major General Oliver Nugent and the Ulster Division 1915–1918* (Stroud 2007), p.22.

18 Ibid.

19 Frank Percy Crozier, *A Brass Hat in No Man's Land* (London, 1930).

20 Cyril Falls, *The History of the 36th (Ulster) Division* (Belfast: M'Caw, Stevenson & Orr, 1922), p.25.

21 Graham Clifford, 'So, just who was the "young Willie McBride"?', *Independent* [website]

<www.independent.ie/life/world-war-1/so-just-who-was-the-young-willie-mcbride-30249256.html>.

22 Interview with author.

23 Cyril Falls, *The History of the 36th (Ulster) Division* (Belfast: M'Caw, Stevenson & Orr, 1922), p.17.

24 Ibid.

25 Ibid.

26 Quoted in Martin Middlebrook, *The First Day of the Somme* (London: Penguin, 1971), p.117.

27 'Victoria Cross', *South Belfast Friends of the Somme Association* [website] <www.belfastsomme.com/vc.html>.

28 Ibid.

29 Martin Middlebrook, *The First Day of the Somme* (London: Penguin, 1971), p.178.

30 Ibid., p.63.

31 Ibid.

32 Kevin Myers, 'The only lessons that could be learnt were through the grievous expenditure of human life' (11 January 2012), *Kevin Myers* [website] <http://kevinmyers.ie/2012/01/11/the-only-lessons-that-could-be-learnt-were-through-the-grievous-expenditure-of-human-life/>.

33 Quoted in Arthur Purefoy, Irwin Samuels, *With the Ulster Division in France* (CreateSpace Independent Publishing Platform, 3 August 2015).

34 *The Irish Times*, 6 July 1916.

35 Thomas Hennessey, *Dividing Ireland: World War One and Partition* (London 1998)

36 Nicholas Perry, *Major General Oliver Nugent and the Ulster Division 1915-1918* (Stroud, 2007)

37 Arthur Purefoy, Irwin Samuels, *With the Ulster Division in France* (CreateSpace Independent Publishing Platform, 3 August 2015).

38 Michael MacDonagh, *The Irish at the Front* (London: Hodder and Stoughton, 1917), p.27.

39 Philip Orr, *The Road to the Somme* (Belfast, 1987).

40 UK National Archives WO32/5868.

41 *The Irish Times*, Monday, 21 November 1921.

42 Mark Coalter, review of Geoffrey Lewis, 'Carson: The Man Who Divided Ireland', *History Ireland*, Vol 13, Issue 5 (Sept./Oct. 2005) <www.historyireland.com/20th-century-contemporary-history/carson-the-man-who-divided-ireland/>.

Chapter 15

1 *The Irish Times*, 12 November 1924.

2 *The Irish Times*, 5 November 1930.

3 Chris Dooley, *Redmond: A Life Undone* (Dublin: Gill and Macmillan, 2015).

4 Ibid.

5 *The Irish Times*, 12 November 1924.

6 Ibid.

7 Ibid.

8 *Irish Independent*, 12 November 1924.

9 Ibid.

10 *The Irish Times*, 12 November 1924.

11 <http://abrahamicfaiths.org/the-abrahamic-faiths-project/>

12 'The National War Memorial Gardens, Islandbridge', *Decade of Centenaries, History Ireland* [website] <www.historyireland.com/decadeofcentenaries/national-war-memorial-gardens-islandbridge/>.

13 Ibid.

14 Richard Holmes, *War Walks* (BBC TV Series 1, Episode 3), first broadcast August 1996.

15 Frederick Whitton, *A History of the Prince of Wales's Leinster Regiment* (Aldershot: Naval and Military Press, 1924), p.305.

16 Quoted in Terence Denman, *Ireland's Unknown Soldiers* (Dublin: Irish Academic Press, 1995), p.75.

17 Ibid.

18 Brigadier-General Sir James Edmonds, *British Official History, Military Operations: France and Belgium, 1916*, Volume II (London: Macmillan, 1923), p.37.

19 'Trones Wood Montauban Guillemont', *Pierre's Photo Impressions of the Western Front 1914–1918* [website] <http://pierreswesternfront.punt.nl/content/2008/03/trones-wood-montauban-guillemont>.

20 Lyn MacDonald, *Somme* (London: Viking, 1983).

21 Michael Stedman, *Guillemont* (Barnsley: Pen and Sword, 1998), p.70.

22 As quoted in ibid.

23 Ibid.

24 Michael Stedman, *Guillemont* (Barnsley: Pen and Sword, 1998), p.91.

25 Quoted in Michael Stedman, *Guillemont* (Barnsley: Pen and Sword, 1998).

26 Francis Hitchcock, *Stand to! A Diary of the Trenches 1915–1918* (London: Naval and Military Press, 1938), p.139.

27 Michael MacDonagh, *The Irish on the Somme* (London: Hodder and Stoughton, 1917).

28 *Cork Examiner*, 20 June 1916.

29 Michael MacDonagh, *The Irish on the Somme* (London: Hodder and Stoughton, 1917).

30 Frederick Whitton, *A History of the Prince of Wales's Leinster Regiment* (Aldershot: Naval and Military Press, 1924), p.279–80.

31 Ibid.

32 Ernst Jünger, *Storm of Steel* (Berlin, 1920).

33 Frederick Whitton, *A History of the Prince of Wales's Leinster Regiment* (Aldershot: Naval and Military Press, 1924).

34 Ibid.

35 Michael Stedman, *Guillemont* (Barnsley: Pen and Sword, 1998).

36 Professor Alfred O'Rahilly, *Father Willie Doyle* (London, 1922), p.255.

37 Michael Stedman, *Guillemont* (Barnsley: Pen and Sword, 1998).

38 'Ginchy', *The Battle of the Somme* [website], Commonwealth War Graves Commission <www.cwgc.org/somme/content.asp?menuid=26&id=26&menuname=Ginchy&menu=main>.

39 'The Somme Day by Day', *Irish Military Online* [website] <http://forum.irishmilitaryonline.com/showthread.php?9058–The-Somme-Day-by-Day/page4>.

40 *The Irish Times*, 11 September 1916.

41 Ibid.

42 'Victoria Crosses', *Chavasse Ferme* [website] <www.chavasseferme.co.uk/victoria-crosses.php>.

43 Frederick Whitton, *A History of the Prince of Wales's Leinster Regiment* (Aldershot: Naval and Military Press, 1924).

44 'John Vincent Holland V.C.', *Hellfire Corner* [website] <www.hellfirecorner.co.uk/holland.htm>.

45 Terence Denman, *Ireland's Unknown Soldiers* (Dublin: Irish Academic Press, 1995), p.83.

46 *The Irish Times*, 5 December 1923.

47 UK National Archives Kew WO 32/5895.

48 *The Irish Times*, Tuesday, 24 August 1926.

49 Ibid.

50 'Irish who fell at Guillemont' (2 February 2007), *Irish Independent* [website] <www.independent.ie/opinion/letters/irish-who-fell-at-guillemont-26273616.html>.

51 *Cork Examiner*, 12 September 1925.

Chapter 16

1 Senia Paseta, *Tom Kettle 1880–1916* (Dublin: UCD Press, 2008).

2 'Andrew Kettle and his son Tom', *Malahide Historical Society* [website] <www.malahideheritage.com/#!kettles/ccbv>.

3 Mary Kettle, *The Ways of War* (London, 1917).

4 Ronan O'Brien, 'The Pity of War', *Studies*, 1 July 2015.

5 'Address to the Houses of Parliament', *President of Ireland* [website] <www.president.ie/en/media-library/speeches/address-by-president-higgins-to-the-houses-of-parliament-westminster>.

6 Senia Paseta, *Tom Kettle 1880–1916* (Dublin: UCD Press, 2008).

7 'Tom Kettle', *Spectator* [online] < http://www.rte.ie/centuryireland/index.php/articles/tom-kettle-i-am-fighting-for-ireland >.

8 Senia Paseta, *Tom Kettle 1880–1916* (Dublin: UCD Press, 2008).

9 Desmond Bowen and Jean Bowen, *Heroic Option: The Irish in the British Army* (Barnsley: Pen and Sword, 2005), p.245.

10 Senia Paseta, *Tom Kettle 1880–1916* (Dublin: UCD Press, 2008).

11 *Freeman's Journal*, 23 October 1916.

12 Senia Paseta, *Tom Kettle 1880–1916* (Dublin: UCD Press, 2008).

13 Quoted in Thomas M. Kettle Papers, UCD Archives, LA34.

14 Ibid.

15 Ibid.

16 Ibid.

17 Ibid.

18 Ibid.

19 Ken Linge, Pam Linge, *Missing but not Forgotten: Men of the Thiepval Memorial* (Barnsley: Naval and Military, 2015).

20 *Leitrim Observer*, 19 August 1916.

21 Tyneside Irish are not counted separately but as part of the Northumberland Fusiliers.

22 Interview with author.

23 'London Cenotaph', *Twentieth Century Society* [website] <www.c20society.org.uk/war-memorials/the-cenotaph/>.

24 *The Irish Times*, 2 August 1932.

25 Ibid., 2 August 1916.

26 <http://www.infomatique.org/statues-memorials-monuments/statues-mounumets-memorials-dublin/thomas-kettle-stephens-green/index.html>

27 *The Irish Times*, 15 December 1967.

28 Ibid.

29 Ibid., 21 December 1996.

Chapter 17

1   *Irish Independent*, 7 June 1967.
2   As quoted in Gary Sheffield, John Bourne, *Douglas Haig: Diaries and Letters 1914–1918* (London: Weidenfeld & Nicolson, 2005).
3   The village is now known as Wijtschate, but for the purposes of this chapter the historic name Wytschaete will be used.
4   As quoted in Peter Oldham, *Battlefield Europe, Messines Ridge* (Barnsley: Naval and Military Press, 1998), p.28.
5   'Battle of Messines', *Everything Explained Today* [website] <http://everything.explained.today/Battle_of_Messines/>.
6   'The Battle of Messines, 1917', *First World War* [website] <www.firstworldwar.com/battles/messines.htm>.
7   'Was the tunnellers' secret war the most barbaric of WW1?', *BBC* [website] <www.bbc.co.uk/guides/zggykqt>.
8   'Mines in the Battle of Messines (1917)', *Wikipedia* [website] <https://en.wikipedia.org/wiki/Mines_in_the_Battle_of_Messines_(1917)>.
9   Brigadier-General Sir James Edmonds, *British Official History, Military Operations: France and Belgium, 1916*, Volume II (London: Macmillan, 1923).
10 Rowland Feilding, *War Letters to a Wife: France and Flanders, 1915–1919* (London: Naval and Military Press, 1929), p.193.
11 Cyril Falls, *The History of the 36th (Ulster) Division* (Belfast: M'Caw, Stevenson & Orr, 1922), p.91.
12 Rowland Feilding, *War Letters to a Wife: France and Flanders, 1915–1919* (London: Naval and Military Press, 1929), p.169.
13 'The Battle of Messines-Wytschaete June, 1917', *Political Irish* [website] <www.politicalirish.com/showthread.php?tid=179>.
14 As quoted in Alfred O'Rahilly, *Father William Doyle S.J.: A Spiritual Study* (London: Longmans, Green and Co., 1932), p.298.
15 Quoted in Tom Burke MBE, *The 16th (Irish) and 36th (Ulster) Divisions at the Battle of Wijtschaete-Messines Ridge 7 June 1917* (Dublin: Royal Dublin Fusiliers Association, 2007).
16 Ibid.
17 Ibid.
18 Rowland Feilding, *War Letters to a Wife: France and Flanders, 1915–1919* (London: Naval and Military Press, 1929), p.192.
19 Willie Redmond, *Trench Pictures from France* (London, 1917, published posthumously), p.32.
20 *Irish Independent*, 7 June 1967.
21 As quoted in J. A. Terraine, 'A Soldier's Soldier' (6 June 1957), *The Spectator* [website] <http://archive.spectator.co.uk/article/7th-june-1957/9/a-soldiers-soldier>.
22 As quoted in Alfred O'Rahilly, *Father William Doyle S.J.: A Spiritual Study* (London: Longmans, Green and Co., 1932), p.299.
23 Interview with author.
24 Peter Oldham, *Battlefield Europe, Messines Ridge* (Barnsley: Naval and Military Press, 1998).
25 Paul Reed, *Walking the Salient* (London: Pen and Sword, 1998).
26 Tom Burke MBE, *The 16th (Irish) and 36th (Ulster) Divisions at the Battle of Wijtschaete-Messines Ridge 7 June 1917* (Dublin: Royal Dublin Fusiliers Association, 2007).
27 Ibid.
28 Rowland Feilding, *War letters to a wife: France and Flanders, 1915–1919* (London: Naval and Military Press, 1929), p.189.
29 'The 4th Australian Division at the Battle of Messines', *In the Footsteps* [website] <www.inthefootsteps.com/history/messines/4AusDivmessines.html>.
30 Brigadier-General Sir James E. Edmonds, *British Official History Volume II: Messines and Third Ypres (Passchendaele)* (London: Macmillan, 1948).
31 Ibid.
32 Rowland Feilding, *War Letters to a Wife: France and Flanders, 1915–1919* (London: Naval and Military Press, 1929), p.191.
33 *The Morning Post*, 9 June 1917.
34 Brigadier-General Sir James E. Edmonds, *British Official History Volume II: Messines and Third Ypres (Passchendaele)* (London: Macmillan, 1948).
35 UK National Archives, Kew, War Memorials WO32/5895.
36 Ibid.
37 *The Irish Times*, 23 August 1926.
38 'Letter from Count Gerald O'Kelly de Gallagh to Joseph P. Walshe (Dublin) (1045/E/26) (Confidential)', *Documents on Irish Foreign Policy* [website] <www.difp.ie/docs/1926/First-World-War-Commemoration/741.htm>.
39 Ibid.
40 *The Irish Times*, Monday, 23 August 1926.

Chapter 18

1 Major William Redmond MP, *Souvenir of the Memorial Fund* (Dublin, 1918).

2 *Irish Examiner*, 16 June 1967.

3 Ibid.

4 Remarks made at Western Front Association conference in Cork, 10 October 2015.

5 Willie Redmond, speech in Cork, November 1914: 'I speak as a man who bears the name of a relation who was hanged in Wexford in '98 – William Kearney'.

6 Quoted in Terence Denman, *A Lonely Grave: The Life and Death of William Redmond* (Dublin: Irish Academic Press, 1995), p.16.

7 Ibid., p.47.

8 Ibid., p.38.

9 Ibid., p.122.

10 'Major William Redmond, M.P.' (obituary, 16 June 1917), *The Tablet* [website] <http://archive.thetablet.co.uk/article/16th-june-1917/5/major-william-redmond-m-p->.

11 Ibid.

12 Ibid.

13 Ibid.

14 Major William Redmond MP, *Souvenir of the Memorial Fund* (Dublin, 1918).

15 'Major Willie Redmond', *The Royal British Legion* [website] <http://branches.britishlegion.org.uk/branches/wexford/branch-information/major-willie-redmond/>.

16 Terence Denman, *A Lonely Grave: The Life and Death of William Redmond* (Dublin: Irish Academic Press, 1995), p.93.

17 Letter to the Bishop of Killaloe, 3 February 1916.

18 Ibid.

19 Redmond's letters are in the Taylor/Monteagle collection. The Monteagles were an old Irish aristocratic family and the correspondence is to Liberal peer Lord Monteagle and his two nieces, London-based socialites Ida and Una Taylor. <www.irishtimes.com/culture/heritage/letters-from-willie-redmond-reveal-pride-in-irish-at-somme-1.1806542>.

20 Terence Denman, *A Lonely Grave: The Life and Death of William Redmond* (Dublin: Irish Academic Press, 1995), p.104.

21 Quoted in William Redmond, *Trench Diaries from France* (New York, 1917, published posthumously).

22 Terence Denman, *A Lonely Grave: The Life and Death of William Redmond* (Dublin: Irish Academic Press, 1995), p.105.

23 Dame Teresa had to evacuate Belgium after German shells blew their convent to smithereens. 'Just before leaving the old Abbey the first bomb fell on it, quite close to us, only about a yard or two away, and we escaped almost by a miracle,' she wrote to Willie Redmond in November 1914.

24 Letter from Fr Edmond Kelly to Willie Redmond's wife, *The Tablet* [website] <http://archive.thetablet.co.uk/article/16th-june-1917/5/major-william-redmond-m-p->.

25 Ibid.

26 *The Tablet*, 16 June 1917.

27 Both he and his brother Samuel, who was a prisoner of war, survived the war, but could not survive the peace. Samuel Meeke died within two weeks of the end of the war, his health severely affected by working in a sulphur mine. John succumbed to tuberculous in 1923. The brothers are buried together in the old churchyard at Dervock in County Antrim. Until 2004, they were in an unmarked grave as neither had a Commonwealth War Graves Commission headstone. That omission was remedied by local historian Robert Thompson in 2004 with money raised from local people. A memorial fund was set up shortly after his death and was heavily subscribed to by his division, but also by the 36th (Ulster) Division and the Tyneside Irish brigade.

28 Terence Denman, *A Lonely Grave: The Life and Death of William Redmond* (Dublin: Irish Academic Press, 1995), p.121.

29 Stephen Gwynn, *John Redmond's Last Years* (New York: Longman's Green and Co., 1919), p.266.

30 Stephen Gwynn, *John Redmond's Last Years* (New York: Longman's Green and Co., 1919).

31 Commonwealth War Graves Commission archives, as seen by author.

32 Ibid.

33 Ibid.

34 Ibid.

35 Ibid.

36 Ibid.

37 Terence Denman, *A Lonely Grave: The Life and Death of William Redmond* (Dublin: Irish Academic Press, 1995).

38 Ibid.

39 Lise Hand, 'Two nations unite in honour of

war dead', *Irish Independent* [website]
<www.independent.ie/opinion/analysis/

lise-hand-two-nations-unite-in-honour-of-war-dead-29854231.
html>.

Chapter 19

1 Interview with author.
2 'Messines Peace Park', Irish Naval
   Association, *YouTube* [website]
   <www.youtube.com/watch?v=npTxEOYGacw>.
3 Ibid.
4 *The Irish Times*, 12 November 1998.
5 The Jesuits have stated that, 'Twenty one
   years after his death, in 1938, the central
   administration of the Society of Jesus
   asked the then Provincial of the Irish
   Province … on their perceptions of Fr. Doyle.
   A questionnaire was sent to fifty members
   of the Province including some living in
   Australia but who had known him during
   their years in Ireland … One of the less
   enthusiastic considered O'Rahilly's judgment
   clouded by "hero-worship".' In Jeffrey
   Burwell, 'Church Militant' (1 June 2015),
   Dublin Review of Books [website] <www.drb.ie/
   essays/church-militant>.
6 Paddy Harte, *Young Tigers and Mongrel Foxes*
   (Dublin: O'Brien Press, 2005). Mr Harte
   was not well enough to be interviewed for

this book, p.322.
7 'Glen Barr's Story',
   International School for Peace Studies [website]
   <www.schoolforpeace.com/content/glen-barrs-story/63>.
8 Paddy Harte, *Young Tigers and Mongrel Foxes*
   (Dublin: O'Brien Press, 2005), p.326.
9 Ibid., p.326.
10 Ibid., p.328.
11 Ibid., p.331
12 Ibid.
13 Interview with author.
14 Interview with author.
15 Paddy Harte, *Young Tigers and Mongrel Foxes*
   (Dublin: O'Brien Press, 2005), p.335.
16 *The Irish Times*, 12 November 1998.
17 Ibid.
18 *Irish Independent*, 12 November 1998.
19 Interview with author.
20 Ibid.
21 Ibid.
22 Ibid.
23 Ibid.
24 *The Irish Times*, Saturday, 14 November 1998.

Chapter 20

1 Frank Hurley was an official First World
   War photographer with the Australian army.
   He was also the photographer on Ernest
   Shackleton's 1914–1916 expedition.
   <https://upload.wikimedia.org/wikipedia/commons/7/79/
   Chateau_Wood_Ypres_1917.jpg>.
2 Gerard Smyth, 'Francis Ledwidge: Farm
   labourer to war poet', *The Irish Times*
   [website] <www.irishtimes.com/culture/heritage/
   francis-ledwidge-farm-labourer-to-war-poet-1.2190739>.
3 *The Irish Times*, 21 November 1992.
4 'Evans, Ellis Humphrey', Commonwealth War
   Graves Commission [website] <www.cwgc.org/
   find-war-dead/casualty/100906/evans,%20ellis%20humphrey>;
   'The Irishman's Diary' (30 July 2005), *The Irish
   Times*: 'He was a poor farmer and shepherd
   from the hills of North Wales. His poetic
   journey, as a peasant in a rural, intensely
   Celtic society, mirrors in many ways that of
   Francis Ledwidge. He and Evans were strong
   nationalists, with Ledwidge an early member of

the Irish Volunteers before joining the British
army. Evans was a reluctant soldier, though he
cherished the fact that in his regiment there
were "plenty of poets, for most of the men
and officers are Welsh". Although he never
approved of the war he willingly took the place
of his young teenage brother Bob, who was
allowed to stay to work the family's small plot.'
5 Seamus Heaney, *Field Work* (London: Faber
   and Faber, 1979).
6 'It is terrible to be always homesick'
   (20 November 2014), *Behind Their
   Lines: Poetry of the Great War* [website]
   <http://behindtheirlines.blogspot.ie/2014/11/it-is-terrible-to-
   be-always-homesick.html>.
7 'Blackbird on the Boyne', *RTÉ
   Radio 1* [website] <www.rte.ie/radio1/
   doconone/2013/0820/647497–radio-documentary-blackbird-
   boyne-francis-ledwidge-doc-on-one/>.
8 Brian Earls, 'Voices of the Dispossessed',
   Dublin Review of Books [website]

<www.drb.ie/essays/voices-of-the-dispossessed>.

9   Quoted in Alice Curtayne, *Francis Ledwidge: A Life of the Poet* (London: Martin, Brian and O'Keefe, 1972).

10 Quoted in Alice Curtayne, *Francis Ledwidge: A Life of the Poet* (London: Martin, Brian and O'Keefe, 1972).

11 Alice Curtayne, *Francis Ledwidge: A Life of the Poet* (London: Martin, Brian and O'Keefe, 1972).

12 Ibid.

13 Dunsany's preface in Francis Ledwidge, *The Complete Poems of Francis Ledwidge with introduction by Lord Dunsany* (New York, 1919).

14 *Freeman's Journal*, 17 February 1914.

15 Alice Curtayne, *Francis Ledwidge: A Life of the Poet* (London: Martin, Brian and O'Keefe, 1972), p.70.

16 Ibid.

17 Ibid., p.50.

18 *Irish Independent*, 8 October 1914.

19 'Francis Ledwidge: quotations from an autobiographical letter written by the post to Prof. Lewis Chase a month before he died', *The Irish Book Lover*, Vol. XII, pp.27–28, October-November 1920 <http://sources.nli.ie/Record/PS_UR_019398>.

20 Alice Curtayne, *Francis Ledwidge: A Life of the Poet* (London: Martin, Brian and O'Keefe, 1972), p.84.

21 *The Irish Times*, November.

22 Alice Curtayne, *Francis Ledwidge: A Life of the Poet* (London: Martin, Brian and O'Keefe, 1972), p.87.

23 Ibid.

24 'Lamp from River Clyde, 1915', *A History of Ireland in 100 Objects* [website] <www.100objects.ie/wp-content/uploads/2015/06/

Worksheet-Lamp-from-the-River-Clyde.pdf>.

25 Ronan McGreevy, 'An Irishman's Diary on the 10th (Irish) Division and Salonika', *The Irish Times* [website] <www.irishtimes.com/opinion/an-irishman-s-diary-on-the-10th-irish-division-and-salonika-1.2457673>.

26 Laura McKenna, 'Francis Ledwidge in Serbia' (15 July 2013), *Laura McKenna* [website] <http://writeso.wordpress.com/2013/07/15/francis-ledwidge-in-serbia/>.

27 Ibid.

28 Alice Curtayne, *Francis Ledwidge: A Life of the Poet* (London: Martin, Brian and O'Keefe, 1972), p.151.

29 Francis Ledwidge, 'In Hospital in Egypt', 'My Mother', 1916. <http://www.archive.org/stream/completepoemsoff00ledwuoft/completepoemsoff00ledwuoft_djvu.txt>

30 *Inchicore* [website] <www.inchicore.info/businesses/view/96/>.

31 'Ledwidge Misunderstood', *The Irish Times* [website] <www.irishtimes.com/opinion/letters/ledwidge-misunderstood-1.1128144>.

32 Alice Curtayne, *Francis Ledwidge: A Life of the Poet* (London: Martin, Brian and O'Keefe, 1972), p.189.

33 Ibid.

34 Ibid.

35 Ibid.

36 Adcock, A. St. John, *For Remembrance Soldier Poets Who Have, Fallen in the War* (London, 1918)

37 <http://www.francisledwidge.com/>

38 Speech given in Bolger at the planting of a tree in memory of Ledwidge in Flanders.

Chapter 21

1   John Keegan, *The First World War* (London: Pimlico Press, 1999), p.395.

2   Andrew Green, *Writing the Great War, Sir James Edmonds and the Official Histories* (London: Frank Cass Publishers), p.173.

3   David Lloyd George, *War Memoirs* (London Little, Brown, And Company, 1934), p.337.

4   Brigadier-General Sir James Edmonds, British Official History, Volume II Messines and Third Ypres (Passchendaele) (London: MacMillan, 1948), p.125.

5   Cyril Falls, *The History of the 36th (Ulster) Division* (Belfast: M'Caw, Stevenson & Orr), p.107.

6   Richard S Grayson, *At War with the 16th (Irish) Division 1914-1918, the Staniforth Letters* (Barnsley: Pen & Sword, 2012), p.125.

7   Terence Denman, *Ireland's Unknown Soldiers* (Newbridge, County Kildare: Irish Academic Press 1992), p.115.

8   Alfred O'Rahily, *Fr Willie Doyle SJ* (London: Longmans, Green and Co., 1922), p.303.

9   <http://www.longlongtrail.co.uk/battles/battles-of-the-western-front-in-france-and-flanders/the-battles-of-ypres-1917-third-ypres/>.

10 <http://www.longlongtrail.co.uk/army/other-aspects-of-order-of-battle/the-british-armies-of-1914-1918/the-british-fifth-or-reserve-army-1916-1918/>.

11 Brigadier-General Sir James Edmonds, *British Official History, Volume II Messines and Third*

Ypres (Passchendaele) (London: MacMillan, 1948), p.138.

12 Alfred O'Rahily, *Fr Willie Doyle SJ* (London: Longmans, Green and Co., 1922), p.320.

13 <http://www.gwpda.org/comment/ypres3.html>.

14 Alfred O'Rahily, *Fr Willie Doyle SJ* (London: Longmans, Green and Co. 1922), p.309.

15 Ibid.

16 Ibid.

17 <http://www.firstworldwar.com/battles/ypres3.htm>.

18 <http://docplayer.net/20775431-Chapter-x-passchendaele-october-november-1917-see-map-9-and-sketches-43-45-the-background-to-third-ypres.html>.

19 <http://forum.irishmilitaryonline.com/showthread.php?11535-The-Battle-of-Passchendaele>.

20 Terence Denman, *Ireland's Unknown Soldiers* (Newbridge, County Kildare: Irish Academic Press, 1992), p.116.

21 Nicholas Perry (ed.), *Major General Oliver Nugent and the Ulster Division 1915-1916*, (Stroud, Gloucestershire: Sutton Publication, 2007), p.163.

22 Private papers of Alfred Glanville, Documents 21037, Imperial War Museum.

23 Myles Dungan, *Irish Voices of the Great War* (Sallins, County Kildare: Merrion Press, 2014), p.203.

24 <http://www.birmingham.ac.uk/research/activity/warstudies/research/projects/lionsdonkeys/j.aspx>.

25 <http://www.1914-1918.net/intobattle_7RIrRif_Frezenberg.html>.

26 Private papers of Alfred Glanville, Documents 21037, Imperial War Museum.

27 <http://www.dublin-fusiliers.com/battaliions/2-batt/campaigns/1917-passchendaele.html>.

28

29 G.A Cooper Walker, *The Book of the Seventh Service Battalion* (Royal Inniskilling Fusiliers), (Dublin, Brindley & Son, 1920), p.121.

30 <http://www.ciroca.org.uk/first-world-war-links/infantry-regiments-1914-18/royal-dublin-fusiliers/>.

31 Cyril Falls, *The History of the 36th (Ulster) Division* (Belfast: M'Caw, Stevenson & Orr), p.106.

32 Ibid.

33 <https://www.facebook.com/permalink.php?story_fbid=1071702446210393&id=115758611804786>.

34 <https://fatherdoyle.com/category/fr-doyle-links/page/10/>.

35 <https://www.jstor.org/stable/24347759?seq=1#page_scan_tab_contents>.

36 Alfred O'Rahily, *Fr Willie Doyle SJ* (London: Longmans, Green and Co. 1922), p.321.

37 <https://www.jstor.org/.stable/24347759?seq=1#page_scan_tab_contents>.

38 Ibid.

39 Ibid.

40 Ibid.

41 Cork Constitution 13 February 1918.

42 <http://www.greatwar.ie/wp-content/uploads/2016/03/The-Blue-Cap-8.pdf>.

43 *Skibbereen Eagle*, 25 August 1917.

44 Ibid.

45 Ibid.

46 *Irish Independent*, 23 August 1917.

47 Nicholas Perry (ed.), *Major General Oliver Nugent and the Ulster Division 1915-1916* (Stroud, Gloucestershire: Sutton Publication, 2007), p.166.

48 Ibid, p.167.

49 Philip Gibbs, *Now It Can Be Told* (London, Harper & Brothers Publishers 1920), p.475.

50 Douglas Haig, diary entry as quoted in Douglas Haig: *Diaries and Letters 1914-1918* edited by Gary Sheffield and John Bourne.

51 Ibid.

52 WO 95/19772 7 Battalion Royal Inniskilling Fusiliers.

53 Brigadier-General Sir James Edmonds, *British Official History, Volume II Messines and Third Ypres (Passchendaele)* (London: MacMillan, 1948), p.197-8.

54 Figures given to author by In Flanders Fields coordinator Piet Chielans.

55 Ibid.

56 Ibid.

57 Ibid.

58 <https://en.wikipedia.org/wiki/Welsh_Memorial_Park,_Ypres>.

59 Interview with author.

60 The dates listed on the memorial are for the Battle of Langemarck, which went on until 18 August, though for the two Irish divisions, it was just a one-day affair.

61 <https://fatherdoyle.com/testimonies/>.

Chapter 22

1 Robert J. Sharpe, *The Last Day, the Last Hour: The Currie Libel Trial* (Toronto: University of Toronto Press, 1988), p.2.

2 Ibid.

3 Ciaran Byrne, *The Harp and Crown, the History of the 5th (Royal Irish) Lancers, 1902–1922* (London, 2007), p.166.

4 Ibid.

5 Norm Christie, *For King and Empire: Canada's Soldiers in the Great War* (2000) <http://www.knowledge.ca/program/king-empire-canadas-soldiers-great-war>.

6 <http://www.nam.ac.uk/research/famous-units/5th-royal-irish-lancers>

7 *Continental Monthly*, Vol. III, No. IV, April 1863 www.gutenberg.org/files/29736/29736-h/29736-h.htm. 'The 5th Royal Irish Light Dragoons refused to charge upon a body of the rebels when the word was given. Not a man or horse stirred from the ranks. Here was a difficult card to play, now, for the authorities, because it would have been inconvenient to try the whole regiment by court martial, and the soldiers were quite too valuable to be mowed down *en masse*. The only course left was to disband the regiment, which was done'.

8 Walter Temple Willcox, *The Historical Records of the Fifth (Royal Irish) Lancers from their Foundation as Wynne's Dragoons (in 1689) to the Present Day* (London: Naval and Military Press, 1908), p.149.

9 Geoffrey Russell Searle, *A New England? Peace and War 1886–1918* (Oxford: Oxford University Press, 2004).

10 Lord Anglesey, *A History of British Cavalry: Volume 7: 1816–1919 The Curragh Incident* (Barnsley: Pen and Sword, 1996), p.9.

11 <http://www.britishempire.co.uk/forces/armyunits/britishinfantry/buffsarthurpaget.htm>.

12 Ibid.

13 Ibid.

14 'The Curragh "Mutiny"', *The Curragh of Kildare* [website] <www.curragh.info/archives/TheCurraghMutiny1914.pdf>.

15 Ibid.

16 Ibid.

17 Ibid.

18 Ibid.

19 H.A. Cape, *The History of the 5th (Royal Irish) Regiments of Dragoons 1689–1922* (Aldershot: Naval and Military Press, 1923).

20 Diary of Lieutenant Rowland Auriol James Beech 16th Lancers, p.122.

21 Ciaran Byrne, *The Harp and Crown: The History of the 5th (Royal Irish) Lancers, 1902–1922* (privately published, 2008), p.54.

22 Ibid., p.129.

23 Ibid., p.217.

24 Neil Richardson, *According to their Lights* (Dublin: Collins, 2015).

25 Michael T. Foy and Brian Barton, *The Easter Rising* (Stroud: The History Press, 2011), p.175.

26 <https://en.wikipedia.org/wiki/Spring_Offensive>

27 'VII Corps', *First World War* [website] <www.webmatters.net/france/ww1_kaiser_08.htm>.

28 'German attack at St Quentin, March 1918', *Dublin Fusiliers* [website] <www.dublin-fusiliers.com/battaliions/1-batt/campaigns/1918-kaisers.html>.

29 Kieron Punch, 'A Brief History of the 16th "Irish" Division' (24 January 2013), *The Wild Geese* [website] <http://thewildgeese.irish/profiles/blogs/a-brief-history-of-the-16th-irish-division>.

30 Ciaran Byrne, *The Harp and Crown: The History of the 5th (Royal Irish) Lancers, 1902–1922* (privately published, 2008).

31 David Bonk, *St Mihiel 1918: The American Expeditionary Forces' Trial by Fire* (Oxford 2011), p.7.

32 Ciaran Byrne, *The Harp and Crown: The History of the 5th (Royal Irish) Lancers, 1902–1922* (privately published, 2008), p.144.

33 James McWilliams, *Amiens: Dawn of Victory* (Toronto, 2001), p.256.

34 Ibid., p.164.

35 Michael Palin, 'The Last Day of the First World War', *Timewatch*, BBC2, 11 November 2008.

Chapter 23

1 'Valenciennes (St. Roch) Communal Cemetery', Commonwealth War Graves Commission [website] <http://www.cwgc.org/find-a-cemetery/cemetery/63800/valenciennes%20(st.%20roch)%20communal%20cemetery>.

2 Ibid.

3 Doug Armstrong, interview with author.

4 'Winter 1921-22 (Age 47)', *The Churchill Centre* [website] <www.winstonchurchill.org/the-life-of-churchill/rising-politician/1920-1932/3089-winter-1921-22-age-47>.

5 'Currygrane House, County Longford', *National Inventory of Architectural Heritage* [website] <www.buildingsofireland.ie/niah/search.jsp?type

=record&county=LF&regno=13400910>.

6 Commonwealth War Graves Commssion
   archives, Robert Armstrong P624.
7 Ibid.
8 Commonwealth War Graves Commission files.
9 Irish Guards archives, Robert Armstrong
   enlistment records.
10 'Armstrong, J H', Commonwealth War Graves
   Commission [website]
   <www.cwgc.org/find-war-dead/casualty/465415/
   armstrong,%20J%20H>.
11 Commonwealth War Graves Commission file.
12 Irish Guards archive files.
13 'Imperial War Graves Commission', *Hansard*
   [website] <http://hansard.millbanksystems.com/
   commons/1920/may/04/imperial-war-graves-commission>.
14 Lieut.-Colonel Sir Frederic Kenyon,
   'War Graves: How the Cemeteries Abroad
   Will Be Designated'
   <www.cwgc.org/media/394532/the_kenyon_report.doc>.
15 Commonwealth War Graves Commission P624.
16 Ibid.
17 Quoted in Ursula Buchan, *A Green and
   Pleasant Land: How England's Gardeners Fought
   the Second World War* (London, 2013).
18 Interview with author.
19 Commonwealth War Graves Commission.
20 'Reg Armstrong', *Wikipedia* [website]
   <http://en.wikipedia.org/wiki/Reg_Armstrong>.
21 Commonwealth War Graves Commission
   P624.

22 Ibid.
23 Ibid.
24 Ibid.
25 '*Aviateurs alliés rassemblés en camps de Comète*',
   *Le réseau COMETE:
   Ligne d'évasion Comète* [website]
   <www.cometeline.org/ficheD370.html>.
26 Ibid.
27 Airey Neave, *Saturday at MI9* (London:
   Hodder and Stoughton, 1969), p.22.
28 Ibid.
29 'Major-Gen Albert-Marie Edmond Guérisse:
   Pat O'Leary of the PAO Allied escape line –
   the "Pat" or "O'Leary" Line', *207 Squadron
   Royal Air Force History* [website]
   <www.rafinfo.org.uk/rafescape/guerisse.htm>.
30 Commonwealth War Graves Commission P624.
31 Isadore Ryan, *Irish Paris* [website].
32 Commonwealth War Graves Commission
   P624.
33 Ibid.
34 Ibid.
35 Ibid.
36 Interview with author.
37 Ibid.
38 Ibid.
39 Ibid.

ACKNOWLEDGEMENTS

I am conscious in writing this book that I am neither the first nor likely to be the last author to write about the Irish in the First World War. There is now a fine body of literature on the subject. There are many informative regimental diaries and soldiers' reminiscences from the 1920s. In the last 25 years, Keith Jeffery (*Ireland and the Great War*), Tom Johnstone (*Orange, Green and Khaki*), Terence Denman (*Ireland's Unknown Soldiers* and *A Lonely Grave: The Life and Death of William Redmond*), Kevin Myers (*Ireland's Great War*), Neil Richardson (*A Coward if I Return, A Hero if I Fall*) and Myles Dungan (*Irish Soldiers and the Great War*) are among those who have greatly expanded our knowledge of Irish involvement in the First World War.

My agent Faith O'Grady of the Lisa Richards Agency and publisher Ronan Colgan encouraged me in this project from the beginning. Beth Amphlett and Chris West from The History Press have been patient editors and designers respectively.

I am grateful for the support of Françoise Scheepers (Visit Belgium), Anita Rampal (Visit Flanders), Marine Catalogna and Agnès Angrand (Atout France) who facilitated my many visits to the Western Front. Angie Grant (Notorious PSG) and Shane Cowley (Canon Ireland) supplied the equipment which allowed me to photograph and film these monuments. I also have a YouTube channel and there are many films relating to stories in this book which can be accessed there using my name in the search bar. I hope this book will inspire other authors to embrace film-making as another means of storytelling.

I would like to thank Peter Francis from the Commonwealth War Graves Commission for allowing me access to its archives. I hope this book highlights some of the wonderful work the commission does in affording to so many men the dignity denied to them in their violent deaths.

The staff of the National Library of Ireland were unfailingly polite and helpful in my many inquiries. Both the former President Mary McAleese and the former Taoiseach Bertie Ahern were generous with their time and deserve great credit for the manner in which they have rescued these proud Irishmen of the First World War from the 'memories in shoeboxes' as Mrs McAleese described it. I would like to thank Mrs McAleese for contributing a foreword to this paperback.

Many relatives shared their knowledge. They include Ben Thomas (Ernest Edward Thomas), Peter Bland SC (Maurice Dease), Thomas Fitzpatrick (Thomas William Fitzpatrick), Willie Malone (William and Michael Malone), William 'Sonny' Condon and John Condon Jnr (John Condon), Tommy Weldon (John Brien), Doug Armstrong and Harry Lindsay (Robert Armstrong), Michael Riordan (John Nash) and Michael McDowell SC (William McDowell).

Tom Burnell has been an invaluable help in his determination to ensure that the Irish war dead are counted and are therefore remembered properly. He also gave me access to his huge database of provincial Irish newspaper cuttings from the war period. Professor Hedley Malloch assisted me in putting together the chapter on the Iron 12 and deserves our thanks for ensuring those unfortunate men who were brutally executed are no longer forgotten.

Similarly, Michael Desmond has resurrected the memory of the Battle of Le Pilly and he advised me on that the chapter. I would like to thank the Mayor of Herlies Marie-Françoise Auger for the hospitality afforded to me on my visit there. Yvon Papeghin showed me the Le Pilly battleground and Franck and Dorothée Gil allowed me access to their home.

Aurel Sercu was generous with allowing me access to his research about John Condon; and Isadore Ryan helped with the chapter on Robert Armstrong.

Tom Burke (Royal Dublin Fusiliers Association), Liam Nolan (Royal Munster Fusiliers Association) and Paul Malpass (Connaught Rangers Association) were patient with all my inquiries.

Many of the chapters in this book arose originally out of articles in *The Irish Times*. I would like to thank my editors, Kevin O'Sullivan, Paddy Smyth, Donncha O'Muirithe and Mark Hennessy, for allowing me the space and time to cover this fascinating period of Irish history. I would like to thank my secondary school teacher Jim Waldron for encouraging me to write and instilling in me a love of history.

I wish to acknowledge Kevin Myers for the inspiration he provided for many years in his dauntless journalism writing about this subject, and also for alerting me to the incredible story of Robert Armstrong. Dermot Bolger did likewise with the chapter on Francis Ledwidge.

I am very fortunate in having a good friend, Tommy Conlon, whose diligent attention to the text improved it immeasurably. Tommy also accompanied me on one of my trips to the Western Front. From start to finish, he has been a great editor, wise counsel and adviser. This book would not be the same without his input. Another friend, Micheál Coughlan, also accompanied me on trips to the Western Front.

Dr Tadhg Moloney from Limerick was another who gave careful attention to the text and supplied me with photographs of the cross at Limburg. His knowledge of the period and passion for the subject was a reassuring resource. Jean Prendergast also helped with the chapters on the Royal Munster Fusiliers.

My wife Rebecca and children Rosamund and Leo proved to be endlessly patient with my absences. I could not have written this book without the support of my wife.

My brother John and his wife Marie Claire helped out while my father Eamonn, brothers Conor and Paul, and sister Nollaig have been a constant support.

Finally, I would like to thank my mother Chris who passed away suddenly during the writing of this book. To her I owe everything. Flights of angels sing thee to thy rest Mum. RIP.

BIBLIOGRAPHY

Anglesey, Lord, *A History of the British Cavalry, Volume 7: 1816-1919, The Curragh Incident* (Pen and Sword, 1996)

Allen, Sam, *To Ulster's Credit* (Plantation Press, 1986)

Atwood, Rodney, *The Life of Field Marshal Lords Roberts* (Bloomsbury, 2014)

Barry, Tom, *Guerrilla Days in Ireland* (Mercier Press, 1949)

Bartlett, Thomas and Keith Jeffery, *A Military History of Ireland* (Cambridge University Press, 1997)

Beatty, Jack, *The Lost History of 1914: How the Great War Was Not Inevitable* (Bloomsbury, 2012)

Blanning, T.C. (ed.) *The Nineteenth Century: Europe 1789-1914* (Oxford University Press, 2000)

Bostridge, Mark, *The Fateful Year: England 1924* (Viking Press, 2014)

Bowen, Desmond and Jean, Heroic Options: The Irish in the British Army (Pen and Sword, 2005)

Brady, L.W, T.P, *O'Connor and the Liverpool Irish* (Royal Historical Society, 1983)

Bridges, Sir Tom, *Alarms & Excursions: Reminiscences of a Soldier* (Longmans, Green and Co., 1938)

Bristow, Adrian, *A Serious Disappointment: The Battle of Aubers Ridge* (L.Cooper, 1995)

Buchan, Ursula, *A Green and Pleasant Land: How England's Gardeners Fought the Second World War* (London, 2013)

Burke, Tom, *The 16th (Irish) Division and 36th (Ulster) Division at the Battle of Wytschaete-Messines Ridge* (Royal Dublin Fusiliers Association, 2007)

Byrne, Ciaran, *The Harp and Crown; the History of the 5th (Royal Irish) Lancers 1900-1922* (London, 2007)

Cannon, Richard, *Historical record of the Fourth Royal Irish Regiment of Dragoon Guards* (London, 1836)

Cape, H.A., *The History of the 5th (Royal Irish) Regiments of Dragoons 1689-1922* (Naval and Military Press, 1923)

Carrington, Charles, *Soldiers from the Wars Returning* (Pen and Sword, 1965)

Churchill, Winston, *The World Crisis* (Charles Scribner's Sons, 1932)

Clark, Alan, *The Donkeys* (Random House, 1961)

Coates, A.J, *The Ethics of War* (Manchester University Press, 1997)

Cogan, Anthony, *The Ecclesiastical History of the Diocese of Meath: Ancient and Modern, Volume 2* (Dublin, 1864)

Cooper, Duff, *Haig: A Biography* (Doubleday, 1936)

Crozier, Frank Percy, *A Brass Hat in No Man's Land* (1930)

Curtayne, Alice, *Francis Ledwidge: A Life of the Poet* (Martin, Brian and O'Keeffe Publishers 1972)

Denman, Terence, *A Lonely Grave: The Life and Death of William Redmond* (Irish Academic Press, 1995)

Denman, Terence, *Ireland's Unknown Soldiers* (Irish Academic Press, 1995)

Dixon, John, *Magnificent But Not War* (Pen and Sword, 2009)

Doyle, Peter and Robin Schäfer, *Fritz and Tommy: Across the Barbed Wire* (The History Press, 2015)

Edmonds, Brigadier-General Sir James E., *British Official History of the War Military Operations France and Belgium* (MacMillan, 1937)

Edmonds, Brigadier-General Sir James E., *British Official History Volume II: Messines and Third Ypres (Passchendaele)* (Macmillan, 1948)

Falls, Cyril, *The History of the 36th (Ulster) Division* (Belfast, 1922)

Feilding, Rowland, *War Letters to a Wife: France and Flanders 1915-1919* (Naval and Military Press, 1929)

Fox, Sir Frank, *Royal Inniskilling Fusiliers in the World War (1914-1918)* (Naval and Military Press, 1928)

Geoghegan, Brigadier General Stannus, *The Campaigns and History of the Royal Irish Regiment* (Naval and Military Press, 1927)

Gibb, Revd Harold, *Record of the 4th Irish Dragoon Guards in the Great War 1914-1918* (Canterbury, 1925)

Gliddon, Gerald, *VCs of the First World War 1914* (The History Press, 2011)

Gosling, Lucinda, *Goodbye, Old Man: Matania's Vision of the First World War* (The History Press, 2014)

Gwynn, Stephen, *John Redmond's Last Years* (Longman's Green and Company, 1949)

Hart, Peter, *Fire and Movement: The British Expeditionary Force and the Campaign of 1914* (Oxford University Press, 2012)

Harte, Paddy, *Young Tigers and Mongrel Foxes* (O'Brien Press, 2005)

Harvey, Lieutenant Colonel Dan, *The Irish at Waterloo* (H Books, 2015)

Heaney, Seamus, *Field Work* (Faber and Faber, 1979)

Hitchcock, Francis, *Stand To! A Diary of the Trenches, 1915-1918* (Naval and Military Press, 1938)

Hitler, Adolf, *Mein Kampf* (Franz Eher Nachfolger, 1925)

Hochchild, Adam, *To End All Wars: A Story of Loyalty and Rebellion* (Mariner Books, 2011)

Holt, Tonie and Valmai, *My Boy Jack* (Pen and Sword, 1998)

Hope, Carole, *Fr Willie Doyle, Worshipper and Worshipped* (Reveille Press, 2013)

Hughes, Brian, *Michael Mallin: 16 Lives* (O'Brien Press, 2013)

Hutton, John, *August 1914: Surrender at St Quentin* (Pen and Sword, 2010)

Jeffery, Professor Keith, *Ireland and the Great War* (Cambridge University Press, 2000)

Jervis, H.S, *The 2nd Munsters in France* (Naval and Military Press, 1922)

Jourdain, H.F.N. and E. Fraser, *The Connaught Rangers, Volume 2* (1926)

Junger, Ernest, *Storm of Steel* (Berlin, 1920)

Keating, Joseph, *The History of the Tyneside Irish Brigade: Irish Heroes in the War* (Naval and Military Press, 1917)

Knott, George H., *The Trial of Roger Casement* (Glasgow, 1917)

Laird, Frank, *Personal Experiences of the Great War* (Dublin, 1925)

Ledwidge, Francis, *The Complete Poems of Francis Ledwidge with introduction by Lord Dunsany* (New York, 1919)

Le Mesurier, George, *The Campaigns and History of the Royal Irish Regiment 1900-1922* (Schull Books, 1997)

Linge, Kein, Pam Linge, *Missing But Not Forgotten: Men of the Thiepval Memorial* (Naval and Military, 2015)

Lucy, John, *There's a Devil in the Drum* (Naval and Military Press, 1938)

MacDonagh, Michael, *The Irish at the Front* (Hodder and Stoughton, 1917)

MacGill, Patrick, *The Great Push: An Episode of the Great War* (Herbert Jenkins, 1916)

MacIntyre, Ben, *A Foreign Field* (London, 2001)

McCance, Captain S., *The History of the Royal Munster Fusiliers* (Naval and Military Press 1922)

McPhail, Helen, *The Long Silence: The Tragedy of Occupied France in World War I* (I.B. Tauris, 1999)

McWilliams, James, *Amiens: Dawn of Victory* (Toronto, 2001)

Meehan, Revd C.P. , *The Rise and Fall of the Irish Franciscan Monasteries and Memoirs of the Irish Hierarchy in the Seventeenth Century* (1872)

Middlebrook, Martin, *The First Day of the Somme* (Penguin, 1971)

Myers, Kevin, *Ireland's Great War* (Lilliput Press, 2014)

Neave, Airey, *Saturday at M19* (Hodder and Soughton, 1969)

Oldham, Peter, *Battlefield Europe: Messines Ridge* (Naval and Military Press, 1998)

O'Rahilly, Professor Alfred, *Father Willie Doyle* (London, 1922)

Orr, Philip, *The Road to the Somme* (Blackstaff Press, 1987)

Parmiter, Geoffrey, *Roger Casement* (Arthur Baker, 1936)

Paseta, Senia, *Tom Kettle 1880-1916* (UCD Press, 2008)

Perry, Nicholas, *Major General Oliver Nugent and the Ulster Division 1915-1918* (Stroud, 2007)

Pinney, Thomas, *The Letters of Rudyard Kipling 1911-1919* (Macmillan, 1990)

Purefoy, Arthur, *Irwin Samuels, With the Ulster Division in France* (Independent Publishing Platform, August 2015)

Redmond, William, *Trench Diaries from France* (New York, 1917)

Richardson, Neil, *According to their Lights* (Collins Press, 2015)

Ryan, Mark, *The First VCs: The Moving True Story of First World War Heroes Maurice Dease and Sidney Godley* (The History Press, 2014)

Searle, Geoffrey Russell, *A New England? Peace and War 1886-1918* (Oxford University Press, 2004)

Seoighe, Mainchín, *Dromin Athlacca: The Story of a Rural Parish in Co. Limerick* (Ath Leachach: Glór na nGael, 1978)

Sheen, John, *Tyneside Irish* (Pen and Sword, 1998)

Sheffield, Gary, John Bourne, *Douglas Haig: Diaries and Letters 1914-1918* (Weidenfeld & Nicolson, 2005)

Spillebeen, Geert, *Age 14* (Collins Press, 2010)

Stedman, Michael, *Guillemont* (Pen and Sword, 1998)

Walker, C.A. Cooper, *The Royal Inniskilling Fusiliers: From Tipperary to Ypres* (London, 1920)

Whitton, Frederick, *A History of the Prince of Wales's Leinster Regiment* (Naval and Military Press, 1924)

Wilcox, Walter Temple, *The Historical Records of the 5th (Royal Irish) Lancers* (Naval and Military Press, 1908)

Wylly, Colonel H.C., *Crown and Company* (Naval and Military Press, 1923)

Yarnall, John, *Barbed Wire Disease: British and German Prisoners of War* (The History Press, 2011)

INDEX

Also from The History Press

IRELAND
AT WAR

The History Press Ireland